MEDIEVAL DUBL

I ndílchuimhne ar Ailbhe MacShamhráin
Gael, scoláire agus Críostaí
1954–2011

Medieval Dublin XI

Proceedings of the
Friends of Medieval Dublin Symposium 2009

Seán Duffy

EDITOR

FOUR COURTS PRESS

Typeset in 10.5 pt on 12.5 pt Ehrhardt by
Carrigboy Typesetting Services for
FOUR COURTS PRESS LTD
7 Malpas Street, Dublin 8, Ireland
www.fourcourtspress.ie
and in North America for
FOUR COURTS PRESS
c/o ISBS, 920 NE 58th Avenue, Suite 300, Portland, OR 97213.

A catalogue record for this title is available
from the British Library.

ISBN 978–1–84682–275–9 hbk
ISBN 978–1–84682–276–6 pbk

This book is published with the active support of
Dublin City Council/Comhairle Chathair Átha Cliath.

Dublin City
Baile Átha Cliath

Printed in England
by Antony Rowe Ltd, Chippenham, Wilts.

Contents

Contributors

TERESA BOLGER is an archaeological consultant and project manager.

NIAMH DALY holds an MA in human osteoarchaeology from University College Cork.

CLARE DOWNHAM is a lecturer in Irish Studies at the University of Liverpool.

ÁINE FOLEY holds a PhD in medieval history from Trinity College Dublin.

PATRICK JAMES HERBAGE holds an MA in history from NUI Maynooth and is heritage course co-ordinator at Dvblinia.

LORCAN HARNEY is an IRCHSS postgraduate scholar in the School of Archaeology, University College Dublin.

RANDOLPH JONES is an independent scholar, based in England, who has an interest in medieval Ireland.

JONATHAN KINSELLA is a research archaeologist with the Early Medieval Archaeology Project (EMAP) at University College Dublin.

DERMOT McGUINNE, formerly of the Departments of Visual Communication Design and Fine Art at the Dublin Institute of Technology (DIT), is the foremost authority on the history of Irish type design and printing.

COLM MORIARTY is a freelance archaeologist.

BARRA Ó DONNABHÁIN lectures in the Department of Archaeology at University College Cork.

MICHAEL O'NEILL holds a PhD in architectural history from Trinity College Dublin.

AIDAN O'SULLIVAN is a senior lecturer in the School of Archaeology, University College Dublin.

MAEVE SIKORA is an assistant keeper in the Irish Antiquities Division of the National Museum of Ireland.

LINZI SIMPSON is an archaeological consultant and project manager.

CHARLES SMITH is a retired civil servant and holds a PhD in history from University College Dublin.

Editor's preface

I am hugely indebted to the team of people who make up Four Courts Press for their willingness to publish this series. This particular volume of essays arises primarily from a one-day symposium held by the Friends of Medieval Dublin in Trinity College Dublin on 23 May 2009. It was the eleventh symposium in the series and this is the eleventh volume of proceedings arising therefrom, along with some additional pieces. We are always anxious to publish original work that has a bearing on the history or archaeology of medieval Dublin (to 1610); so if you would like to present your research at our annual symposium and/or publish in a future volume in the series, do please contact the editor at sduffy@tcd.ie.

The venue costs associated with the symposium were paid by the Department of History at Trinity College, for which the editor is very grateful. A subvention towards the cost of publication has been generously provided by Dublin City Council: I would like to take this opportunity to thank the City Manager, Mr John Tierney, the City Heritage Officer, Mr Charles Duggan, and the City Archaeologist, Dr Ruth Johnson, for the enthusiasm with which they have embraced the efforts of the Friends of Medieval Dublin to bring to a wider audience an appreciation of the city's great medieval inheritance.

The most recent manifestation of this cooperation has seen the Friends and the City Council join forces in organizing a very successful series of monthly lunchtime talks called 'Tales of Medieval Dublin', the first season of which ran from July to December 2010 in the wonderful new Wood Quay Venue, and the 2011 season is now underway. Like the annual medieval symposium, these talks have enjoyed spectacular success: it is not every day that a lecture on medieval history can attract an audience in excess of 150!

Finally, readers of Linzi Simpson's important study in this volume, entitled 'Fifty years a-digging: a synthesis of medieval archaeological investigations in Dublin City and suburbs', may wish to know that a major project by the same author entitled *The archaeological remains of Viking and medieval Dublin: a research framework*, funded under the Heritage Council's initiative known as the Irish National Strategic Archaeological Research (INSTAR), was completed in November 2010 and is available online at www.heritagecouncil.ie.

Seán Duffy
Chairman
Friends of Medieval Dublin

Fifty years a–digging: a synthesis of medieval archaeological investigations in Dublin City and suburbs[1]

LINZI SIMPSON

INTRODUCTION

Ten years ago the writer published, in *Medieval Dublin I*, an exercise attempting to summarize the results of all archaeological excavations carried out within the historic core of medieval Dublin and its immediate environs since the era of professional excavation began forty years earlier. The exercise was confined, for the most part, to those sites within the known circuit of the mural defences, apart from some material from the immediate south-eastern suburb (Simpson 2000, fig. 1). That first synthesis – henceforth, 'Forty years a-digging' – relied heavily on the *Excavations* bulletin, a publication that provides brief summaries of all licenced excavations carried out in the Republic of Ireland (Bennett 1997–), and also on personal communications with the excavation directors, in advance of detailed analysis and publication.

Since that first publication, however, there have been major and ground-breaking excavations that have added significantly to our knowledge of the medieval city and its complex evolution, from monastic settlement to a fully-fledged English colonial metropolis, and the purpose of the present essay is to synthesize their results. This new information relates, for the most part, to the suburbs, which has served to highlight a glaring omission from 'Forty years a-digging', namely the exclusion (for reasons of space) of excavations results from the immediate suburbs of the city, which I have attempted to address in this update. Finally, it is also the case that the majority of the large excavations reported on in 'Forty years a-digging' have now been published, mainly in the *Medieval Dublin* series, and this has produced a vast corpus of additional information, including dating evidence, which I have now attempted to add in, reducing the previous reliance on personal communication.

On a slightly negative note, however, it should be noted that the update does not purport to include every investigation carried out in Dublin in the past fifty years, but is confined to those where significant or new information was received. In addition to this, the *Excavations* bulletin was, at the time of

[1] This essay is dedicated to the memory of my father, Arthur J. Simpson, a tireless supporter of medieval Dublin for many years.

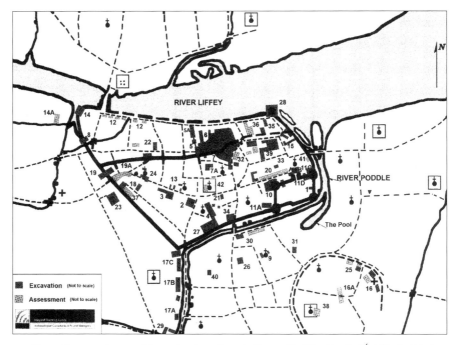

1.1 Map of excavations and investigations (2000) (*key*: 1 Dublin Castle (Ó hEochaidhe); 2 High Street 1 (Ó Riordáin); 3 High Street 2 (Ó Riordáin); 4 Christchurch Place (Ó Riordáin); 5–5a Winetavern Street (McMahon; Halpin); 6–7a Wood Quay/Fishamble Street (Wallace); 8 Bridge Street (O'Rahilly; McMahon); 9 Church of St Michael le Pole (Gowen); 10 Dublin Castle (Lynch and Manning); 11 Dublin Castle (Lynch); 12 Merchant's Quay (Meenan/Murtagh?); 13 High Street (Murtagh; Gowen); 14–14a Usher's Quay (Gowen); 15 Parliament Street/Essex Gate (Scally; Simpson); 16 Stephen Street/Aungier Street (Hayden; Halpin); 17a–c Patrick Street/Nicholas Street (Walsh); 18 Back Lane (Walsh); 19 Bridge Street (Hayden; Healy); 20 Castle Street (Byrne); 21 Christ Church Place (Gowen); 22 16–17 Cook Street (Meenan); 23 Cornmarket (Hayden); 24 St Audoen's Church (McMahon); 25 Stephen Street (Meenan); 26 Bride Street (McMahon); 27 Christ Church Place/Ross Road (Walsh); 28 Isolde's Tower (Simpson); 29 Patrick Street/Dean Street (Walsh); 30 Ship Street (Scally; Simpson); 31 Dublin Castle (Simpson); 32 Fishamble Street/Kinlay House (Simpson); 33 Lord Edward Street (Gowen); 34 Werburgh Street (Hayden); 35 Essex Street West (Simpson); 36 Essex Street West (Gowen; Kehoe); 37 Back Lane (Coughlan); 38 Whitefriar Street (Gowen; Kehoe); 39 Temple Bar West (Simpson); 40 Bride Street (Gahan); 41 City Hall (Kehoe); 42 Christ Church Cathedral (Simpson)).

writing, available only up to 2007, which may mean that some smaller sites investigated between 2007 and 2011 have been missed in the following discussion (although every effort has been made to reduce this risk through personal communication).

As was the case with 'Forty years a-digging', the information below is presented in chronological order according to the findings, rather than the date of excavation; thus, information from individual sites has been divided up into the relevant time-periods and spread throughout the article. *Italicized* numbers after sites refer to figure 1.1; **bold** numbers after sites refer to figure 1.2.

ADDITIONAL PROJECTS, STUDIES AND SURVEYS

In addition to the new and exciting information coming from the archaeo-logical excavations, a range of research projects have been completed in the intervening ten years, which have added greatly to our knowledge of medieval Dublin. One of the first, which was to kick-start other significant projects, was the publication of *The conservation plan for Dublin city walls and defences*, edited by Margaret Gowen, which originated as an action of the Dublin City Heritage Plan, 2002–6 (Gowen 2000). This conservation plan contained a series of proposed actions, the main one of which was to 'formulate an over-arching development-focused strategic plan for enhancing the physical and visual identity of the 'old city' with a realistic, phased long-term view to implemen-tation' (Policy 6.2).

The result was the commissioning by the Heritage Office of Dublin City Council of the *The Ship Street/Werburgh Street framework plan*, by McCullough-Mulvin Architects, which proposes innovative ways of enhancing the medieval city through new build and the development of eight key sites within the historic core (McCullough 2005). This was followed by the *The Ship Street/Werburgh Street archaeological research agenda*, commissioned by the City Archaeologist as a pilot study, which placed the designated sites within their historical and archaeological context, identified research gaps and detailed the potential impact while suggesting mitigating strategies (Simpson 2008d). Funding was then sought by Dublin City Council, and subsequently received from the Irish National Strategic Archaeological Research (INSTAR), for a project entitled *The archaeological remains of Viking and medieval Dublin: a research framework*, compiled by the writer and submitted in November 2010 (Simpson 2010d) (available online at www.heritagecouncil.ie).

In tandem with this, Dublin has benefited hugely from a second INSTAR-funded project entitled the Early Medieval Archaeology Project, AD400–1100 (EMAP), which is based in the School of Archaeology, University College Dublin (www.emap.ie) (see Harney et al., this volume). This nationwide study examines in particular the wealth of information relating to early medieval Ireland generated by the huge increase in archaeological excavations in Ireland during the construction boom and is a wonderful resource for anyone interested in medieval Dublin.

The benefits of intensive research can also be seen by the significant output from Module 1 of the Medieval Rural Settlement Project (MRSP), which was set up in 2002 by the Discovery Programme, a state-funded research body.

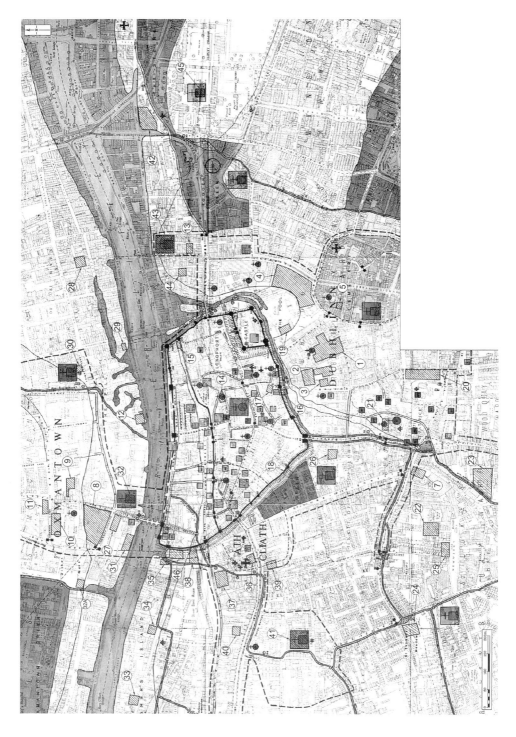

This study examines settlement and land-use in the region surrounding the medieval capital city, following the Anglo-Norman invasion of Ireland in 1169. The success of this intensive and academic research can be measured in the major and ground-breaking book that has just been published by Margaret Murphy and Michael Potterton, the worth of which is self-evident (Murphy and Potterton 2009).

Finally, the *Medieval Dublin* series itself and other publications, including the National Museum Publications series and *Dublin in the medieval world: studies in honour of Howard B. Clarke*, have added significantly to our knowledge of historic Dublin, the *Medieval Dublin* series alone adding 100 articles by 73 authors, at the time of writing, with a further two volumes in press. The benefits to the subject of such intensive academic coverage are obvious and particularly well-articulated in a question posed by Stout in his final comments in a recent review of the above: 'Is there any town in Europe so rich in medieval scholarship?' (Stout 2009–10, 196).

THE POOL OF 'DUIBLINN'

As 'Forty years a-digging' discussed ten years ago, the Viking settlement at Dublin was known in the contemporary sources by two names, *Áth Cliath* ('Ford of the hurdles') and *Duiblinn* ('Black pool'), both obviously prominent topographical features somewhere near the mouth of the River Liffey (Clarke 2002, 17; Simpson 2000, 52–3). The site of the pool has been traditionally identified as the garden attached to Dublin Castle, an association now recreated in its modern name, the Dubhlinn Gardens. While it is not yet possible to confirm the location as that of the historic 'Black pool', several boreholes on the site in the early 1990s did locate the remains of a silty marshland, likely to be associated with a standing body of water such as a pool (Meenan, *Excavations 1991*, 35). However, the date of these deposits could not be established as the investigation was very limited.

1.2 Update of excavations and investigations (2011)
(*key*: 1 Golden Lane; 2 Chancery Lane; 3 Bride Street; 4 South Great George's Street; 5 Longford Street Little; 6 Longford Street Little; 7 The Coombe; 8 Hammond Lane/Church Street; 9 Church Street East; 10 Jameson's Distillery; 11 May Lane; 12 Ormond Quay; 13 Crow Street/Temple Lane; 14 Fishamble Street; 15 Lower Exchange Street; 16 Werburgh Street; 17 Werburgh Street; 18 Iveagh Market; 19 Assay Office; 20 Kevin Street Garda; 21 St Patrick's Cathedral; 22 The Coombe bypass; 23 New Street; 24 Ardee Street; 25 Newmarket; 26 John Dillon Street; 27 Hammond Lane; 28 Strand Street Little (Walsh); 29 Strand Street Little (Walsh); 30 6 Mary Abbey Street; 31 Arran Quay; 32 Innes Quay; 33 Strand Street/Usher's Island; 34 Bridgefoot Street/Strand Street; 35 Usher's Quay; 36 St John the Baptist; 37 National College of Art and Design; 38 Augustine Street; 39 Thomas Street; 40 Thomas Street; 41 St Thomas' Abbey; 42 Westmorland Street; 43 Cecilia Street; 44 Sycamore Street/Meeting House Square; 45 Trinity College; 46 Augustine Street).

South Great George's Street

Since then, confirmation that the location contained a natural body of water in
use in antiquity was obtained during a large-scale excavation carried out by the
writer at South Great George's Street, along the supposed southern rim of the
pool (4). This edge is preserved in the modern streetscape by a distinctive
curving eighteenth-century property boundary, with a drop in height of 4m
from south (South Great George's Street) to north (the Dubhlinn Gardens).
The excavations revealed the remains of Viking habitation and burials, centred
on an inlet that fed directly into the pool and which was used by Vikings to
moor their boats (Simpson 2005, 11–62; ibid. 2010, 63–4).

This narrow inlet displayed evidence of periodic inundations and, critically,
the layers included the distinctive orange gravel found in the channel of the
Liffey, demonstrating unimpeded ingress and egress to the Liffey and
ultimately the sea. More recently, boreholes within the Gardens have provided
additional information establishing that the silt deposits, originally found in
this location in 1991, are at least 6m in depth, suggesting that the pool was
originally very deep (pers. comm., William R. Frazer).

Assay Office, Dublin Castle

There have been other developments in attempting to define the limits of the
pool. In 'Forty years a-digging', it was suggested that the distinctive turn in
Ship Street Little may have been influenced or dictated directly by the western
edge of the pool. However, excavations within the Assay Office building (just east
of the Chester Beatty Library (19)), have established that this area was outside
the pool, as a water channel excavated there could be dated to the fourteenth
century (Myles 2008). Thus, the western limit must have been further east
than the Assay Office, perhaps along the current line of the modern gardens.

Summary

The conclusion that must be drawn from the evidence to date is that the castle
garden was originally a body of water at least 6m in depth and fed by both the
Poddle and the tidal Liffey. This phenomenon was exploited by the Vikings in
the ninth century when establishing their raiding camp at Dublin, the availability
of sheltered waters emphasizing what is emerging as a defining characteristic
of such raiding bases: direct and unimpeded access to a major river.

Whether or not this body of water is the remnants of the actual *Duiblinn*
referenced in the historic records is far more difficult to establish and cannot
be done by archaeological means. Duffy has even suggested that the term
Duiblinn may occur in certain Irish-language sources to mean what is now
Dublin Bay, and that there remains the slight possibility that the early medieval
monastic site of that name was located further upstream at Islandbridge, where
a pool just above the tidal reaches of the Liffey is mentioned in the documentary

sources throughout the medieval period (Duffy, 'Tales of Medieval Dublin' lecture series, Lecture 1, 2010).

THE ECCLESIASTICAL SETTLEMENT

One of the major research questions of 'Forty years a–digging' was the location of the monastery of Duiblinn, referred to in the contemporary annals before the arrival of the Vikings in Ireland (Simpson 2000, 15–19). This site was thought to be located in the south-eastern suburb of the later walled town, close to the pool mentioned above and marked by a distinctive street pattern, forming a characteristic oval shape (ibid., 56–60). The northern end was presumed to have been formed by the curving streets of St Peter's Row, Stephen Street Upper and Lower and Whitefriar Street, and is most visible on Rocque's map of Dublin, dated 1756. This type of street pattern has been identified at other historic towns with monastic origins, the streets preserving the outline of the long-vanished enclosing banks.

The oval street pattern and St Stephen's Church
Some archaeological investigations had already been carried out within the putative enclosure at the time of the last synthesis, but these were concentrated in the north-east quadrant, in and around St Stephen's Church, with limited investigation in the interior, at the Carmelite friary and Aungier Street (Simpson 2000, 16). The excavations at St Stephen's Church (25) have since been published by Hayden and Buckley, providing much needed additional detail; in particular, the fact that nothing was found to suggest that there was early activity at this site, the primary deposits dating to the twelfth century (Hayden and Buckley 2002, 172). What is of relevance, however, is that the investigations by Hayden included test-trenching along the curving street alignment of Stephen Street Lower, which attempted to establish whether this boundary originated in the Early Christian period as part of an enclosing feature around the early monastery. However, this work found that there was no evidence earlier than the twelfth century, leading Hayden to suggest that the origin of the curving street lies in an expansion of the northern boundary of the church of St Stephen in the Anglo-Norman period (ibid.). This, however, does not preclude the possibility that the twelfth-century alignment mirrors an earlier smaller curving alignment, which has since disappeared.

St Peter's Church
A large excavation has been carried by Coughlan within the putative enclosure at the north-western side, at the corner of Longford Street Great and Stephen Street Upper (5). This is the known site of St Peter's Church and the work

there initially was thought to have identified part of the monastic ditch, but set back from the modern streetscape, to the rear of the properties fronting onto the street, as suggested above (Coughlan 2003, 22). This ditch was very large, measuring 5m in width, but, while at the northern end it followed the curving alignment of the streets, at the southern end it turned sharply east, suggesting that it is more likely to have enclosed St Peter's Church and cemetery. In addition, the director suggests that the ditch can probably be dated to c.1100, too late to be part of the monastic enclosure (ibid., 26).

Longford Street / Digges Lane
A possible link between this ditch and a second ditch was suggested by O'Neill, although this was located some distance to the east, to the rear of Longford Street/Digges Lane. The second ditch, although similar in size, was curving to the north-west but was positioned to the rear of the properties along Longford Street/Digges Lane, and thus well within the putative enclosure (O'Neill 2004, 73–90; see Coughlan 2003, fig. 5). The information received was limited, as only a small section was excavated, between 6m and 7m in length, and it was not bottomed, due to health and safety considerations. The fill did, however, produce eleventh-century artefactual evidence in the form of a curved roof tile, suggesting that the ditch was being infilled by this date, probably making it unlikely that it was Early Christian.

Digges Lane and Stephen Street Lower
Testing by O'Neill on the adjoining site at the corner of Digges Lane and Stephen Street Lower (behind Drury Lane Hotel) further suggested that the ditch, 6m in width at this location, was possibly continuing for a further 14m, curving towards the north-west, in the direction of St Peter's Church. If this was the case, it would suggest the presence of a large oval enclosure, measuring 150m east–west by 50m north–south, with St Peter's Church at the western end, rather than in the centre (O'Neill 2004). However, the significant distance between both excavations and the limited stretch of the ditch actually excavated (150m) suggests that a degree of caution should be exercised in this instance.

This may also be supported by the fact that an excavation by the writer on this site, to the north of the projected line of the ditch at Longford Street/Digges Lane, found that the earliest deposits produced no finds, suggesting that, although they may have been pre-Anglo-Norman, there was little evidence of activity in this location. By the Anglo-Norman era, the land appears to have been under cultivation, although some ceramic finds may be indicative of domestic habitation close by. The only activity identified was several small pits suggestive of dumping (Simpson, *Excavations 2003*, 0582).

THE SITE OF THE MONASTERY

The church of St Michael le Pole

'Forty years a-digging' highlighted the importance of another site very close by, to the west of the pool and centred on the known church site of St Michael le Pole (*9*) (Simpson 2000, 17–18; Campbell, *Excavations 1989–90*, 99). A section of this important site had been partially excavated in the 1980s and produced the earliest medieval occupation levels at that time from Dublin, quoted in 'Forty years a-digging' as mid-to-late eighth century (Simpson 2000, 17). This important site has now been published by Gowen, providing much-needed detail on these primary deposits (Gowen 2001, 13–52). The carbon-14 determinations confirm that the earliest activity has a 94.6 per cent probability of dating to between 663 and 872, with a 68 per cent probability of dating to between 679 and 779 (ibid., 31).

The nature of the early activity is also very significant and the features included at least one substantial hearth and evidence of intensive burning, some of which was clearly industrial (ibid., 28–31). However, the lower levels also produced a series of fourteen large post-holes, stake-holes and spreads of ash along with three parallel gullies cut into the boulder clay. The hearths and post-holes, some of which were stone-packed, are suggestive of large timber buildings at these early levels, most likely to be domestic, and thereby indicative of occupation. While obviously the post-holes may represent the earliest church on the site, which was probably of timber, the presence of the hearth makes this unlikely.

The stone foundations of the church and integrated round tower were located during the excavation and dated stratigraphically to c.1100. Of extreme interest was the fact that the south wall was constructed on top of a Christian east–west lintel grave, that displayed a 94.6 per cent probability of dating to between 895 and 1269 and a 68 per cent probability of dating to between 999 and 1189 (Gowen 2001, 31). Thus, the evidence suggests that there was an earlier cemetery at this site, which pre-dated the construction of the church in c.1100 and which contained a least one high-status individual, as suggested by the lintel grave.

Bride Street

The early evidence from St Michael le Pole was supported by the findings of a second very important site (*26*: 3), 100m to the west at Bride Street, excavated by McMahon and included in 'Forty years a-digging' (McMahon 2002; Simpson 2000, 18–19). This site also produced evidence of habitation at the primary levels, which was dated to between the eighth and tenth centuries, suggesting that it was associated with the church of St Michael le Pole (Simpson 2000, 18–19). This site has since been published by McMahon, the primary evidence suggesting the presence of an early medieval settlement on the south bank of the Poddle, not far from the church site of St Michael le Pole (McMahon 2002). At least one structure and two non-formal burials were also identified, the latter in the second phase of activity. The published carbon-14 determinations span the period between 726 and 979, and 877 and 1001, suggesting that the primary occupation levels were even earlier (ibid., 81).

Golden Lane
The cumulative evidence, then, presented in 'Forty years a-digging', was starting to highlight the importance of the Poddle valley, to the west of the site of the pool, as potentially a settlement area, coeval with the monastery and perhaps even the monastic site itself. Since then, there have been significant advances made by several excavations in the Golden Lane and Chancery Lane area (**1, 2**) (O'Donovan 2008; Walsh 2009). The first excavated was Golden Lane, directed by O'Donovan in 2005, the excavation site positioned deliberately to the south of the known site of the church, in advance of development (O'Donovan 2008, 36–130).

The subsequent excavation located a significant section of an Early Christian cemetery, suggesting that the ecclesiastical site of St Michael le Pole was considerably earlier than hitherto thought, a significant find and one that was hinted at by the lintelled grave, mentioned above, found as part of the first excavations in the 1980s (Simpson 2000, 27). The new excavation located a total of 272 burials to the south of the church, within an area measuring 22m east–west by 10m approximately, and positioned 15m from the south wall of the church. The type of graves, orientated east–west, with evidence of plank lining, shrouds and ear-muff stones along with clustering of graves is consistent with Early Christian burial practice (ibid., 47). This must have been a discrete burial ground, demonstrated by the fact that no burials were found on the western side during the St Michael le Pole excavations (see Gowen 2001, fig. 9), or on the northern side, which was tested by O'Donovan (pers. comm., E. O'Donovan).

The grave sequence was dated to between *c.*700 and 1200, based on grave morphology and artefactual association, and therefore spanned the taking of Dublin by the Vikings in the mid-ninth century (ibid., 46). The evidence also suggests that the interments were continuous, with no identifiable period of abandonment, the cemetery evidently having been adopted when the Viking Dubliners converted to Christianity in the tenth century or later. While there was no physical evidence of an enclosure, the burials' distinct concentration within an arc suggests that there was originally some sort of boundary, perhaps not very substantial if it was within a larger enclosure and certainly not on a par with the massive ditch around St Peter's Church further west.

The excavations also produced limited evidence of other activity at boulder clay level in the form of three pits that may have pre-dated the use of the ground as a cemetery but are likely to represent early habitation activity (ibid., 44). In addition to the Christian burials, three (possibly four) outlying non-Christian burials were found, two of which were ninth-century furnished pagan Viking burials, a male and female (see below) (O'Donovan 2008, 44–5). Their siting outside the cemetery, which was still in use at the time, may have been a deliberate avoidance although they are more likely to have formed part of a group of similar burials, found along the Poddle valley (see below).

Chancery Lane
The limited evidence of pre-Viking settlement at Golden Lane and St Michael le Pole was expanded very considerably by the findings from four important sites at Chancery Lane to the south-west of Golden Lane, excavated by Walsh from 2002 to 2006 (2) (Walsh 2009, 9–37). These investigations provided evidence of an organized formal settlement spread over a large area (approximately 75m by 50m) and dated to the early medieval period. The carbon-14 determinations span the years 680 to 964 and the director suggests that this primary settlement evidence is most likely to be attributable to native Irish living here sometime between the eighth and tenth century (ibid. 2009, 14).

One of the most significant finds was a substantial semi-sunken road, which was traced over 20m in length at Chancery Lane (2) (Walsh 2009, 14). This major feature was 2.35m in width, mettled and bounded by gullies on either side. The road cut through the truncated remains of a skeleton, which returned a 95.4 per cent probability to dating to between 684 and 885 (with an intercept date of 781), suggesting that the road was laid down at around this time. The road was orientated north-west/south-east, extending past the church of St Michael le Pole, which lay approximately 50m to the west, and was possibly heading to the pool or its environs. The northern destination is not known, but the orientation prompted the director to suggest that it may be heading towards the later Bride Street, perhaps to a crossing on the River Poddle. This route might even represent the *Slige Dála* (see Clarke 2002, fig. 2).

A second roadway, 2m in width, was also found and Walsh thinks this may be identified with a similar feature found by McMahon at Bride Street (3), suggesting that it was at least 60m in length (Walsh 2009, 16). If this is the case, this possible road was running perpendicular to the main road, suggesting the presence of a major junction in this location, an indication of street grid or layout by the mid-ninth century. Both routes had the remnants of boundary fences and structures, aligned to the roads, the structures at Chancery Lane (2) dating from the late eighth/ninth century (McMahon 2002, 75; Walsh 2009, 18). At the latter site, this also included stake-lines respecting the orientation of the road and at least one possible structure measuring 5m in width, along with a second possible hut measuring 4m by 2.5m. An area of mettling was also found that produced evidence of metalworking in the form of slag (Walsh 2009, 21).

The site also produced four graves, orientated east–west, with a fifth suggested by the presence of a skull (ibid., 12). One of the burials was cut by the roadway but three were associated with this feature and these were all in shallow unmarked graves, the evidence suggesting that they were shrouded, as was the Irish custom, similar to the burials at Golden Lane (ibid., 12). They were generally spread far apart and can probably be linked to the group of burials found further west at Bride Street (McMahon 2002). The director suggests that the burials at Chancery Lane (2) were most likely to be native Irish rather than Viking. The collection of artefacts supports this, as no diagnostically Viking artefacts were found. The dates from the burials (94.5 per cent probability) ranged from 680 to 883 (intercept date of 778) and 780 to 964 (intercept date of 885), indicative of ninth-century native occupation west of the pool (Walsh 2009, 19).

Also of interest was the discovery of a stone-lined well, associated with the roadway, which was square but had two steps on the southern side and could be dated to the ninth century (ibid., 21). This well was far more elaborate than a well of a similar date found at Golden Lane (1), and the fact that the well could be accessed suggests that it might have been a holy well, as such features are common, both within monastic enclosures and in the general environs.

Summary
The remains of a street grid and related plot layout at Chancery Lane at this very early date are compelling evidence that this low-lying ground formed part of the monastic settlement, tucked in behind the ridge and on the banks of the pool. The carbon-14 determinations from a layer of silt over the mettled road suggest that the road was out of use by the mid-ninth century (ibid., 15), an indication, perhaps, of some sort of significant event that had a major impact on the continuing evolution of settlement in this area. This may, of course, have been the arrival of the Vikings in the early to mid-ninth century, the recent discoveries demonstrating that they overran the Poddle valley, although it is likely that they would have adopted such a significant piece of infra-structure. Alternatively, the road may have fallen into disuse when the Viking settlement was attacked and destroyed in the mid-ninth century and when attention was refocused along the Liffey frontage site to the north (see below).

Despite this, the area did continue to be utilized by Vikings, as demon-strated by the general spread of Viking burials in the Poddle valley and the continuing habitation at Golden Lane (1) into the tenth century and onwards, as well as evidence of occupation further west at South Great George's Street (4) (see below). However, the evidence suggests that this habitation was relatively sparse, especially from one of the sites at Chancery Lane, where there was no demonstrable occupation into the Viking and Hiberno-Norse period on that specific site.

THE FORD OF DUBLIN

The second name of Dublin, *Áth Cliath* ('ford of the hurdles') evidently refers to one of the most important and defining features of the settlement on the banks of the River Liffey, but surprisingly little is known about its whereabouts (Clarke 2002, 17; Simpson 2010e, 54–5). As is well known and reported in 'Forty years a-digging', two possibilities are consistently cited: the site of the later bridge (Bridge Street Lower and Church Street) or just west of the bridge, along the alignment of Bow Lane (Clarke 2002, 17).

3–15 Hammond Lane / 161–168 Church Street
There has been some advancement in our knowledge in the intervening years, provided by a large excavation along the west side of Church Street (8) (3–15 Hammond Lane; 161–168 Church Street) along the medieval river frontage, which was excavated in three separate sections. Church Street is identified in Speed's map of Dublin, dated 1610, as the main street in Oxmantown (see below), the pre-Anglo-Norman date of the route established by the presence of St Michan's Church, which was certainly in existence by 1095–6, if not earlier (Purcell 2009, 19).

The pre-Anglo-Norman date of the Church Street route was confirmed by the Phase 2 excavations by Phelan in the north-east corner of the large block (8), fronting onto Church Street (Phelan 2010, 164–97; Phelan and Weldon 2007). This work established that the main approach to the bridge (Church Street) was on an elevated route, which had a substantial bank and ditch bordering it along the western side. The earthworks were likely to be defensive, guarding this important route, and a date-range of 1122–61 was determined for a fence cutting the top of the bank, suggesting that the bank proper was constructed in the late eleventh/early twelfth century. The excavations did not locate the actual road surface of Church Street, unfortunately, which the director suggests lies 3m below the present surface, and, as a result, it is impossible to establish whether or not the route was any earlier than the late eleventh century, although it was certainly the main access route by that time.

The first phase of this large excavation (8) fronted onto what was the original river foreshore along the Hammond Lane frontage, and this encompassed the proposed northern landing point of the ford, west of the bridge, as suggested by Clarke (Cryerhall 2006, 9–51; Clarke 2002). The excavation revealed the remains of flood banks and ditches, running parallel to the river, which had a 94.5 per cent probability of dating to between 1010 and 1160, suggesting that they were constructed sometime in the late eleventh century, a similar date to the defences along Church Street (ibid., 20). However, there was a gap in the earthworks that measured 20m in width, allowing unrestricted access to the riverfront in an area with a gentle gradient towards the river. This, the director suggests, may mark the landward site of the ford but of a later date, dated to the late eleventh century/twelfth century. It is certainly the case that the bridge and ford may have been operating simultaneously, well into the Hiberno-Norse period as the width of the river at low tide was probably only 5m (ibid., 22). This crossing point, if it was such, was out of use by the late twelfth century.

THE VIKINGS: OCCUPATION AND BURIAL IN NINTH-CENTURY DUBLIN

One of the major preoccupations at the time of 'Forty years a-digging' was the location of the first Viking settlement at Dublin, the *longphort* or 'ship camp', where the Vikings first over-wintered in 841. This was prompted by the fact that the extensive excavations at Fishamble Street/Wood Quay in the 1970s and 1980s suggested that the main settlement on the ridge above the Liffey could be dated to the early tenth century, at the earliest, although there was evidence of sporadic activity along the river foreshore, which pre-dated the construction of the flood banks in the early tenth century (Wallace 1982). The excavations, then, did not produce firm evidence of intensive pre-tenth-century habitation such as that found at Temple Bar West to the east (Halpin 2005, 102).

Ship Street Great and South Great George's Street
This research question has been advanced significantly since then, accelerated mainly by the identification of a ninth-century grave-field, spread out along the Poddle valley, along with a discrete area of habitation, centred on an inlet of the pool and defended by a series of earthworks and palisades (Simpson 2005, 11–62; ibid. 2010, 62–8). The first indication was the unexpected discovery by the writer of a severely damaged Viking warrior grave at a large site at Ship Street Great/Golden Lane (1), which had been almost completely removed by deep cellars (ibid., 32–4). Unfortunately, all that survived in the shallow grave was the skull and part of the upper torso, but enough was left to establish that it was a male aged between 25 and 29. He was in a supine position and was orientated east–west, with the head to the west, in the Christian tradition. But the skeleton also had a group of objects around his neck, identified as grave goods, and this was not consistent with Christian burials. These included a delicate finger ring, a silver twisted ring, a decorated glass bead and a fragment of square iron disk, which could not be identified. The most diagnostic find, however, was a fragment of a pattern-welded sword found next to the burial, identifying the grave as a Viking furnished warrior burial. This was supported by the date determined for the remains, which had

a 94.5 per cent probability of being between 665 and 865 (intercept date 790) (ibid.).

When a second large block (100m by 50m) came up for redevelopment, to the east of the Ship Street Great site, at South Great George's Street (4), the entire site was excavated by the writer and a further four warrior burials were found, suggesting that the area was possibly part of a large grave-field or cemetery that stretched out along the Poddle valley (Simpson 2005, 34–53). The excavation was on the southern lip of the pool (now the Dubhlinn Gardens next to the Chester Beatty Library) and at the lowest levels, the remains of a ninth-century Viking settlement were uncovered, bounded by a waterway or inlet on the western side. This inlet fed directly into the pool and thus there was access via the Poddle and Liffey to the open sea from this sheltered site upstream on the Liffey–Poddle confluence. The primary levels suggested occupation, demonstrated by hearths, domestic refuse pits, drainage gullies and evidence of buildings, along with large amounts of butchered animal bone and shell. Various fragments of human remains found in these early levels suggested that a mixed population resided here, which included women, children and at least one neonatal, of thirty-six months' gestation.

Although the levels were very truncated, the remains of one large aisled rectangular hall, at least 10.5m in length (but an estimated 15m) and supported by substantial large internal stone-packed posts, were also found, the first phase of which is most likely to date to the late ninth century (ibid., 49). The middle aisle, 3m in width, was mettled and was replaced at least twice, while the hearth was off-centre but substantial, measuring 65cm in width. Other structures and at least one large industrial hearth/kiln were also identified in the immediate environs, along with post-holes, stake-holes and refuse pits – all indicators of domestic habitation.

The area of occupation was flanked by the inlet and divided off from the water by two successive palisade fences within slot-trenches and a ditch along the break in slope, later converted into a bank. While these features were originally thought to represent an effort to control flooding, as they were subsumed by silt (Simpson 2005, 36), they are now thought to form part of a boundary or defence system, as they compare favourably with similar features at Wood Quay, which were not very substantial (Russell and O'Brien 2005; Harrison 2007). In support of this, the ditch was cut into higher ground, above the tidal reaches of the water (Simpson 2005, 56; 2010e, 76).

The inlet or river channel was obviously in use in the ninth century, as the excavation of the river gravels produced diagnostically Viking Age finds, which were predominantly of metal. These included two lead weights, a drop-bearded axe, a knife blade, an iron shears and six ship rivets, suggesting that boats were moored in this location, presumably in the pool directly north (ibid.). What was most surprising was the fact that the four warrior burials were identified in the habitation deposits, all in shallow graves, perhaps suggesting that they were originally sealed by cairns (Simpson 2005, 11–62; 2010e, 78–9). They were aged between 17 and 29 and were strong physically, one possibly with a severed right arm, suggesting that he died in battle. Three had surviving grave-goods and these included two shield bosses, a dagger, an antler comb, a zoomorphic bone pin and an unidentified metal object, possibly part of a knife guard (Daly 2005, 63–77). One of the burials lay on a hearth (although the skeleton was not burnt) and a second was on a thin layer of charcoal.

All of the skeletons were dated by carbon-14 determination and three produced a 94.5 per cent probability of dating to between 670 and 882 (intercept dates of 770, 786 and 790), while the fourth had a wider span, of between 786 to 995 (intercept date of 885) (Simpson 2005, 43–7). Isotope analysis was also carried out and proved very informative, suggesting that this was a heterogeneous group of warriors, as two of them came from Scandinavia, while the other two came from somewhere closer to Ireland, possibly the Viking colonies in Scotland and the Isles.

Golden Lane
More recently, an additional two furnished Viking burials were located at Golden Lane (1), right beside the Ship Street Great warrior. The Viking burials lay between 10m and 30m from the Early Christian cemetery and were 150m west of the South Great George's Street burials. They are likely to form part of the same group, surviving in small pockets of intact ground where the houses later built on the site had no cellars to destroy the archaeology. Osteological examination by Buckley identified a male, as expected, but also a female, the first women of the Poddle valley group. The skeleton was in relatively good condition, consisting of the full torso, pelvic region and part of the legs and arms although the skull was unfortunately missing (see O'Donovan 2008, 51, pl. 9). She was orientated slightly north-east/south-west with the head to the south-west and was in a slightly curved supine position, with the hands over the pelvis. Analysis suggests that she was a middle-aged or older female, buried with an unusual decorated bone buckle.

The second burial was also an exceptional find. It was a male aged between 20 and 30, who was evidently a high-status individual, as his grave-goods included a spear-head, a decorated belt buckle, a strap end, an iron knife and two lead weights (possibly originally in a leather pouch) (ibid., 50–1). He was also in a supine position and was orientated slightly north-east/south-west, with the head to the west (see O'Donovan 2008, 49, fig. 7). The carbon-14 determinations of both graves suggest a 95.4 per cent probability of the burials dating to between 678 and 869, and 680 and 870, almost identical to the Ship Street Great and South Great George's Street burials.

Two additional outlying burials, without grave-goods, were orientated east–west, suggestive of Christian burials. The first was the almost intact skeleton of an older male, buried in a supine position and orientated east–west with head to the west. This burial had a 94.5 per cent probability of dating to between 772 and 900, suggesting that he too could potentially be a Viking warrior. The second, which was badly damaged, was also a male but was a younger adult, making him a contender for warrior status, especially as he was only 10m to the south-west of the Ship Street Great burial.

What is immediately very striking at Golden Lane is that all four outlying burials are orientated roughly east–west, with the head to the west, in what is essentially the Early Christian tradition. The burial at Ship Street Great, only 10m from one of the burials at Golden Lane, was also orientated east–west with the head to the west but, at the time, this was simply attributed to a coincidental orientation (Simpson 2005, 33). At South Great George's Street, although not as striking, one of the burials was orientated north-west/south-east with the head to the west, while a second was orientated south-west/north-east with the head to the south-west (Simpson 2005, 41). The orientations at Golden Lane/Ship Street Great (1) are unlikely to be coincidental, given the numbers, but suggest that the grave-diggers may have been influenced in some way by the burial tradition of the adjoining Christian cemetery. This is despite the fact that three of the burials were accompanied by grave-goods and were clearly pagan warrior burials.

The combination of carbon-14 determinations (seven in total) suggests that, statistically, the warriors are likely to be early in the sequence and it is certainly the case that all the dates of the Poddle valley group area are remarkably consistent, especially in their intercept dates. If the orientations of the Viking pagan warrior graves are influenced by the Christian burial rite, and this is not merely coincidental, this may suggest a certain merging of traditions from the very start, the Vikings displaying, perhaps, an adaptability to the existing population at Dublin rather than being bent on their extinction. It is also the case, of course, that this merging of traditions may suggest that the graves are later in the Viking warrior sequence rather than earlier. One point to notice is that the belt buckle found with the male warrior at Golden Lane could be paralleled with other examples from the Irish Sea region, dated to the early tenth century (O'Donovan 2008, 53), while another warrior burial, found at Bride Street in the nineteenth century but not discussed here, has a sword that has been reclassified by Harrison and re-dated to the early tenth century (Harrison 2010, 139).

Islandbridge
There have been other recent developments involving Viking warrior burials, but not in the known core of the Viking Age settlement at the confluence of the Poddle and Liffey. The truncated remains of a male warrior, 1.5km upstream at Islandbridge, was excavated by the National Museum of Ireland after a sword and spearhead were recovered during service works. The skeleton was

badly truncated but was evidently a furnished warrior burial, similar to those
found as part of the larger burial field (see Maeve Sikora et al., this volume).
The find site was not unexpected, as it was within a known Viking burial-
ground, stretching from Islandbridge to Kilmainham, on the south bank of the
Liffey, where a minimum of fifty-two burials were found between in the late
nineteenth and early twentieth century (O'Brien 1998; Ó Floinn 1998, 35–44;
Harrison 2010, 127; Simpson 2010e, 69–70).

Finglas
The Viking warrior burials are not confined to the south side of the river but,
critically, are found on both sides, as at least two potential cemeteries have also
been identified on the north side of the river, at Phoenix Park and Parnell
Square/Granby Row, extending east to Mountjoy Square (Ó Floinn 1998,
134–6). These burials can be found further afield, however, as a surprise find
was made at 4–8 Church Street in Finglas, where a female grave was located
during an excavation (Kavanagh, *Excavations 2004*, 0599; Sikora 2010). She
was aged between 25 and 35 and was orientated east–west in a shallow grave.
Her grave-goods were spectacular: two oval brooches, gilded in gold and silver,
along with copper, textile and an unusually long comb.

Chancery Lane
The evidence suggests that there was a certain contraction in the settlement at
Chancery Lane after the roadway went out of use, perhaps because the Viking
settlement further west, at South Great George's Street, took precedence. The
evidence from the excavation certainly records some degree of reorganization
in the general layout after the roadway fell out of use, as one of the sites in
Chancery Lane (2) identified flimsy structures within plots, 5m in width,
which respected the line of Chancery Lane rather than the early roadway.
Numerous pits, some of which were a very regular size and possibly originally
timber-lined, indicate that the activity in this location is likely to be domestic,
rather than dumping, with some evidence of industrial activity, perhaps
smithing (Walsh 2009, 22). But elsewhere, parts of the site contained a silt
deposit, which was identified as cultivation or plough-soil, suggestive of open
ground in this location, and the director noted that there was no evidence of
occupation or direct continuity of usage into the tenth and eleventh centuries
(ibid., 21).

Summary
The combination of evidence coming from these crucial excavations in the
Poddle valley indicates that there was a ninth-century Viking encampment on
the south bank of a natural pool (possibly the 'Black Pool' implied in the place-
name *Duiblinn*), and thus set back from the main River Liffey. The selection of

a location without a river frontage might have been dictated by the position of the sheltered pool (which was used to moor boats) and/or by the existing infrastructure, in the form of the Early Christian settlement known to have existed in the Chancery Lane/Golden Lane area, a short distance to the west.

The carbon-14 determinations suggest that this first encampment on the banks of the pool was set up early in the sequence of Viking contact at Dublin, possibly even pre-837, when the Vikings are first recorded as taking Dublin, presumably occupying it intermittently before finally staying the winter in 841, a reflection of the fact that the raiding base had probably rapidly evolved into a trading base, the highly portable plundered booty becoming a trading commodity. The camp must have taken on some sort of a semi-permanent status when the burials occurred, perhaps operating as a way-station, as suggested by Downham, but one that was militarily secure (Downham 2010, 116). It is also the case that little is understood about the make-up of the large Viking warrior gangs, although isotope analysis from South Great George's Street indicates that it was a mix, from Scandinavia and the early colonies. It is possible, therefore, that there were a series of different encampments scattered around the mouth of the Liffey, on both sides of the river.

It is also not known how long burial continued in the Poddle valley, although, in general, these types of burials are dated to the ninth century, with this type of burial rite being largely abandoned by the tenth century (Harrison 2010, 145).

It may also be the case that initially both the monastic settlement and the Viking camp coexisted side-by-side for a time, especially when the latter was first established, but that the Vikings eventually appear to have dominated the entire area is suggested by the fact that at least two Vikings were interred at the ecclesiastical centre (Golden Lane (1)), close to what must have been the centre of the Early Christian settlement. What is clear, however, is that this period of Viking occupation in this location was relatively limited in time and this area did not develop in tandem with the tenth-century *dún* further north along the Liffey frontage. While the excavations at Chancery Lane (2), St Michael le Pole (9), Golden Lane (1) and South Great George's Street (4) did produce evidence of tenth-century activity (apart from one of the four sites at Chancery Lane), in general, these deposits were not indicative of intensive occupation.

The Poddle valley group may also have been associated with the known cemetery that has been identified east of the tenth-century Viking settlement, at the Hoggen Green, now College Green (Simpson 2010e, 66–7). The importance of this suburb is highlighted by the fact that the place-name is derived from the Old Norse word *haugar*, meaning burial mounds, two of which survived into the seventeenth century. The Thingmoot or public assembly place was also located in this area outside the main area of settlement (Duffy 2005, 354). The evidence to date suggests that there were at least four male warrior burials in Hoggen Green, which probably date from a similar phase to the Poddle valley group. This may suggest that the warriors were buried in a large swathe or grave-field that stretched from Hoggen Green to Bride Street and even potentially as far as Islandbridge and Kilmainhan.

The pattern at Dublin, then, is of a concentration of at least seventy-five Viking burials, most likely to be ninth century, interred in individual graves around the mouth of the Liffey, extending up as far as Kilmainham. It has been calculated that this large number represents a fifth of all known Viking Age examples from Britain and Ireland (Harrison 2010, 127), which is difficult to explain unless there was a significant Viking population in Dublin at this time, far bigger than the excavated evidence at South Great George's Street would suggest.

THE LONGPHORT OF DUBLIN

The findings at South Great George's Street, coupled with the recent discoveries in regard to Viking camps or *longphuirt* at Woodstown, Co. Waterford, and at Annagassan, Co. Louth, must prompt a review of the data presented in 'Forty years a-digging', not least because of what is now known about the potential size of such encampments, even if they were transitory. In the case of Woodstown, which was still operating into the tenth century, the settlement was almost half a kilometre in length (O'Brien and Russell 2005). Dublin was a major base in a position of prominence in Ireland and is likely therefore to have been at least as large as Woodstown. This may suggest that the *longphort* occupied all the area between the pool and the Liffey frontage, including the Temple Bar West site (35) (Simpson 2010e, 73, 79). Thus, the site of the *longphort* at Dublin was potentially huge, measuring over 400m north–south by potentially 200m in width.

When we compare the early dates coming from the Poddle valley (early to mid-ninth century) with the slightly later dates coming from the intensive habitation deposits at Temple Bar West (in and around the late ninth century), reported on 'Forty years a-digging', we can perhaps chart a pattern in occupation over time: thus, it would appear that there was a shift northwards, from the concentrated activity at South Great George's Street within a defended area of the pool, to the high ridge on the banks of the Liffey.

Temple Bar West
The critical evidence comes from a large site excavated by the writer, to the west of Wood Quay (*6–7a*), at Temple Bar West (*39*) included in 'Forty years a-digging', the stratigraphic report of which has subsequently been completed (Simpson 2001). This excavation was within the north-east corner of the later

tenth-century *dún* and was deliberately sited there, as a previous excavation at Parliament Street (15) by Scally had located evidence of late ninth-century domestic habitation, along with flood banks on the River Poddle (Simpson 2000, 21; Gowen with Scally 1999; Scally 2002). A similar stratigraphy was identified at Temple Bar West (*39*), but a far larger area was excavated as part of a research programme. In general, the results confirmed the presence of ninth-century levels in this location, followed by intensive habitation by the late ninth century (Simpson 1999; 2001).

Past interpretations: The primary levels at Temple Bar West (*39*) suggested that there was occupation on the banks of the Poddle and the Liffey from an early period, possibly even pre-dating the arrival of the Vikings in the mid-ninth century. After this, the evidence was more scattered but by the late ninth century the area was certainly densely settled and formally laid out, divided into property plots containing houses and was clearly part of a large Viking settlement at the confluence of the Poddle (Simpson 1999; 2000, 21–2). While an earthen bank was identified at Temple Bar West (*39*) running parallel to the Liffey, it was interpreted as a flood bank similar to those found at Parliament Street to the east, and deemed by its size unlikely to be defensive. On the basis of this, the interpretation was that the habitation was an 'urban sprawl' associated with the *longphort*, which was assumed to have been positioned somewhere upstream on the Poddle (ibid., 22).

   This emphasis by the writer on the apparent lack of defences at Temple Bar West was, however, probably a mistake, as the excavations at Woodstown, Co. Waterford, also enclosed by a bank and ditch system, established that neither of these features was particularly substantial (Harrison 2007). In addition, at South Great George's Street (4), the defences consisted of two successive slot-trenches, originally holding palisades, and a small bank and ditch. The slot-trenches can now be paralleled by a similar distinctive slot-trench that was identified at the earliest levels, running parallel to the Liffey (Simpson 2010e, 81).

   With this in mind, a review of the evidence for the early levels of Temple Bar West may suggest that this area was within the documented *longphort*, which stretched from the crook of the Poddle and Liffey as far south as the Black Pool on the Poddle, in a topographical location that is very typical of this kind of Viking site (ibid.). This early site may have been bounded by Fishamble Street on the western side, as first suggested in 'Forty years a-digging', the continuation of this boundary being perhaps the Werburgh Street alignment, as suggested by Halpin in his convincing paper on the evolution of Dublin (Halpin 2005, 78–114).

The primary levels: Six potentially ninth-century levels were identified on the banks of the river (see below). The primary phase was associated with an inlet of the Liffey, which was bordered by a post-and-wattle fence, continuous apart from a 3m gap, presumably for access to the water (Simpson 2010e, 80–1). Two large upright posts in the channel may be all that survives of mooring posts set into coarse gravels, the gravel returning a 94.5 per cent probability of dating to between 630 and 905 (64 per cent probability of dating between 665 and 885), with an intercept date of 705.

This activity was protected by a palisade within a slot-trench, mentioned above, which ran along the bank of the Liffey, orientated east–west. Up on the river bank, there was evidence of scattered habitation and industrial processes, most likely Viking in date, as the finds included a fragment of amber, probably from the Baltic region (Simpson 2010e, 81; 2001, 40). The habitation evidence consisted of large stone-packed post-holes, suggesting structures, although the plan and formation were difficult to decipher. The industrial activity was at the southern side of the site, where the remains of hearths and spreads of ash and charcoal, along with mettled and clay surfaces were found, suggesting that some sort of industrial metalworking was taking place.

The ploughing episode: All of this phase of activity was ploughed out in what appeared to be a single act, described in 'Forty years a-digging' (Simpson 2000, 20), which stretched from the Poddle on the east as far west as Fishamble Street at least, and possibly into Wood Quay. If this is the case, the curving line of Fishamble Street may not have marked the western limit of the early activity at this level, as suggested above, but was still likely to have been a pre-tenth-century boundary (Simpson 2000, 23–4; Halpin 2005, 102). The industrial activity at the southern side of the site continued in the same area uninter-rupted after the ploughing, suggesting that this activity may not have been associated with cultivation per se, as one would expect, but rather an attempt by the Vikings to clear the land and lay it out anew, perhaps after the longphort was destroyed in the mid-ninth century.

Late ninth-century activity in Temple Bar West: What is certain is that industrial activity intensified after the ploughing and this processing was finally identified as iron smelting (by Robert Barklie and Christopher Stillman, TCD), an activity that was also very well represented at the Woodstown site in Co. Waterford. The surprise, however, was that the iron source was not bog iron but hematite, the closest source of which is in the Wicklow Mountains. If the ore was being mined by the *longphort* inhabitants of Dublin rather than imported, this has implications for the degree of intimate connections that must have existed between the Vikings and the inhabitants, which went beyond the supply of meat, food and timber. It also attests to the amount of investment in Dublin as a trading rather than a raiding base.

Burial evidence: The western side of the site produced evidence of burial, which was very different from the warrior burials mentioned previously and likely to date to the late ninth century (Simpson 2001). The first was at the western end of the site and was that of a small child, with the head to the west, in the Christian tradition, but associated with a pit, which contained a bull skull, fully fleshed on deposition. This was probably a pagan votive offering and it returned a 94.5 per cent probability of dating to between 690 and 1025 (64 per cent chance of dating between 790 and 880), but with an intercept date of 865. This burial may have been associated with a second curious burial/charnel pit a short distance to the east, which contained seven complete cattle skulls, five with horns, all lined up deliberately along the eastern edge, surrounding fragments of two human crania in the middle. A third pit also contained human remains in the form of one limb, but also several articulated vertebrae, the latter suggesting that there was still skin and sinew attached when the bones were deposited.

The burials were within an area that was actually occupied, similar to the site at South Great George's Street (4), the evidence for occupation including a well preserved clay-domed kiln, most likely (judging by its type) to be for corn-drying, although no cereal was found. This was associated with some sort of large structure defined by post-pits and at least two large hearths. The remains of a possible fence were also found, suggestive of small-scale settlement in this location.

The sunken structures: The scattered occupation and usage of the ground on the western side of the site was replaced by three sunken structures or *grubenhauser*, which were positioned along the banks of the Liffey (along Essex Street West) and described in 'Forty years a-digging' (Simpson 2000, 22–3). In summary, they measured 3.2m by 2.25 in width by 60cm and each had a sunken passageway, returning a 94.5 per cent probability of dating to between 790 and 890 (64 per cent chance of dating between 790 and 880), but with an intercept date of 865. The eastern end of the site also produced evidence of two additional possible sunken structures, although these were very truncated.

Property layout and reorganization: These sunken structures were infilled in a single event, probably in preparation for the rapid development of this quarter, which was then laid out into property plots containing houses, some of which had animal pens at the rear of the plots. This phase of occupation, as described in 'Forty years a-digging' (Simpson 2000, 21–2), was relatively short-lived as there were only two phases of housing, but the type of post-and-wattle house (Type 1, after Wallace) was identical to those found in the tenth-century levels at Wood Quay (6), suggesting that the form was established even by this early date in the late ninth century.

The plots were orientated north-east/south-west, respecting the line of the Poddle rather than the Liffey to the north, and space may have been at a premium, suggested by the fact that the river inlet was infilled and reclaimed by this time. A sophisticated level of communal organization was demonstrated by the construction of a stone roadway, leading down to the Liffey in the second phase. The land to the west of the houses, towards Wood Quay and where the sunken structures were infilled, was divided into three large properties and the ground was levelled up with domestic refuse where it sloped northwards down to the river. A series of animal pens and one square house were then constructed within the existing properties, suggesting less intensive habitation on this side of the site.

This early habitation phase was also identified by Scally to the east, between Temple Bar West (*39*) and the Poddle at Parliament Street/Exchange Street Upper (*15*), where it was similarly short-lived (Gowen with Scally 1996, 10; Scally 2002). The first house (orientated north–south) returned a 94.5 per cent probability of dating to between 690 and 888, while one of the subsequent houses returned a 94.5 per cent probability of dating to between 779 and 983. Statistical analysis carried out by Scally suggests that there is an 82.6 per cent chance that these structures pre-dated the tenth century (ibid., 14). A house at Temple Bar West returned a 94.5 per cent probability of dating to between 775 and 1015 (64 per cent chance of dating to between 865 and 985), with an intercept date of 895, while a second house had a 94.5 per cent probability of dating to between 780 and 1000 (64 per cent chance of dating to between 865 and 975), with an intercept date of 890 (Simpson 2001).

These houses were subsequently demolished and the area was subsumed by the industrial processes noted to the south, suggesting a complete change of usage along the river. This change was also identified at Parliament Street/Essex Street/Exchange Street Upper (*15*) by Scally, suggesting that the entire north-east corner, bounded by the Poddle on the east and the Liffey on the north, became one large open industrial area in the early tenth century (see below).

LATE NINTH–CENTURY DEFENCES AT DUBLIN

Parliament Street
An earthen bank, measuring 3.7m in width, was identified running along the Poddle riverbank at Parliament Street/Exchange Street Upper (*15*) and this, the director suggests, pre-dates the tenth-century phase of activity, a development that is mirrored by a similar although more substantial bank at Temple Bar West (*39*) (Gowen with Scally 1996, 11–12; Simpson 2001). At Parliament Street, the low height prompted the director to suggest that this is unlikely to have functioned as a flood bank, mainly because it is at least 3m above the high-tide mark of the river (ibid., 16).

Temple Bar West

At Temple Bar West, only the southern flank of the bank was within the excavation cutting, but this was founded on an elaborate wattle screen that was pegged into the ground and may have originally represented a pathway along the river (Simpson 2001). These banks are not substantial, but the evidence to date suggests that the massive defensive ramparts, which encircled the settlement or *dún* in the mid- to late tenth century, evolved from these smaller flood banks and an intermediary defensive bank, like those found at Woodstown, Co. Waterford, is not an impossibility.

Ross Road

The southern extent of ninth-century activity on the ridge is not known, although a bank was located by Hayden at Werburgh Street (*34*: **17**) and reported on in 'Forty years a-digging', when it was dated to the early tenth century, relatively early in the sequence (see below) (Simpson 2000, 27). Since then, however, this site has been published along with a second important site at Ross Road further west (*27*) (Hayden 2002, 44–68; Walsh 2001, 65–87).

The relevance of the site at Ross Road (*27*) is that it is positioned along the southern line of the tenth-century defences, but Walsh included an interpretation of an earlier excavation (by the National Museum of Ireland) at Christ Church Place, in which she identified some kind of earthen embankment, which was 10m north of the tenth-century banks. This bank was almost 4m in width and pre-dated the tenth-century bank sequence, raising the possibility that it dates to the late ninth century. The rampart appeared to contain habitation material to the north, which included a possible mettled roadway or surface, suggestive of formal layout in this location (Walsh 2001, 95). If this can be dated to the late ninth century, it places this rampart outside the epicentre of activity further east, the western boundary of which was suggested by Halpin to be the Fishamble Street/Werburgh Street alignment (Halpin 2005, 102). However, this bank was only identified in section, after the excavation, and its function and route are difficult to establish.

Werburgh Street

This rampart may have extended as far west as Werburgh Street (*34*: **17**), however, as post-excavation analysis of the site mentioned above by Hayden suggests that the bank can probably be dated to the late ninth/early tenth century (Hayden 2002, 46–7, 66) and may, therefore, represent the late ninth-century rampart and the early tenth-century flood banks noted at Ross Road, coalescing at this point. The full extent of the bank at Werburgh Street was not within the excavation footprint, but what survived measured at least 3m in width, with the remains of a palisade/fence within a slot-trench along the internal (northern) side, partially sealed by bank material (Hayden 2002, 47).

OCCUPATION IN THE PODDLE VALLEY INTO THE TENTH CENTURY

South Great George's Street
The identification of possibly late ninth-century defences in Ross Road on the ridge is significant as, coupled with the evidence from Temple Bar West (*39*), it indicates a focus on the ridge, while there was still occupation in the Poddle, at South Great George's Street (*4*). This continued occupation is suggested by a rebuilding of the hall-type structure, which returned a 94.5 per cent probability of dating to between 895 and 1011, with an intercept date of 976, along with associated deposits (Simpson 2005, 50).

St Michael le Pole
Further west, at the church site of St Michael le Pole (*9*), there was also evidence of later activity, in the form of spreads of clay, mortar and ash, which sealed the primary features but was not scientifically dated, although it pre-dated the church (*c*.1100) and some of the earlier graves. The spreads of mortar suggest the presence of some sort of earlier mortared building, possibly an earlier church, which was then truncated by the foundations of the later church (Gowen 2001, 28–9).

Golden Lane
The excavations at Golden Lane (*1*) also suggest continuous occupation, and one of the major features was the well-preserved remains of a corn-drying kiln, complete with fire-box, flue and drying chamber, which was dated to the tenth century (O'Donovan 2009, 55). Two large rubbish pits were also located, one of which produced a 94.5 per cent probability of dating to between 830 and 1018. The finds included five perforated bone pins, perhaps suggesting manu-facturing close by (ibid., 59). While the evidence does suggest that this area was utilized in the tenth century, the intensive habitation deposits found further north on the ridge of Dublin are noticeably absent, suggesting a shift in focus northwards, towards the banks of the river.

THE TENTH- AND ELEVENTH-CENTURY *DÚN*

'Forty years a-digging' summarized the evidence for habitation within the *dún* or defended area, dating from the tenth century to the early twelfth century, and this has not altered significantly, as there have been no major new excavations in the intervening years. However, more detailed information is now available for at least two of the large sites discussed previously, Temple Bar West and Werburgh Street. The evidence from Temple Bar West (*39*) is particularly important as this site continued to be occupied *after* the Vikings are said to have been expelled from Dublin in 902 and *during* their supposed period of exile until their triumphant return in 914, an indication that only the ruling class are likely to have been forced from Dublin.

Temple Bar West
As mentioned previously, the stratigraphic report from Temple Bar West (*39*) was completed in 2001 and a summary account was included in 'Forty years a-digging' although little detail was included (Simpson 2000, 30–1). The evidence suggests that the eastern side of the site, towards the Poddle, was developed as a large industrial quarter, an expansion of the activity that was occurring along the southern side of the site since the ninth century. The most significant development in the early tenth century, however, occurred on the western side of the site, closest to Wood Quay (*6*), where the ground to the rear of the plots, containing animal pens and small sub-structures, was rapidly developed as a domestic quarter.

Redevelopment at Temple Bar West: The new development involved the conversion of the three large properties into six (and later eight) property plots, orientated north–south and backing onto the River Liffey. The houses were at the southern end and they fronted onto an east–west path or street, made of wattle and timber, the precursor of Copper Alley on the southern side. A minimum of ten habitation levels (Levels 7–16) were identified, which could be dated from early tenth century to the mid- to late twelfth century, in a continuous sequence. The houses at the southern end of the plot unfortunately extended partially beyond the limit of excavation and so the fronts were not excavated, but the rear plots were exposed in their entirety. Each plot was defined by individual post-and-wattle walls, the lower levels woven in a specific way, creating a slanted pattern, not identified in Dublin previously. Most plots had a wattle path extending centrally down the plot, which were replaced over time along with various little outhouses, fronting onto the paths. At one level, all the paths were replaced in stone. The wattle and timber road that the houses fronted onto was exposed in one of the excavations, where it was identified as an enduring route, perhaps the forerunner of the medieval Preston's Lane.

The development of this side of the site as a residential quarter is most likely to be associated with the emerging importance of the Fishamble Street area in the early tenth century and the increase in domestic habitation is probably related to an influx of population associated with the documented return of the exiled Vikings in 917, as discussed in 'Forty year a-digging' (Simpson 2000, 25). However, the evidence does suggest that the site was continually occupied during the period of exile and at least one building straddled the late ninth- and early tenth-century levels.

The buildings at Temple Bar West: A total of nine levels were identified dating from the early tenth century to the early twelfth, with a total of sixty-four buildings spread between five to seven plots. The boundaries at this side of the site continued in use up into the Anglo-Norman period, apart from one slight shift of just over 1m to the east in/or around the early eleventh century. There were indications of continual access from one plot to another, perhaps among familial groups, and this was also suggested by the fact that at least two houses were founded on the same clay foundation. At the western end of the site, the well-preserved remains of a small semi-sunken structure were identified in the rear of the plot, 90cm in depth and with a sunken passageway, lined with granite stones. It was relatively small and extended beyond the limits of the excavation, the excavated section measuring 2m square. The walls were originally stave-built and the wattle floor survived almost intact (Simpson 2001).

The industrial area: The eastern and southern side of the site developed very differently from the western side, especially the eastern side, which was clearly not a domestic quarter, the earlier post-and-wattle houses being sealed deliberately with dumps of clays and converted into an industrial area. The features included clay platforms, hearths and spreads of ash and charcoal along with clay and stone surfaces, and this industrial activity could be traced over a considerable period of time, from the Hiberno-Norse period into the Anglo-Norman period. The larger hearths were extraordinary for their longevity of use and one of the biggest hearths was over 1.2m in depth, representing a considerable period of time. The type of activity could not be identified, although extensive investigations were carried out. Some of the hearths may have been kilns or ovens with clay domes, as the layers of charcoal and ash were interleaved with layers of burnt and baked sod. Dumps of cockle shells were a notable feature and an examination found that these shells included very small examples that were unlikely to have been consumed (depending on the gathering process) and perhaps suggesting that they were used in lime production.

33–34 Parliament Street/Upper Exchange Street
This general phase of industrial activity extended as far as the Poddle by the late tenth century, as it was also located at 33–34 Parliament Street/Upper Exchange Street (*15*) by Scally, where it was equally perplexing (Gowen with Scally 1996, 18). The features in this location were very similar, in particular four free-standing hearths, one of which was stone-kerbed although there was no indication of associated buildings. The processes could not be identified in this location, but the artefact assemblages of pins and combs suggested that people gathered here, possibly engaged in some sort of industrial activity involving hearths and burnings (ibid.). In the late eleventh century, a large clay embankment was constructed across the site and this also contained several hearths, the macro-fossil analysis suggesting use for food processing rather than anything industrial (ibid., 19). This platform was subsequently sealed by large deposits of clay along with cockle shells, also possibly used for lime-making.

Werburgh Street

The second important site within the *dún* was on the western side of Werburgh Street (*34*: **17**), where excavations by Hayden located dense habitation deposits first reported in 'Forty years a-digging'. This site has now been published, in summary form, and the site plans reveal an impressive sequence of houses and buildings within properties, which could be dated from the mid-tenth century to the late eleventh century (Hayden 2002, 44–68). The primary deposits were represented by the remains of a defensive rampart, already mentioned, at the southern end of the site, while a curious feature was also exposed on the western side. This consisted of the south-east corner of a square of infilled ground (approximately 9m north–south by 7m) retained by a stout post-and-wattle fence. The infill consisted of organic material, silt and stones along with dumps of ash and clays. This feature was similar in type to the large reclamation cages found at Temple Bar West (*39*), which preceded the construction of property plots in the early tenth century (west side of the site), the main function of which was to level the slope from south to north towards the river (Simpson 2001).

Formal layout: There is evidence that formal layout was already occurring at this side of the site in the early tenth century, as the remains of a substantial mettled roadway were identified skirting around the reclamation cage and heading westwards (Hayden 2002, 47). This surface, which was replaced at least once, was subsequently sealed by organic refuse before the construction of the first house, but the alignment was preserved in the plot formation, in the form of a small property sandwiched between two adjoining plots.

The first plot and house was orientated east–west, aligned to the banks, and included a sub-circular animal pen, almost identical to pens in Temple Bar West (*35*) (where one included a possible farrowing pen for pigs), a reminder of the rural nature of the defended settlement in spite of the sophistication of a new stone road. Dendrochronological analysis from the path produced a date of AD924±9, although the director suggests that this may be been reused (see below) (Hayden 2002, 48). The subsequent properties that evolved on the site were curving to the north-east, following the orientation of the road long gone and are an indication of the importance of these early features in establishing enduring property alignments, as identified at Temple Bar West, where the alignment of the reclamation cages continued into the twelfth century.

The houses: The Type 1 houses at Werburgh Street were very well-preserved and were similar to those uncovered at Fishamble Street/Wood Quay. A total of nine house levels were identified, the first of which was dated to the early tenth century, as mentioned above, but the next level was dated by coins to the late tenth century. This time gap is difficult to explain, although the director suggests that the dated timber might have been reused and therefore in a later house (ibid., 53).

A sunken structure was also identified in the second level of housing, but representing the first house in that specific plot, as is often the case. This measured just over 3m in width by at least 4.5m in length, but it was truncated at the western end, the passageway unfortunately not surviving. The sunken structure was plank-lined, and the roof was supported on circular posts in the corners and midway down the building (Hayden 2002, 51, fig. 6). While the plank-lining is more akin to the type of later sunken structure found at Temple Bar West (eleventh-century), the size and use of internal circular posts (rather than large rectangular timbers) to support the roof is similar to the group of early sunken structures dated to the late ninth century. This may suggest that the sunken structure represents a hybrid type, straddling the two different types.

The houses at Werburgh Street were accessed by long wattle paths, suggesting that they represent subsidiary or secondary housing, lying to the rear of the houses fronting onto the street; a similar layout to the houses found at Kinlay House, on the eastern side of Fishamble Street (Simpson 2000, 31). Almost all were typical Type 1, as categorized by Wallace, although one did have a slight variation as the door was in the side wall (Hayden 2002, 67). There appears to have been substantial evidence of metalworking in the form of furnaces and hearths along with slag (ibid., 53). One of the features of this site was the many gullies and pits filled with cockle shells, which, the director suggests, may have been used for drainage: perhaps this is the function of the copious amounts of shell used in both Temple Bar West and Parliament Street mentioned above. The finds were also very significant from this site, the upper levels of houses containing late eleventh-century pottery, while the lower levels produced a hoard of Anglo-Saxon silver pennies, dated to the late tenth century. The director also comments on the very fine assemblage of timber and small finds.

Dublin Castle

The findings from Werburgh Street match an earlier site some distance to the east, outside the north-west corner of Dublin Castle (*10: 11*), excavated by Lynch and reported on ten years ago (Simpson 2000, 33). A summary account of these excavations has been published in the *Medieval Dublin* series, revealing additional information about this important phase of the site, including details of some of the more unusual finds (Lynch and Manning 2001, 169–204). The habitation deposits were up to 1m in depth and a total of nine phases of activity were identified. All were aceramic, suggesting that they potentially pre-dated the late eleventh/twelfth century. The phases of activity included the establishment of property boundaries and the construction of post-and-wattle houses along with evidence of metalworking, with a period of abandonment also identified.

High Street

There has been very little work carried out within the city walls, especially at the western end. However, very limited investigations at 11 High Street in 2011 by McQuade did locate over 1m of surviving habitation deposits, which correlates with other investigations that had taken place in the location (pers. comm., Melanie McQuade).

THE DEFENCES OF THE *DÚN*

Ross Road

As previously mentioned, the excavations at Ross Road by Walsh and, to a lesser extent, Werburgh Street by Hayden, have revealed evidence of the tenth-century defences surrounding the settlement and summary details were included in 'Forty year a-digging', but the sites have since been published (Walsh 2001, 88–127; Hayden 2002, 44–68). At Ross Road (*27*), the excavation was deliberately placed along the known southern line of the defences and a total of four successive banks were identified. The first was a flood bank, as previously mentioned, dated to the early tenth century and paralleled directly with Parliament Street (*15*) and Wood Quay (*6*) (Walsh 2001, 96–8). A second bank was constructed on the first and this too is likely to have been a flood bank containing the Poddle to the south, but this, interestingly, was raised over time, as the layers of the banks were interleaved with habitation deposits from the north (ibid., 100).

Fire at Ross Road: While the bank was a flood bank, there were several fences down-slope from the bank, which may have had a defensive function and were destroyed in a catastrophic fire, which burnt the settlement and destroyed the bank, the scattered material of which contained several male skulls and fragments of crania. This, the director suggests, may suggest that the fire was the result of an attack, perhaps that recorded in 936 (ibid. 101). A third embankment was created in the mid- to late tenth century, the northern edge of which was probably scarped to create a significant fall towards the river, and there is evidence of plot layout and the creation of paths at the same time. This embankment was subsequently raised and extended southwards in the late tenth century and a post-and-wattle fence was constructed in a palisade trench on the top of the bank, along with what might have been planking, similar to the bank at Wood Quay (6) (Walsh 2001, 106). Dating evidence from the fence suggests a date from 900 to 990 and it represents the final earthen defence, which eventually measured 6m high by 4m wide. This survived as the main defence until the early twelfth century, when the first city wall was constructed (ibid., 88–127).

The Poddle: The course of the Poddle was also located during the excavation, running along the base of the banks, suggesting that the river flowed along the base of the ridge at this date rather than meandering across the Poddle valley, as previously thought. The river was later re-channelled and pushed further south as part of the reorganization of the defences on this side after the Anglo-Norman invasion (see below) to act as a water-filled moat at the base of the wall (Walsh 1997, 26–7).

Parliament Street
A defensive earthen bank, dated to the late tenth century, was also located by Scally at Parliament Street (15), and the results were published in summary format in 1996 and included in 'Forty years a-digging'. However, a more detailed and substantial account has now been published in the *Medieval Dublin* series, which provides additional information (Scally 2002, 11–33). At this important site, the primary and low bank from the late ninth century became obsolete when a second bank was constructed 12m further east, towards the river. The area between both banks was then reclaimed by dumping in stony clays (ibid., 19). The remains of a timber riverfront structure were also identified as part of the this secondary bank and this returned a date-range of 897–1017, which, the director suggests, indicates that the bank was built in the late tenth century. A wattle path was also identified, which was relatively well preserved.

    The dating of the bank to the late tenth century suggests that there is potentially a gap of a hundred years between the two banks, which is probably unlikely and may suggest that there was an additional bank beyond the limit of the excavation, closer to the river. A third bank was then constructed over the second bank and the reclamation layers, and this bank was founded on a platform of wattle and timber, most of which was reused. It was a similar size to the previous bank, 3.7m in width, and had a facing of post-and-wattle on the internal side in one location (see Scally 2002, 23, pl. 3). This bank could not be dated accurately, but it evidently post-dated the previous bank (dated to the late tenth century) perhaps suggesting a date-range in the late tenth/eleventh century. This would suggest that this bank forms part of the second large bank found at Wood Quay and the fourth at Ross Road (ibid., 24).

Dublin Castle
'Forty years a-digging' included some of the detail from the large-scale excavations at Dublin Castle (*11c*), specifically those by Lynch at the Powder Tower, where the remains of a stone-revetted bank were located and identified as part of the earthen embankment on this side of the settlement (Simpson 2000, 26). This site has now been published and more information is available (Lynch and Manning 2001, 169–204). The outer face of the north–south clay

bank was exposed, constructed on the rocky shoreline of the Poddle, measuring 2.7m in width and with a dry-stone stone facing set a slope of 45 degrees. A second bank was also located on top of the first, and this had the remains of a timber-revetted facing. Interestingly, this stretch of the defences also had a possible ditch or fosse, similar to a fosse identified outside the bank at Wood Quay (Wallace 1981).

THE WESTERN BANK

'Forty years a-digging' highlighted the fact that the location of the western bank of the defended settlement or *dún*, first identified at Fishamble Street and then at Parliament Street, Ross Road and Werburgh Street, was not known (Simpson 2000, 27–8). The defences at the western end of the settlement at Cornmarket (*19*) were found, on investigation by Coughlan, to be later in date and most likely not, therefore, the original western limit (Simpson 2000, 27). Although investigations by Walsh at Winetavern Street (*5*) had found a dump of clay that was interpreted as possibly representing a continuation of the banks further east at Wood Quay, this interpretation had its problems. Firstly, the curving alignment of the banks at Wood Quay (*6*) suggested that they turned southwards, up towards Christ Church, defining the 'core' of the settlement (Wallace 1992a, 46; Simms 1979, 23) and perhaps continuing along the Nicholas Street alignment (Halpin 2005, 102). Secondly, the continuation of the banks along the riverfront at Winetavern Street suggested that the land to the west of the Nicholas Street/Winetavern Street north–south divide was also settled extensively in the tenth century, which is not borne out by the excavation results along High Street. The latter suggests that this area was not settled or laid out until the early eleventh century, although there was evidence of earlier artefactual material, possibly even dating to the late ninth century (Murray 1983, 43–4; Ó Riordáin 1973, 135–55).

Christ Church Cathedral
A limited investigation carried out by the writer on the site of the cloisters at Christ Church (*42*) may have located what remains of a clay bank, clad with stone on the western side and lying 3m below the present ground level (Simpson 2010a). The bank was only exposed in a test-trench in an area that was much disturbed in the post-medieval period, but the alignment suggests that it may have been a continuation of the banks found at Wood Quay. If this is the case, the banks must have continued southwards up the hill, curving east but kinking at the southern end towards Ross Road (*27*), where they were located by Walsh, as suggested by Halpin (Halpin 2005, 104, fig. 9). If this is the western bank, extending through the Christ Church complex, certain conclusions can be drawn.

Archaeological testing within the cathedral established that the building, which is twelfth-century in date, was founded on boulder clay (Simpson 1999a; Kehoe 1999) and the earlier remains were limited: they included the foundations of an earlier stone structure and several shallow pits. What was not found were deep deposits of organic habitation deposits, as found elsewhere within the historic core of the *dún*. In 'Forty years a-digging', this was presumed to infer that there had been little activity prior to this in and around Christ Church and the recent testing probably confirms this, as the organic deposits in the cloister area were limited in depth (Simpson 2000, 28; Simpson 2010a).

The right of way: The location of the bank in this location may also explain the enigmatic passageway or right-of-way that appears to have extended along the western side of the cloister, dividing the Christ Church complex from the archbishop's palace and the church of St Michael's of the Hill on the other side of Winetavern Street. Although the canons got permission to move the road to its current position in 1234 when extending the nave, the original route or right-of-way was maintained and is still visible in the upstanding architecture of the cathedral, at the western end of the crypt (fifth bay). This passageway, then, orientated north–south, extended through the last bay of the crypt and is probably the reason that the crypt has one bay fewer than the nave.

The mettled surface: Archaeological investigations at this end of the crypt confirmed the presence of this passageway, composed of brown sticky clay with a mettled or cobbled surface. It was positioned at a lower level than the finished pier bases of the crypt, suggesting that it was earlier (Kehoe 1999). Although these earlier investigations did not find evidence of the defensive embankment, the remains of a wall foundation, orientated north-east/south-west, were found beneath one of the end pier bases in the western wall of the crypt (Simpson 1999a). It lies to the west of the laneway, mentioned above, and may originally have been associated with the early defences in some way (O'Neill 2000, 207–56; Kinsella 2009, 31–75).

THE QUAY OF THE *DÚN*

The enclosed settlement or *dún* was a river frontage site, but, despite the large-scale excavations along the river, there is no firm evidence of where exactly the port or quay of the *dún* was located. The banks at Wood Quay (6) were positioned on higher ground, but the stretch excavated was continuous with no visible breaks, which would have been necessary for a quay front. In addition, there were sloblands in front of the settlement, making access to the river difficult at low ride. What is surprising is that the extensive excavations at

Wood Quay outside did not locate a myriad of wooden pathways and routes, which would have provided access across the mudflats at low tide in the tenth and eleventh centuries.

There are several alternatives for a quay site. The boats may have been coming in along the present line of the river, as they were in the late twelfth century, confined to the deeper water of the main channel, or else brought closer and beached before being re-launched on the tide (Wallace 1981). If this is the case, however, the lack of temporary riverfront structures or causeways that could be inundated by the tide but usable at low tide is somewhat surprising. A third possibility is that the ships might only have been brought as far as the confluence of the Poddle and unloaded there, perhaps explaining the early interest in occupying the Temple Bar West area in the ninth century (Simpson 2001).

Another possibility is that the shoreline or strand west of Winetavern Street, where there has been almost no archaeological excavation, contains the remains of the old riverfront in an area that was already known as 'the strand' by the early thirteenth century. This might be supported by the fact there is evidence that suggests that St Audoen's Gate, on this side, may have been on the site of the earlier pre-Anglo-Norman gate through the *c.*1100 wall (Simpson 2000, 39). Finally, perhaps there was an ancillary quay that could be used at high tide, possibly at the other end of the eastern suburb at the Steine, where there was a landing point from at least the Hiberno-Norse period onwards, and which was still recorded as operating in the sixteenth century.

EARTHEN EXTENSION DEFENCES IN THE LATE ELEVENTH
CENTURY

'Forty years a-digging' attempted to establish an evolution for the medieval city, which has been developed significantly since the new information from the Poddle valley has become available (Simpson 2010e, 89, fig. 10). This suggests that, on the evidence to date, the Poddle valley was the main area of settlement in the Early Christian period and one of the first places of contact for the Vikings in the mid-ninth century. An expansion by the Vikings north-wards is a possibility, towards the confluence of the Poddle and Liffey, which by the late ninth century was extensively settled, perhaps defined by Fishamble Street/Werburgh Street, as suggested by Halpin (2005, fig. 14). This was followed by a rapid a growth towards the west (Wood Quay) by the mid-tenth century, when the settlement was enclosed by banks, the alignment of which may be preserved in the Winetavern Street/Nicholas Street route (ibid.). These banks defined the main settlement from the mid- to late tenth and eleventh century and represented the epicentre of activity, along with whatever was occurring outside the *dún* at this date.

The evidence from the excavations at both Wood Quay (*6*) and Ross Road (*27*) suggested that these earthen banks were then replaced by a stone wall, but this wall, dated to between 1100 and 1120, also encompassed a much larger triangular swathe of land as far west as the road down to the bridge, now Bridge Street. Archaeological evidence, however, now suggests that a new phase in the defences can be added, not to the sequence of the *dún* but to the triangular extension on the western side, which appears to have been enclosed by an earthen bank system prior to the construction of the new city wall in *c*.1100. The wall, then, may have simply followed the alignment of this earlier enclosure, which can be identified as an intermediate phase of defences between the earthen embankments of the *dún* constructed in the mid- to late tenth century and the enclosing city wall built between *c*.1100 and 1120.

Cornmarket

The first indication of additional defences was suggested by the findings at Cornmarket by Hayden just outside the city wall at Newgate (*23*) on the western side of the city, which were included in 'Forty years a-digging' (Hayden 2000, 84–116). The published account, however, provides far more detail about this site, in particular the remains of two large ditches running parallel to but outside the line of the city wall at this end of the town (Hayden 2000, 86) (*23*). Both were substantial, measuring between 5.8m and 8m in width, and they may have continued northwards, as a similar but smaller ditch (*c*.5m in width by 1.9m in depth) was located to the north during a separate excavation at Bridge Street (19) (ibid., 87). At the time, Hayden suggested that they may form part of a ditched defensive system built in the late eleventh or early twelfth century protecting the vulnerable western side of the settlement where there was no natural watercourse (ibid., 94).

High Street

The ditches were presumably part of the same defence system that included a substantial bank running along the alignment of the city wall at Lamb Alley and identified by Healy during monitoring works along the southern side of High Street and on the south-western side of Cornmarket (*19a*) (Healy 1974). Healy found a 24m-stretch of the bank and established that it was pre-Anglo-Norman, measuring at least 8m in width by 2.5m in height and representing a formidable construction. Healy found that it was partially levelled, probably to form the foundation of the *c*.1100 city wall, which did not survive in this location. This bank, then, is likely to be pre-1100 (ibid.).

The top of the bank lay 20cm below present ground level and was composed of compact redeposited yellow-brown clay with stones, containing numerous animal bones, fragments of charcoal and layers of red ash. The only finds were a bronze strap tag with animal head terminal and traces of interlace, and a broken antler tine, along with what was possibly an intrusive find of white pottery with yellow glaze (ibid., 5; Simpson 2010e).

Back Lane

A short distance south, evidence of pre-Anglo-Norman defences was also found by Coughlan at Back Lane (*18*), where the remains of a substantial palisade fence were located and tentatively dated to the early twelfth century, although not scientifically (Coughlan 2000, 203–34). This defence was augmented significantly by the construction of a large clay bank, presumably a continuation of the bank further north, which also lay just below the modern surface and which must have been Hiberno-Norse in date, sealed by Anglo-Norman cultivation soils. Like Healy's bank, the bank at Back Lane was composed of redeposited boulder clay and was found to have formed the foundation for the city wall in this location, although it is not clear if it is the *c.*1100 wall or a later Anglo-Norman replacement (ibid., 205–7). The addition of a large palisade fence may have been required as this was the main entrance into the settlement on this side and, in the absence of a watercourse, is likely to have required additional protective measures in the form of the palisade and possibly the two ditches found by Hayden.

Mother Redcap's Market

The evidence for a clay bank that preceded the construction of the city wall appears relatively strong along the southern side of the settlement, but this new data was confined to the western end of the settlement, where, arguably, the bank may simply have been related to the importance of the route to the bridge and the need to defend the bridge itself. However, a small but very important site may provide the missing link between the western end of the town and the *dún*. A small investigation was meticulously carried out by hand by Myles was carried out at Mother Redcap's Market, on Back Lane, which lies to the west of the Nicholas Street/Winetavern Street alignment and, therefore, is likely to be outside the *dún* (Myles, *Excavations 2006, 600*). During this work, Myles opened up four test-pits along the alignment of the wall and found the remains of a clay bank also close to the modern surface. The wall in this location was identified as eighteenth or nineteenth century, but the remains of what is likely to have been a mural tower on the wall were found further west, at Back Lane (37), confirming the earlier alignment (Coughlan 2000, 229–30). The bank, then, is likely to have served as a foundation for the city wall in this location also.

Winetavern Street

There is less evidence for an earthen bank along the northern side of the settlement, along the Liffey, not helped by a lack of excavation west of

Winetavern Street in general. However, excavations by Walsh at Winetavern Street (*5*) did locate what was possibly the remains of a levelled bank, 5m in width, along the riverfront (Walsh 1997, 92). The director suggested that this bank may have been part of the earthen banks that enclosed the tenth-century *dún*, this alignment suggesting that the curving banks found at Wood Quay straightened out to head westwards across the Nicholas Street/Winetavern Street divide (ibid., 104). The alignment of the banks, however, and the possible bank identified by the writer at Christ Church may now suggest that they continued to curve southwards and headed up towards Christ Church, as first suggested by Wallace (Wallace 1992, 41).

If this is the case, this would place the bank found by Walsh outside the enclosed *dún* and may perhaps support the suggestion that there was a second later bank that pre-dated the c.1100 wall. In support of this, the director also notes that the c.1100 wall was founded on the northern end of the bank (Walsh 1997, 92), in a similar sequence that is immediately identifiable at Back Lane, Cornmarket and Mother Redcaps.

Summary

The evidence, then, suggests that the western end of the settlement was probably enclosed by an earthen bank of redeposited boulder clay when settlement spilled out along the ridge, something that probably occurred relatively early in the evolution of the settlement. This additional enclosure was probably required to protect the industrial and habitation quarter, immediately outside the dún, ample evidence of which was found during the excavations at High Street. However, the distinctive triangular shape was probably dictated by the additional necessity of protected the vulnerable bridge and crossing at the western end of the settlement, as suggested by Clarke (1977, 45). It is certainly the case that the western piece of land enclosed by the new city wall was not intensively inhabited, as the evidence from the two excavations at Back Lane (*15* & *16*) indicates that it was under cultivation in the late eleventh/early twelfth century (Coughlan 2000; Walsh, *Excavations 1992*, 46).

THE SOUTHERN SUBURB

The importance of the southern suburb to the *dún* has always been flagged by the fact that there are five documented pre–Anglo-Norman churches spread throughout this relatively small area, lying outside the defended settlement. The ecclesiastical significance can probably be traced back to what is now known about the early date of the church of St Michael, which is likely not to be the only early church in this location. The five churches, St Peter's, St Patrick's, St Bridget's, St Michael le Pole's with the fifth, St Kevin's, positioned further south, reflect what must have been a strong Christian population in this location for which there is little archaeological evidence.

St Peter's Church

There have been excavations at two of the church sites in the southern suburb at St Michael le Pole's, already mentioned, and St Peter's to the north-east, both of which have been published in the *Medieval Dublin* series. At St Peter's Church (5), investigations by Coughlan at the corner of Stephen Street Upper and Longford Street Great revealed part of the cemetery attached to the church, where approximately 150 burials were excavated between 2001 and 2002 (Coughlan 2003, 11–39). The cemetery was defined by a large ditch on the western side, already discussed, which was recut several times in the Anglo-Norman period and finally replaced with a stone wall. The curving ditch was substantial, measuring 5m in width, but lay to the rear of the properties fronting onto the street, where there were no cellars.

Coughlan suggests that the ditch can probably be dated to *c*.1100, a similar date proposed for the church of St Michael le Pole to the west (9) (ibid., 26; Gowen 2001, 36). Four simple Christian burials could be associated with the earliest phase of the ditch and these were relatively well-preserved although two were missing skulls. All four were males between 25 and 45 and had suffered significant bone trauma, although not leading to their death (ibid., 23–6).

St Michael le Pole / Golden Lane

The second site investigated, as previously discussed, was the church of St Michael le Pole (9), which is recorded in the documentary sources and is pre-Anglo-Norman, granted to Christ Church by the 'son of Pole', the ruling Hiberno-Norse family when the Anglo-Normans invaded Ireland (Bradley 1992, 51; Clarke 2002). The western end of the stone church and tower was identified during the excavations and has been published in the *Medieval Dublin* series (Gowen 2001, 13–52). The west wall measured 7.2m long and was between 90cm and 95cm in width. It was of mortar-bonded masonry with a heavily mortared rubble core and, in general, only one course of the actual wall survived, founded on the plinth. There was a noticeable difference in the masonry of the plinth, the latter of which was composed of small, irregular stones, which was in contrast to the distinctive square block masonry of the main build (ibid., 38–9).

The door of the church was also located in the west wall of the church, off-centre and at the southern end, measuring 88cm in width and subsequently blocked-up with masonry. The remains of a clay-bonded wall directly north of the door was identified as possibly representing the foundations of the engaged tower known to have existed at St Michael's Church and similar to St Kevin's Church in Glendalough, Co. Wicklow (ibid., 40). A series of burials were also identified at the site, but the bulk of these are thought to date to after the fourteenth century, on the ceramic evidence found in the clay deposits. Burial and construction continued at this site into the mid-nineteenth century, which caused considerable damage to the underlying graves and church foundations (ibid., 41).

Golden Lane

The construction of the stone church in this location in *c.*1100 is not surprising, as the archaeological evidence in the immediate environs suggests occupation and habitation at this date. The excavations by O'Donovan at Golden Lane (1) suggested that a lime-making complex was located outside the southern boundary of the cemetery (O'Donovan 2002, 36–130). The features consisted of a pit/kiln with evidence of burning stone and a well-preserved slaking-out pit and a well, the latter producing a timber that had a 94.5 per cent probability of dating from between 1022 and 1164, thus correlating with the estimated date for the construction of the church of *c.*1100 (ibid., 60). This, then, may have been the source of lime for the construction of the church or the earlier stone building, suggested by spreads of mortar found by Gowen (Gowen 2001, 38).

The cemetery: O'Donovan exposed a significant section of the cemetery, as previously mentioned, and 272 burials were excavated, almost all of which were Christian, clustered together in a dense cemetery. These skeletons were in the supine position, orientated east–west, with the head to the west, and were probably originally shrouded, as was the native Irish custom (ibid., 46). Ear-muff stones were also a feature of some of the graves, and these were used to stabilize the head on interment, presumably as a mark of respect. The evidence from the burial ground is consistent with a resident population that included men, women and children of different ages. One of the most important elements was the fact that burial continued at this site from the Early Christian period through into the twelfth century, with no evidence for a period of abandonment when the pagan Vikings were in control.

The Coombe

The evidence from Golden Lane suggesting that the southern suburb outside the defended settlement was inhabited in the Hiberno-Norse period was spectacularly confirmed by excavations by Walsh at the Coombe (7), where she identified three formal properties or plots containing domestic houses along the Coombe waterway, some distance from the main centre of settlement along the ridge (C. Walsh: 11th Medieval Dublin Symposium, 2009). Each property contained a rectangular domestic house, but these were a hybrid type, built using a combination of post-and-wattle and sill-beam, probably suggesting that they were late in the Hiberno-Norse sequence. The houses were partially built over a large stone road, which was positioned south of the modern route but was evidently a much earlier route.

Although the antiquity of this area has long been advocated by Clarke, the discovery of the cluster of properties is very significant, as they represent the first evidence of Hiberno-Norse habitation outside the walled city on the southern side. The implications are considerable: that the Coombe was laid out and densely inhabited so far from the main town may suggest a much larger settlement in the suburbs than hitherto suspected, although the implications of an area serviced by five churches outside the walls were always known. But the archaeological remains are disappointing if this is the case. The extensive excavations by Walsh along the western side of Patrick Street (*17a–c*), between the Coombe and the town, did not locate comparable material or even hint of formal plot layout in this area prior to the Anglo-Norman period, which is somewhat surprising. It may have been, of course, that they were concentrated along a channel of the Poddle, which had been constructed in the late twelfth century (Walsh 1997).

It may also be the case that the lack of comparable material is because the Coombe was a separate small nucleated settlement that evolved around the Cross Poddle, a very important crossing over the Coombe and Poddle waterway, as it was the tidal point of the Liffey.

THE NORTHERN SUBURB

The identification of Hiberno-Norse habitation in the southern suburb has implications for other suburbs also, including the northern suburb, known as Oxmantown, which was not included in 'Forty years a-digging'. Finally, archaeological investigations are starting to shed some light on this enigmatic suburb, which was centred on the main route Oxmantown Street (now Church Street), which led to the bridge and across the Liffey.

The oft-repeated traditional view was that this suburb was established when the Anglo-Normans took Dublin in 1170 and cast out the surviving Hiberno-Norse people, allowing them to establish another settlement on the northern side of the river. However, the suburb was served by St Michan's Church, a pre-Anglo-Norman foundation, in existence at least as far back as 1095, an indication that the suburb certainly pre-dated the Anglo-Norman arrival in Dublin in 1170 (Purcell 2003; 2005; 2009). Indeed, the earliest record of the name, dating from Henry II's expedition to Ireland in 1171–2, is in the form *Houstmanebi*, evidently of Scandinavian origin and attesting to the place-name's prior existence (Duffy 2005, 95–117).

The importance of the suburb was secured when St Mary's Abbey was established at the eastern end on the River Bradogue. This monastic house was founded in 1139, becoming Cistercian in 1147, and the monastery had a substantial precinct and held considerable land in the area, the direct access to the river frontage being one of its greatest assets.

There have been significant advances in attempting to locate traces of this Hiberno-Norse settlement in the last ten years, which had remained elusive until relatively recently. The evidence is provided by archaeological investigations at Church Street, most notably of a large block at 3–15 Hammond Lane/161–168 Church Street (8), which straddled the original line of the river and fronted onto Church Street on the eastern side. A series of smaller excavations and investigations have also been carried out in and around St Michan's Church itself.

Hammond Lane/Church Street
At Hammond Lane/Church Street (6), the large site was excavated in three separate sections: the southern end by Cryerhall (2006); the north-east corner by Phelan (2010); and the south-east corner by Moriarty (forthcoming, *Medieval Dublin XII*). The northern boundary of the site was approximately 50m south of St Michan's Church, downslope, while the southern end was bounded by Hammond Lane, a medieval route known originally as Hangman's Lane, as it led to the gallows on Oxmantown Green.

Flood banks and reclamation: The first and largest of the excavations by Cryerhall was located along the Hammond Lane frontage (8), and this important excavation located the original pre-Anglo-Norman river frontage, bounded by Hammond Lane (Cryerhall 2006, 9–50). What was most revealing was that the foreshore contained a series of flood banks and ditches, with evidence of reclamation deposits, suggesting that land creation was actively underway well before the Anglo-Normans arrived in Dublin in 1170 (ibid., 15–19). One of these ditches has a 68.2 per cent probability of dating to between 1030 and 1160, suggesting that these reclamation deposits were probably underway by the mid- to late eleventh century, with concerted efforts being made to keep out the tidal river. A gap in these significant flood defences may have marked the position of the crossing point or ford across the river in this location (see above).

The defensive bank and ditch: The north-eastern side of the site fronted onto Church Street (8) and this was excavated by Phelan, producing very different information from the river frontage site (Phelan 2010, 165–97). Unfortunately, the excavation did not locate part of Oxmantown Road, but a substantial bank and ditch was found to border this route, which was probably constructed in the late eleventh/early twelfth century, as a carbon-14 determination from a later fence cutting the bank returned a date of between

1121 and 1261 (ibid., 176–82). The bank, though probably quite low (1m in height), was a substantial 8m in width and is therefore likely to have been a defensive feature, protecting the elevated route of Church Street as it headed to the all-important bridge. This road might have, by the alignment of the bank and ditch at the northern end, curved to the north-west towards St Michan's Church, the foundation of which was similarly dated although it may be earlier (Purcell 2003). The proposed date of the late eleventh century also ties in with the construction of the extension to the earthen defences across the Liffey in the main settlement, which was dated similarly.

The buildings: The excavations by Phelan (8) also exposed the remains of habitation that lay outside this defensive earthwork to the west, opening out onto the reclaimed land, above the flood banks along the Liffey frontage found by Cryerhall. Two structures, which can be dated similarly to the bank, were found in this location – a small sunken structure and the base of some sort of substantial building defined by post-holes, which the director suggests might have been a tower or platform ditch (ibid., 182–3). In addition to this, there were occupation layers (ash and burning) and a curious series of linear parallel lines of posts (approximately eighty), orientated east–west and extending westwards from the bank. The layers of ash and burning were suggestive of industrial activity outside the line of the bank, but the first formal layout dated only from the late twelfth century, when the bank was out of use (see below).

Hiberno-Norse houses: The adjoining site, further south (the south-east corner of the block) was excavated separately by Moriarty and this also located the line of the foreshore but there was no sign of the bank, suggesting that it must have curved eastwards presumably towards the bridge, as suggested by the alignment uncovered by Phelan. Moriarty did locate the flood bank system identified by Cryerhall, however, running along the line of the river (Moriarty 2010; idem, *Medieval Dublin XII*, forthcoming).

This important excavation also located the first definitive evidence of domestic occupation along the eastern side of Church Street, where the almost complete ground plan of a post-and-wattle Type 1 house (after Wallace) was identified within a property plot, orientated east–west. The house, which sealed a large curving wattle-lined sunken ditch, was dated by carbon 14, which suggested a date in the late eleventh to early twelfth century. It was protected from the river on the southern side by the flood banks, and must have fronted onto a route north–south along the outside (western side) of the bank.

The house, which was within a 7m-wide plot, was rectangular in plan, with slightly rounded corners, measuring 6.8m long by 5m wide. The hearth was central, flanked by two aisles, although a good section of it had been truncated. It is most likely to have formed one of a terrace of such houses and the artefacts suggest that it was the residence of a relatively wealthy individual and was therefore not a poorer quarter down by the river, as one might expect.

27–31 Church Street

Limited excavations on the eastern side of Church Street (9) (rear of nos 27–31) also exposed the remains of Hiberno-Norse activity, composed of post-and-wattle structures likely to be domestic houses and including at least one sub-rectangular building defined by four large post-holes and ten domestic pits (Nelis, *Excavations 2003*, 508). The evidence also suggests that some sort of 'cottage-type' industries were being carried out at the rear of the site, where layers of burnt clay and slag indicate metalworking, while a collection of antler tines is suggestive of horn-working. Interestingly, a large amount of cockle shells was also found at this site, which can be paralleled on other sites across the river, at Parliament Street, Temple Bar West and Werburgh Street, where suggestions for their use include lime production and drainage.

St Michan's Church

St Michan's Church, as mentioned earlier, was the only parish church in Oxmantown, its location on Church Street a testament to the importance of this street. The traditional date of foundation is *c*.1095, which places it at a similar date to St Michael le Pole across the river, in the southern suburb, and to the church of St Peter of the Hill, suggested by the date of the ditch found by Coughlan (Gowen 2001; Coughlan 2003). However, Purcell has suggested that it may pre-date the eleventh century (Purcell 2009, 119). The church of St Michan is also likely to have been enclosed: Rocque's 1756 map of Dublin depicts the graveyard as extending further north than the current enclosure, but it was probably even larger than this originally (Purcell 2003, 218). However, the archaeological excavations in the immediate environs have produced mixed results.

May Lane

Excavations by Meenan at the northern corner of Church Street and May Lane (11) revealed the presence of a V-shaped ditch, orientated roughly east–west and positioned 80m to the north of St Michan's Church (Meenan 2004, 91–110). The ditch was quite substantial, measuring approximately 4m in width by 2m in depth, and this can be compared directly with the ditch at St Peter's Church on the southern suburb, which measured 5m in width (Coughlan 2003, 22). The remains of a minimum of ten human skeletons were recovered, six of which were intact and had probably been placed deliberately along the base of the ditch. These were orientated east–west, with heads to the west, suggesting that they were Christian burials and two were dated scientifically. The earliest date produced a 95.4 per cent probability of dating to between 890 and 1020, which is very early for the northern suburb and one which suggests that the ditch is earlier than the church, if any credence is to attach to the traditional foundation date of 1095. However, as mentioned, Purcell has recently argued that there was an earlier church on this site, and this may be supported by this evidence (Purcell 2009, 119). The second burial of the group produced a potentially slightly later date of between 980 and 1160, a combination of both dates suggesting a date range of 950–1050 for the graves (68.2 per cent probability) (Meenan 2004, 109).

Despite the Hiberno-Norse dates for the cluster of burials along the base of the ditch, the actual ditch fill itself produced Anglo-Norman pottery down to the base (ibid., 97). As it is unlikely that the ditch was an open feature from the mid-eleventh to the late twelfth century, this suggests that the lower level was an earlier ditch, which was subsequently recut in the Anglo-Norman period. At the time of publication (2004), the director posited that the ditch may have originally enclosed St Michan's Church, as a second similar ditch was tentatively identified after a testing campaign by Hayden on the opposite (southern) side of the church, at 3–15 Hammond Lane (8) (Hayden, *Excavations 2001*, 82). However, this was subsequently found not to be a ditch during the large-scale excavation by Cryerhall on the same site.

152–155 Church Street
The continuation of this ditch, however, was possibly identified further west, at a large excavation by Dawkes at 152–155 Church Street (10), immediately south of May Lane (bounded by May Lane to the north, Church Street to the east, Bow Street to the west and by St Michan's Church to the south) (Dawkes 2010, 198–219). The earliest levels at this important site exposed activity in the form of numerous small pits, ditches and gullies, cut into the natural clays and sands and the director suggests it probably pre-dated the late tenth century, although no scientific dating was presented and several features contained medieval pottery (ibid., 203). This activity was sealed by a layer of introduced soil, which in turn was cut by a ditch thought to date to the late tenth/early eleventh century but with no dates presented.

The next phase of activity revealed a possible double ditch arrangement on the western end, on roughly the same alignment as Meenan's ditch, orientated north-east/south-west. The main ditch was similar, but was narrower than Meenan's, extending for a substantial 30m in length. It measured 2m in width by a shallow 1.2m in depth, but the upper levels are likely to have been truncated. The presence of a second, outer ditch was suggested by the director, located just west of the main ditch, but only a small stretch survived, less than 3m in length, measuring at least 2.8m in width by 1.36m in depth. The director suggested that a third ditch may have represented the eastern arm of the enclosure on the eastern side of the site. This was orientated north–south and measured at least 11m in length by 3.79m in width by 95cm in depth (ibid., 208). Although dated to the late tenth/early eleventh century, the ditches were filled with clays that contained medieval pottery, similar to the May Lane ditch found by Meenan further east (11). Dawkes suggests that the ditches were infilled by the thirteenth century (ibid., 205).

Despite the medieval pottery in the fill to the base of the ditch, the presence of pre-Anglo-Norman Christian burials at the base of such an early ditch at May Lane is likely to have had an ecclesiastical connection, presumably related to St Michan's Church despite the early date. Whether or not the ditch had an enclosing function, encircling the church, is more difficult to establish. The excavations by Phelan at Church Street (8) did locate a north–south ditch and bank along the eastern side of the much larger site (161–168 Church Street) on the southern side of the church, and Dawkes suggests that it may represent the eastern extent of an enclosing ditch (Dawkes 2010, 216). However, Phelan's excavation demonstrated that the ditch was curving to the north-west, to the south of St Michan's and was late eleventh/early twelfth century (Phelan 2010, 165).

24–27 Ormond Quay

A third site produced a series of human bones at 24–27 Ormond Quay (Bermingham, *Excavations 2000*, 280). The remains pre-dated the seventeenth-century reclamation levels in this location and might be related to St Michan's Church, although the site is some distance from the church and the bones were not dated. They consisted of just long bones (no teeth or skulls) and represented five adults and four juveniles (three males and at least one female positively identified).

Summary

The collective evidence for the Hiberno-Norse period confirms the existence of the northern suburb of Oxmantown on the north bank of the river in the Hiberno-Norse period, prior to the Anglo-Norman invasion in 1170. The earliest activity probably dated to the mid- to late tenth century. St Michan's is likely to have been the focus of activity at this end of Oxmantown, the evidence of a possible enclosing or boundary ditch on the northern side perhaps supporting the notion that there was a church in this location that may have pre-dated 1095, although further evidence is required. The river frontage was prone to flooding and was protected by a series of flood banks, while reclamation occurred on the higher ground by the mid-eleventh century.

The defences along the Church Street route dating to the late eleventh century are not a surprise as the bridge was the main lynch-pin between Oxmantown and the walled city, and an easily identifiable 'back door' weakness of the settlement. The defences revealed the importance and vulnerability of this route, and it is not a coincidence that comparable developments were occurring on the south side of the bridge at the same time, when an additional area was enclosed by earthen defences, which also extended as far west as the southern route down to the bridge. By the early twelfth century, there were significant remains of domestic habitation within plots orientated east–west, to the west of Church Street. The well-preserved house suggests that a relatively wealthy population-group was residing here, living in large Type 1 houses, identical to those found on the southern side of the river.

THE EASTERN SUBURB

The eastern suburb has always been something of an enigma in the archaeo-logical record for medieval Dublin, in that the historical and place-name evidence for its importance has not been backed up by the archaeological record. While Viking warrior graves discovered in antiquity (discussed above) revealed the potential of the suburb to produce evidence of Viking and Hiberno-Norse activity, this has not been matched in the more recent past. There are several reasons for this: the last ten years have seen little construction development in the city centre and when it did occur on a large scale prior to this, it was confined to Temple Bar, which was mostly reclaimed after 1600. In addition, demolition was kept to a minimum in this historic quarter. Despite this, several small sites have produced important results, most important of which was the Green Building in Crow Street (13), within the confines of the Anglo-Norman Augustinian friary on Cecilia Street.

The Green Building
This significant excavation, on Crow Street/Temple Lane (13), located a small group of human burials dumped in a pit in estuarine mud in what later became the cemetery attached to the Anglo-Norman Augustinian friary at Cecilia Street (Reid, *Excavations 1994*, 91; Duffy and Simpson 2009, 300–33). Surprisingly, the carbon-14 determinations suggested that they dated to the eleventh century, despite the fact that they were in a thirteenth-century cemetery. In all, there were six skeletons, most of which were aligned north–south, but several of which were in a crouched position, clearly not formally buried. The group consisted of three adult females and three juveniles, and a fragment of an iron knife blade was found beside the skull of one of them (Reid, *Excavations 1994*, 91; Ó Donnabháin and Hallgrímsson 2001, 69).

The location of this gruesome discovery, which may indicate a familial or at the very least a community group, may be coincidental and it is not known how they died, although their mode of burial is not suggestive of high-status individuals. Their presence in this suburb, however, is indicative of Hiberno-

Norse activity for which there is little other evidence. Their location, off Temple Lane, is also interesting, as this was originally known as Hoggen Lane, a Scandinavian place-name derived from the word *haugr*, meaning burial mound. Thus this corroborates the antiquity of this lane.

The ford of St Mary
Hoggen Lane or Temple Lane led down to a ford, possibly the ford of St Mary's Abbey, which was still in existence as late as the sixteenth century (Duffy and Simpson 2009; Clarke 2002). During archaeological investigations in the Liffey by the writer at low tide, a high ridge of bedrock was identified stretching diagonally westwards from what would originally have been the termination of Hoggen Lane (Temple Lane) across the river to Ormond Quay (Simpson 2010e). This probably marks the line of the ford, which, from its location at the end of this Viking Age lane, was probably in use in pre-Anglo-Norman times. More recent excavations by Hayden at Meeting House Square, to the west of this route, have located the remains of a slipway cut into the bedrock, which may mark the position of the ford, although this has been dated to the Anglo-Norman period (pers. comm., Alan Hayden).

The priory of All Hallows
The priory of All Saints or All Hallows (45) was founded by Diarmait Mac Murchada at the eastern end of the suburb in c.1162 (Budd 2001; Simpson 2002a, 195, 256). In 1592, the precinct of the dissolved monastery was granted to the University of Dublin as a site for a new college (Trinity). The pictorial evidence suggests that at least some of the monastic buildings were reused, including a curious octagonal steeple and possibly a hall in the north range, and this possible reuse pinpoints the location of the medieval quadrangle as being one and the same as that of the new college (Budd 2001). The college was spectacularly constructed of brick, as shown in the Hatfield depiction, dated to *c*.1598, and it survived largely intact until the mid-eighteenth century, when it was mapped by Rocque (1756).

The location of the priory at this end of Trinity College (the north-east corner of the medieval quadrangle is marked by the campanile) was confirmed during monitoring works by the writer within Library Square, to the east of Parliament Square (or Front Square) (45). This square is one of the oldest spaces in the college, bounded on the east by the earliest surviving buildings, the Rubrics started in 1699 (Simpson 2002a, 225). Monitoring of services running across the green revealed that the space is earlier still and was originally the medieval burial ground, attached to the priory (ibid., 219–20).

More recent monitoring works by the writer in Parliament Square (Front Square) in Trinity have located part of what is likely to represent the western range of the medieval priory quadrangle, confirming that at least this range was reused in the late sixteenth century when the college was constructed. A solid medieval wall was located in a narrow trench, measuring 1.2m in width by at least 1.1m in height, and composed of limestone blocks, mortared with a distinctive yellow lime mortar. The wall had an offset or projecting plinth on the western side.

As part of the same monitoring programme, part of the eastern range was also found, but this was identified as dating to *c.*1592, when the college was first constructed, and thus represented a new construction at this time. That this was not the original priory wall was suggested by the fact that, on the Rocque map (1756), the northern range extended beyond the east range and the eastern range was visibly narrower. This wall was also very substantial, measuring between 90cm and 1m in width and composed of solid limestone foundations, topped with brick wall foundations (Simpson, Monitoring report, forthcoming, 2011). The brick is a distinctive bright red and its use, less than 30cm below present ground level, suggests that the college had no cellars.

THE WESTERN SUBURB

The western suburb, by way of contrast, has produced no evidence of pre-Norse activity, which is somewhat puzzling, especially as there have been several large excavations, although these have been confined to the rear of the street. This must always have been a pivotal thoroughfare, leading, as it does, to Kilmainham and Islandbridge, where the Viking grave-fields are located, possibly associated with some settlement of the same date, as yet not located.

Usher's Island
Further downstream, just west of the bridge at Dublin, there has been some additional work carried out on Usher's Island (*14–14a*), a place first suggested by Clarke as the possible site of a second ninth-century settlement at Dublin and mentioned in 'Forty years a-digging' (Clarke 2002; Simpson 2000, 20–1). Various sites have been tested on the 'island', but with mixed results. An assessment at the extreme eastern side of the island (15–21 Usher's Quay) found only natural silt layers over most of the site apart from the south-east corner (closest to the possible ford site) where deposits dated to the Anglo-Norman period were located, suggesting that this end of the island was formed by this date (Gowen, *Excavations 1994*, 86).

Additional testing on the north side of Island Street (**33**) (in the middle of the island), however, at 29–31 Island Street, indicates that this part of the island was formed in the post-medieval period, the archaeological deposits consisting of late seventeenth-century layers overlying naturally deposited sand and silts, the product of the silting problem at Dublin so well documented in the medieval period. Thus, there were no medieval levels in this location (Walsh, *Excavations 2003*, 540). A third site, off Island Street/Strand Street and Bridgefoot Street (*34*), at the eastern end of the island, revealed organic silt up to 7m in depth, but these could be similarly dated to the seventeenth and eighteenth centuries, representing naturally deposited layers of sand and silt, probably from periodic inundation (Walsh, *Excavations 1999*, 208).

THE c.1100–1120 CITY WALL

The circuit of the early twelfth-century walled town is thought to be relatively well known, but, as Halpin has pointed out, there are still major questions to be answered. The most basic is confirmation of the original circuit and whether or not it was on the same alignment as the Anglo-Norman circuit. The most recent information from Ross Road suggests that it clearly was not, as the Anglo-Norman wall at Ross Road and Ship Street Little lay 11m south of the original alignment (Simpson 2000, 38–41; Halpin 2005, 109). The location of the quay area when the primary wall was constructed in *c*.1100 is also still problematic. The wall was found between the two earlier clay banks at Wood Quay, but this stretch was continuous and there was no indication of a quay in front of the wall, as one might expect. There is a possibility that the quay was located further west, on the western side of Winetavern Street, in and around the mural gate known as St Audoen's Arch (see below).

Ross Road
The most significant investigation was carried out by Walsh at Ross Road/Christ Church Place (*29*) on the southern side of the town, where the remains of two walls were located (Walsh 2001, 88–127). The earliest was more of a stone facing, standing 80cm in height and 1.2m in width, but extending for less than 5m where it was preserved as a foundation for a later tower (see below). The second wall founded on the earlier foundations was in a more complete state, cut into the southern slopes of the defensive embankment, and this survived for approximately 17m but was dated slightly later than the excavated section at Wood Quay, to *c*.1120. The surviving wall foundation was constructed of large limestone blocks and stood 3.5m in height with a slight batter on the southern side. The western side was comprehensively robbed out, but the cut for the wall was clearly identifiable (see Walsh 2001, 109, fig. 8). Thus, the Hiberno-Norse wall, which was located on a break in slope and had the Poddle lapping against its base, was rendered obsolete and was plundered for building material, most likely for the new wall constructed in the late twelfth century.

Surprisingly, the *c*.1120 wall was found to lie 11m to the north of the previously supposed alignment along Ship Street Little, where, further east, an extant section survives in the modern streetscape close to Dublin Castle. Thus, Walsh established a new alignment for the primary mural defences. The results of the excavation suggest that the Anglo-Normans then embarked on an ambitious refortification on this side of the town, which involved demolishing the first city wall and wall-facing and replacing them with a new wall, 11m further down the slope. Part of the *c*.1120 wall was retained, however, along with the earlier section, as previously mentioned, and was reused as a foundation for a mural tower that straddled both the old and the new Anglo-Norman wall (see below). This new alignment reclaimed land on this side of the settlement and the new programme of works included the re-channelling of the Poddle to flow in a city moat at the base of the new wall (Walsh 1997, 26–7).

13–15 Werburgh Street

This new Anglo-Norman alignment was confirmed during a small excavation at 13–15 Werburgh Street (**17**), on the western side of the street, also along the Ship Street Little alignment. Testing by the writer located the city wall, which had been incorporated within a still-standing eighteenth-century boundary wall (Simpson 2008, 150–77). Initially, the conclusion was that the wall represented two walls, the Anglo-Norman wall on top of the Hiberno-Norse one, as reported in 'Forty years a-digging' (Simpson 2000, 41). However, the site was subsequently excavated by the writer and it was established that the entire wall was, in fact, Anglo-Norman, constructed on top of a clay bank, the upper levels of which were dated similarly. This bank was exposed but not excavated (Simpson 2008, 150–77).

This suggests, then, that the Hiberno-Norse wall is likely to have been further north along the Ross Road alignment and this was suggested during the excavations by Hayden to the north, also on the western side of Werburgh Street (**17**) (Hayden 2002, 44–68). Part of the defensive earthen embankment was found along the southern end of the site, but the full extent was not within the excavation footprint, and thus the southern slope of the bank was not excavated. If the sequence is similar to that found at Ross Road, this may suggest that the city wall lay just outside the southern limit of the site.

Parliament Street

A similar approach was taken by the Anglo-Normans in the north-east corner of the walled town, at Parliament Street (*15*), where the city wall was also completely rebuilt, evidently because of weaknesses identified by the Anglo-Normans in the existing mural defences. In this location, the position of the wall was probably restricted because of the Poddle confluence and the ability for expansion did not exist. Thus, unlike the southern defences, in this location the new wall was found to abut the earlier wall (c.1100) (Scally 2002, 27–8). The primary wall survived in a stretch measuring 6.6m in length by 1.4m in

width and 1.48m in height, with a batter on the external side and a plinth on
the internal face. This wall was also located outside the bank defences, in a
similar location to the wall further west at Wood Quay and south at Ross Road.

Bridge Street
There is less evidence for the western side of the town as excavations at Bridge
Street (*19*) by Hayden, across the supposed line, found no trace of the wall
(Hayden 2000, 84–116). The director suggests that the wall must have been
positioned a few metres to the east of the current proposed alignment.

Dublin Castle
A series of archaeological campaigns have been carried out at Dublin Castle,
but these did not expose the *c.*1100 or any previous stone fortification (Lynch
and Manning 2001, 169–204). While the remains of a stone-revetted bank and
possible ditch were identified within the Powder Tower (*11c*), this was
identified by Lynch as likely to represent the pre-Anglo-Norman earthen
rather than stone defences, which creates a gap in the defence sequence on this
side of the settlement.

Wood Quay
Additional works have been carried out to various sections of the city wall,
some of which did not involve excavation. A digital scaled survey of the city
wall at Ship Street Little, Power's Square, Lamb Alley and Cook Street has
been carried out on behalf of Dublin City Council (Simpson and Ancinelli
2008b) as part of general conservation works, which also involved stabilizing a
vulnerable section along Ship Street Little. The other major project was the
refurbishment of the basement space beneath the Dublin Civic Offices at
Wood Quay (6), which contains a significant stretch of the *c.*1100 wall
measuring over 22m in length by 4.2m in height. This is now the City Wall
Exhibition Space, or Wood Quay Venue, designed by McCullough-Mulvin
architects.

   The wall, which was numbered and underpinned as part of the works
during the Wood Quay excavation, was surveyed digitally and photographically
in advance, and a written description was also produced (Simpson and
Ancinelli 2008b). The conservation of the wall was supervised by Carrig
Conservation (John Beatty). The wall extended out of the basement building
on the western side in an additional stretch that measured 9m (east–west) by
4m in height. This work, carried out by the writer under Ministerial Consent
(C251:W27), exposed a large plinth at the base of the wall, which was founded
on hard boulder clay. The excavation also revealed that some of the foundation
stones to the west were removed in the relatively recent past, in advance of
underpinning during the Wood Quay campaign in the 1980s.

A second section of the city wall was located a further 18m to the west during a small excavation by the writer also under Ministerial Consent (C329 ext.:E4058). This work exposed the northern face of the Hiberno-Norse wall, which, until now, had been sealed by late seventeenth-/early eighteenth-century buildings. It was approximately 2.3m below present ground level and was at least 1m in width, probably extending for a further 2.3m in depth at this location, based on the levels from the exposed section further east towards the Dublin Civic Offices. The wall was composed of large limestone blocks, copiously mortared with a rubble core, identical to the build further east under the Civic Offices. The small excavation also established that there were at least 2.2m of intact archaeological deposits, on both the north and the south face of the wall, an indication that the entire site was not excavated during the campaigns at Wood Quay.

THE ANGLO-NORMAN CONQUEST OF DUBLIN, 1170

'Forty years a-digging' identified that the Anglo-Norman takeover of Dublin in 1170 completely transformed the Hiberno-Norse city, which underwent a period of rapid change. The archaeological evidence now suggests that there was an immediate massive reorganization of the defences, a substantial reclamation programme towards the river, the construction of a new city wall enclosing the newly reclaimed land along the river and a programme of rapid expansion into the adjoining suburbs.

THE CITY WALL

Although it was for long thought that there was relatively little activity in the immediate years after the conquest, the new evidence now suggests that the complete opposite occurred, and that a robust and ambitious plan was executed almost immediately to refortify the entire walled city. The strength of the walls had been found wanting in 1170 (which is the reason the Anglo-Normans had managed to capture it) and the new rulers at Dublin were only too aware where the deficiencies in the city defences lay, and it is likely that work began almost immediately to strengthen the existing walls. Weak sections on the circuit of the walls were identified and attempts were made to remedy them, including the western gate, which was replaced and renamed New Gate by 1177 (Simpson 2000, 41).

Elsewhere, the refurbishment works involved demolishing sections of the existing wall along part of the southern stretch, probably from Ross Road (*27*) at least as far as 14–16 Werburgh Street (**17**: *34*) (Walsh 2002; Simpson 2008), and also along the eastern section, in the north-east corner at Parliament Street (*15*) (Scally 2002). Elsewhere, the wall was possibly just renovated, for example at Lamb Alley (Coughlan 2000, 209; Halpin 2005, 108–9). At Ross Road, as mentioned previously, Walsh established that the works were substantial and involved the demolition of the Hiberno-Norse wall and the construction of a new wall 11m to the south. The ground in between, formerly occupied by the earthen banks, was infilled and reclaimed, expanding the size of the settlement on this side (Walsh 1997, 112).

Earlier excavations by Walsh at Patrick Street and Nicholas Street (*17a–c*), published in 1997, also found significant evidence of this refortification programme. The excavations outside the city at Patrick Street pinpointed the location of the wall and also found a well-preserved lime-kiln, which Walsh suggests was used to make lime for the refurbishment programme at this location (Walsh 1997, 77). These important excavations also located the artificial ditch that was excavated at the base of the city wall, which measured a massive 20m in width by between 7m and 8m in depth. The work by Walsh also established that the Poddle was channelled through timber revetments into the ditch forming a moat.

Dublin Castle

Probably the most important part of the city defences was the citadel or stronghold, Dublin Castle, where a series of archaeological campaigns have been carried out, both within and without the precinct of the castle (Lynch and Manning 2001, 169–204). While mentioned in the previous synthesis ten years ago, a summary of these excavations has now been published, providing additional information. These investigations exposed part of the precinct wall, the foundations of the north-east corner tower (*11c*) (the Powder Tower), part of the north-west corner tower (*10*) (Corke Tower) and a square tower attached to and coeval with the south-west corner tower (*11a*) (Bermingham Tower). Excavations on the northern side of the castle, outside the main gate, suggest the presence of a possible drawbridge pit, evidently part of the main access route into the castle.

The excavations also explored various sections of the castle moat, which was found to measure 22m in width and which was diverted from the city moat to flow around the castle. The moat was up to 7m in depth and was full of well-preserved organic deposits that contained a large number of artefacts (ibid.).

SECTIONS OF SURVIVING CITY WALL

Power's Square

'Forty years a-digging' included a description of the upstanding sections of the city wall at Ship Street Little and Lamb Alley, but a third section, at Power's

Square (west of Nicholas Street), first identified by Healy, was inadvertently omitted. This section survived as a boundary wall, running to the rear of the St Vincent de Paul shelter at Nicholas Street and extending westwards, forming the northern boundary of Power's Square. The significant stretch extends for approximately 55m, standing between 3m and 4m in height and between 1.2m and 1.9m in width (Simpson and Ancinelli 2008b).

The wall is constructed of the distinctive limestone blocks of the mural defences, but has significant brick additions and repairs, some of which are probably sixteenth and seventeenth century in date. It was reduced in width by the removal of facing stones from both the internal and the external face in the post-medieval period, but the medieval core can be readily identified (Simpson 2008b). What is not known is whether or not this represents the Hiberno-Norse or the Anglo-Norman wall, although the alignment may suggest that it represents the Anglo-Norman wall, if the two separate alignments identified at Ross Road extended as far west as this location.

The Poddle

As mentioned above, the excavations at Patrick Street and Nicholas Street (*17a–c*) established that the Poddle was re-chanelled into the newly dug city ditch forming an impressive water-filled moat, as reported on in 'Forty years a-digging' (Walsh 1997, 26–7). Since then, the location of the eastern stretch of this river has also been confirmed at a site fronting onto Dame Street excavated by the writer at 3–6 Palace Street, close to Dublin Castle (Simpson 2005a; Simpson, *Excavations 2006*, 636). The remains of a substantial post-medieval stone building were tentatively identified as possibly the successor to the medieval mill known as the 'Doubleday mills', known to be in this location (Clarke 2002).

The strategy at this site was one of preservation *in situ*. The structure was not removed, and thus the medieval deposits were not examined in detail. However, a series of investigative bore-holes were undertaken, which established that the active river channel was between 6m and 7m in depth in this location, infilled with compact organic remains containing animal bone and shell. Medieval post-and-wattle structures were also identified between 4m and 5m below present ground level (Simpson 2005a).

Dame Street

It should be noted that the monitoring works just east of the site at Palace Street, along the western end of Dame Lane, while exposing cellars at the extreme western end, fronting onto Palace Street, also located soils that were probably medieval in date, lying 60cm from present ground level (Simpson 2003). Thus, medieval horizons do survive in this location, on the eastern side of the river channel.

THE MURAL TOWERS

There has been no advance in knowledge in the last ten years in regard to the mural towers and gates on the city wall, but the evidence of a realignment of the defences on the southern side of the city has significant implications. The excavations at Ross Road (*27*) by Walsh, where the new city wall was constructed 11m further south, must have involved the relocation of the Pole Gate (Werburgh Street Gate) further south, on the new Anglo-Norman Ship Street Little alignment. Thus the site of the original Pole Gate is probably approximately 11m north of the junction with Bride Street.

The only other additional information is the detail provided by the publication by Walsh of her excavation of Geneville's Tower (Walsh 2001, 112–14). This established that the tower dates from the first part of the thirteenth century and measured 11.8m by 6.4m, composed of mortar-bonded limestone walls (ibid., 112). The tower survived to first-floor height and the second-floor was supported by large wooden posts founded on stone piers. Two doorways were also identified, in the east and west wall, both of which were blocked. The tower is described as D-shaped and Walsh suggests that the 'D' element, probably late twelfth century in date, lay outside the limit of excavation, while the square element was slightly later, dating to the first quarter of the thirteenth century (ibid., 114).

A large, arched building was identified abutting the western side of the tower, and probably built soon after it. This was badly damaged, but a series of large piers were located, which originally supported walls. The director suggests that this may be identified as Geneville's Inns, which are recorded in the documentary sources (ibid.).

THE CITY DITCH

Cornmarket and Bride Street
'Forty years a-digging' dealt with sections of the Anglo-Norman city ditch found at Cornmarket (*23*, *19*) and Bridge Street by Hayden and these have since been published, providing more detail about these important sites (Hayden 2000, 84–116). At Cornmarket, the ditch measured at least 11.2m in width (the eastern side was not within the cutting) by 5.1m in depth, while at Bridge Street, further north, it measured 22m by at least 10.5m (ibid., 94). At Cornmarket, while initially it had water, the ditch began infilling by the mid-thirteenth century and had deposits to a significant depth by the mid-fourteenth century, which is somewhat surprising, given that it was a defensive feature. The finds from the ditch clearly suggest that they were used as convenient dumps by the local inhabitants.

At Bridge Street (*19*), further north towards the Liffey, the massive feature began infilling in the fourteenth century but was still visible in the landscape in the eighteenth century as there was an active watercourse, coming from Thomas Street (Hayden 2000, 95). In addition to this, the northern end, where it met the Liffey, was tidal. Both sections of ditch excavated by Hayden produced an important chronological and stratified sequence of artefacts including probably the earliest bone spectacles in Ireland and Britain, which would be dated to the early-to-mid-fourteenth century (ibid., 97).

Iveagh Markets
A section of the Anglo-Norman city ditch has also been investigated by Myles at the Iveagh markets (18) (Myles, *Excavations 2000*, 262), establishing its alignment in this location. Myles also found an enigmatic stone structure on the southern (external) lip of the ditch, which was five courses in height, totalling 1m, and founded within a construction trench. Although only a small section survived, where it had slid into the ditch, the director concluded that this did not represent a domestic building but was more likely to be a bridge abutment or mill, the former probably the most plausible since there is no documented mill in this location. The excavations at Cornmarket (*23*) by Hayden also located the remains of a timber revetment, founded on stone, set on the outer (west) lip of the ditch. The revetment was back-braced but relatively short, measuring only 2.5m in length by 2m in height (Hayden 2000, 95).

John Dillon Street
The excavations suggest that ditches were a familiar feature in the environs of Dublin, especially in the southern suburb, and, while these might have been for individual defence purposes, they must have had other functions also, perhaps as boundaries or drainage. Excavations by Walsh on the south side of the walled city, at John Dillon Street (**26**), revealed the remains of what appears to have been quite a substantial ditch, running north–south along the eastern side of the street (Walsh, *Excavations 2001*, 388). This feature measured 4.5m in width by 1.4m in depth and was bounded by a strong post-and-wattle fence along the eastern side.

The director suggests that the ditch is unlikely to have held water, as it was filled with cess material and sterile clays, but it was truncated by two medieval pits, one of which was dated to *c.*1267. This opens up the possibility that the ditch can be associated with the reorganization of the defences that occurred on this side of the city in the late twelfth century, with the cutting of a large city moat at Nicholas Street and the diversion of the Poddle (see Walsh 1997, 26–7). Thus, there may have been additional earthen and ditched defences that protected the main routes before the suburban gates were constructed.

Molyneaux House

Two similar ditches were found by the writer at the rear of the modern
Molyneaux House, on Bride Street, the first of which was pre-Anglo-Norman.
This ditch was at the northern end of the site and was orientated east–west,
extending for at least 7.7m in length and measuring 2.1m in width by 80cm in
depth (although truncated). This feature was sealed with redeposited clays,
similar to the ditch at John Dillon Street (Simpson, *Excavations 2002*, 520).
The ditch had steep sides and did not appear to have been a drainage ditch.

A second ditch, orientated north–south, truncated the earlier ditch and was
far more substantial, measuring 4m in width by 1.6m in depth and extending
for over 22m. The primary deposit consisted of silty clays probably indicative
of water, with iron-panned stained gravel suggesting that it was fast-flowing
water, presumably associated with the Poddle. Domestic refuse was evidently
cast in, an indication of occupation close by, and in the fourteenth century the
northern end was recut. This was subsequently filled in with clays that contain
limestone and rubble, suggesting demolition of the buildings in this location.

RECLAMATION ON THE NORTHERN SIDE OF THE WALL

The swathe of open foreshore that lay immediately north of the Hiberno-
Norse wall was actively reclaimed by the Anglo-Normans (Simpson 2000, 39).
This land reclamation was most actively demonstrated by the findings at Wood
Quay (6) and the impressive range of timber revetments used to achieve this
(Wallace 1981). The newly formed land was then enclosed by a strong city wall
between c.1240 and 1260, but the old wall was retained, perhaps as some
secondary line of defence. There has been some advance in regard to our
knowledge of reclamation on the south side of the city, most notably from
Winetavern Street and Augustine Street.

East of Winetavern Street

Since 'Forty years a-digging', the large-scale excavations by Halpin at Winetavern
Street have been published in a single impressive volume, documenting the
reclamation process, which was found to be a continuation of the same activity
found at Wood Quay to the west (Halpin 2000). A similar dating sequence was
also identified, at the western end (6) towards Winetavern Street, dated by
dendrochronology to between 1190 and 1208. Thus, the reclamation was
started within twenty-five years of the invasion and was presumably a follow-
on to the other improvement works the Anglo-Normans embarked on immediately after the invasion. These excavations also crucially located the western
boundary of the reclaimed area of Wood Quay, which was formed by two parallel
north–south timber revetments, dated to between 1190 and 1213 (ibid.).

There is no doubt, however, that the primary function of the revetments was to reclaim the land by retaining dumped organic material, as occurred elsewhere in Dublin. But, in addition to this, Wallace had suggested that the revetments at Wood Quay (24) were probably also used to dock boats, and the excavations at Winetavern Street support this conclusion (Wallace 1981, 250). This was prompted by the discovery of a cobbled surface near the top of the revetment, suggesting that dry-shod access was possible, perhaps even being, as Halpin suggests, the primary function of the revetment in this location (Halpin 2000, 180). Thus, for the first time in Dublin, the quay can probably be identified. Halpin also confirmed that the type of revetments at Wood Quay were not paralleled anywhere else in Dublin and were clearly of superior build.

West of Winetavern Street
On the west side of Winetavern Street, the single excavation at 16–17 Cook Street (22), mentioned in 'Forty years a-digging', has now been published, providing important additional information (Meenan 2002, 128–39). The large-scale reclamation of deep organic deposits evident at Wood Quay does not appear to have occurred in this location. Instead, the excavation result suggests the presence of the river, confirmed by the discovery of a sunken boat dated by dendrochronology to the late twelfth or early thirteenth century (ibid., 131). While there was no evidence of continual habitation in this location, there were indications of some low-grade activity in the form of wattle fences (possibly structures) and several pits, which may suggest that the water may only have been present at high tide or during flooding episodes. However, there was no formal domestic habitation here until the late thirteenth century at least. The findings at this site were also supported by a monitoring programme at 32 Cook Street, which also suggested that the layers in this location were made up of gravels and silts, including some of the orange gravel usually associated with the Liffey (Turrell, *Excavations 2004*, 526).

It should be noted that the excavations on the eastern side of Winetavern Street by Halpin did provide evidence of at least one inundation as the north–south revetments were under construction in the thirteenth century, indicative of water in this area also, probably the result of a flood (Halpin 2000, 52). This ingress of water, close to the junction of Cook Street, supports the findings at Cook Street of water in this location and may suggest a body of water still present on the west side of Winetavern Street while occupation was occurring further west (see Halpin 2000, fig. 17).

It should also be noted that, despite the fact that the area at Wood Quay was still being reclaimed in the thirteenth century, there was a jetty or boardwalk on a bank in the northern section of Winetavern Street, just north of the Cook Street alignment. This was constructed between 1188 and 1189, establishing the line of the river at this date (Walsh 1997, 92, pl. 7). Further north, a north–

south timber revetment was uncovered, founded on stone and on a projecting tongue of ground which projected into the Liffey (ibid., 106).

Essex Street West
Further east, two small investigations since 'Forty years a-digging' have revealed more evidence of reclamation north of the primary city wall (*c*.1100). Investigations by Nelis at the corner of Exchange Street Lower and Essex Street West exposed deposits related to reclaiming land (Nelis, *Excavations 2000*, 260), while a substantial stone lime-kiln was also found in a similar location (15) by Kehoe. This latter discovery is very important as it is likely to have been producing the mortar for the new city wall extension in the mid- to late thirteenth century (Kehoe, *Excavations 2004*, 541) and can be paralleled by another similar kiln at Patrick Street (Walsh 1997, 77) and Cecilia Street in the eastern suburb (Duffy and Simpson 2009, 229–32).

Temple Bar West
The excavations at Temple Bar West (*27*) by the writer revealed the scale of reclamation works that were clearly not confined to the river frontage and involved excavation elsewhere. At part of this site, the existing ground was dug out to between 2m and 3m in depth, the extracted deposits presumably tipped north of the *c*.1100 wall to aid in the reclamation process. The result was a general lowering of the ground level in part of the site at Temple Bar West, which became a garden area (Simpson 2001).

THE NEW CITY EXTENSION WALL *c*.1240

'Forty years a-digging' described the new city wall found down by the Liffey, which was exposed at the north-east corner at Lower Exchange Street (*28*) (Simpson 2000, 54). The north-east angle was protected by a round mural tower, known as Isolde's Tower (Simpson 1994), but the river frontage wall was also exposed, where it was over 2m in width, refaced in the fourteenth century (ibid.). The remains of a communal stone drain and a river-washed stone sluice were also identified to the west of the tower, but there was no indication of a quay front in this location. Further west, at Wood Quay, the riverfront wall was also identified where it was a recorded 3m in width (Wallace 1981, 251).

Usher's Quay and the timber dock
The supposed western extension wall was located at Usher's Quay (*17*), and this was referred to ten years ago in 'Forty year a-digging' and published in the same volume (Swan 2000, 126–58). Swan located an east–west riverfront wall and what appeared to be an enclosed stone and timber dock, dated by

dendrochronology to between *c*.1180 and *c*.1190. Thus, not much more than ten years after the invasion, construction had already started along what must have been the line of the river (almost along the modern line), the work taking place before the land to the north of the Hiberno-Norse wall was reclaimed.

The western side of the site was bordered by a substantial north–south wall, which, from the alignment, would appear to be have been the extension city wall (*c*.1260), but which Swan suggests may have been earlier. This wall extended for 14m and measured 1.8m in width by 1.7m in height, which is similar to other sections of the city wall (ibid., 136–7). However, surprisingly, it had a straight joint at the northern end, which was possibly founded on an earlier masonry build, containing some sort of projecting pier and the remains of a socket. Thus, this wall is likely to be earlier than the extension wall constructed in the mid- to late thirteenth century.

Confirming this, a gap was identified between the north–south city wall and the riverfront wall, which was interpreted as some sort of water-gate. This provided access into a well-preserved dock, fed water from an arched culvert and protected from silting up by two timber revetments. This dock measured at least 18m east–west by 20m north–south, but the full extent was not excavated. The revetments were of oak and produced dendrochronological dates of 1101±9 to 1185±9, suggesting that this feature must have been built shortly after the invasion (ibid., 154).

The riverfront east–west wall, by way of contrast, was not as substantial as the north–south wall and this was only 81cm to 1.02m in width, making it unlikely that it represents the extension riverfront wall proper, either by morphology or by the dating of associated features. This wall certainly formed part of the dock as it contained a complicated sluice mechanism related specifically to this function. It is possible that the new extension wall, built between 1240 and 1260, was located further north and that it replaced this earlier wall, although this is not certain. The findings of this excavation suggest that there was significant activity in this location immediately after the Anglo-Norman invasion, as part of the great refurbishment works that were occurring at this time, but, critically, it established the line of the river at this date, roughly along the modern line today.

THE EXTENSION CITY DITCH *c*.1240

Augustine Street

As mentioned previously, the area north of the Hiberno-Norse walled circuit was enclosed by a new city wall, which was under construction by *c*.1240 and was probably completed about twenty years later. This extension to the city was protected on the eastern side by the Poddle and at the western side by the construction of a new ditch, which was a continuation of the old ditch (although there must have been a pre-existing watercourse, allowing the water from the old ditch to drain into the Liffey, as discussed above). This new stretch, however, has not yet been located, despite substantial excavations by Hayden at a large site on the west side of Augustine Street (46), along what was thought to be its alignment. The director suggested that ditch must have been positioned directly under Augustine Street, outside the site to the east (Hayden 2010, 241–66; see fig. 1, p. 242).

RECLAMATION OUTSIDE THE CITY WALLS

Augustine Street

The same site has produced important information with regard to reclamation on the south side of the river but outside the walled city. The investigations at Augustine Street (46) proved that reclamation was also occurring outside the walled settlement on the western side, down by the bridge, confirming the evidence of early activity in this location found by Swan at Usher's Quay and mentioned above (Hayden 2010, 241–66). The work by Hayden revealed that this area was under reclamation from the late twelfth century (ibid., 244), and thus well in advance of the construction of the extension city wall, in the mid-thirteenth century. The reclamation was marked by the construction of post-and-wattle fences, orientated east–west, which retained refuse material to the south, levelling out sloping ground. This was later augmented by the construction of a flood bank.

This area was still subject to inundation, however, and only the eastern end of the bank survived. The evidence suggests rapid accumulation of river silt and gravels, as documented further east at Wood Quay. There was usage of the river frontage in this location, however, as the remains of a wattle path were found, which led down to an inlet on the Liffey (ibid., 246). By the fourteenth century, the land had dried out and two watercourses were identified.

ANGLO-NORMAN SETTLEMENT WITHIN THE TOWN

As previously mentioned, there has been little excavation within the city walls and, as a result, little advancement of knowledge in regard to Anglo-Norman settlement within the walls. In general, layers dating after the early twelfth century tend to have been truncated by cellars, which has caused significant damage in Dublin. Despite this, however, some of the larger sites do include some Anglo-Norman material, as part of the tail-end of the stratigraphic sequence.

Temple Bar West

At Temple Bar West (27), the large site in the north-east of the city, the sequence of Viking and Hiberno-Norse plots on the western side of the site continued in use into the Anglo-Norman period. Thus this sector remained a domestic quarter after the invasion, and the plots were maintained, whether by the original inhabitants allowed to stay on or by newcomers, having taken over the plots. While these layers were very truncated, at least one of the wattle paths in the rear of the plots was replaced by a timber pathway, a reflection of the preference the Anglo-Normans had for working in timber rather than in wattle exclusively (Simpson 2001).

This preference for timber was also demonstrated by the well-preserved remains of seven timber-lined cess pits, which were positioned within the original property boundaries, although there was no trace of any surviving boundary fences. Thus, all that survived were the deep pits, the location a clear indication that the properties were still in use, probably associated with sill-beamed houses fronting onto the street at the southern end. The pits were very substantial and elaborately constructed of overlapping timber planks, some with collapsed timber lids. What was interesting was that these pits displayed evidence of having been emptied out in a regular way. They were almost identical to pits excavated by Coughlan in Back Lane (18), where they were directly associated with timber-sill domestic houses (Coughlan 2000, 203–33).

This continuation of activity was also identified on the eastern side of the site, towards the Poddle, which continued in use as an industrial quarter, represented by clay platforms, hearths and mettled and clay surfaces, along with layers of burning and ash. The upper levels of this sequence could be dated to this period by the increasing number of ceramic finds, but, in the mid- to late thirteenth century, as mentioned above, this entire area was scarped or dug out and probably dumped over the *c.*1100 wall that ran along Essex Street West. This extraordinary act consisted of the wholesale removal of large amounts of the existing ground at the eastern side of the site: the western side, which was occupied by the house plots, escaped the general destruction.

This removal of material, as mentioned above, is likely to have been related to the large-scale development works in this area prompted by the need to construct a new quay/city wall along Lower Exchange Street. Excavations by the writer at Essex Street West (35–36), immediately north of Temple Bar West, found that the ground was infilled with domestic refuse, which produced Anglo-Norman finds subsequently sealed by 2m of black silt, presumably dredged from the Liffey (Simpson 1995). The former deposits are likely to have originated in Temple Bar West. It may also be the case that the material was used for constructing earthworks out in the river to enable the new wall to be constructed, as the excavation at Essex Street West did locate an earthen bank (Simpson 2001).

MEDIEVAL CHURCHES

There have been some advances in our knowledge of medieval churches in Dublin as there have been several investigations concentrated on some of the important church sites. Some of these – the churches of St Audoen, St Stephen and St Michael le Pole – were reported on in 'Forty years a-digging', but all have now been published, along with the new site at St Peter's Church (**19**) by Coughlan (Coughlan 2003, 11–39). Other investigations have been limited in size and scope, but have produced important information.

The church of St Audoen

St Audoen's Church (*24*) is the only extant medieval church in the Dublin, located at the western end of the walled city. The comprehensive investigations by McMahon have been published in a detailed volume, which documents the evolution of the complex building sequence (McMahon 2006). McMahon located the original church and dated it to the late twelfth century, suggesting that the primary church was a small two-cell structure with a smaller chancel at the eastern end. A laneway was also identified, running past the church on the eastern side, the origins of which were pre-Anglo-Norman.

This original simple nave-and-chancel building was followed by the construction of a long narrow nave, built in the early to mid-thirteenth century over the original church, and this subsequently became St Anne's chapel. The church was then doubled in width in the late thirteenth/early fourteenth century and by the early to mid-fourteenth century it was extended at the eastern side by the construction of the north chancel. The tower was added at the western end in the early to mid-fifteenth century and the Portlester chapel was added onto the northern chancel in the fifteenth century (McMahon 2006, 87).

The church of St John

The primary church of St Audoen's may have had parallels with a second important church to the east, at the top of Fishamble Street (**14**). Emergency excavations in this location were carried out by the writer, at the site of the church of St John of Bothe Street (Simpson 2008a). This work exposed masonry foundations that had been previously located during the excavations at Wood Quay but had been covered and preserved. This church was an important parish church, which was in existence before 1170, as it was granted by a Gillamichael to the priory of the Holy Trinity (Christ Church) (Clarke 2002, 16). The documentary sources indicate that it was rebuilt several times during the medieval period and had a graveyard attached, which is preserved *in situ* as a green space outside the Civic Offices. The church was only demolished in 1884 but the western gable probably survived until the 1960s, as a terrace of houses was built onto this side (ibid.).

The excavations to repair a water main at the southern end of Fishamble Street revealed part of the medieval church and the main structure uncovered was almost square in plan, measuring 6.14m north–south by 5m, and composed of solid limestone walls measuring 1.5m in width (Simpson 2008a). It had a small stone projection in the eastern face (fronting onto Fishamble Street) at the northern end and this corner also showed evidence of having been refaced or repaired. Only a small section was investigated and this could not be dated accurately.

The main square of masonry was very substantial and appeared, by type, to be medieval. In addition, there was a medieval soil deposit, which was still *in situ* along the northern face. The general external width of 6.3m suggests that it represents the eastern end of a small church, possibly a two-cell structure comprising a nave and chancel at the eastern end. A similar small church was located during the excavations at St Audoen's, which was built *c.*1200 (McMahon 2006, 86). This small structure had a long nave with a smaller chancel at the eastern end, which was subsequently subsumed by a large church. The nave measured 15.5m long by *c.*8m, with the narrower chancel measuring approximately 6.5m in width (ibid., 88).

Christ Church Cathedral
There has been some advance in attempting to decipher the evolution of Christ Church (*42*) in the Anglo-Norman period, although much remains a mystery. The cathedral chapter was originally Benedictine, but the Augustinian rule was introduced in 1163, before the invasion of Dublin in 1170, and the precinct was laid out around the cloister and garth at the western end of the precinct. The location was identified by Sir Thomas Drew in the nineteenth century when he located and excavated the chapter house (*c.*1225) in the east range, which is still extant today (Stalley 2005; Kinsella 2009). Drew also found what was interpreted by him as the remains of the cloister, although his reconstructions have to be treated with some caution.

In the early seventeenth century, the monastic precinct was developed as the Four Courts and it is possible that some of the existing monastic buildings were reused or incorporated during this rebuilding programme (Kinsella 2009, 31–75). A recent investigation by the writer concentrated on the site of the cloister, now a green space, where three trenches were excavated (Simpson 2010a). These immediately established the presence of substantial stone remains relating to the Four Courts just beneath the surface of the modern ground. The foundations consisted of a series of large limestone piers and the court of the common pleas, a building that was built anew in the green space of the cloister, was immediately identified and could be matched to the cartographic sources.

Part of the chancery court was also identified, which was of interest as this was potentially the original refectory of the monastery. Only a small section was exposed (and not the main walls), but this was found to have been supported by identical piers to the common pleas, suggesting a major rebuild in the early seventeenth century. However, it is still possible that there are medieval remains in this location, which were not located within the area investigated (Simpson 2010a). The small investigation also located natural undisturbed ground in the north-east corner of what would have been the cloister (beneath the 'old church yard'), establishing that the level of the cloister is likely to have been roughly equivalent to the level of the top step leading up from the extant chapter house (Simpson 2010a).

The church of St Michael of the Hill
A small excavation was also carried out by the writer just to the west of Christ Church in the courtyard attached to the former Synod Hall, at the site of the church of St Michael of the Hill. This important intra-mural church is reputed to have been built on the site of the episcopal palace, constructed by Bishop Dúnán in the mid-eleventh century. It functioned as a parish church throughout the medieval period and had a cemetery attached, which is depicted on Rocque's map of Dublin (Clarke 2002, 17). The church was comprehensively rebuilt in 1670 and only the fifteenth-century tower was preserved, which was again retained by the builders of the Synod Hall in 1875.

The recent investigations by the writer in the northern courtyard, in advance of the construction of a new porch, were limited in depth to the upper deposits (Simpson 2010c). Despite this, the investigation established that this area was densely inhabited in the Hiberno-Norse period and the remains of post-and-wattle houses do survive in this location, most likely to be orientated north–south. At least 2m of well-preserved organic habitation deposits suggest a well-preserved sequence, although this was not investigated. The modern courtyard was found to lie outside the cemetery of the church (Simpson 2010c).

The church and leper hospital of St Stephen
The new information has not been confined to churches within the walls. A series of investigations have been carried out in and around the church and leper hospital of St Stephen (*25, 16*), and these were included in 'Forty years a-digging', as mentioned previously, but have now been published (Buckley and Hayden 2002, 151–94). These excavations located the stone church, the walls measuring 80cm in width by 1m in height, and ceramic analysis suggests a date in the late twelfth/early thirteenth century for the construction of the church. The remains of a stone terrace were also found on the northern side of the church. A significant find from this site included a broken granite high-cross shaft, which was used as a grave-marker, but was not closely datable.

The church was also enclosed in the Anglo-Norman period by a bank and ditch (ibid., 153). The ditch was badly truncated but was originally V-shaped and measured at least 2.15m in width by 1.3m in depth. The bank was also badly damaged and measured less than 30cm in height by 1.8m in width. Hayden also located the remains of a north–south route extending to Stephen Street Upper, as well as several burials, none of which were of lepers. Over 120 burials were excavated as part of an earlier campaign at this site. Many of these were infants, dating from the medieval into the post-medieval period (Halpin, *Excavations 1992*, 58). Other excavations in and around the church site of St Stephen suggest that there was not much activity in this location, the stratigraphy consisting of a 1m-deep layer of garden soil, sealing a number of cultivation gullies (Halpin, *Excavations 1993*, 58).

The church of St Peter
The church of St Peter (5), as previously mentioned, can probably be dated to *c.*1100, suggested by the remains of an enclosing ditch found by Coughlan during excavations close to the site (Coughlan 2003, 11–39). While this site did not include the site of the church, a later phase was identified which involved infilling the ditch and replacing it with a mortared stone boundary wall. The eastern wall foundation extended for at least 8.5m and was 1.2m in width, while the southern wall was little more than a robber trench with an entrance in the south-west corner (ibid., 26–7). A total of 146 burials were associated with the stone boundary walls and an introduced burial soil, which produced medieval pottery. Some of the burials cut earlier graves, but, in some instances, other long-bones and skulls were re-interred with care.

In addition to this major excavation, testing at 7 Upper Stephen Street revealed disturbed disarticulated bones and a stone wall that may also have been related to the church boundary, which were Anglo-Norman in date (pers. comm., Franc Myles, 2000). The remains of a ditch (with a burial in the upper levels) were also located during additional testing by Moriarty along Stephen Street Upper, and this was presumably part of the enclosing ditch located by Coughlan, although this was not established (pers. comm., Colm Moriarty). Finally, testing at the site of the church by Walsh did locate the remains of a demolition layer over a clay floor, the demolition layers including limestone spalls and mortar along with lime render, the latter suggestive of a building rather than a boundary wall (Walsh, *Excavations 2007*, 488). The director suggests that this represents the remains of a large robbed-out medieval building, most likely to be St Peter's Church.

STONE BUILDINGS IN THE RECLAIMED LAND

The excavation at Cook Street (22) by Meenan was reported on in 'Forty years a-digging', but this important site has now been published (Meenan 2002,

128–39). The findings included the north-west corner of what must have been a substantial stone building, as it measured 8m in length by at least 1.8m in height, with walls 1m in width. The building was orientated north–south and probably fronted directly onto Cook Street on the southern side. It was founded on boulder clay, cutting through earlier riverine deposits, and was dated to the fourteenth or fifteenth century (ibid., 137–8). The excavations at Winetavern Street by Halpin also located the remains of two stone structures, one of which was L-shaped and very substantial, dated to the late thirteenth century on ceramic evidence (Halpin 2000, 56–7). The director suggests that this may have been the tholsel or guildhall, the location of which is mentioned in the documentary sources. This location, however, would place the tholsel outside the walled city rather than within, which would be unusual perhaps.

THE ANGLO-NORMAN SUBURBS

'Forty years a-digging' did include some of the more important Anglo-Norman sites from the suburbs, but only those in the immediate environs of the walled city. Since then, as previously mentioned, there have been very important sites excavated on both the southern and northern side of the river.

THE SOUTHERN ANGLO-NORMAN SUBURB

Ship Street Little

There have been several significant excavations in the southern suburb in the last ten years. The site at Ship Street Little excavated by the writer, mentioned in 'Forty years a-digging' ten years ago, has since been published, revealing important information about the new Anglo-Norman colony (Simpson 2004, 9–51). This site was located just outside the line of the city moat and the lowest levels consisted of two river channels, associated with the Poddle, which were open and flowing from the tenth to the early twelfth century (Simpson 2004, 21–2). These were subsequently infilled, probably as part of a reclamation programme in the late twelfth century, most likely to be associated with the construction of the city moat.

After this reclamation was completed, the formerly wet and marshy ground was made available for habitation and the partial foundations of four successive post-and-wattle house structures, as well as a possible tanning pit and stone drain, were found during the excavations. The fifth building in the sequence was part of a sill-beamed house, dated by dendrochronology to 1289±9, which can be compared directly to similar structures at the other end of the city, at Back Lane (Coughlan 2000) and to one of the structures at Christ Church (CP 13/2 2; Murray 1983, 178).

The sequence of buildings at Ship Street Little is very important as it charts the development of the Anglo-Norman structures in an area that was reclaimed immediately outside the city walls. The use of the post-and-wattle technique up until *c*.1289 is interesting as it represents an adoption of the vernacular Irish style of building, by people competent in coppicing and in post-and-wattle construction. The last house was a sill-beamed one, dated by dendrochronology to *c*.1285, rather than a post-and-wattle house, which can be compared directly to similar structures at the other end of the city, at Back Lane (Coughlan 2000, 203–34). The final phase of structural activity was industrial and was identified as a tanning complex, probably late medieval in date, which included a rectangular timber pit and three barrels (Simpson 2004, 43).

Golden Lane and Stephen Street
Adjoining Ship Street Little to the west was the important site at Golden Lane (1), excavated by O'Donovan, which also revealed significant evidence of occupation in the Poddle valley, which could be dated to the Anglo-Norman period. One of the major features was a large double-ditched sub-rectangular enclosure, which could be dated from the thirteenth to the sixteenth century and which the director tentatively suggests may have represented a moated site, a type of defended farmstead in use in Ireland at this date (O'Donovan 2008, 63–7). This appears as a type of residence found extensively in frontier locations and usually constructed between the late thirteenth and early fourteenth century. The enclosure was relatively small, measuring 20m east–west by 15m, but was within a field system, defined by a network of field boundaries (ibid., 68–9). Thus, it may well have been a defended residence, constructed in the late thirteenth century in the exposed southern suburb when the very capital of the English colony was under severe pressure from the Irish rebels in the Leinster mountains (Simpson 1994a).

Longford Street
In general, the evidence suggests that the south-eastern side of the southern suburb was in use predominantly for industrial use and some cultivation. This was suggested by excavations at Longford Street Little (bounded by Stephen Street Lower on the north) by O'Neill (O'Neill 2004, 73–90), where the Anglo-Norman activity consisted of earthen banks, surfaces and some sort of wall-slot, indicative of a structure in this location. The orientation of these features bore no relationship to the earlier pre-Anglo-Norman ditch, mentioned above, which was infilled by this date. By the thirteenth and fourteenth century, a new ditch had been opened up on roughly the same alignment of the earlier ditch, perhaps suggesting that it was some sort of a boundary that was still maintained into the fourteenth century. This site also produced evidence of industrial activity in the form of some sort of an hour-

glass shaped furnace, measuring 1.44m in length, which contained traces of a
metallic residue (ibid., 80).

Kevin Street Garda station
A much larger excavation was carried out further south by the writer along the
eastern side of Kevin Street Garda station (20), to the east of St Patrick's
Cathedral (Simpson 2009b). The Garda station, which comprises a number of
historic buildings, was originally the medieval palace of John Cumin, the first
Anglo-Norman archbishop of Dublin, in the late twelfth century. The palace
was not only the domestic residence of the archbishop but also the administration centre for the manor of St Sepulchre (Clarke 1998, 52). It was
constructed deliberately in this location, on an elevated position overlooking
the Poddle valley and church of St Patrick but, crucially, outside the city walls
and thereby outside the jurisdiction of the citizens of Dublin.

The extant remains of the palace: An architectural investigation of the
walls and building fabric of the Garda station, by Arthur Gibney Architects,
has confirmed that the original medieval quadrangle survives almost intact,
although there have been considerable additions throughout the centuries,
including a new block in the central courtyard (O'Donovan 2003, 253–78).
Sections of the wall were stripped, both externally and internally (Arthur
Gibney Architects) and the medieval masonry was exposed, revealing that the
western range and parts of the southern, northern and eastern range are still
extant, disguised beneath a modern render. Part of a tower also survives within
the block, along with a small medieval building at the northern side, which is
orientated east–west and was probably the chapel of the palace, mentioned in
the documentary sources.

The archaeological excavation: The archaeological excavation was confined
to the eastern side of the complex, fronting onto Bride Street on the east and
Kevin Street on the south and, as a result, lay outside the footprint of the main
quadrangle but within the palace precinct (Simpson 2009a). The finds include
numerous cut stone fragments (the quality and style of which suggests that the
palace was lavishly decorated in the medieval period), which were found reused
in the post-medieval buildings and dumped in this location (report by Michael
O'Neill).
    The site had been badly truncated in the post-medieval period, the intact
stratigraphy confined to the mid-western part of the site. In this location, two
boundary ditches, which were probably pre-Anglo-Norman in date, suggest
that there was some Hiberno-Norse activity at this site, but this was extremely
limited. By the Anglo-Norman period (after 1170), however, there was
occupation in the central area, suggested by the remains of cess and refuse pits,

which are usually found associated directly with domestic dwellings, although none survived here. One of these pits produced the skull of a young man, which could be dated to the late twelfth/early thirteenth century and which shows signs of decapitation. The head had been laid on a wattle mat and buried with a putrefying dog along with a collection of interesting animal bones. These included remains of a sparrow hawk and a hen harrier, presumably from a falconry attached to the palace, as well as hare, fallow and red deer. Deep-water fish were also represented (cod and ling), as well as conger eel (report by Jonny Gerber).

The defensive ditches: In the mid-thirteenth century there was a major intervention in the form of the construction of substantial ditches along Bride Street and Kevin Street, which are most likely to have enclosed the medieval precinct, perhaps providing an outer defence to an inner walled precinct. The ditches were between 4m and 5m in width by at least 1.5m in depth (although the upper levels were truncated) and at least two entrances were identified: an east–west route onto Bride Street on the northern side, and a second parallel route in the central area. The remains of an internal clay bank were also identified along the Bride Street frontage.

Habitation and industrial activity: The main ditches were recut in the mid-fourteenth century, but were narrower (between 1.5m and 2.5m), although they probably still performed an enclosing function, possibly even still defensive if bolstered by a palisade or some other type of defensive feature. The remains of a sunken stone cellar (4.3m by 1.3m by 70cm in depth) was also identified, suggesting occupation in this location in the fourteenth/fifteenth century, dated by a line-impressed tile within the fill. This area was then divided into three large property plots or fields, suggesting a general open plan. Within the western area, there was evidence of intensive industrial activity in the form of a large kiln, the chamber of which measured at least 3.7m north–south by 3.5m. It was cut to a depth of 1.7m and had a well-formed flue and fire-box at the southern end.

The lower fill deposits of the kiln contained bronze flecks, slag, fragments of moulds and possible crucible fragments, suggesting that the primary function initially was metalworking, and this is supported by the activity surrounding the kiln, which included scorched areas, also producing metal-working evidence in the form of fire-pits. The presence of at least two large structures was suggested by the remains of substantial post-holes. This activity was also not confined to the western end of the site as there was evidence of metalworking on the eastern side also.

The kiln appears to have had a range of other uses over a period of time, including domestic, agricultural and industrial. It seems likely that some of the features located to the east of the kiln may have been secondary working areas, spread out over the lifetime of the kiln, possibly a series of small structures, wind breaks and work areas associated with it. A small furnace was identified along with a possible smithing area, and this was associated with two large post-holes, perhaps from a temporary structure around it. The area to the west of the furnace was also burnt or scorched. In addition, further east, a second bowl furnace or hearth was located close to the Bride Street boundary ditch and this feature was linked to the same activity as it contained similar small inclusions of bronze and burnt clay.

The recutting of the boundary ditches: The boundary ditches were recut for a third time, but this time they were far more substantial, measuring nearly 3m in width, perhaps suggesting a more defensive role, dated roughly to the early to mid-fifteenth century. The southern end of the site was divided into long narrow plots, measuring approximately 24m in length by 7m in width, which backed onto the Kevin Street ditch on the southern side. There was access on this side to the street, probably via a stone gate with a corresponding entrance at the south–east corner, through a gap in the ditch. The evidence suggests that at least two of the plots had semi-basemented buildings, the cellars being used for storage. In confirmation of this domestic habitation evidence, two well-preserved wells were also found, which provided fresh water and one of which contained a complete Dublin jug at the base. This may have been lost while water was being retrieved.

Plot reorganization: After the ditches were infilled, the evidence suggests that plots now extended over the infilled ditch and fronted directly onto Kevin Street on the south. The remains of a mettled road were found, sealing the infilled ditches and evidently forming the east–west route, now Kevin Street Upper. The levels were very truncated, but at least one stone wall survived, which is all that remains of houses in this location. The infilling of the boundary ditches along Kevin Street and Bride Street was obviously a major shift in land usage in this area and may suggest that this area was no longer part of the palace complex, although the plots may still have been owned by the archbishop of Dublin. Once the ditches were infilled, there was direct access to both Bride Street and Kevin Street, which probably increased the value of the land.

The construction of the road is also an interesting feature: clearly a route was already established along Kevin Street Lower prior to this, but the infilling of the ditches provided the impetus for the construction of a new road. Unfortunately, the ground was very truncated and it was difficult to establish whether or not this reconstruction included the relocation of the houses within the plots. That the plot alignments were maintained is evident by the fact that

they survive into the post-medieval period and can be traced in the Early
Modern cartographic sources.

Bride Street
Additional excavation was carried out just north of the large site at Kevin
Street Garda station and this suggests that significant remains survive on this
site also; a continuation of the activity identified further south at the Garda
station itself (Cosgrave, *Excavations 1998*, 143). The features uncovered by
Cassidy and O'Brien include stone wells, indicative of domestic habitation,
along with stone drains, mettled surfaces, large pits filled with domestic waste
and at least one medieval wall running parallel to Bride Street. Additional
features were located in the second phase of excavation by Cosgrave, which
included clay-bonded walls, architectural fragments, hearths and kilns, along
with cobbled and mettled surfaces (ibid.).

St Kevin's Church
The southern end of the suburb was serviced by the small parish church of St
Kevin, the site now occupied by a post-medieval church with no trace of
medieval build. Testing to the north of the church by Conway, on a site parallel
to Liberty Lane, uncovered an east–west ditch along the Kevin Street Lower
frontage, which was possibly a continuation of a similar ditch found the
previous year at the corner of Kevin Street Lower and Church Lane (Conway,
Excavations 1997, 46; *Excavations 1998*, 169). The ditch fill contained medieval
pottery, suggesting that it was beginning to fill in by the Anglo-Norman
period, but it may have been earlier in date.
   The director suggests that the ditch may have been part of the city ditch,
although this is perhaps too far south, lying some distance from the medieval
city. Despite this, it may form part of a second line of defensive earthworks,
perhaps protecting the suburbs (see below). However, its close proximity to St
Kevin's Church, a pre-Anglo-Norman foundation, makes it much more likely
that it is a ditch associated with the church, perhaps even enclosing it,
suggesting an enclosure of at least 8om in diameter. However, Dublin and its
immediate environs are full of ditches, many of them drainage or boundary
fences, and it may have been either of these, running along the medieval route
of Kevin Street Lower.

St Patrick's Cathedral
There have been other investigations in the immediate area of the palace,
including in the environs of St Patrick's Cathedral (21), to the north-west of
Kevin Street. This work, by the writer, produced evidence of disarticulated
disturbed human remains on the northern side of the cathedral, although these
could not be dated, as they had been moved when a boiler house was

constructed in the nineteenth century. However, the findings suggest that burial took place on this side also, in addition to the extant burial-ground on the south-eastern side of the cathedral. The investigations on this side also established that there is good preservation of organic deposits, over 1.5m in depth, an indication that St Patrick's Park probably has the potential to contain significant archaeological deposits (Simpson 2009b).

50 Patrick Street / 31–32 Kevin Street and Minot Tower
A smaller excavation at 50 Patrick Street/31–32 Kevin Street revealed a channel thought to be associated with the Poddle, which survived beneath basemented buildings in an area that was originally part of the cathedral precinct. The channel was filled with organic remains that contained high-status artefacts including ceramic floor tiles, which presumably originated in the cathedral. Also of considerable interest was the large number of medieval Dundry stones (an imported English oolite used extensively in the thirteenth century in high-status buildings), which had been reused in the existing building (Walsh, *Excavations 2005*, 463). These can probably be paralleled by a similar collection of stones found at the archbishop's palace of St Sepulchre described above (Simpson 2009a). Finally, investigations carried out by Kehoe in the late fourteenth-century Minot Tower during the construction of toilets revealed disarticulated human remains, probably disturbed in the nineteenth century (Kehoe, *Excavations 2002*, 573).

105–109 the Coombe
Further to the south-west, a series of excavations and investigations were carried out along the Coombe valley, which confirm the importance of this location, suggested by the findings of pre-Anglo-Norman houses by Walsh (see above). Excavations by McQuade at 105–109 the Coombe identified an artificial watercourse on the south side of the main road, presumably siphoned off from the Coombe stream, which ran along the northern boundary of the site (McQuade, *Excavations 2004*, 528). Evidence of land reclamation in what was evidently boggy ground was also identified, marked by post-and-wattle fences, and there was some indication of plot layout, presumably a continu-ation of the habitation discovered by Walsh although dated to the Anglo-Norman period.

Small-scale industrial activity was also occurring within the plots, evidenced by the finding of at least one substantial hearth, which included a firing pit containing burnt cereal. This can be paralleled with a similar corn-drying kiln found by Hayden further east as part of the Coombe bypass excavations (22) (see below). McQuade also found six tanning pits, along with a stone-lined pit, evidently the remains of a tanning complex, exploiting the supply of water. This tanning may have continued on the site until the post-medieval period (ibid.).

The Coombe bypass

Further east, similar evidence was retrieved by Hayden in advance of the new Coombe bypass road (**22**) (close to St Luke's Church), where a total of five sites were investigated and dated to the Anglo-Norman period (Hayden, *Excavations 2000*, 372). The earliest evidence at the Coombe consisted of medieval pits and gullies, but of great interest was the discovery of a large east–west counterscarp medieval ditch, which suggests that this early settlement was defended, as the remains of a palisade were located on the southern side (Hayden, *Excavations 2001*, 372). This ditch can probably be dated to the early years after the invasion, as a stone-lined corn-drying kiln was constructed in the bottom of the ditch, which has been dated to the thirteenth century, suggesting that the ditch may have been out of use by this time. These features, however, were not long-lasting, as they were sealed by cultivated soil, probably indicative of a certain contraction in settlement in this location from the late thirteenth to the fifteenth century (ibid.).

The discovery of the earthen defences in the western suburb, some distance from the city walls, is very significant as it raises the possibility of additional outlying defences around the medieval city, about which little is known. These may have been secondary defences to the main city wall and ditch system, ringing the main walled settlement. Alternatively, of course, the ditch may be all that remains of an individual defensive feature around a specific smaller settlement or site.

Ardee/Cork Street

St Thomas' Abbey (**41**) was very well positioned on the western side of the city as the Poddle was included within the demesne land attached to the abbey (Simpson 1997, 24–5). Although the Poddle originally had a very direct north–south route, skirting around the eastern boundary of the abbey lands, the monks quickly redirected the river to flow on a much more circuitous route, called the 'Abbey Stream', on which they constructed at least three mill complexes (ibid.). This work was probably done shortly after the abbey was established in 1177 and this is confirmed by a reference to a 'pond below St Thomas' Court' (McNeill 1950, 31–2), which is also mentioned at a later date as a landmark in the 'Riding of the franchises', a ceremonial procession around the city boundaries, which was carried out by Dublin's mayor and citizens (Myles 2009, 193).

Large-scale excavations at Cork Street/Adree Street (**24**) by Myles have revealed evidence of what is possibly that millpond, associated with the abbey mills and in use throughout the later medieval period (Myles 2009, 183–212). This presented as deep deposits of silt approximately 3m in depth fed by the Commons Water, the pond measuring between 50m and 53m in width (ibid., 188, 191). Myles suggests that the millpond might even be pre-monastic in origin and directly related to an original mill mentioned in the grant of Donore to the abbey of St Thomas (ibid., 196). That the pond was clearly related to the milling industry of the abbey was confirmed by the discovery of six millstones at the site. This, the director suggests, probably indicates that the actual mill building was close by (ibid.).

Other evidence of milling activity was found during a second investigation at the site of the Woodenmill mentioned above, also belonging to the abbey (Myles 2009, quoting Walsh). A timber from what was possibly the mill building produced a felling date of 1172±9 (Q10670M), thus potentially in and around the abbey foundation date of 1177 (Simpson 1997, 24). This date is particularly significant as it confirms results of research by the writer in the early 1990s that the diverted stream, previously thought to date to after the construction of the city watercourse in 1244 (Ronan 1927), was significantly earlier in date, dating to just after the grant to the abbey in the late twelfth century (Simpson 1997, 24).

Ardee Street and Emerald Terrace
At Ardee Street, Hayden also identified a branch of the medieval abbey stream, divided into two channels, while additional investigations to the west identified two late twelfth-/thirteenth-century watercourses or channels at Emerald Terrace, one of which was contained within timber planks and by a number of large post-holes, suggesting that it may have been a millrace servicing a horizontal mill (Hayden, *Excavations 2002*, 531). A shallow pool of water was also identified.

Fumbally Lane, Newmarket and New Street
The results of the Coombe bypass excavations suggest a certain contraction in this area of settlement in the fourteenth century, marked by layers of cultivation soil. This was also suggested by excavations at a second large site, which was excavated by Lohan at Fumbally Lane. This site produced evidence of medieval occupation but also medieval cultivation, in a similar sequence to the Coombe bypass site (Lohan, *Excavations 2006*, 618). The lowest levels produced evidence of furrows, but in the south-east corner there was evidence of domestic dumping, usually associated with habitation. A similar profile was identified at 48–50 Newmarket/14–16 Newmarket Street (25), where excavations by Frazer also produced evidence of habitation and cultivation dating to the thirteenth and fourteenth centuries (Frazer, *Excavations 2003*, 560).

By way of contrast, large-scale excavations by Giacometti further south at New Street (23) exposed the remains of a medieval industrial tannery that continued operating into the early modern period, suggestive of a secure situation in this location from the medieval into the early modern period (Giacometti, *Excavations 2004*, 564). This site comprised over a hundred circular and rectangular pits, which were connected to the Poddle by a series of drains and ditches. In at least one instance a water channel was diverted from the river to supply the vast amount of water that must have been required for such a large tannery. The pits were unlined and the circular ones measured between 83cm and 1.65m in diameter, while the rectangular pits were between 1m and 1.28m square by between 1m and 2m in depth.

THE WESTERN ANGLO-NORMAN SUBURB

Cornmarket and Bertram's Court: There have been significant advancements in our knowledge of the development of the western suburbs, outside the New Gate on the western side of the walled city. One of the most important sites lay outside the western gate at Cornmarket (*29*), known in the medieval period as 'Bertram's Court'. This site was included in 'Forty years a-digging' but was also published in the same volume, which provides more detail (Hayden 2000, 84–6). While the preservation of organic material was poor, the excavation revealed an area that can be identified from the documentary sources as Bertram's Court and a total of nine levels were identified on this site, spanning the time period from the late twelfth into the fourteenth century. The findings included a mettled surface or road, probably Cesus Lane, and this was associated with boundaries of post-and-wattle fences from the earliest levels, as well as flimsy post-and-wattle buildings.

A more substantial building (early to mid-thirteenth century) was also identified, and this was particularly interesting as, although the main walls were of post-and-wattle, there was also a series of structural internal posts, abutting the walls, representing a mix of the Hiberno-Norse (post-and-wattle) and Anglo-Norman building techniques (ibid., 102). This house was re-floored at least eight times and could be identified as a metalworking workshop, where belt buckles were manufactured. A second, though less well-preserved, building contained the remains of two wooden troughs.

Metalworking continued on the site throughout the mid- to late thirteenth century, and in the fourteenth century a large timber building was constructed, denoted by a clay floor and earthfast posts. Curiously, one wall was of post-and-wattle while the others might have been sill-beamed, again representing a mix of Hiberno-Norse and Anglo-Norman building traditions. The later level contained a large stone-walled clay structure edged with roof tiles, which was probably a tile kiln, the first identified at Dublin.

Francis Street
There have been limited archaeological investigations along Francis Street but excavations at one important site, at 123–133 Francis Street/1–4 Swift Alley,

located the remains of a stone house, dated to the thirteenth/fourteenth century. This house, excavated in the south-east corner of the site in an area measuring 10m2, only survived because the eighteenth-century houses in this location had no basements, unlike the houses in the remainder of the site. The medieval house was very unusual as it measured 9m in length but its long axis was parallel to the street rather than fronting onto it. In addition to this, the walls were built of clay and rubble, which is relatively unusual (Walsh, *Excavations 1997*, 132). A second excavation at 97 Francis Street revealed medieval soils and, most significantly, a thirteenth-century metalled surface, which was resurfaced in the medieval period and which the director suggests may represent the original Francis Street, a very rare survival in Dublin (Walsh, *Excavations 2000*, 263).

The development of Francis Street is likely to have been promoted by the Franciscan friary in this suburb (Clarke 2002, 19). At the time of the Dissolution, this house included a church, a cemetery, a cloister and other buildings on a total of two acres, presumably in the immediate environs. The site of the friary is currently occupied by the substantial church of St Nicholas of Myra, which presumably has destroyed most of the monastic precincts and claustral buildings (ibid., 14). However, excavations did locate part of the cemetery attached to the monastery. A total of eighty-four burials were located at 34–36 Francis Street, some of which were originally in wooden coffins (Murtagh, *Excavations 1994*, 67).

The hospital of St John the Baptist

The western suburb was dominated by the Augustinian hospital of St John the Baptist (Fratres Cruciferi), which was founded between 1185 and 1188 (Clarke 2002, 26; Gwynn and Hadcock 1988). It was on the north side of Thomas Street, just outside the Newgate and the site is now occupied by the modern church and monastery of SS Augustine and John. The only trace of the friary was found during an extensive excavation at Augustine Street/16–17 John Street West (**36**), where the cemetery was identified. During this work, a total of 168 burials were excavated, although it is not clear how many of these were medieval (see Cosgrave, *Excavations 1998*, 136). The burials were found to seal medieval pits, suggestive of occupation before the cemetery, which was known to have been extended in 1350. Finds included shroud pins and coffin nails.

Augustine Street and National College of Art and Design

At the time of the Dissolution in the sixteenth century, the property of the hospital included at least three mills known as 'St John's mills', presumably on the north side of the precinct, taking advantage of the steep slope, from south to north (Simpson, *Excavations 1996*, 116; Clarke 2002, 17). Another mill is recorded as being built in 1478 somewhere close by (Clarke 2002, 26). The excavations at Augustine Street (**38/46**) carried out by Hayden immediately west of the walled city produced very significant evidence of milling (Hayden 2010, 241–66). At least two artificial medieval watercourses were identified, but the major find was the well-preserved remains of a double mill dated by Hayden to between 1601 and the 1690s. Despite the post-medieval date, the location is significant, as it is likely that it is very close to the site of one of the medieval mills mentioned in the documentary sources, as mill sites have a documented longevity due to the complexities of channelling their water-supply.

National College of Art and Design
The importance of the area for milling was further established by the results of an excavation carried out by the writer to the south-west (**37**), at the base of the slope from south to north at the National College of Art and Design (bordering Oliver Bond Street on the north). This excavation located the remains of two medieval watercourses, most likely to be millraces, running along the natural ridge (from south to north) and then turning down the steep slope towards the river (Simpson 1996; Simpson, *Excavations 1996*, 116). These must have been related to the mills attached to St John's hospital or a mill just outside the city walls (Oliver Bond Street) known as 'Mullinahack' in the documentary sources (Clarke 2002, 17). These medieval millraces were replaced in the late sixteenth century by distinctive stone-lined channels, at a similar date to the construction of the Augustine Street mill (**46**), and they may have been part of this complex.

Additional investigations at the junction of Oliver Bond Street and Augustine Street, conducted by Walsh, exposed the remains of medieval silt deposits with low-grade dumping of organic material. A later brick culvert may have housed the original medieval watercourse known as the 'Glib', which flowed into the Liffey at this location (Walsh, *Excavations 1997*, 3). This watercourse was also identified by Hayden at the northern end of Augustine Street, where it flowed in several channels that could be dated to between the thirteenth and fifteenth centuries and was probably associated with milling in the general vicinity. There was also evidence of the channels being realigned in the fifteenth and sixteenth centuries, correlating with the evidence from the site at the National College of Art and Design.

St Thomas' Abbey
The most important ecclesiastical foundation in the western suburb was St Thomas' Abbey (**41**), at the western end of St Thomas' Street and the establishment of this house was to have a major impact on the development of the western suburb, especially Thomas Street (Clarke 2002, 7; Duddy 2003, 70–97). The abbey was founded in 1177. The precinct of the abbey was extensive and the lands included the liberty of Donore, which bestowed additional

privileges on the house, as it was administered independently and lay outside the jurisdiction of the city of Dublin (Gwynn and Hadcock 1988, 172).

A series of very important excavations have been carried out by Walsh, and these have established that there are extensive subterranean remains of the abbey spread throughout Earl Street, Meath Street and Hanbury Lane (41), so well-preserved and of such significance that the site has now been purchased by Dublin City Council (Walsh 2000, 105–202).

Earl Street: The southern boundary of the precinct was identified at Earl Street and this took the form of an enclosing ditch, similar to that identified around the archbishop's palace of St Sepulchre at Kevin Street Garda station (see above). This ditch, however, was massive, measuring between 6.2m and 8m in width by at least 2.1m in depth, and dated to the late twelfth century (ibid., 191). The ditch was infilling in the late thirteenth/early fourteenth century and was replaced by a substantial stone wall boundary in the fourteenth century, founded along the alignment of the earlier ditch except at the eastern end of the site, when the ditch swung away to the south. The stone wall was 90cm in width by 65cm in height with a plinth on the southern side (ibid.).

Meath Street: A second site at Meath Street, to the north-east, revealed a spectacular find, the foundations of the church of the abbey, one of the most important buildings of the complex (ibid., 195–8). The southern wall was identified, which was an impressive 2.75m in width, establishing that it was a building of substantial size (Walsh 2000, 195). The identification of it as the church was supported by the exposure, in the interior, of two sections of a tiled pavement and a small area of cobbling, the former very rare in Dublin. A second wall was also uncovered, parallel to the southern wall of the church but 3m to the south. The director suggested that this represents the remains of the cloister.

Hanbury Lane: The third site, at Hanbury Lane, lay to the east and excavations here located part of a burial ground, lying to the north of the church. A total of seventeen unmarked burials were uncovered in the north-east corner of the site and these were dated to the thirteenth century but the low number of burials and the manner in which they were spread out suggested that this represents a peripheral burying area, rather than the main cemetery of the abbey (ibid., 200). The investigation also found that grave markers and unexcavated burials remain *in situ* on the western part of the site at Hanbury Lane, however, suggesting that the cemetery proper may be in this location.

Finally, the investigations at Hanbury Lane also identified what may be the remains of part of the eastern boundary of the abbey in the form of a stone wall, dated to the medieval period. This clay-bonded wall was not very substantial, however, measuring just 70cm in width. It is not known if there was a ditch in this location also (ibid., 19).

Thomas Street

Thomas Street was one of the most important thoroughfares in medieval Dublin, following the route of a natural gravel ridge that extends along the southern bank of the Liffey as far as Kilmainham and beyond. It appears to have developed rapidly within the first decade after the Anglo-Norman invasion, and this was actively encouraged: the original grant to St Thomas' Abbey, included a grant of 'burgage' (property plots to which certain privileges were attached), which was designed to stimulate development at this end of the suburb (Duddy 2003, 89).

Several important excavations have been carried out along the Thomas Street/James' Street alignment, which supports the documentary evidence of domestic occupation along the street by the late twelfth century, but these investigations have been confined to the rear of the existing houses. This 'rear plot' evidence consists of pits and spreads of animal bone, along with latrines and post-and-wattle fences clearly related to the houses that would have fronted onto the street. But there is also evidence of industrial activity at some of the sites, all suggestive of intensive occupation.

119–121 Thomas Street

One of the largest sites was investigated by O'Donovan on the north side of Thomas Street, to the rear of nos 119 and 121 (**40**) (O'Donovan 2003, 127–71). This excavation behind the houses fronting onto the street revealed widespread evidence of habitation along with small-scale local manufacturing, suggested by the presence of slag and metalwork debris. The features included a pit with an oak box, six clay-lined and interlocking pits filled with cess, and a stone-lined trough, as well as other cess pits and a barrel.

A wide range of artefacts was retrieved, including clay roof and floor tiles, evidently originating from medieval houses along the street frontage (ibid., 164). This activity was dated by finds and by dendrochronology to the period from the early years of the thirteenth century (1206±9) into the fourteenth century (ibid., 136, 164). The early date is an indication that this street was developed soon after the invasion.

Additional sites on Thomas Street

There have been other smaller investigations along the street and, in general, the picture is one of habitation and small-scale industrial activity carried out to the rear of the street. At 131 Thomas Street a small site to the rear of the property produced evidence of medieval storage pits, cess pits and a fine assemblage of medieval pottery suggesting relatively prosperous residents (Hayden, *Excavations 2004*, 590). At 34–36 Thomas Street (south side), also behind the houses to the rear, investigations by the writer revealed what may represent a watercourse; either Colman's Brook or the millrace attached to the Watte Will (owned by St Thomas' Abbey). The evidence also suggested a possible leather tanning complex (Gowen and Simpson, *Excavations 1996*, 115), although testing to the rear of no. 38 produced no evidence of archaeological material (Walsh, *Excavations 1998*, 14).

This is something of a surprise, since investigations by O'Carroll at 58–59 Thomas Street (on the south side) (39) found cess pits along with evidence of iron-working, represented by slag waste and fire-reddened clay, a familiar usage of this suburb. This site also produced a good collection of ceramic pottery, dating from the late twelfth/thirteenth century, similar to the site at no. 131 investigated by Hayden (Carroll, *Excavations 1997*, 170; Hayden, *Excavations 2004*, 590).

St James' hospital
The urban sprawl appears to have extended as far west as James' Street, although it is not known how continuous the activity was and whether or not the street was laid out in regular plots as far as this end of the suburb. The evidence suggests that this end was certainly occupied and formed part of the developed suburb, serviced by the parish church of St James. This church was founded in *c.*1190 and was granted to the abbey of St Thomas (Clarke 2002, 18). The evidence comes from important excavations at St James' hospital by Walsh, which, unusually, almost fronted onto the street and produced the remains of a rectangular timber house, within property boundaries. A possible corn-drying structure was also found, a reminder of the nature of the settlement in the environs of Dublin (Walsh, *Excavations 2001*, 402). This house was sealed by a layer of cultivation soil, suggesting a contraction of habitation in this area, the soil forming the foundation for a mettled roadway, flanked by ditches on either side. The latter was seventeenth-century in date but respected the line of the earlier medieval boundaries.

THE EASTERN ANGLO-NORMAN SUBURB

The eastern suburb was also settled extensively in the Anglo-Norman period, the importance of this suburb elevated by the fact that it fronted directly onto the river and that there was a landing stage at the Steine, which was in use throughout the medieval period (see above). Unfortunately, as previously mentioned, the historical evidence is not matched by the archaeological evidence for several reasons, not least because there has been little modern development in the medieval suburb, the main concentration of new construction being along Temple Bar, reclaimed in the 1600s.

The Holy Trinity friary
Despite this, some important excavations have been carried out that hint at the potential of this quarter to yield important information. The foundation of the

Augustinian friary at Cecilia Street (43) after 1265 was probably the most important event in the eastern suburb in the Anglo-Norman period. The friary was founded perhaps by the Talbot family and the order followed the rule of St Augustine and was mendicant, and thus they administered aid to the poor of Dublin. The site was on the south bank, at what is now Cecilia Street, close to a crossing point on the river, possibly the ford of St Mary's Abbey, mentioned in the documentary sources (Duffy and Simpson 2009, 202–48).

Recent archaeological investigations have confirmed the general location of the friary first suggested by Clarke (1978) as in and around Cecilia Street. Thus, the precinct was bounded by the river at the northern end, Upper Fownes Street on the east and either Temple Lane or Eustace Street on the west (ibid., 211–12, 222–3).

5–6 Cecilia Street: The excavation at 5–6 Cecilia Street (43) by the writer established that foundations of the friary did survive, as the eighteenth century-building on this plot had no cellars (Duffy and Simpson 2009, 227–47). A substantial arched stone wall was identified as the eastern precinct wall of the friary and was found to be a substantial build with evidence of either an entrance or buttresses on this side. The alignment of the wall, along the western boundary of Fownes Street Upper, established that this street owed its origins to the medieval period and was not laid out in the seventeenth century when the Temple Bar area was developed, as had previously been thought. The wall measured between 1.05m and 1.2m by 2m in height and was founded on a series of distinctive open segmented arches, often used on unstable ground. Four small wall projections were also identified on the eastern side, and these are likely to be buttresses of some sort (ibid., 237).

Other investigations located various smaller stretches of the northern precinct wall running along the medieval river frontage and this wall was a similar type to the eastern wall, although it was battered on the riverside. It was badly truncated, however, and the only sections surviving were those incorporated within post-medieval boundary walls (ibid.). The excavation also located the remains of at least two stone buildings, one of which respected the line of Cecilia Street, suggesting that this street too has its origins in the medieval period.

The church and the lime-kiln: The other building was a substantial structure at the northern end of the site, which was orientated east–west and was possibly part of the church of the friary. This building measured at least 9m in length by 5m in width and was constructed slightly later than the other walls and set at a slight angle (ibid., 243). The primary levels produced an intact lime-kiln, most likely to have produced mortar when the friary was under construction and subsequently truncated by one of the walls (ibid., 231).

This kiln was square in plan and measured 4.3m north–south by 3.9m in width and was 40cm in depth, with vertical sides, which were vitrified. The surrounding clay was fired a bright orange colour and there were burnt rods at the base of the kiln, along with layers of burnt limestone chips. A truncated slaking pit was also located close by, which measured at least 1.4m in length by 45cm in width and was 3cm in depth, filled with soft slaked lime.

23–4 Temple Lane: A section of the cemetery attached to the friary was identified halfway between Dame Street and Cecilia Street during excavations at 23–24 Temple Lane/Crow Street (**13**) (Reid, *Excavations 1994*, 91; Ó Donnabháin and Hallgrímsson 2001, 69). This site, set back from Temple Lane, produced evidence of at least sixty-five burials, all orientated west–east and some of which were buried in coffins. The ceramic collection suggests a date from the early thirteenth to the fourteenth century, which correlates with the historical information about the friary (Reid, *Excavations 1993*, 92).

32 Dame Street
There have been few excavations along Dame Street, which must have been the main thoroughfare of the eastern suburb in the Anglo-Norman period leading down to the priory of All Hallows and beyond to Ringsend. However, one excavation by Giacometti located the remains of a large curving ditch (orientation and size not ascertained), which was infilled in the twelfth to the fourteenth century but which the director suggests may have formed a significant boundary in this location, perhaps defining Hoggen Green to the east (Giacometti, *Excavations 2007*, 471). It was also located just south of the site of a suburban fortified gate.

The River Liffey
Throughout the medieval period, the eastern suburb was bounded on the northern side by the River Liffey, the line of which has been identified through various investigations and some excavation. The medieval shoreline lay just south of the line of East Essex Street and Temple Bar, and this is marked in the modern topography by a drop in level of over 1.5m from south to north. At Cecilia Street, the rear wall of the properties fronting onto the street mark the line of the river, which was subsequently infilled with organic deposits from the 1600 onwards.

This reclamation was carried out in much the same way as the medieval reclamation at Wood Quay, using timber revetments, holding dumped organic cess material. These deposits (extending as far north as the present quay wall) are very rich in artefacts, especially ceramic material dating from the late sixteenth/seventeenth century onwards. The actual medieval Liffey bed was characterized by deep mud-flats and riverine deposits, the result of sand and silt being swept up the mouth of the river and then deposited along the banks of the river, a problem that is first recounted in the historical sources as early as 1305 (Simpson 1994, 4–5).

The chapel of St Clement

The chapel of St Clement was located to the north of the priory of All Hallows (now Trinity College) on the banks of the River Liffey, but the site is unknown and it was closed by *c.*1530 (Clarke 2002, 20). Works in the late nineteenth century at the site of the Allied Irish Bank at College Street reputedly uncovered the remains of an *in situ* tiled floor, which could be dated to the medieval period (Eames and Fanning 1988, 67). In the absence of any other known ecclesiastical site, this probably marks the site of the chapel. However, there is confusion over this and the floor may be part of the abbey of Mary de Hogges within the city, close to Dame's Gate (see below). A recent testing programme identified the site of the 'tiled pavement' as 5 College Street, but this work revealed that there were river gravels in this location less than 2m below present ground level with no indication of an old medieval ground level (Reid, *Excavations 2000*, 251).

College Street, Westmorland Street and Fleet Street

Further east, towards the landing stage known as the Steine at Pearse Street, several important investigations provide details of the river shoreline in the medieval period. A testing programme was carried out in 1997 on a large block bounded by College Street, Westmorland Street and Fleet Street (42), and this revealed that the northern end of the site was under water up until the late seventeenth century (Carroll, *Excavations 1997*, 117). Subsequent excavation on this site in 1999 revealed that most of it had been reclaimed in the seventeenth century, as suggested in the testing, and that the natural deposits were of gravel and silt, derived from the river (Desmond, *Excavations 1999*, 189). However, a small section of the southern side represented a medieval foreshore and produced a small quantity of medieval finds, suggesting that this area was in use during the medieval period (Desmond, *Excavations 1999*, 189).

The western side of the site, along the Westmorland Street frontage, preserved the remains of a river or stream, either the Steine or a tributary, which was culverted in the post-medieval period. East of the river a series of well-preserved seventeenth-century timbers was located, indicative of possible mooring posts in an area that was constantly flooded, while the remains of buildings, dating to the eighteenth century, were also located along Westmorland Street, Fleet Street and College Street frontages.

Townsend Street

Archaeological investigations suggest that the area to the north-west of this large site was also under water during the medieval period. A series of timber revetments was found during an archaeological excavation at Townsend Street, which was dated by dendrochronology to the mid- to late seventeenth century (Walsh, *Excavations 1999*, 192). Townsend Street was the medieval route that headed out from the city to Ringsend, bordered by the river on the northern side. The results of the excavation suggest that, by the seventeenth century, reclamation was already underway.

24a D'Olier Street / 3–4 Leinster Street and 9–11 Hawkins Street

In addition to the information from Townsend Street, archaeological works at 24a D'Olier Street/3–4 Leinster Street, 9–11 Hawkins Street, just north of the large site at Westmorland Street (42), revealed that this area was also in the river in the seventeenth century (Simpson, *Excavations 2002*, 534). This monitoring programme produced evidence of the footings of a seventeenth-century wall, which may have been associated with land reclamation in the area but had been comprehensively demolished. The wall was orientated east–west, lying parallel to the river but had been badly damaged.

The River Poddle

The Poddle channel was used extensively for milling in Dublin and there was a dam or sluice just south of the Dame Street/Cork Hill junction. The documentary sources record various mills on the eastern stretch of the river, including the Doubleday mills (at Palace Street), the King's mills and Dame's mills, along with others opposite the castle and further upstream at Ship Street Little. An important excavation at Meeting House Square (44) (10–14 Sycamore Street/31–33 East Essex Street) located the remains of a branch or channel of the Poddle, which contained several large timbers, dated by dendrochronology to 1349±9 (Reid, *Excavations 1993*, 76).

This site is currently under archaeological investigation by Hayden and the river channel has been identified along with significant earlier activity. This indicates that there was a spit of land projecting into the Liffey, which was being reclaimed, as Hayden located reclamation cages constructed of post-and-wattle, along with evidence of a hearth. A significant north–south watercourse was identified extending through the site on the eastern side, feeding into the Liffey (pers. comm., Alan Hayden).

3–6 Palace Street

The river was located in a second excavation by the writer at 3–6 Palace Street, just north of Dublin Castle, and this investigation established that the river was between 6m and 7m in depth, infilled with organic and silt layers, filled with domestic refuse (Simpson, *Excavations 2006*, 636). Post-and-wattle fences were located between 4m and 5m below present ground level, but they were truncated by a large post-medieval masonry structure. This massive structure is likely to be the Doubleday mill recorded in this location in the post-medieval period, most likely to be the successor of the medieval mill.

Assay Office, Dublin Castle

The remains of a fourteenth-century water channel were also found by Myles during redevelopment of the Assay Office (**19**) in Dublin Castle (in front of the Chester Beatty Library), and this is likely to have been associated with a mill mentioned in the documentary sources, the exact location of which is not known (Clarke 1978).

The church of St George

The church of St George was located to the west of Dublin Castle, to the south of St Andrew's, on South Great George's Street, which was known originally as George's Lane (see below). It belonged to the priory of All Hallows and was rebuilt in the mid-fifteenth century but by 1607 it had been demolished (Clarke 2002, 18). The site of the church is unknown, but it is thought to have been located on the western side of South Great George's Street, at the junction with Exchequer Street.

Archaeological investigations by the writer to the rear of 59–64 South Great George's Street, at the Methodist church known as George's Hall, revealed the remains of a large stone wall, which was tentatively dated to between 1600 and 1650. Boulder clay was not exposed, but this was identified as possibly representing a boundary wall, which was replaced with a second wall, possibly associated with the church (Simpson 2000c; Simpson, *Excavations 2001*, 382). In addition to this, the truncated remains of a male supine burial were found on the adjoining site on the south during the excavations at South Great George's Street (4). While initially thought to be a Viking warrior burial, this grave was dated, by carbon-14 determinations, to the fifteenth century and was more likely to be associated with the church (Simpson 2008c).

THE NORTHERN ANGLO-NORMAN SUBURB

'Forty years a-digging' did not include any sites on the northern side of the river, but there have been significant advances in this area. The new evidence suggests that this suburb, known as Oxmantown, is most likely to have been occupied by the eleventh century and the Church Street route, down to the bridge, was probably the most developed street by this date. This settlement was certainly intensively inhabited after the Anglo-Norman invasion in 1170, Speed's map suggesting that, by the seventeenth century, it was almost as large as the walled city on the southern side of the river (Clarke 2002, 19). The north side of the river was held predominantly by St Mary's Abbey, the great

Cistercian house, but also by the priory of St Saviour's, founded in 1224 by the Dominicans (Gwynn and Hadcock 1988, 224). The improvement works carried out by the Anglo-Normans on the walled city were mirrored on the northern side of the Liffey and it is likely that this area saw an influx of Hiberno-Norse, who had been forced to move outside the city walls, into the established settlement of Oxmantown.

Reclamation along the banks of the Liffey
There have been significant advances in what is known about riverfront activity on the north side of the river, mostly the result of a large excavation carried out at a block (8) bounded by Hammond Lane on the south and Church Street on the east, which was excavated in three sections, as previously mentioned (Cryerhall 2006; Phelan 2010; Moriarty 2010; forthcoming, *Medieval Dublin XII*).

3–15 Hammond Lane
The first phase of this important excavation established the line of the river in the Hiberno-Norse period, along 3–15 Hammond Lane (8) (Cryerhall 2006) and the marginal ground along the foreshore, which was protected by artificial flood banks. This discovery was important as it established the line of the river, its tidal reaches and the fact that the river flooded periodically (ibid., 15). One of the ditches was dated by carbon-14 determinations to between 1010 and 1160, suggesting that control of the tempestuous river was of primary importance in the pre-Anglo-Norman period and that land reclamation had already begun before the arrival of the Anglo-Normans and the subsequent putative expulsion of the Dubliners to the north side of the river.

After the Anglo-Norman arrival in 1170, however, concerted efforts to reclaim the area began and this was done by means of large wattle reclamation boxes, filled with organic clays, which were used to rapidly fill in the ground (ibid., 23). This was in complete contrast to the method used on the southern side of the river, at Wood Quay and Winetavern Street, where timber revetments were used, the difference possibly a reflection of differing functions, as the southern side was also probably the quayside. The cages ensured rapid reclamation, the land then laid out for cultivation in long property boundaries, orientated roughly north–south, presumably fronting onto the forerunner of Hammond Lane. This area, however, may have remained as marginal ground and it was used extensively for dumping in the thirteenth century, marked by the large number of domestic rubbish pits, indicative of intensive habitation close by (ibid.). The sources also indicate that the area was used extensively for dumping in the fifteenth century, when it was known as 'Hankeman's Dunke Hollow': a large number of rubbish pits revealed during the excavation support this interpretation (Cryerhall 2006, 38).

Hammond Lane

By the mid-thirteenth century, the line of the river was pushed back beyond the southern line of Hammond Lane (27) and this was established during excavations by the writer on the block on the southern side of Hammond Lane, where the robbed-out remains of a timber-revetted channel, orientated east–west, were located along the northern side of the site. The channel was parallel with Hammond Lane and survived for a distance of 11.4m (Simpson, *Excavations 1993*, 50) and, as the revetment was of oak, it was dated by dendrochronology to the mid-1240s. The type of revetment was also unusual as it was both front- and back-braced. The watercourse was substantial, with the fall from west to east. It presumably turned south and eventually discharged into the Liffey.

While the wooden structure may have been a millrace associated with a mill somewhere in Oxmantown Green (there was a windmill in this location), by the fifteenth century the *Prese Mese*, a device either for catching herrings or for storing them, is recorded in this location. Unfortunately, not enough of the structure survived, although it was evidently originally substantial.

52–56 Strand Street Great (28)

The identification of timber revetments at the western end of the suburb, at Strand Street Great, may suggest that there was another quayside at this end of Oxmantown, some distance from Church Street and the bridge (28). This substantial structure was located on a site bounded by 52–56 Strand Street Great on the south and Byrne's Lane on the north, thus south-east of the precinct of St Mary's Abbey (Walsh 2005, 160–87). It was an impressive front-braced revetment/waterfront structure, which survived for at least 25m and was very well preserved, constructed of oak and dated by dendrochronology to the early thirteenth century.

The revetment was on a small inlet to the south-east of the abbey, and is most likely to have been related to it, although the main harbour was probably further west, at the mouth of the Bradogue (see Walsh 2005, 164). The director suggests that it may represent an attempt to construct a harbour in this location, which was thwarted by repeated flooding.

24–28 St Mary's Abbey and 150–12 Capel Street

Reclamation works along the river were also suggested by the discovery by Kehoe of thirteenth-century oak revetments, further to the south-west (29), along the early shoreline just north of Ormond Quay (Kehoe, *Excavations 2003*: 552; Keogh [*sic*], *Excavations 2004*, 586). They were orientated north-east/south-west and extended southwards beyond the Strand Street Little frontage. That it is likely to represent some sort of quay-front is suggested by the remains of a limestone platform over the revetment, which measured 9m long by 2.3m in width (Keogh [sic], *Excavations 2004*, 586). In addition, there was little evidence of reclamation deposits. Further west, however, and also along the river, excavations by Bolger (12) produced a timber platform or walkway along the river, which was prehistoric; an indication of the longevity of riverine waterfronts along the Liffey (pers. comm., Teresa Bolger).

9–14 Arran Quay

The revetments: The most significant Anglo-Norman riverfront excavation on the north side of the river was probably that carried out by Hayden at 9–14 Arran Quay (31), 65m west of the medieval bridge and fronting onto the modern quay frontage (Hayden 2004, 149–242). This important excavation located wooden front-braced revetments, the earliest of which yielded a dendrochronological date of *c*.1305, over a hundred years later than the revetments at Wood Quay (Wallace 1981a, 109). The first revetment was orientated north–south but had been robbed out, surviving to up to 45cm in height at the western end. It ran parallel to a naturally deposited bank of sand and silt, and organic refuse, river silt, stones, sand and gravel were then dumped in behind it, to build up the ground level to a depth of 1.05m.

A second revetment (2) was then constructed, which tied into the first but was aligned roughly east–west. It was dated to the first half of the fourteenth century by pottery associations (ibid., 173). Revetment 1 was then extended southwards into the river by the construction of a stone wall or stone-footed structure. The presence of a third revetment was suggested by the further deposition of reclamation deposits but no timbers survived (ibid., 175). The dating of the revetment construction process is interesting, as it suggests that the reclamation process was still underway on the north side of the river approximately a hundred years later than on the south side, in the Wood Quay area (Wallace 1981). In general, similar carpentry techniques were used, although the revetments were not as well constructed, probably because, as the director suggests, they were never designed to be seen.

Berthage on the river: Only a small area was actually reclaimed and Hayden suggests that the revetments were probably built to provide a better frontage along the riverbank, perhaps even to dock boats rather than to gain land. The natural silting up of the Liffey, a well-documented problem in Dublin in the Middle Ages, must have greatly facilitated this process as it did on the southern side of the river at Wood Quay a hundred years earlier. The revetments allowed expansion onto land that was originally part of the river and subject to flooding. The revetments also facilitated the construction of the stone quay in the fourteenth century.

A stone quay wall: The revetments were replaced with a strong quay wall, constructed in the late fourteenth/early fifteenth century, which bears testimony to permanency of access to the river in this location, but lags about a hundred years behind the main settlement on the southern side of the river. The wall was constructed in two sections and measured between 85cm and 1m in width by up to 80cm in height. There was evidence of sand and silt accumulating rapidly on the riverside, suggesting that the problem of silting up of the Liffey was still an issue, after the construction of the quay wall (ibid., 180). Of even more significance was the overwhelming evidence of fish-processing on this site, unique in Dublin (ibid., 189). Hayden suggests that fish were continually landed at Arran Quay and processed before being brought to the fish market and this theory is supported by the faunal evidence from the site. The specimens caught were very informative as they included cod and ling, both deep-water fish suggestive of a well-developed fishing industry at Dublin by the early fourteenth century (Hayden 2004, 189).

HABITATION WITHIN THE NORTHERN ANGLO-NORMAN SUBURB

3–15 Hammond Lane / 161–169 Church Street

A series of excavations along Church Street, the most important thoroughfare in Oxmantown, have also produced significant information about the organization of the northern suburb and how it was laid out in the Anglo-Norman period. The results suggest that the street was occupied by houses, probably on either side of the street and most likely extending as far south as the bridge. A significant amount of information has been gleaned from the large site on the western side of the street (**27**) (3–15 Hammond Lane and 161–169 Church Street), previously discussed, which revealed evidence of houses and plots along the eastern side of Church Street in the Hiberno-Norse period (Phelan 2010; Moriarty forthcoming, *Medieval Dublin XII*). The excavations also suggested the presence of plots fronting onto both Church Street and Hammond Lane along the southern side of the site.

Stone properties and houses: At Hammond Lane (**27**) the excavations produced limited evidence of stone properties fronting onto the lane along the southern boundary of the site, but they were relatively late, dating to the fourteenth and fifteenth centuries. One of the stone buildings was a substantial survival as it was incorporated into a seventeenth-century house (Cryerhall 2006, 38–9). However, the evidence for the eastern side of the site was far earlier. This side of the site was excavated in two sections, as mentioned previously; the north-east corner by Phelan (2010) and the south-eastern section by Moriarty (forthcoming, *Medieval Dublin XII*). The combined evidence suggests a total of ten plots fronting onto the street in the Anglo-Norman period, representative of intensive habitation.

The north-east section of the site produced evidence of a total of five properties dated by the ceramic assemblage to the late twelfth century and post-dating the Hiberno-Norse bank that extended along the western side of Church Street (Phelan 2010, 188). These properties were defined by post-and-wattle fences and the plots measured, on average, 7m wide by 21m in length. The remains suggested that the houses were also of post-and-wattle (rather than being sill-beamed), each one occupying a long plot, with gardens to the rear. Evidence within the rear of the plots included domestic waste and cess pits and one of the plots had a well-preserved stone-lined well.

At least one of the occupants of the plots was a local craftsman, perhaps a smith, as the remains included a smelting furnace and a number of iron clench bolts, similar to the type used for shipbuilding, in the process of being melted down. The evidence for cultivation at the rear of the plots was the fact that there were no structures, pits, wells or cess refuse at the western end of the plots (ibid., 188). The layers also produced evidence of a severe fire, which swept across the site and can possibly be associated with a recorded fire that occurred in 1303 or 1304 (ibid., 190), if not the famous destruction of the suburbs that occurred during the Bruce Invasion.

Redevelopment of the northern suburb

The fire may have initiated a major redevelopment in this location in the early fourteenth century when the post-and-wattle houses were replaced in stone, a development that had occurred probably a hundred years previously on the southern side of the settlement. On this site, however, the pre-stone houses were not sill-beamed timber houses but were still of post-and-wattle. The evidence of the stone houses was very truncated but enough survived to indicate that the five plots were maintained although the east and west boundaries were shifted to the east, over the demolished earthen bank along Church Street (ibid., 190–1).

The final phase of this substantial excavation was carried out by Moriarty in the south-east corner closest to the bridge and this also located five property plots fronting onto Church Street, including the possible remains of one post-and-wattle house that could be dated to the late twelfth century (Moriarty forthcoming, *Medieval Dublin XII*). The plots were very narrow, perhaps relating with their close proximity to the bridge, and measured between 4.3m and 5m in width (as compared to further north, where the plots were 7m in width). These post-and-wattle houses were also replaced in stone but these were badly truncated.

152–155 Church Street

A series of excavations by Dawkes at 152–155 Church Street (10), to the north of St Michan's Church, also revealed significant evidence of occupation in the thirteenth and fourteenth centuries in the form of houses in the north-east corner of the site (Dawkes 2010, 198–219). These houses did not front onto Church Street but were set back between 20m and 30m from the street frontage and thus they represented back-plot habitation. At least three very truncated buildings, orientated east–west, were tentatively identified, marked by the survival of foundation trenches with some masonry surviving (ibid., 211–12).

The buildings at Church Street: The first possible building was at least 8.1m in length, which is very long, but only 2m in width and all that survived was a sunken rectangular pit (17cm in depth) and possible clay floor, suggesting that it was some sort of storage chamber (see Dawkes 2010, fig. 4).

The former presence of a second possible building was suggested, but this was also very truncated. A grey clay floor was identified, the straight edges indicative of walls that were probably robbed out. The remains of stone alignments may have represented sill-beam foundations rather than post-and-wattle, as stones were often used as foundation for the base-plates. The third building was a granary, as suggested by the botanical remains, and this was at least 5.7m in length by 2m in width by 29cm in depth. This building was possibly extended on the eastern side and was associated with a stone drain. Both buildings were burnt down in the Middle Ages after a period of abandonment (ibid., 125).

145–150 Church Street and St Michan's Church
Small-scale investigations by Murtagh at 145–150 Church Street, on the north side of May Lane (Comyn Lane) also revealed truncated evidence of habitation that could be dated to the Anglo-Norman period. This survived in the form of a cobbled surface with associated drainage channel along with a stone-lined lime-pit, dated to the mid- to late thirteenth century, that was indicative of tanning (Murtagh, *Excavations 1996*, 80). In support of this, a deed in the Christ Church collection records that a family of dyers occupied land in this immediate area from the mid-fourteenth into the early fifteenth century (ibid.).

Occupation material indicative of habitation immediately adjacent to the south wall of St Michan's graveyard was found during investigations by Cassidy (Cassidy, *Excavations 1993*, 60). The findings were archaeologically poor but environmentally rich, as the excavation revealed a series of disturbed deposits dating from the fourteenth century to modern times, overlying natural gravels.

East side of Church Street
The eastern side of the street was also intensively settled in the Anglo-Norman period, as suggested by excavations by Nelis to the rear of 27–31 Church Street (9) (Nelis, *Excavations 2003*, 508). This work located the remains of medieval deposits, with a series of ten domestic pits indicative of intensive settlement. A large amount of cockle shells and antler tines suggest that industrial processing was also carried out on site, perhaps lime-production and

comb- and/or bone-working. The lowest levels also produced evidence of at least one sub-rectangular structure, the dimensions of which were difficult to establish.

St Mary's Abbey

The abbey of St Mary (**30**) dominated the eastern end of Oxmantown, the precinct evolving over time but presumably expanding significantly after the Anglo-Norman invasion. The precinct was extensive, originally occupying the block now defined by Capel Street to the east, Arran Street and Boot Lane to the west, Little Mary Street to the north and the river to the south (Purcell 2003, 204). The position of the monastic quadrangle is preserved in the modern streetscape and the chapter house and slype (a passageway), built *c.*1190, are still extant at Meetinghouse Lane, off Mary's Abbey (ibid.). These were rediscovered in 1880 during the demolition of a bakery. The chapter house has a groin-vaulted chamber with a single light Gothic window in the western façade and now houses an interpretive centre (ibid.).

6 St Mary's Abbey

However, more recent investigations at 6 Mary's Abbey (**30**), close to the presumed south-eastern side of the cloister, have suggested that there may be more extant remains of the abbey than hitherto suspected. An inspection of the standing building by Doyle revealed that, at basement level, there may be medieval remains, both below ground and incorporated within the eighteenth-century building. Testing, while inconclusive, did identify earlier walls and a cobbled surface beneath the existing post-medieval building, presumably related to the abbey (Doyle, *Excavations 2000*: 272).

Subsequent investigations by Hayden revealed that the standing wall to the rear of the site was medieval and evidence of an additional medieval wall was located during the excavation of a single test-trench. This dry-stone limestone wall was orientated east–west and was positioned within a foundation trench that was 1m in depth (Hayden, *Excavations 2003*, 551).

The boundary walls surrounding the abbey are referred to in the documentary sources in the fifteenth century, as is the main gate on the northern side. Fisher's Lane, the laneway on the southern side of the abbey, led to a harbour attached to the river. The riverfront harbour was also probably developed at this point and this was known as 'the Pill'. The revetments located by Walsh (**28**) and described above may have been related to an attempt to establish a harbour in this location, although the main harbour was probably further west, at the mouth of the Bradogue (see Walsh 2005, 164).

St Saviour's priory

The Dominican priory of St Saviour's was the second major ecclesiastical establishment in Oxmantown, said to have been founded in 1224, and this was positioned on the eastern side of the bridge (**32**). A new church was dedicated in 1238 (McMahon 1988, 273; Gwynn and Hadcock 1988, 224; O'Sullivan 1990). The site is now occupied by the Four Courts, which is bordered on the south by Inns Quay. While the priory is not named on Speed's map of Dublin (1610), the monastic quadrangle is immediately identifiable, albeit with the southern range missing. The priory extended beyond its precincts: there was a quay attached to the priory on the eastern side of the bridge by the late fifteenth century (Purcell 2003, 214) and Speed's map depicts a large break in the wall at the riverfront with the suggestion of a small inlet or quay on the eastern side.

The boundaries of the priory have been traced in Rocque's map (1756) by McMahon, defined by Inns Quay, Mass Lane, Charles Street and Pill Lane (**32**) (McMahon 1988, 276). Excavations at Inns Quay by McMahon located significant archaeological remains, including deposits dated to the late twelfth/thirteenth century, which contained architectural fragments likely to have originated in the monastic quadrangle. Structural remains included a stone-built channel, along with a timber sluice, presumably associated with an artificial water-supply. The most significant find, however, was a large sixteenth-century stone building, founded on segmented relieving arches not unlike the remains of the Augustinian friary on the southern side of the river at Cecilia Street, the fifteenth-century Geneville's Inns at Ross Road and a stone wall dated to the fourteenth century at Hammond Lane (see above).

The site of the cemetery attached to the priory was known previously, as thirty burials were found at Inns Quay (**32**) in the 1960s during the construction of a ballroom, while building works at the Public Record Office also produced medieval deposits, dated by medieval pottery (ibid.). Thus, there is significant potential for other survivals in this location.

Oxmantown Green
Oxmantown was bordered on the east by a large expanse of commonage known as Oxmantown Green, which is referred to in the documentary sources throughout the medieval period. This was an importance public space, and represented a hub of communal activity on this side of the river, used for grazing, industrial activity and public gatherings, although the primary function was probably as pastureland (Purcell 2005, 221).

The green is first mentioned in the historical sources in the mid-thirteenth century, but it existed earlier than this and was associated with the Hiberno-Norse settlement at Oxmantown (Clarke 2002, 24). In the sixteenth century it is recorded that the grazing was reserved for freemen of the city, but a source dated to 1635 provides more information on the ancient rights:

> the municipality ordained that no part of the three greens at the edge of the city be sold or leased, but that the same shall be wholly kept for the

use of the citizens and others to walk and take the open air, by reason [that] this city is at this present time growing very populous (Gilbert 1888, II, 253).

The green was also used for industrial purposes, as suggested by the documentary sources, which mention a quarry, a horse mill and lime-pits (see below). By the fifteenth century, there was a gallows somewhere on the green, probably near Parkgate Street (Clarke 2002, 22), which was accessed by Hammond Lane, originally known as Hangman's Lane. Some investigations have occurred in the green, but these have produced little information.

Smithfield
A large site excavated by Myles on the western side of Smithfield produced limited evidence of an old ground surface at the earliest levels, and the director suggests that this was probably medieval, based on the ceramic assemblage (Myles 2006). More information was gleaned from a much smaller investigation at the bottom of Smithfield (32), to the west of the Hammond Lane (Gahan, *Excavations 1999*, 272). This investigation produced evidence of a complex system of water management and drainage at this end of the green, which the director suggests could be dated to the late thirteenth and fourteenth centuries. More significantly, the earliest levels also produced considerable amounts of ceramic material of a similar date, suggestive of domestic occupation of a generally wealthy quarter. However, these important levels also produced ceramic roof and floor tiles indicative of medieval stone houses in the immediate vicinity.

The evidence also suggests a contraction in settlement in this area in the late fourteenth century as these earlier levels were sealed by large dumps of redeposited subsoil, which was then cultivated, as suggested by a series of furrows and a drainage ditch. A large ditch was identified parallel to the Liffey. It did not appear to be a drainage ditch, as it contained no silt deposits indicative of water. The director suggested that it was more likely to be a major property boundary or division on the banks of the river (ibid.).

3–15 Hammond Lane
There is archaeological evidence that Oxmantown Green originally extended as far east as the rear of the properties fronting onto the western side of Church Street, an area that was in use partially as an industrial area. The excavations at 3–15 Hammond Lane/161–169 Church Street (8) by Cryerhall revealed the remains of what was probably a horse mill (Cryerhall 2006, see fig. 12, 31), mentioned in the documentary sources as being located in Oxmantown Green (Purcell 2005, 214). The circular horse-track, which was 15m in diameter by 2m in width, was relatively well preserved, although nothing of

the superstructure of the actual mill survived. An artificial watercourse, contemporaneous with the horse mill but not physically attached, may have been associated with it, although the nature of the connection is not clear. The location was also used extensively for dumping, as suggested in the documentary sources and evidenced by the discovery of at least two 'dumping complexes'.

By the late fourteenth century, the archaeological evidence suggests a period of abandonment and decline, with the earlier activity sealed by a layer of cultivation soil, as located at Smithfield and mentioned above. Despite this, the area did recover, as there is evidence of new building by the fifteenth and sixteenth centuries. A fragment of a late medieval building was located by Cryerhall along the Hammond Lane frontage (8) incorporated within the new seventeenth-century houses and was dated at the earliest to the fifteenth century, with continued occupation into the post-medieval period (Cryerhall 2006, 39–40).

The house can be identified on Rocque's map (1756) but, critically, was probably only one of an entire streetscape of stone or timber-framed buildings as opposed to mud and thatch (ibid., 40). This was suggested by the deep deposits of demolition debris (cobbles, roof tiles, roof slates, floor tiles, mortared rubble) dating to the fifteenth and sixteenth centuries, which were identified across the eastern side of the site, towards the Church Street frontage (ibid., 40). Thus, at Hammond Lane the process of occupation and domestic habitation had come full circle.

CONCLUSION

This update of 'Forty years a-digging' serves as a reminder of the vast amount of data that has now been generated by the archaeological investigations at Dublin, and, more importantly, is now available to a wider audience in the form of publications. Through the publication of these excavation reports, the building blocks have been generated for further research that will help sustain and provide new and invigorating material for those interested in medieval Dublin, now that the frantic period of excavation associated with the 'Celtic Tiger' has finally come to a halt. Even a brief account such as this, based on what is for the most part summary excavation reports, highlights the potential of this material so carefully gathered in the last fifty years in the interest of the people of Ireland. It can only be hoped that the scholarship which the study of medieval Dublin attracts, will continue and will be recognized for its worth and will be suitably supported.

BIBLIOGRAPHY

Bennett, Isabel 1987-present *Excavations: summary accounts of archaeological excavations in Ireland*. Dublin.

Brady, John and Simms, Anngret (eds) 2001 *Dublin through space and time (c.900–1900)*. Dublin.

Bradley, John, Fletcher, Alan, Simms, Anngret (eds) 2009 *Dublin in the medieval world: studies in honour of Howard B. Clarke*. Dublin.

Brooks, Eric St John (ed.) 1936 *Register of the hospital of S. John the Baptist without the Newgate, Dublin*. Dublin.

Bradley, John 1992 The topographical development of Scandinavian Dublin. In F.H.A. Aalen and Kevin Whelan (eds) *Dublin city and county: from prehistory to present*, 43–56. Dublin.

Buckley, Laureen 2003 Health status in medieval Dublin: analysis of the skeletal remains from the abbey of St Thomas of the Martyr. In Seán Duffy (ed.) *Medieval Dublin III*, 98–126, Dublin.

Buckley, L. and Hayden, A. 2002 Excavations at St Stephen's leper hospital, Dublin: a summary account and analysis of burials. In Seán Duffy (ed.) *Medieval Dublin IV*, 151–94. Dublin.

Budd, Roland 2001 *The platforme of an universitie: All Hallows priory in Trinity College, Dublin*. Dublin.

Clarke, H.B. 1997 The topographical development of early medieval Dublin, *Journal of the Royal Society of Antiquaries of Ireland* 107, 29–51.

— 1978 *Dublin c.840–c.1540: the medieval town in the modern city*. Dublin.

— 1998 *Urbs et suburbium*: beyond the walls of medieval Dublin. In Con Manning (ed.) *Dublin beyond the Pale: studies in honour of Paddy Healy*, 45–58. Bray.

— 2002 *Dublin Part 1, to 1610: Irish historic town atlas no. 11*, Dublin.

Clarke, H. and Ambrosiania, B. 1995 *Towns in the Viking Age*. Leicester.

Conway, Malachy 1998 Archaeological assessment and excavation of a development site at 1 Cecilia Street, 17–19 Temple Lane, Dublin 2. Submitted to the former Dúchas, now National Monuments and Architectural Protection Division, and National Museum in July 1998.

Coughlan, Tim 2000 The Anglo-Norman houses of Dublin: evidence from Back Lane. In Seán Duffy (ed.) *Medieval Dublin I*, 203–33. Dublin.

— 2003 Excavations at the medieval cemetery of St Peter's Church, Dublin. In Seán Duffy (ed.) *Medieval Dublin IV*, 11–39. Dublin.

Cryerhall, Abi 2006 Excavations at Hammond Lane, Dublin: from hurdle-ford to iron-foundry. In Seán Duffy (ed.) *Medieval Dublin VII*, 9–50. Dublin.

Dawkes, Giles 2010 Interim results of excavation at 152–3 Church Street, Dublin: St Michan's early enclosure and late medieval timber-framed buildings. In Seán Duffy (ed.) *Medieval Dublin X*, 198–219. Dublin.

Deery, Siobhan and Simpson, Linzi 2008 Archaeological desk study, Christ Church Cathedral, proposed cloister scheme, Dublin 8. Submitted to the Department of the Environment, Heritage and Local Government and National Museum in June 2008

Doran, Bill and Doran, Linda 2009 St Mary's Cistercian abbey, Dublin: a ghost in the alleyways. In Bradley et al. (eds) 2009, 188–201. Dublin.

Downham, Clare 2010 Viking camps in ninth-century Ireland: sources, locations and interactions. In Seán Duffy (ed.) *Medieval Dublin X*, 93–125. Dublin.

Dublin Archaeological Research Team 1981 Preliminary report and recommendations on the site of St Michael le Pole and surrounding area. Unpublished report lodged with the Office of Public Works, 51 St Stephen's Green.

Duddy, Cathal 2003 The role of St Thomas' Abbey in the early development of Dublin's western suburb. In Seán Duffy (ed.) *Medieval Dublin IV*, 79–95. Dublin.

Duffy, Seán 1993 'The political narrative': historical background for the Archaeological excavation at 33–34 Parliament Street/Exchange Street Upper Stratigraphic report by Georgina Scally lodged with the former *Dúchas*: the Heritage Service and the National Museum.

— 2000– (ed.) *Medieval Dublin I–XI* (11 vols). Dublin.

__ 2005 A reconsideration of the site of Dublin's Viking thing-mót. In Tom Condit and Christiaan Corlett (eds) *Above and beyond: essays in memory of Leo Swan*, 351–60. Bray.

Duffy, Seán and Simpson, Linzi 2009 The hermits of St Augustine in medieval Dublin: their history and archaeology. In Bradley et al. (eds) 2009, 300–30. Dublin.

Eames, E.S. and Fanning, Thomas 1988 *Irish medieval tiles*. Dublin.

Elliott A.L. 1990 The abbey of St Thomas the Martyr near Dublin. In Howard Clarke (ed.) *Medieval Dublin: the living city*, 62–7. Dublin.

Gilbert, J.T. 1854–9 *A history of the city of Dublin*, 3 vols. Dublin.

— 1889, *Calendar of the ancient records of Dublin.*

Gowen, Margaret (ed.) 2004, *Conservation plan: Dublin city wall and defences*. Dublin, Wicklow. Commissioned and published by Dublin City Council 2004.

— 2001 Excavations at the site of the church and tower of St Michael le Pole, Dublin. In Seán Duffy (ed.) *Medieval Dublin II*, 13–52. Dublin.

Gowen, Margaret with Scally, Georgina 1999 *A summary report on excavations at Exchange Street Upper/Parliament Street*, Dublin. Temple Bar Archaeological Report 4. Dublin.

Gwynn, Aubrey and Hadcock, Neville 1988 *Medieval religious houses: Ireland*. First published 1970; Dublin.

Halpin, Andrew 2000 T*he port of medieval Dublin: archaeological excavations at the Civic Offices, Winetavern Street, Dublin 1993*. Dublin.

— 2005 Development phases in Hiberno-Norse Dublin: a tale of two cities. In Seán Duffy (ed.) *Medieval Dublin VI*, 94–113. Dublin.

Harrison, Stephen 2007 *Woodstown 6*, Supplementary Research Project, July 2007, Chapter 1 Academic Review 3–95 (Archaeological Consultancy Services Ltd).

— 2010 The Suffolk Street Sword: further notes on the College Green cemetery. In John Sheehan and Donnchadh Ó Corráin (eds) *The Viking Age: Ireland and the west*, 136–44. Dublin,

— 2010 Bride Street revisited: Viking burial in Dublin and beyond. In Seán Duffy (ed.) *Medieval Dublin X*, 126–52. Dublin.

Hayden, Alan 2000 West side story: archaeological excavations at Cornmarket and Bridge Street Upper, Dublin – a summary account. In Seán Duffy (ed.) *Medieval Dublin I*, 84–125. Dublin.

— 2002 The excavation of pre-Anglo-Norman defences and houses at Werburgh Street: a summary. In Seán Duffy (ed.) *Medieval Dublin III*, 44–68. Dublin.

— 2004 Excavations of the medieval river frontage at Arran Quay, Dublin. In Seán Duffy (ed.) *Medieval Dublin V*, 149–242. Dublin.

— 2010 Archaeological excavations at the west side of Augustine Street. In Seán Duffy (ed.) *Medieval Dublin X*, 241–66. Dublin.

Healy, Patrick 1974 Road work excavation in High Street and Cornmarket, report 25 April 1974.

— 1990 The town walls of Dublin. In Howard Clarke (ed.) *Medieval Dublin: the making of a metropolis*, 183–92. Dublin.

Johnson, Ruth 2004 *Viking Age Dublin*. Dublin.

Kehoe, Helen 1999 Archaeological monitoring at Christ Church Cathedral, Dublin 8 (Licence 99E0539), unpublished report submitted to National Monuments and

Architectural Protection Division, and National Museum in 1999 (Margaret Gowen and Co. Ltd).

Kinsella, Stuart 2009 Mapping Christ Church Cathedral, Dublin, *c.*1028–1608: an examination of the western cloister. In Bradley et al. (eds) 2009, 143–67. Dublin.

Lydon, James F. 2002 Dublin Castle in the Middle Ages. In Seán Duffy (ed.) *Medieval Dublin III*, 115–27. Dublin.

Lynch, Ann and Manning, Conleth 2001 Excavations at Dublin Castle, 1985–7. In Seán Duffy (ed.) *Medieval Dublin II*, 169–204. Dublin.

MacShamhráin, Ailbhe 2002 *The Vikings: an illustrated history*. Dublin.

Manning, Conleth 1998 *Dublin and beyond the Pale: studies in honour of Paddy Healy*. Wicklow.

Meenan, Rosanne 2002 Archaeological excavations at nos 16–17 Cook Street, Dublin. In Seán Duffy (ed.) *Medieval Dublin III*, 128–39. Dublin.

— 2004 The excavation of pre-Anglo-Norman burials and ditch near St Michan's Church. In Seán Duffy (ed.) *Medieval Dublin V*, 91–110. Dublin.

McCullough, Niall 2005 Ship Street/Werburgh Street Framework Plan. McCullough-Mulvin Architects, Dublin City Council.

— 2007 *Dublin, an urban history: the plan of the city*. Dublin.

Milne, Kenneth (ed.) 2000 *Christ Church Cathedral: A History*. Dublin.

McMahon, Mary 1988 Archaeological excavations at the site of the Four Courts Extension, Inns Quay, Dublin, *Proceedings of the Royal Irish Academy* 88C, 271–319.

— 1991 Archaeological excavations at Bridge Street Lower, Dublin, *Proceedings of the Royal Irish Academy* 91C, 41–71.

— 2002 Early medieval settlement and burial outside the enclosed town: evidence from the archaeological excavations at Bride Street, Dublin, *Proceedings of the Royal Irish Academy* 102C6, 67–135.

— 2006 *St Audoen's Church, Cornmarket, Dublin: archaeology and architecture*. Dublin.

Moriarty, Colm 2010 Phase 11B archaeological excavation at 3–5 Hammond Lane/161–169 Church Street, Dublin 7. Licence 09E517. Submitted to the National Monuments and Architectural Protection Division, and the National Museum in November 2010.

— 2012 (forthcoming) Excavations at 3–5 Hammond Lane/161–169 Church Street, Dublin 7. In Seán Duffy (ed.) *Medieval Dublin XII*. Dublin.

Murphy, Margaret and Potterton, Michael, 2005 Investigating living standards in medieval Dublin and its region. In Seán Duffy (ed.) *Medieval Dublin VI*, 224–56. Dublin.

— 2009 Mapping a medieval landscape? The Civil Survey and land use in County Dublin. In Bradley et al. (eds) 2009, 316–45. Dublin.

— 2010 *The Dublin region in the Middle Ages: land-use, settlement and economy*. Dublin.

Murray, Hilary 1983 *Viking and early medieval buildings in Dublin*, British Archaeological Reports 119. Oxford.

Myles, Franc 2006 Archaeological excavations at Smithfield, Dublin. Licence 00E0272. Submitted to the relevant heritage authorities, August 2006.

— 2008 Archaeological excavations at the Assay Office, Dublin Castle, Dublin 2 (Margaret Gowen and Co. Ltd), Licence 06E0530.

— 2009 Archaeological excavations at the millpond of St Thomas' Abbey, Dublin. In Seán Duffy (ed.) *Medieval Dublin IX*, 183–202. Dublin.

O'Brien, Elizabeth 1998 A reconsideration of the location and context of Viking burials at Kilmainham/Islandbridge, Dublin. In Manning (ed.) 1998, 35–44. Bray.

O'Brien, R. and Russell, I. 2005 The Hiberno-Scandinavian site of Woodstown 6, Co. Waterford. In J. O'Sullivan and M. Stanley (eds) *Recent archaeological discoveries on the National Road scheme 2004: archaeology and National Roads Authority Series 2*, 111–29. Dublin.

Ó Donnobháin, Barra and Hallgrímsson, Benedikt 2001 Dublin: the biological identi-fication of a Hiberno-Norse town. In Seán Duffy (ed.) *Medieval Dublin II*, 65–87. Dublin.

O'Donovan, Danielle 2003 English patron, English building? The importance of St Sepulchre's archiepiscopal palace, Dublin. In Seán Duffy (ed.) *Medieval Dublin IV*, 253–78. Dublin.

O'Donovan, Edmond 2003 The growth and decline of a medieval suburb? Evidence from excavations at Thomas Street, Dublin. In Seán Duffy (ed.) *Medieval Dublin IV*, 127–71. Dublin.

— 2008 The Irish, the Vikings and the English: new archaeological evidence from excavations at Golden Lane, Dublin. In Seán Duffy (ed.) *Medieval Dublin VIII*, 36–130. Dublin.

Ó Floinn, Raghnall 1998 The archaeology of early Viking Age in Ireland. In H. Clarke, M. Ní Mhaonaigh and R. Ó Floinn (eds) *Ireland and Scandinavia in the early Viking Age*, 132–65. Dublin.

O'Keeffe, Grace 2009 The hospital of St John the Baptist in medieval Dublin. In Seán Duffy (ed.) *Medieval Dublin IX*, 166–82. Dublin.

O'Keeffe, Tadhg 2009 Dublin Castle's donjon in context. In Bradley et al. (eds) 2009, 277–94. Dublin.

O'Neill, John 2004 Excavations at Longford Street Little, Dublin: an archaeological approach to *Dubh Linn*. In Seán Duffy (ed.) *Medieval Dublin V*, 11–73. Dublin.

O'Neill, Michael 2000 Design sources for St Patrick's Cathedral, Dublin and its relationship in Christ Church Cathedral. *Proceedings of the Royal Irish Academy* 100C6, 207–56.

— 2004, St Patrick's cathedral and its prebendal churches: Gothic architctural relation-ships. In Seán Duffy (ed.) *Medieval Dublin V*, 243–76. Dublin.

— 2006 *St Patrick's cathedral, Dublin*. Dublin.

— 2009 Christ Church cathedral as a blueprint for other Augustinian buildings in Ireland. In Bradley et al. (eds) 2009, 168–87. Dublin.

Ó Riordáin, Breandán 1973 The High Street excavations. In B. Almqvist and D. Greene (eds) *The proceedings of the seventh Viking Congress Dublin, 15–21 August 1973*, 135–55. Dublin.

O'Sullivan, Benedict 1990 The Dominicans in medieval Dublin. In Howard Clarke (ed.) *Medieval Dublin: the living city*, 83–99. Dublin.

O'Sullivan, Aidan et al. 2009 Early Medieval Archaeological Project (EMAP). University College Dublin (http:/www.emap.ie).

Phelan, Sinead 2010 The bank, the ditch and the water: Hiberno-Norse discoveries at Church Street and Hammond Lane. In Seán Duffy (ed.) *Medieval Dublin X*, 165–97. Dublin.

Phelan, S. and Weldon, K. 2007 Archaeological stratigraphic report, 3–15 Hammond Lane/161–169 Church Street, Dublin 7. Submitted to the National Monuments and Architectural Protection Division, and the National Museum in June 2007.

Purcell, Emer 2003 Land-use in Oxmantown. In Seán Duffy (ed.) *Medieval Dublin IV*, 193–228. Dublin.

— 2005 The city and the suburb: medieval Dublin and Oxmantown. In Seán Duffy (ed.) *Medieval Dublin VI*, 188–223. Dublin.

— 2009 Michan: saint, cult and church. In Bradley et al. (eds) 2009, 119–40. Dublin.

Scally, Georgina 2002 The earthen banks and walled defences of Dublin's north-east corner. In Seán Duffy (ed.) *Medieval Dublin III*, 11–33. Dublin.

Sheehan, John and Ó Corráin, Donnchadh (eds) 2010 *The Viking Age: Ireland and the west*. Dublin.

Sikora, Maeve 2010 The Finglas burial: archaeology and ethnicity in Viking-Age Dublin. In Sheehan and Ó Corráin (eds) 2010, 402–17.

Simpson, Linzi 1994 *Excavations at Isolde's tower, Dublin*. Dublin Temple Bar Archaeological Report 1.

— 1994a Anglo-Norman settlement in Uí Briúin Cualann. In Ken Hannigan and William Nolan (eds) *Wicklow: history and society*, 191–235. Dublin.

— 1995 Excavation at Essex Street West, Dublin. Temple Bar Archaeological Report 2.

— 1996 Excavations at the National College of Art and Design, Dublin 2. Licence 95E045. Submitted to the former Dúchas now National Monuments and Architectural Protection Division, and the National Museum in May 1996.

— 1997 The historical background. In Clare Walsh (ed.) *Archaeological excavations at Patrick, Nicholas and Winetavern Streets, Dublin*, 17–33. Dingle.

— 1999 *Director's findings: Temple Bar West* Temple Bar Archaeological Report 5. Dublin.

— 1999a Archaeological Assessment in the crypts of Christchurch Cathedral, Dublin (Licence 99E0091) (Planning Reference 1886/98). Submitted to the National Monuments and Architectural Protection Division, and the National Museum (Margaret Gowen and Co. Ltd).

— 2000 Forty years a-digging: a preliminary synthesis of archaeological investigations in medieval Dublin. In Seán Duffy (ed.) *Medieval Dublin I*, 11–68. Dublin.

— 2000a The historical background. In Andrew Halpin, *The port of medieval Dublin: archaeological excavations at the Civic Offices, Winetavern Street, Dublin 1993*, 7–14. Dublin.

— 2000b The historical background. In Alan Hayden, West side story: archaeological excavations at Cornmarket and Bridge Street Upper, Dublin – a summary account. In Seán Duffy (ed.) *Medieval Dublin I*. 101–3. Dublin.

— 2000c Archaeological excavation to the rear of 59–64 South Great George's Street (Licence 99E0710). Submitted to the former Dúchas now National Monuments and Architectural Protection Division, and the National Museum, in February 2002.

— 2001 Stratigraphic report on excavations at Temple Bar West, Dublin 2. 4 Vols. December 2001. Submitted to the former Dúchas, now National Monuments and Architectural Protection Division, and the National Museum in December 2001.

— 2001a Monitoring at Christ Church cathedral, Dublin. Submitted to the former Dúchas now National Monuments and Architectural Protection Division, and the National Museum in April 2001.

— 2002 History and topographical survey. In Mary McMahon, Early medieval settlement and burial outside the enclosed town: evidence from archaeological excavations at Bride Street, Dublin. *Proceedings of the Royal Irish Academy* 102C4, 67–70.

— 2002a The priory of All Hallows and Trinity College, Dublin: recent archaeological discoveries. In Seán Duffy (ed.) *Medieval Dublin III*, 195–236. Dublin.

— 2003 Monitoring of a service trench at the western end of Dame Lane submitted to the former *Dúchas*, the Heritage Service and the National Museum of Ireland in April 2003.

— 2004 Understanding the site. In Margaret Gowen (ed.) *Conservation plan: Dublin City walls and defences*. Dublin.

— 2004a Excavations at the southern side of the medieval town at Ship Street Little, Dublin. In Seán Duffy (ed.) *Medieval Dublin V*, 9–51. Dublin.

— 2005 Viking warrior burials in Dublin: is this the longphort? In Seán Duffy (ed.) *Medieval Dublin VI*, 11–62. Dublin.

— 2005a Archaeological excavation, 3–6 Palace Street, Dublin 2. Licence 02E0244; Planning ref. 2368/01. Submitted to the National Monuments and Architectural Protection Division, and the National Museum.

— 2006 *Dublin city: walls and defences.* Dublin.

— 2008 The medieval city wall and the southern line off Dublin's defences: excavations at 14–16 Werburgh Street. In Seán Duffy (ed.) *Medieval Dublin VIII*, 150–77. Dublin.

— 2008a Archaeological monitoring in the grounds of Dublin City Council, including excavation at the junction of John's Lane South and Fishamble Street. Submitted to National Monuments and Architectural Protection Division, and the National Museum in October 2008.

— 2008c Archaeological excavation of a site bounded by 42–50 and 52–57 South Great George's Street and 58–67 Stephen Street Upper. Submitted to the former Dúchas, now National Monuments and Architectural Protection Division, and the National Museum in May 2008.

— 2008d 'Ship Street/Werburgh Street Archaeological Research Agenda'. Report commissioned by Dublin City Council, submitted 2008.

— 2009a Archaeological excavations at the site of archbishop's palace of St Sepulchre, Kevin Street Garda station, on the eastern side of Kevin Street, to the rear of 35–47 Bride Street, Dublin 8. Submitted to the Department of the Environment, Heritage and Local Government and National Museum in May 2009.

— 2009b Archaeological excavation and monitoring works at St Patrick's Cathedral, St Patrick's Close, Dublin 8. Licence 07E1125. Report submitted to Department of the Environment, Heritage and Local Government and National Museum in October 2009.

— 2010 Pre-Viking and early Viking-Age Dublin: research questions. In Seán Duffy (ed.) *Medieval Dublin X*, 49–92. Dublin.

— 2010a Archaeological assessment at the 'cloister' of Christ Church Cathedral, Christ Church Place, Dublin 8. Licence 10E202. Submitted to the Department of the Environment, Heritage and Local Government and National Museum in October 2010.

— 2010b The first phase of Viking activity in Ireland: archaeological evidence from Dublin. In Sheehan and Ó Corráin (eds), 2010, 418–29.

— 2010c Archaeological excavation at Dublinia (the former Synod Hall), St Michael's Hill, Christ Church, Dublin 2. Licence 09E331. Submitted to the Department of the Environment, Heritage and Local Government and National Museum in May 2010.

— 2010d 'The archaeological remains of Viking and medieval Dublin: a research framework'. Submitted to Dublin City Council and Heritage Council (Irish National Strategic Archaeological Research).

— and Andrea Ancinelli 2008b Measured survey of sections of the city wall of Dublin, submitted to Dublin City Council, August 2008.

— and Seán Duffy 2009 The hermits of St Augustine in medieval Dublin: their history and archaeology. In Bradley et al. (eds) 2009, 300–33. Dublin.

Sikora, Maeve 2010 The Finglas burial: archaeology and ethnicity in Viking-Age Dublin. In Sheehan and Ó Corráin (eds), 2010, 402–17.

Speed, John 1610 *Dublin, from theatre of the empire of Great Britain*, reproduced by Phoenix maps (1988), Dublin.

Stalley, Roger 2000 The architecture of the cathedral and priory buildings, 1250–1530. In Kenneth Milne (ed.) *Christ Church cathedral, Dublin: a history*, 95–128. Dublin.

— 2005 Christ Church Cathedral. In Christine Casey (ed.) *The buildings of Ireland: Dublin*, 318–36. London.

— 2005a St Patrick's Cathedral. In Christine Casey (ed.) *The buildings of Ireland: Dublin*, 602–18. London.

Stout, Matthew 2009–10 Review article: medieval Dublin (vols viii–x). In *Studia Hibernica* 36, 179–96.

Swan, Leo 2000, Archaeological excavations at Usher's Quay, 1991. In Seán Duffy (ed.) *Medieval Dublin I*, 126–58. Dublin.

Wallace, P.F. 1981 Anglo-Norman Dublin, continuity and change. In Donnchadh Ó Corráin (ed.) *Irish Antiquity*, 247–66. Dublin.

— 1981a Dublin's waterfront at Wood Quay, 900–1317. In G. Milne and B. Hobley (eds) *Waterfront archaeology in Britain and Northern Europe* Council for British Archaeology 41, 109–18. London.

— 1982 Carpentry in Ireland, 900–1300: the Wood Quay excavations. In Seán McGrail (ed.) *Woodworking techniques before AD1500*, British Archaeological Report, Interim Series 192, 263–300. Oxford.

— 1984 A reappraisal of the archaeological significance of Wood Quay. In John Bradley (ed.) *The Wood Quay Saga*, 112–33. Dublin.

— 1988 Archaeology and the emergence of Dublin as the principal town in Ireland. In John Bradley (ed.) *Settlement and society in medieval Ireland*, 123–60. Kilkenny.

— 1990 The origins of Dublin. In Clarke (ed.) 1990, 70–97.

— 1992 The archaeological identity of the Hiberno-Norse town. *Journal of the Royal Society of Antiquaries of Ireland* 122, 35–66.

— 1992a *The Viking age buildings of Dublin*, Part 1 and 2. Medieval Dublin excavations, 1962–81. Series A. Dublin.

— 2001 *Garrada* and *airbeada*: the plot thickens in Viking Dublin. In A.P. Smyth (ed.) *Seanchas: studies in early and medieval Irish archaeology, history and literature in honour of Francis J. Byrne*, 261–74. Dublin.

— 2004 The big picture: mapping Hiberno-Norse Dublin. In H.B. Clarke et al. (eds) *Surveying Ireland's past: multidisciplinary essays in honour of Anngret Simms*, 31–40. Dublin.

Walsh, Claire 1997 *Archaeological excavations at Patrick, Nicholas and Winetavern Streets, Dublin*. Dingle.

— 2000 Archaeological excavations at the abbey of St Thomas the Martyr. In Seán Duffy (ed.) *Medieval Dublin I*, 185–200. Dublin.

— 2001 Dublin's southern defences, tenth to fourteenth century: the evidence from Ross Road. In Seán Duffy (ed.) *Medieval Dublin II*, 88–127. Dublin.

— 2005 Archaeological excavation of an Anglo-Norman waterfront at Strand Street Great. Dublin. In Seán Duffy (ed.) *Medieval Dublin VI*, 160–87. Dublin.

— 2009 An early medieval roadway at Chancery Lane: from *Duibhlinn* to *Áth Cliath*? In Seán Duffy (ed.) *Medieval Dublin IX*, 9–37. Dublin.

County Dublin: some observations on the historiography of early medieval excavation and research, 1930–2005

LORCAN HARNEY, JONATHAN KINSELLA
AND AIDAN O'SULLIVAN

INTRODUCTION

This paper builds upon research by the Early Medieval Archaeology Project (EMAP) to investigate the history, character and results of early medieval excavations in Co. Dublin. Dublin is a particularly suitable case study because it has experienced profound changes across its landscape as a result of sustained development throughout recent decades and particularly during the 'Celtic Tiger' years. This has impacted almost the entire county from the foothills of the Dublin Mountains at Tallaght, to the western county borders at Lucan, and northwards as far as Swords and beyond. Excavations have occurred within the historic core of Dublin city which has led to detailed analysis of the town's topographical development (for example, Simpson 2000; Halpin 2005; Kerr et al. 2009). Therefore, this paper will instead focus on significant excavations outside the town, because large-scale development-led excavations, particularly in recent years, have also revealed a variety of previously unknown and important early medieval sites across Co. Dublin (see Appendix 2.1 for a summary of excavated sites and licences). These exciting discoveries have the undoubted potential to inform us about the people who lived and worked in Co. Dublin throughout the early Middle Ages. Building on previous EMAP research (see www.emap.ie), this paper will investigate:

- how the changing economic, social and political climate from the early twentieth century influenced the changing character of early medieval excavations in Co. Dublin;
- how the changing character of excavations resulted in the discovery of new forms of archaeology and new interpretations of the early medieval past of Co. Dublin.

EXPLORING THE HISTORIOGRAPHY OF EARLY MEDIEVAL
EXCAVATION AND RESEARCH IN COUNTY DUBLIN

Antiquarian excavation and research, c.AD1750–1920

From the seventeenth to the early nineteenth century, archaeology in Ireland was practised mostly by a small group of interested amateurs or gentlemen scholars drawn predominantly from the professional gentry classes, clergymen and ex-military figures. Particularly from the later eighteenth century, these scholars were intrigued by the picturesque ruins of early church sites, frequently describing the mythologies and history associated with these places. Although these early antiquarian surveys were extremely valuable, some of their conclusions were rather fanciful, based on scant archaeological evidence and arguably tainted by the political and religious upper-class background of the authors. One such scholar was Edward Ledwich who, in his *Antiquities of Ireland* (1790), credited the 'Ostmen' with the introduction and construction of early medieval Irish stone roofed churches and round towers (Danish architecture), such as those he described at Clondalkin, Tallaght and St Doulagh's (all Co. Dublin). Also, in the later eighteenth century, there was a tendency among some of these antiquarians, such as Major General Charles Vallancey (1721–1812), to employ artists such as the Dutchman Gabriel Beranger (1730–1817) to sketch panoramic views of early church ruins and castles. Prior to his tour of Connacht in 1779, Beranger had acquired considerable experience in the 1760s sketching the remains of early churches and castles in the Dublin area, including the church and tower of St Michael le Pole, St Patrick's Cathedral and Clondalkin round tower (Harbison 1998; see fig. 2.1).

The mid-nineteenth century marked a gradual transition as archaeological inquiry was placed upon a more 'scientific' basis as the resources available to early antiquarians greatly expanded. The precedent for this transformation was the formation of the Ordnance Survey of Ireland, which, under the supervision of Thomas Colby (1784–1852) and latterly Thomas Larcom (1801–79), undertook an ambitious project of mapping the entire country in the 1830s and 1840s The remit of the survey extended far beyond merely mapping the island to also determining townland boundaries and acreage as a means of equalizing local taxation and recording the history, folkloric tradition and antiquity of every antiquarian site across the Irish landscape. As has recently been observed (Prunty 2009, 476–80), the OS emphasized close observation and objective description and classification of sites through fieldwork (decrying earlier mythical explanations) and, for the first time, allowed sites to be plotted on a countrywide basis using the 6-inch maps; an advancement which laid the basis for modern archaeology and landscape studies. The fieldwork of the OS expanded the number of known antiquarian sites from stone-built monuments, such as churches and round towers, to include other site types, such as raths, crannogs and prehistoric tombs, which prompted a new emphasis among

2.1 Clondalkin church and tower (after Harbison 1998, 89).

nineteenth-century antiquarians on identifying and cataloguing the character-istics of these site types in the Irish landscape through site excursions and fieldwork. The Dublin OS letters, written between March and September 1837 and almost exclusively by Eugene O'Curry and John O'Donovan, focused predominantly on sites in the southern half of the county (Herity 2001). Also working for the survey was a young artist, George Du Noyer, who sketched various archaeological sites including prehistoric tombs, promontory forts and raths in Co. Dublin.

Shortly afterwards, William F. Wakeman published his *Handbook of Irish antiquities* (1848), which produced descriptions and illustrations of a whole range of site types, from prehistoric cromlechs and sepulchral tombs, to raths and dúns, oratories, churches, crosses and round towers, and finally Anglo-Norman abbeys, castles and town walls. The guide book focused on those antiquities in close proximity to the metropolis (Dublin city) and proved so successful that further editions were republished into the early twentieth century. In Dublin, there was also considerable interest in studying the art and architecture of ecclesiastical monuments. Local surveys of ancient churches, crosses and cross-slabs in the county were produced by various antiquarians including Wakeman (1890–1, 1892), Robert Cochrane (1893) and P.J. O'Reilly (1901a, 1901b, 1901c). From the mid-nineteenth century, accounts of excursions to antiquarian sites in Dublin, most notably its early churches, were regularly reported in the local and national journals such as the *Irish Literary Gazette*, culminating in the six-volume *History of the County Dublin* (1902–20), produced by Francis Elrington Ball, one of Dublin's most noted local antiquarians in the early twentieth century. Although regional surveys of raths and crannogs were very common in other counties, Westropp's (1922) review of promontory forts was one of the relatively few surveys of earthen secular sites in Co. Dublin in the later nineteenth and early twentieth centuries.

Furnished Viking graves were arguably the earliest and best recorded archaeological discoveries in Co. Dublin in this period. This indicated the Viking (and foreign?) character of early medieval Dublin to antiquarians and placed Scandinavian influence at the forefront of their perceptions and understandings of early medieval Dublin city and county by the beginning of the twentieth century. One of the earliest of these finds was at College Green in 1685 in the vicinity of the Viking Thingmoot and near the levelled mound known as the Hogges (see Duffy 2005). Since these discoveries, other finds have been made at various sites in Dublin city, including the Phoenix Park in 1847 and inside a levelled mound at Mount Erroll, Donnybrook, in 1879 (see Ó Floinn 1998). The most notable discovery (and possibly the most important excavated early medieval site in nineteenth-century Ireland), was the Viking cemetery at Kilmainham, exposed between 1836 and 1866 during gravel-quarrying, and the construction of the Great Southern and Western Railways (O'Brien 1995, 1998). Elsewhere, some of the earliest and most reputable early medieval excavations in the mid-nineteenth century were undertaken at round towers, particularly in Ulster, by Edmund Getty (1855a, 1855b, 1855c), secretary of the Belfast Harbour Board. These were perhaps driven by a desire to resolve the 'round tower controversy', one of the most heated debates among antiquarians at this time regarding the origins and functions of these monuments (we have yet to establish if any of the Dublin round towers were excavated in the nineteenth century for similar purposes). Shortly later, the disestablishment of the Church of Ireland in 1869 transferred the vast bulk of early church sites (including round towers) into state care, prompting the Office of Public Works (OPW) to direct conservation works on these stone monuments in Dublin and elsewhere in the late nineteenth century.

Excavations during the mid-twentieth century, 1920–70: Independence and the 'Golden Age' state-centred narrative
Irish independence and partition in 1922 brought about major changes in the development of Irish archaeology on the island. Political self-consciousness, north and south of the new border, and an awareness of the potential role of

archaeology in promoting state identities ensured that the investigation of the archaeological heritage was removed from the purview of the amateur and placed firmly in the hands of state-controlled and university-based organizations (Evans 1968, 7; O'Sullivan 2003). In the Irish Free State (and latterly Irish Republic), there was considerable popular and scholarly interest in investigating the existence of a pre-Anglo-Norman early medieval Golden Age (see O'Sullivan 1998, 178–81) and it was this ethos that shaped the early archaeological and historical research of this period. The description of this period as 'early Christian' highlighted the common belief that Christianity was the central ideological force, defining and shaping this island's cultural history from the fifth to the twelfth century. Indeed the churches' rich ruins and relics – round towers, high crosses, chalices, brooches and manuscripts – were seen as verification of a unique highly sophisticated pre-invasion 'Golden Age' civilization of 'Saints and Scholars' in the 'Dark Ages' of early medieval Europe.

Oddly enough, few Irish ecclesiastical sites were actually comprehensively excavated in Ireland between 1920 and 1970, with the exceptions of Nendrum, Co. Down (Lawlor 1925), and Church Island, Co. Kerry (O'Kelly 1958). Frequently, many of the archaeological excavations on these sites were part of conservation work on buildings and monuments. Indeed it has been observed that early church sites were traditionally perceived by the Irish state bodies as 'enduring monuments' to be studied for their art and architecture, rather than investigated as dwelling spaces within a complex landscape of settlements and other sites (O'Sullivan 1998, 184). Only two excavations of early medieval Dublin church sites occurred in this period. A trial excavation of an area to the north of the early medieval church on Dalkey Island was excavated by the English archaeologist G.D. Liversage (1968). It revealed evidence for two phases of early burial, an eleventh-century Norman coin and a boundary wall associated with the early ecclesiastical site. The only other notable excavation took place at a small forgotten nave and chancel church, 300m away from the round tower, at Clondalkin (Rynne 1967). The church was surrounded by a small enclosure and may have been built as a small parish church in the later eleventh or twelfth century.

Instead, archaeologists in the mid-twentieth century tended to focus on high-status secular sites such as crannogs and raths; a precedent set by the highly significant Harvard Archaeological Mission to Ireland (1932–6) under the leadership of Hugh O'Neill Hencken (1902–81). The expedition was strongly promoted by the Irish Free State as it focused largely on pre-Anglo-Norman sites of prominence and historical importance such as the royal crannog at Lagore, Co. Meath (Hencken 1950), and high-status cashels like, for example, Cahercommaun, Co. Clare (Hencken 1938). Hencken and his team were also broadly welcomed by Irish archaeologists for introducing new excavation techniques and consistently publishing their findings.

A series of important university-led research excavations at prominent sites such as Garranes, Co. Cork (Ó Riordáin 1942), and Knockea, Co. Limerick (O'Kelly 1967), mostly in Munster, followed the Harvard Expedition. Michael Tierney (1998) and Jerry O'Sullivan (1998) have explored how the myth of an 'early Christian Golden Age' was mobilized in the politics of the Irish Free State and suggest that these site excavations were hugely influential in the development of normative ideas about early Irish society as rural, pastoral and largely based upon the activities of self-sufficient, small farming households inhabiting raths; ideas which (in terms of the socially conservative ethos of mid-twentieth-century Ireland) could be usefully portrayed as living in a manner that was not dissimilar to that of Irish rural communities in the 1930s and 1940s.

In contrast, there was no similar early medieval research tradition in Dublin, with only two notable excavations in this period of a cashel at Feltrim Hill (Hartnett and Eogan 1964) and a promontory fort on Dalkey Island (Liversage 1968; Doyle 1998). Threatened by an extension to Dublin airport, the cashel at Feltrim Hill revealed occupation deposits from the Neolithic to the early medieval period and evidence for a large number of hearths, paving horizons, animal bone and early medieval artefacts. The promontory fort at Dalkey was intermittently occupied in the Neolithic and the Bronze Age, in the form of temporary encampments, before it was reoccupied in the early medieval period. Associated with this latter phase was evidence for fortifications, a possible field system, a shell midden, a house and significant quantities of imported Mediterranean B and Frankish E ware. The lack of interest among archaeologists in investigating early medieval settlement sites in Dublin can perhaps be explained by the relative scarcity of recorded raths across Co. Dublin and the historic province of Laigin in general. This is perhaps because of an intensive medieval and post-medieval tillage tradition (Stout and Stout 1992; Stout 1997, 61–2), and the fact that the remains of earthen monuments almost never survive above ground in urban contexts such as Dublin city and its expanding suburbs since the nineteenth century. It might also indicate a general apathy among archaeologists in investigating early medieval sites in Dublin, particularly because there were more 'interesting' sites to be studied in the rugged landscape of the Gaelic west compared to the strongly Anglicized character of the Dublin region. Finally, perhaps simply because the county, with its foreign Viking archaeology, just did not conform to the dominant Gaelic 'Golden Age' narrative.

Following earlier precedents in the nineteenth century, burials and cemeteries continued to be the most common form of excavated early medieval site in Dublin, particularly by Nation Museum staff following various forms of development. Further Viking burials were recovered during the laying out of the War (First World War) Memorial Park at Islandbridge in 1933–4 and these

2.2 A Viking grave under excavation at Islandbridge, 20 October 1934 (from the National Museum of Ireland; after Harbison 2001, 63).

required the attention of the National Museum (O'Brien 1995, 13, 1998, 214; Harrison 2001, 62–4) (see fig. 2.2). Frequently, in isolated contexts, stone-lined burials were also reported to the National Museum between the 1920s and the 1960s at Baltrasna, Mount Offaly, Sutton and Lambay, all in Co. Dublin. Although these long cist burials were generally orientated east–west and lacked any grave-goods, they were initially dated by Joseph Raftery (1941) to the early Iron Age. However, their orientation, form and lack of grave-goods seem to fit more appropriately within a later Iron Age/early Christian milieu and this is supported by more recent excavations and carbon-14 determinations.

Wood Quay and EU accession: the birth of 'contract archaeology'
In the 1960s, urban redevelopment began to reveal valuable information about the origins and topographical development of Ireland's major cities and towns including Dublin. The National Museum's campaign of excavations of Viking and medieval Dublin at High Street through the late 1960s and early 1970s (Ó Ríordáin 1971, 1976), culminated in the Wood Quay and Fishamble Street excavations in the later 1970s in advance of construction of the Dublin Civic Offices (see, or example, Wallace 1984, 1985, 1992a, 1992b, 2001, 2004a). The publicized nature of the Wood Quay saga ensured the popularization of Dublin city as a 'Viking town'; arguably introduced entirely new subjects into Irish archaeology (for example, 'urban archaeology', 'Viking Age archaeology') and

politicized a generation of Irish archaeologists, alerted to the need for rescue archaeological programmes as well as stronger monument conservation policies as part of the planning process. There have been extensive excavations in Viking/ medieval Dublin since the 1960s, and these have been recently summarized by Simpson (2000; this volume) and EMAP (Kerr et al. 2009).

Ireland and the UK's membership of the European Economic Community in 1973 (and latterly the European Union) had a significant impact on archaeology on the island of Ireland. EU-supported farm improvement schemes and land reclamation projects resulted in state-funded rescue excavations of early medieval sites in the 1970s and 1980s. These occurred mostly in rural Ireland, with almost none in Dublin. However, a key development occurred in Irish archaeology in the later 1980s, when EU Structural Fund mechanisms were reformed and there was increased capital expenditure on regional development and infrastructural projects. These ultimately led to the first 'contract archaeology' excavations and, with the emergence of developer funding based on the 'polluter pays' principle, commercial archaeological companies devoted to mitigating development impacts were established and expanded significantly.

Since this period, Dublin's rich early medieval archaeology has been extensively revealed. One of the earliest infrastructural projects was the University College Cork-directed Bord Gáis Cork–Dublin Pipeline scheme in 1981/2. Excavations revealed a shallow-ditched drain and pit at Brownsbarn, which may have formed part of an early medieval settlement, the greater part of which lay outside the pipeline corridor (Sleeman and Hurley 1987, 71–3). The Brownsbarn–Ballough Bord Gáis Pipeline (originally known as the North-Eastern Pipeline) scheme in 1988 (and reinforcement works in 1999) uncovered a whole range of previously unknown early medieval burial grounds at Kilshane (Gowen 1988a; Conway 1999b), Gracedieu (Gowen 1988b; Conway 1999b) and Westereave (Gowen 1988d; Conway 1999c). More recent excavations along the route of the Bord Gais Pipeline to the west excavated early medieval cereal-drying kilns at Flemington (Bolger 2009) and Jordanstown (Tobin 2002, 2007, 221–5). Another possible early medieval cereal-drying kiln was excavated in Flemingtown in north Co. Dublin (Byrnes 2002, 2007, 219). The M50 ring-road was one of the earliest major road schemes in the Republic of Ireland. Since the mid-1980s, a variety of early medieval sites, including enclosures at Ballymount Great (Stout 1982), Scholarstown (Keeley 1985) and Laughanstown/ Glebe (Seaver 2004, 2005), have been excavated along its route.

Digging through the 'Celtic Tiger' economic boom: new archaeology and new interpretations of the early medieval past
Since the 1980s, there has been a gradual shift in emphasis from state to commercial sector-led excavations and, secondly, new legislative changes with the aim of protecting our archaeological heritage. European Union membership placed the Irish archaeological resource under the protection of tighter planning

legislation and the 1992 *European Convention on the Protection of the Archaeological Heritage* (commonly referred to as the Valetta Convention), has had a major impact on the nature of archaeology in Ireland. This has led to the establishment of uniform codes of practice and conduct agreed with state agencies (for example, the Department of the Environment, Heritage and Local Government and the National Roads Authority) as well as the commercial sector by the late 1990s. The greatest impact of Valletta on archaeology in Ireland has undoubtedly been the legislative incorporation of archaeology into the planning and pre-planning process under the various Planning and National Monuments Acts (1930–2004). These have introduced new forms of protection for archaeological 'Sites and Monuments' across the island. In real terms, this has meant that new forms of 'testing' and 'monitoring' excavations, under the supervision of licensed archaeologists, must be undertaken near and within the delineated boundaries of protected monuments (for example, raths, cashels, souterrains and ecclesiastical sites) in advance of any form of development initiative. The Urban Archaeological Survey of Ireland has also delineated areas of archaeological potential in the historic cores of Irish towns and cities as the state has recognized its obligation to protect both urban and rural 'archaeological landscapes'.

A combination of these legislative changes and the impact of the 'Celtic Tiger' resulted in an explosion of archaeological excavations from 1995 to 2005 across the country. The vast bulk of early medieval excavations in Co. Dublin occurred between the late 1990s and the mid-2000s due to the vast scale of residential and commercial infrastructural projects. The various recent motorway developments in Ireland proceeded under new codes of practice in this period and they have revealed a large number and variety of early medieval sites across the country. However, excavations in advance of road schemes in Dublin have produced few early medieval sites except those along the M50 (see above), two late Iron Age/early medieval transitional-period cemeteries at Bellinstown (Lynch 2002) and Coldwinter (Opie 2001) along the M1, and a cereal-drying kiln and metalworking site at Cherryhound (Fitzgerald 2006, 32; McGowan 2004) along the line of the N2 Finglas–Ashbourne road.

The construction of sprawling residential and industrial estates throughout the county of Dublin has uncovered the vast bulk of the early medieval archaeological evidence discovered in recent decades, including a wide variety of features and sites such as isolated ironworking hearths and furnaces, charcoal-production pits, cereal-drying kilns, field systems, unenclosed settlements, cemeteries and settlement/cemeteries, for example. These testify to a diversity of settlement types, social practices, occupational endeavours and religious influences by early medieval communities in Dublin and emphasize an archaeological discourse far removed from one that once focused uniquely on churches, raths and crannogs.

GENERAL OBSERVATIONS AND STATISTICS OF EARLY MEDIEVAL
EXCAVATIONS IN COUNTY DUBLIN, 1930–2005

EMAP has identified 118 excavations which have revealed early medieval (that
is, AD400–1100) archaeological evidence in Co. Dublin between 1930 and 2005.
These 118 excavations occurred on approximately seventy-nine designated
EMAP sites.[1] These figures exclude all excavations of early medieval sites
within the historic core of Scandinavian Dublin and those excavations which
have occurred on, or in close proximity to, early medieval recorded sites and
monuments such as churches, souterrains and raths. The vast majority of these
excavations have been undertaken since the late 1980s, but particularly from
2000 to 2005 during the 'Celtic Tiger' economic boom. Before the 1980s,
excavations at sites of early medieval archaeological significance in the county
were very rare, averaging about 1–2 per decade (see fig. 2.3). Indeed, Stout and
Stout (1992, 17) refer to just two rath excavations in Dublin by the early 1990s.

EMAP has classified and assessed early medieval sites according to the
significance of their excavated archaeology and not by their extant structural or
morphological features. This evidence has been categorized as 'general',
'significant', 'highly significant', 'uncertain' and 'no archaeological significance'.
The latter has been excluded from discussions in this paper and describes
excavations on or in close proximity to early medieval monuments (for example,
raths), which have revealed no excavated early medieval archaeology of
significance. Those of 'highly significant' status have revealed the richest early
medieval archaeological evidence in terms of structures, features, artefacts and
multiple-phasing; those of 'general' significance are at the other end of the
spectrum; and, finally those of 'uncertain' status are currently undated excavated
structures and features that are potentially of early medieval date. The information from figure 2.4 illustrates that 31 per cent (25) of sites with excavated early
medieval evidence are of 'general' status, 32 per cent (25) are of 'significant'
status, 19 per cent (15) are of 'highly significant' status and 18 per cent (14 of the
79 sites) are of potential early medieval significance but remain undated.

---

1 This survey of early medieval excavated sites, 1930–2005, is based on a review of available
published material and www.excavations.ie. Although we have consulted unpublished
reports in the archives of the (former) Department of the Environment, Heritage and Local
Government and from commercial companies, we have not examined unpublished files in
the Office of Public Works and the National Museum of Ireland. The appendix to this
paper includes a selection of important early medieval sites in Co. Dublin excavated after
2005, but these sites are excluded from the statistics in this section. Characterizing
archaeological complexes as 'sites' can be problematic in some instances, as excavation
licences can involve the investigation of a whole series of early medieval sites and
monuments such as enclosures, ecclesiastical sites, field systems, isolated kilns and
metalworking features, not all of which are always stratigraphically or chronologically
associated with each other. Where all these monuments are excavated together under the
same licence, they are listed and described here under the same 'archaeological site'.

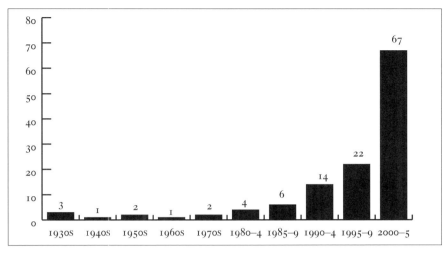

2.3 Early medieval excavations in Co. Dublin, 1930–2005.

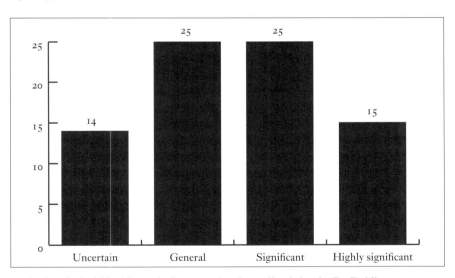

2.4 Archaeological 'significance' of excavated early medieval sites in Co. Dublin, 1930–2005.

The types of early medieval excavated sites in Co. Dublin range from small 'single feature' sites, such as isolated burials and pits, cereal-drying kilns and iron/metalworking features, to larger and more complex sites including enclosures, ecclesiastical sites and settlement/cemeteries with a range of internal features, to entire early medieval landscapes with multiple sites, monuments and features, some of which are not always directly associated with each other (see fig. 2.5). Early church sites are the most common early medieval excavated site type in Co. Dublin, as excavations have occurred in many instances on

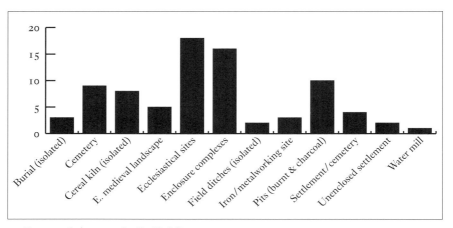

2.5 Excavated site types in Co. Dublin, 1930–2005.

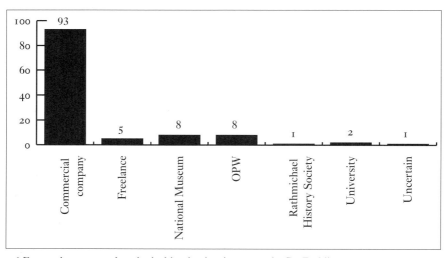

2.6 Excavations per archaeological institution/company in Co. Dublin, 1930–2005.

portions of their enclosing ditches and banks. They are followed by early medieval enclosures with some of the most significant of these containing associated field-systems, buildings and structures such as cereal-drying kilns and industrial hearths and furnaces. In contrast, there are few securely dated early medieval unenclosed settlements in Co. Dublin.

There is also growing evidence for excavated early medieval isolated burials, unenclosed and enclosed cemeteries, and cemeteries with associated settlement evidence (increasingly referred to as settlement/cemetery sites in the archaeological record). Excavations at the latter two site types have revealed a high proportion of both 'highly significant' and 'significant' archaeological evidence.

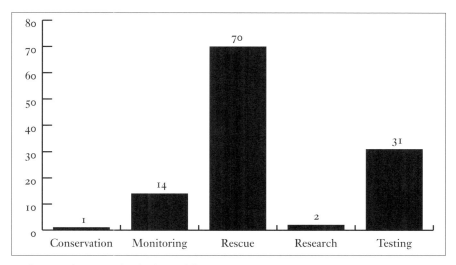

2.7 Reasons for excavation in Co. Dublin, 1930–2005.

There is a relatively high number of excavated 'single feature' early medieval pits, frequently charcoal-rich and with *in situ* firing, that may have been charcoal-production pits. Other structures that do not occur in association with any early medieval settlements include isolated field boundaries, cereal-drying kilns and iron/metalworking features. Isolated burials, charcoal-rich pits, metalworking features and cereal-drying kilns account for a high proportion of the 'uncertain' sites in the appendix, but many of these are potentially early medieval.

The vast majority (93; or 79 per cent) of the excavations on these early medieval sites are of recent date and were undertaken by commercial archaeo-logical companies (see fig. 2.6). These are a direct product of the expansion of the archaeological profession during the 'Celtic Tiger' boom. Private freelance archaeologists, independent of archaeological companies, accounted for a further 5 (4 per cent), indicating that the commercial sector was involved in approximately 83 per cent of excavations of early medieval sites in Co. Dublin between 1930 and 2005. Government bodies and organizations, most notably the OPW and the National Museum, were responsible for just 16 (14 per cent) of the excavations, while the remaining 3 per cent were undertaken by, or on behalf of, local history societies (1), universities (2) or are uncertain (1).

The majority (70; or 59 per cent) of sites with early medieval archaeological evidence were uncovered through 'rescue' excavations, while 'testing' and 'monitoring' investigations account for a substantial 45 (38 per cent) of excavations (see fig. 2.7). Notably, there is a lack of an early medieval research tradition in Dublin city or county, excavations elsewhere across the country frequently being undertaken by state or university bodies. The only known exceptions in Co. Dublin are Liversage's excavations at Dalkey Island (1968)

and Elizabeth O'Brien's investigations at Ballyman in the late 1970s and early
1980s (1977–9, 1984, 1985a, 1985b, 1986, 2005) on behalf of Rathmichael
Historical Society, which produced evidence for an early medieval cereal-
drying kiln and a fulacht fiadh: the latter representing one of the very few
known early medieval examples in the entire country. Also, there is a notable
absence of conservation excavations undertaken by OPW staff on early medieval
churches, round towers and high crosses – something that has occurred
outside Dublin. EMAP's provisional survey has only identified one such
excavation at St Doulagh's Church, Kinsealy, Balgriffin (Swan 1989, 1990a),
though others may have taken place and remain unpublished.

Most excavations in Co. Dublin were undertaken in advance of recent
commercial and residential developments (see fig. 2.8). It is also worth noting
that, although a considerable area of Co. Dublin was quite rural and agricultural
until very recent times, it is surprising that no early medieval site appears to
have been excavated due to farm improvements between 1930 and 2005. So far,
the only identified excavation that was a direct product of farm-work identified
a stone cist grave at Baltrasna, inspected by museum staff in 1922 (see Stout
1991). However, like the OPW excavations, it is quite possible that others were
undertaken in the intervening years but also remain unpublished.

THE ARCHAEOLOGY OF EARLY MEDIEVAL COUNTY DUBLIN

Early medieval rural settlement in Co. Dublin
Recent excavations have demonstrated that the Irish early medieval rural
landscape was populated by a variety of settlement forms such as enclosures
(including raths, cashels and raised types), souterrains (both enclosed and
unenclosed), unenclosed dwellings, settlement/cemetery sites, crannogs,
hillforts, promontory forts and caves. Co. Dublin contains a relatively low
number of recorded early medieval settlement enclosures. Stout and Stout
(1992, 16) record 105 examples, a small number compared to other parts of the
country, but this is probably due to centuries of intensive tillage and urban
sprawl which has obliterated above-ground archaeological features. Dublin also
contains a relatively small number of known souterrains, while no crannogs or
caves are recorded. Much of our understanding of early medieval rural
settlement in Co. Dublin has only developed relatively recently and is primarily
due to the scale and scope of excavations in this part of the country. When
Stout and Stout (1992) analyzed the settlement evidence in Dublin twenty
years ago, they identified two excavated early medieval settlement enclosures.
There are now at least eighteen known excavated examples in Co. Dublin and
all were excavated after the mid-1980s (although our graphs focus on excavated
sites 1930–2005, this figure of eighteen includes other known excavated
settlement enclosures post-2005). Some of these, including enclosures at

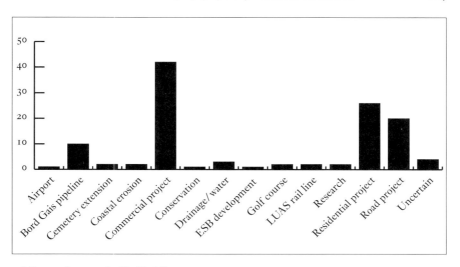

2.8 Excavation type in Co. Dublin, 1930–2005.

Laughanstown/Glebe (Seaver 2004, 2005), Rosepark (Carroll 2008), Flemington (Bolger 2009), Barnageeragh (Corcoran 2009), Ballynakelly (McCarthy 2009; see fig. 2.9), and Lusk (Giacometti 2006, 2007) are highly significant, as they were associated with field systems, internal features, structures and industrial evidence. Many of the settlements were excavated in the northern part of Co. Dublin and none were evident above ground prior to archaeological assessment and testing. This has relevance to Stout and Stout's (1992) assertion that northern Dublin was thinly settled in comparison to the southern part of the county and highlights the problems in devising settlement models based on surviving archaeological monuments and a limited archaeological record. Road schemes and large-scale development projects across Ireland have revealed a large body of previously unrecorded settlements and related features that have obvious implication for our understanding of past settlement practices at both micro and macro scales.

An investigation of Dublin's settlement enclosures demonstrates their morphological diversity. Although traditionally classified as 'raths' or, more commonly, 'ringforts', there has been some debate about the possible discovery of new settlement site types such as 'plectrum-shaped enclosures' (Coyne and Collins 2003; Coyne 2006; Collins and Coyne 2007). More recent publications do not attempt to classify these sites based on their shape, arguing instead that people in early medieval Ireland lived in enclosures of various sizes and shapes, which were modified and reconstructed across time, that served a variety of functions and were the dwelling places of people of differing social status (Kinsella 2010; Fitzpatrick 2009). Indeed, it is clear that many early medieval settlements in Dublin and across the country had dynamic 'cultural biographies'

2.9 Ballynakelly, Newcastle (after McCarthy 2009).

whereby they had a 'lifecycle' or 'biography' from production, through use and abandonment that mirrors the patterns of birth, life and death of its inhabitants (see O'Sullivan 2008), and these may be best understood as places that changed in social and cultural meaning across time (Gerritsen 2003; Van de Noort and O'Sullivan 2006).

A very small number of souterrains have been excavated in Co. Dublin and nearly all are associated with enclosure complexes, such as Rosepark (Carroll 2008), Barnageeragh (Corcoran 2009) and possibly Ballymount Great (Ó Néill 2000a), though the example from the latter site is not definite, as well as immediately outside the ecclesiastical enclosure at Lusk (O'Connell 2009). Clinton (1998, 2001a) has argued that excavated souterrains associated with enclosures frequently post-date the main phase of rath occupation (between the sixth and ninth centuries AD) and were instead often associated with a later early medieval (between the ninth and twelfth centuries AD) open settlement phase. Such a scenario has been demonstrated at Knowth, Co. Meath (Eogan 1968, 1974, 1977), and also significantly now at Rosepark, where some souterrains were cut into the ditch fills of the earlier phases, while others were located downhill from the enclosures (Carroll 2008, 105; see fig. 2.10).

Two souterrains and a number of pits and hearths at Barnageeragh were located to the west of the nearby excavated settlement enclosure (Corcoran 2009). These potentially represent an unenclosed settlement that succeeded the abandonment of the rath. South-west of the village of Balrothery (also in north Co. Dublin), in the townland of Stephenstown, are the remains of a

2.10 Rosepark souterrains, Balrothery (after Carroll 2008, 74).

souterrain exposed by gravel quarrying in the 1990s. An excavation close to the souterrain in 2005 revealed the remains of a hearth and post-holes and these were interpreted as forming a circular structure, probably prehistoric or related to the nearby early medieval souterrain (Devine 2005). Another potential early medieval unenclosed circular structure was excavated at Ballycullen, Oldcourt, in the foothills of the Dublin Mountains, although this could also be a prehistoric building (Larsson 2002a, 2002b). Perhaps the most intriguing settlement comprises a number of potential Scandinavian structures within a former early medieval enclosed cemetery at Cherrywood in south Co. Dublin (Ó Néill 2006; Ó Néill and Coughlan 2010). This may represent the remains of a rural Scandinavian farmstead: one of the very few such sites known in the Scandinavian kingdom of Dyflinarskiri and Dublin generally.

Living with the dead: the evidence for 'settlement/cemeteries'
Since the mid-1990s, there has been growing evidence for settlement/ cemetery sites in the Irish archaeological record. Many of these sites were initially confined to the north-eastern counties of modern Leinster (Meath, Louth, Dublin) in the area of the earliest major road schemes (M1, M4, N2) and there was initially some suggestion that this new site type may have had this particular regional expression (Stout and Stout 2008). However, the expansion of major road schemes outside this region (M6, M7, M8, N9/N10) since the early 2000s indicates that settlement/cemeteries have a broader island-wide distribution, although the majority remain in north Leinster. In

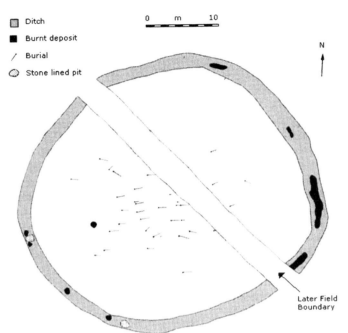

□ Ditch
■ Burnt deposit
／ Burial
◯ Stone lined pit

0   m   10

N

2.11 Cherrywood
(sixth-/seventh-
century enclosed
cemetery (after
Ó Néill 2006, 68).

Later Field
Boundary

Dublin, four settlement/cemetery sites have been excavated, although the
exact number is open to debate depending on how we differentiate these sites
from unrecorded early medieval ecclesiastical sites and the type of criteria we
employ regarding the required extent and character of burial and settlement
evidence (for example, dwellings, agricultural and industrial evidence). These
sites appear to have frequently originated in the late Iron Age/early medieval
transitional period (Kinsella 2010). Mount Offaly, Co. Dublin (Conway
1999d), is a very interesting site because it appears to have developed from its
inception, possibly as a *fert*, into a larger settlement/cemetery. Of interest were
a number of religious artefacts including box or book mounts and a composite
bronze cross from the site's final phases. The lack of domestic evidence from
the final enclosure may suggest that the site functioned solely as a cemetery by
this stage and was under the control of the Church.

It has been suggested that the settlement/cemetery site at Butterfield,
Rathfarnham (Carroll 1997), represents the remains of an unrecorded ecclesiastical enclosure, yet this is more likely a large settlement and cemetery site
that was utilized by the local community independently of the church across a
number of centuries. The site at Corcagh Demesne (Carroll 2001a, 2001b) is
another example of an excavation in Dublin that revealed burials and settlement
evidence in the form of artefacts, animal bone and cereal-drying kilns.
Cherrywood (Ó Néill 2006; Ó Néill and Coughlan 2010; see fig. 2.11) could be

loosely classified as settlement/cemetery because a potential Scandinavian group constructed their dwellings within the confines of an earlier (former) enclosed cemetery. This site highlights the problems that archaeologists are faced with when trying to box sites within certain categories and we can be sure that these modern constructs had little relevance to communities in the past. However, what these Dublin sites demonstrate is the diversity of settlement/cemetery types in terms of their chronologies, morphologies and use. Similarly to enclosed settlements throughout the county and country, each site has its own unique history and cultural biography in which a wide range of social, ideological, religious and political factors influenced what we see in the archaeological record today.

Death and burial in early medieval Co. Dublin: deconstructing the 'Golden Age' narrative?
The problems pertaining to identifying settlement/cemetery sites are further highlighted with the excavated evidence at Gracedieu (Gowen 1988b, 1988c) and Gallanstown (Purcell 1999, 2000). At the former site, sixty-five burials were uncovered that appear to be associated with an enclosure. Artefacts were rare but included a sherd of E ware and scraps of both ferrous and non-ferrous metal. Animal bone was retrieved from the ditch fills and a gully. Another enclosed cemetery was excavated at Gallanstown, while features in proximity included a well of uncertain date and pits, all of which contained cereal remains. It was also noted that some animal bone was present with the burial of a young child. Although it could be argued that there is tentative settlement evidence at both sites, in terms of features and artefacts, the presence of small quantities of animal bone, cereal remains and metallurgical waste may indicate ritual deposition practices at these ancestral cemeteries.

Excavations in Dublin have also revealed a variety of other burial grounds. A small number of isolated stone-lined burials of probable early medieval date have been identified, including examples at Margaretstown (Stout 1991), Baltrasna (Stout 1991) and Sutton (Raftery 1941, 303), while larger unenclosed early medieval cemeteries are more common, for example at Kilshane (Gowen 1988a), Westereave (Gowen 1988d), Mount Gamble (O'Donovan and Geber 2009, 2010), Pelletstown East (Frazer 2003; pers. comm., Denise Keating) and Darcystown (Carroll et al. 2008). Excavations at Glebe South (Carroll et al. 2008) and Bellinstown (Lynch 2002) have revealed ring-ditches cut by late Iron Age/early medieval transitional-period inhumations and perhaps represent the sites of pagan *ferta* cemeteries: places castigated by Tírechán, the Armagh-based hagiographer at the turn of the eighth century. Evidence for Viking furnished graves appears later in the ninth century, and these have been identified in considerable numbers in Dublin city (see, for example, O'Brien 1998; O'Donovan 2008; Ó Floinn 1998; Simpson 2000, 2005). Elsewhere in Co. Dublin, the evidence is less common, although, as we have seen, examples occurred at Donnybrook and in the Phoenix Park. More recently, the skeleton of a possible Viking woman associated with a gold and silver gilded oval brooch was excavated to the north of St Canice's Church at Finglas, in north Co. Dublin (Wallace 2004b, 7). The occurrence of isolated stone-lined cists, unenclosed and enclosed cemeteries, settlement/cemetery sites and Viking furnished graves in Dublin, and throughout Ireland, highlight the diversity of burial practices in early medieval Ireland. They show us that communities buried their dead according to religious beliefs, social practices, ideologies and even political influences that differed from place to place and over time. Although the centuries from AD400 to 1100 are traditionally regarded as the 'early Christian period', there is abundant archaeological evidence now for the diversity and complexity of burial practices and the long-lived nature of pagan practices or, more appropriately, the slow conversion of Irish society (or elements of it) to Christian belief and practice in the early medieval period.

The Church in early medieval Co. Dublin
Co. Dublin contains a relatively dense distribution of early medieval ecclesi-astical sites reflected in the high proportion of excavations at these sites from 1930 to 2005. Altogether, there are approximately nineteen ecclesiastical sites with early medieval excavated evidence. The most comprehensive excavations of a Dublin ecclesiastical site have been completed recently at Kilgobbin in south Co. Dublin (Bolger 2004; Kerr et al. 2009; Larsson 2004a, 2004b, 2004c). Here, excavations revealed multiple phases of enclosure ditches, field boundaries, hearths, pits, iron and metalworking evidence, cereal-drying kilns and a possible structure, as well as a large quantity of early medieval artefacts. Evidence for structures is relatively scarce at all of the excavated ecclesiastical sites (except for one possible structure associated with a kiln at Kilgobbin), while elsewhere a souterrain and an early cemetery have been investigated at Lusk, in north Co. Dublin (O'Connell 2009). Recently, geophysics and test excavations at a site at Mooretown North/Oldtown outside Swords exposed a previously forgotten multivallate ecclesiastical enclosure with associated field systems (Halliday 2004; Baker 2004, 2010, 9–13). Radial divisions were also identified between the second and outer enclosures, with a graveyard in the centre of the site (Baker 2004).

However, most ecclesiastical sites in Dublin, including some of the major monasteries at Finglas (Halpin 1994a, 1994b; Hayden 2003; Kavanagh 2004; Wallace 2004b), Swords (Baker 2004; Dunne 1997; O'Carroll 1998, 2000), Clondalkin (Rynne 1967) and Tallaght (McConway 1994, 1995; Newman 1990; O'Brien 1990; Walsh 1997), for example, have only been partially investigated and mostly through sections of their enclosure ditches. In contrast, there have been many fewer excavations within the ecclesiastical cores (for example, area of the churches, cemetery and round tower) and this is principally because these church sites in Co. Dublin are still frequently in use. One of the exceptions to this is the

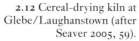

2.12 Cereal-drying kiln at Glebe/Laughanstown (after Seaver 2005, 59).

conservation works undertaken at St Doulagh's Church, Balgriffin (Swan 1989, 1990a). Building on an earlier antiquarian tradition established by Petrie, Stokes and Champneys, scholarly interest at church sites has long been focused on the art, architecture and basic layout of these stone monuments and buildings. However, recent excavations, including those in Co. Dublin, are beginning to shed valuable light on these places as settlements, in which different communities (clerics, tenants and craftworkers) lived, worked, worshipped and buried their dead during the early medieval period.

Agricultural evidence in early medieval Co. Dublin
One of the most significant characteristics of the 'Celtic Tiger' boom was the scale of its archaeological excavations. In many cases, developments avoided areas where upstanding or recorded archaeological monuments were present (for example, raths, souterrains and churches), yet were to discover a host of related archaeological features in the surrounding landscape. These included those related to agriculture, such as field systems, cereal-drying kilns and watermills, and industry, including charcoal-production pits and metalworking smelting and smithing furnaces.

Excavations have uncovered eight isolated early medieval cereal-drying kilns, including examples at Cherryhound (McGowan 2004; Fitzgerald 2006, 32), Jordanstown (Tobin 2002; Tobin 2007, 221–5) and the Brehons' Chair, Taylorsgrange (Lynch 1998). Cereal-drying kilns have also been excavated at various other enclosed settlements, church sites and cemeteries (see Appendix 2.1), for example at Laughanstown/Glebe (Seaver 2004, 2005; see fig. 2.12), Rosepark (Carroll 2008), Lusk (McCabe 2002a & 2002b) and Flemington (Bolger 2009). It is likely that the majority of corn-drying kilns were constructed and used in the fields surrounding early medieval enclosed settlements, as they were an obvious fire hazard and those revealed within enclosures were probably not contemporary with the settlement phases. These excavations have considerably advanced our understanding of the extent of crop husbandry in early medieval Ireland and the chronology and evolution of cereal-drying kilns. It is apparent now that cereal cultivation was an essential aspect of a mixed early medieval economy, whereas previously its role had been downplayed by archaeologists, largely as a result of a lack of archaeological evidence. Initial archaeological analysis of cereal-drying kilns suggests that earthen-cut figure-of-eight-shaped kilns were constructed during the late Iron Age/early medieval transitional period and were replaced centuries later by larger stone-lined keyhole-shaped kilns from approximately the tenth century onwards.

EMAP has identified other evidence for cereal processing in Co. Dublin by the presence of two early medieval watermills. The first is a tenth-/eleventh-century millrace associated with field ditches and ironworking features on the banks of the River Liffey at Chapelizod and close to the medieval church of St Laurence (Walsh 2002). Another watermill was excavated at Carrickmines Great and was dated to AD1123±9 or later (Clinton 2001b, 2002; Brady 2006, 48, 67). There has also been an explosion of evidence for early medieval field systems, most frequently associated with enclosed settlements, such as Ballynakelly (McCarthy 2009), Laughanstown/Glebe (Seaver 2004, 2005), Rosepark (Carroll 2008) and Lusk (Giacometti 2006, 2007), although isolated early medieval examples also occur at various places including those found in advance of the construction of Grange industrial estate just outside Clondalkin (Doyle 2000a, 2000b, 2005).

Industrial evidence in early medieval Co. Dublin

Finally, there have also been considerable developments in our understanding of early medieval iron and metalworking in recent years, largely as a result of specialist residue and geochemical analysis, notably by Tim Young and Effie Photos-Jones. In Co. Dublin, archaeological evidence for early medieval iron and metalworking (in the form of smelting furnaces, smithing hearths and finds such as slag, crucibles and moulds, for example) is not abundant and evidence has been identified primarily on enclosed settlements, such as Flemington (see fig. 2.13), church sites, settlement/cemeteries and cemeteries. There have been relatively few dated early medieval industrial sites; the best example being Cherryhound (McGowan 2004; Fitzgerald 2006, 32), but as early medieval ironworking was dependent on charcoal production, other indirect evidence for this activity in Co. Dublin might also be suggested by the presence of charcoal-rich pits at sites such as Grange, Baldoyle (Elder 2004a, 2004b). Again, however, evidence for this is limited in Co. Dublin.

CONCLUSION

Although there is a long tradition of early medieval excavation in Dublin, the vast bulk of the excavations have been undertaken since the late 1990s. Before then, excavations of early medieval sites were scarce, due to a number of different reasons: namely the paucity of surviving early medieval earthen sites and the lack of a research tradition in the county. Viking furnished graves were one of the earliest and best-recorded archaeological discoveries in the eighteenth and nineteenth centuries in Dublin, developing perceptions of the city and county as strongly Scandinavian (and foreign in terms of the 'Golden Age' narrative) by the beginning of the twentieth century. From the mid-1990s onwards, with the links between 'Celtic Tiger' infrastructural developments, increased planning and legislative requirements, and a growth in the commercial sector, there has been a clear increase in the number, scale and quality of archaeological excavations in Co. Dublin. This has expanded the range of known early medieval site types from traditional monuments, such as churches, raths and souterrains, to also include settlement/cemeteries, unenclosed dwellings, cereal-drying kilns, watermills, field systems and industrial features.

Some regions of Dublin have now been extensively excavated, particularly Lusk and Balrothery in north Co. Dublin. Stout and Stout (1992) suggested that this was a thinly settled area during the early Middle Ages, but they did not have the benefit of, nor could they have foreseen, the scale of excavations that would occur in this part of Dublin two decades later. What the Celtic Tiger years have shown is that above-ground archaeological monuments represent only a small portion of this country's and county's archaeology and that much of our history lies hidden beneath the landscape.

Our knowledge of Co. Dublin has radically changed over the last quarter of a century and now is the time, as things slow down to a manageable pace, to get to grips with Dublin's vast volume of archaeological data. Much can be gleaned by the increase in known settlements and their relationship to surrounding agricultural and industrial features. Politically, Lusk and Balrothery were originally part of the larger kingdom of south Brega between the seventh and tenth centuries. Co. Dublin sprawled the contested boundary between the Southern Uí Néill and the Laigin in this period and the archaeological evidence is now available to support regional multi-disciplinary case-studies in Dublin of the Gailenga and Ciannachta of Brega and the Uí Dúnchada and Uí Chellaig Chualann, both political groups of the Northern Laigin.

There is also great potential to investigate the archaeology of the later early medieval Scandinavian kingdom of Dyflinarskiri and study the developing and

2.13 Ironworking furnace at Flemington, Balriggan (after Bolger 2009, 32).

changing relationships between its primary town at Dubh Linn and the wider county from the tenth to the twelfth century. Although Dublin may have been a political backwater for archaeologists in the mid-twentieth century, the sheer scale and richness of the early medieval archaeological evidence generated from recent excavations now firmly places the archaeology of Co. Dublin and city at the heart of our emerging understandings of early medieval Ireland.

ACKNOWLEDGMENTS

EMAP would like to thank the Heritage Council's INSTAR funding, which supported and facilitated the completion of this paper. We would also like to acknowledge Denise Keating and Stuart Elder for providing unpublished carbon-14 determinations for sites at Pelletstown East, Castleknock and Grange, Baldoyle. Thanks to Brian Dolan for information on ironworking in Dublin and burial on Lambay Island. A special thanks must go to everyone from the commercial and academic archaeological sector who has contributed to EMAP's previous research, most recently the Settlement Gazetteer. Finally many thanks to the editor, Seán Duffy, for his support, encouragement and assistance with this paper and for facilitating the inclusion of the inventory.

... MEDIEVAL SITES IN DUBLIN COUNTY, 1930–2005[2]

Site name	Site type and brief description	Year	Significance	Licence	Company	Excavation type	Reason for excavation	Reference
Baldonnell Lower	Cereal-drying kiln.	2003	Uncertain	03E0374	Margaret Gowen	Rescue	M50 Outer ring road	Phelan 2003 (2003:457)
Ballycoolen, Astagob and Mitchelstown	Pit containing charcoal and slag-like material.	2000	Uncertain	00E0043	Margaret Gowen	Monitoring	Bord Gais Brownsbarn–Kilshane Pipeline	Doyle 2000c (2000:0213)
Ballycullen, Oldcourt, Site 1	Unenclosed habitation site. Possible early medieval unenclosed house.	2002	Uncertain	02E0190 & Ext.	Arch-Tech	Monitoring	Residential development	Larsson 2002a (2002:0639)
Ballycullen, Oldcourt, Site 1	Unenclosed Habitation Site. Possible early medieval unenclosed house.	2002	Uncertain	02E1373	Arch-Tech	Rescue	Residential development	Larsson 2002b (2002:0640)
Ballymount Great	Possible Iron Age enclosure with later ditch re-cuts. Ditches. Pits. Finds suggest 10th–14th-century activity.	1997	Significant	97E0316	Margaret Gowen	Rescue	Luas Network Line A (Tallaght–Middle Abbey Street)	Conway 1997 (1997:079)
Ballymount Great	Enclosure. Possible Iron Age enclosure with later ditch re-cuts. Ditches. Pits. Finds suggest 10th–14th-century activity.	2000/2002	Significant	00E0538	Margaret Gowen	Rescue	Luas Network Line A (Tallaght–Middle Abbey Street)	Ó Néill 2000 (2000:0205), 2002 (2002:0462)
Ballymount Great	As above.	1982	Significant	N/A	OPW	Rescue	M50 Western Parkway Motorway	Stout 1982
Ballynakelly, Newcastle	Early human burial predating enclosure, internal pits, ironworking, post-holes and gullies and kilns. Small associated enclosures.	2007	Significant	06E0176	Arch-Tech	Rescue	Development	McCarthy 2009
Baltrasna, Milverton	Burial. Cist, possibly associated with another burial site in adjacent townland at Margaretstown.	1922	Uncertain	N/A	National Museum	Rescue	Farmwork	Stout 1991 (1991:052) (H.E. Kilbride Jones, excavator)

2 This appendix mainly lists excavated early medieval sites and licences from 1930 to 2005, but some important post-2005 excavations are also included.

Site name	Site type and brief description	Year	Significance	Licence	Company	Excavation type	Reason for excavation	Reference
Barnageeragh, Skerries	Enclosure, souterrain, structure, hearths, pits. Multi-phase site with enclosed and later unenclosed settlement.	2004/2005	Highly significant	04E209 ext.	Margaret Gowen	Monitoring/rescue	Development	Corcoran 2009
Barnageeragh, Skerries	As above.	2005	Highly significant	04E1639	ADS	Rescue	Development	Corcoran 2009
Barnageeragh, Skerries	As above.	2006	Highly significant	06E0477	ADS	Rescue	Development	Corcoran 2009
Bellinstown	Cemetery. Ring-ditch cut by five inhumations.	2001	Significant	01E0744	Valerie J. Keeley	Rescue	M1 Airport–Balbriggan Motorway Bypass Contract 2	Lynch 2002 (2002:0473)
Brownsbarn	Field boundary? Ditched drain and pit (finds comprised a 9-/10th-century bone comb, lignite bracelet and animal bone)	1981	General	N/A	UCC	Rescue	Bord Gais Cork–Dublin Pipeline 1981/1982	Sleeman and Hurley 1987, 71–3
Butterfield, Rathfarnham	Settlement/cemetery. Multi-phase enclosure. Settlement and industrial evidence. C.233 burials within the enclosure.	2005	Highly significant	05E0959	Judith Carroll	Monitoring	Development	Carroll 2005 (2005:519)
Butterfield, Rathfarnham	As above.	1997	Highly significant	97E0140	Judith Carroll	Rescue	Development	Carroll 1997 (1997:184)
Carrickmines Great	Medieval ringwork castle site with kilns, industrial areas, houses and agrarian enclosures. A water mill was dated to 1123± 9 years or later (Brady 2006, 48 & 67) but it is unclear if any of the other features also date to the twelfth century.	2001/2002	Significant	00E0525	Valerie J. Keeley	Rescue	M50 South-eastern Motorway	Clinton 2001b; Clinton 2002; Brady 2006, 48 & 67

	description					Excavation type	Reason for excavation	Reference
Cherryhound (Site 2)	Cereal-drying kiln and metalworking. Phase of metalworking to the east followe d by phases of kiln use to the west.	2004	Significant	03E1360 & ext.	CRDS	Testing/rescue	N2 Finglas–Ashbourne Road Scheme	McGowan 2004 (2004:0483); Fitzgerald 2006, 32
Cherrywood	Settlement/cemetery? Multi-phase enclosure utilized initially as a cemetery, between approximately the 6th and 7th centuries, before it was settled by a potential Scandinavian group between the 8th/9th and 12th centuries.	1998/1999	Highly significant	98E0526	Margaret Gowen	Testing	Development	Ó Néill 2006; Ó Néill and Coughlan 2010.
Cherrywood	As above.	1999	Highly significant	99E0523	Margaret Gowen	Rescue	Development	Ó Néill 2006; Ó Néill and Coughlan 2010.
Cobbe's Hill, Mount Gamble, Miltonsfields, Swords	Cemetery. Unenclosed cemetery of approximately 300 inhumations on a low hill overlooking Swords radiocarbon dated to between AD550 and AD1150.	2002	Highly significant	02E0608	Margaret Gowen	Rescue	Development	O'Donovan and Geber 2009; O'Donovan and Geber 2010.
Coldwinter	Cemetery. Enclosed cemetery, 7 inhumations, iron slag from ditch base. Other finds included a quern stone, Mesolithic flakes, a small stone bead, a stone ring, hammer stones and animal bone.	2001/2002	Significant	99E0548 ext.	Valerie J. Keeley	Rescue	M1 Airport–Balbriggan Motorway Bypass Contract 2	Opie 2001 (2001:344)
Corcagh Demense, Clondalkin	Pit. Possible pit furnace.	2000	Uncertain	00E0935	Judith Carroll	Rescue	Saggart–Rathcoole–Newcastle Drainage Scheme	Elliott 2001 (2001:338)
Corcagh Demesne, Clondalkin	Settlement/cemetery. Probable enclosed cemetery, cereal-drying kilns, iron slag, ditches and possible structures.	2001	Significant	01E0849	Judith Carroll	Monitoring	River Camac Improvement Scheme	Carroll 2001a (2001:339); Monk and Kelleher 2005, 109

Lorcan Harney, Jonathan Kinsella and Aidan O'Sullivan

Site name	Site type and brief description	Year	Significance	Licence	Company	Excavation type	Reason for excavation	Reference
Corcagh Demesne, Clondalkin	As above.	2001	Significant	01E0911	Judith Carroll	Rescue	River Camac Improvement Scheme	Carroll 2001b (2001:340); Monk and Kelleher 2005, 109
'Cross Church of Moreen', Balally	Ecclesiastical site. Drystone walling.	1990	Significant	N/A	OPW	Rescue	Bord Gais pipeline extension	Cotter 1990a (1990:030)
'Cross Church of Moreen', Balally	Ecclesiastical site. Bivallate enclosure, rotary quern stone found.	2003	Significant	01E1078	Valerie J. Keeley	Rescue	M50 South-eastern Motorway	O'Donnchadha 2003 (2003:455)
'Cross Church of Moreen', Balally	Ecclesiastical site. Bivallate earthwork enclosure possibly associated with church.	2001	Significant	00E0370	Valerie J. Keeley	Testing	M50 South-eastern Motorway	Desmond 2001 (2001:322)
'Cross Church of Moreen', Balally	Ecclesiastical site. Three pits with large amounts of charcoal. One contained a bronze strap tag or belt buckle and animal bone.	1990	Significant	N/A	OPW	Testing	M50 Southern Cross Route Motorway	Mount 1990 (1990:029); Mount and Keeley 1990
Crumlin	Ecclesiastical site. Enclosing ditch, pits, medieval ridge and furrow.	1998	General	98E0362	Archaeological Projects	Testing	Development	Hayden 1998 (1998:130)
Crumlin	Ecclesiastical site. Enclosure ditch.	1999	General	99E0305	ACS	Rescue	Residential development	Murphy 1999 (1999:173)
Dalkey Island	Early medieval settlement Landscape. Promontory fort and church.	1956/1957/1958/1959	Highly significant	N/A	University of Bermingham Archaeological Field Unit	Research	None	Liversage 1968
Darcystown 1, Balrothery	Pit (charcoal-rich). Late Iron Age/early medieval pit.	2003/2004/2005	General	03E0067	Judith Carroll	Rescue	Residential development	Carroll, Ryan and Wiggins 2008
Darcystown 2, Balrothery	Ring-ditch, late Iron Age/early medieval cereal-drying kiln, hearth, two pits.	2004	Significant	04E0741	Judith Carroll	Rescue	Residential development	Carroll, Ryan and Wiggins 2008, 72–83.

Site type and other description	Year	Significance	Licence	Company	Excavation type	Reason for excavation	Reference
Darcystown/Glebe South, Balrothery — Early medieval settlement landscape. Inhumation burials and 10 cereal-drying kilns. Two kilns radiocarbon dated to between the early 4th and late 6th century AD.	2004	Significant	02E0043	Judith Carroll	Rescue	Residential development	Carroll 2004 (2004:0495); Carroll, Ryan and Wiggins 2008, 82.
Drinan/Nevinstown East, Swords — Enclosure. Two internal inhumations and early medieval brooch.	2005	Significant	03E1362 EXT	Margaret Gowen	Monitoring	Residential development	Moriarty 2005 (2005:419)
Feltrim Hill — Hillfort.	1947	Significant	N/A	OPW	Rescue	Airport development	Hartnett and Eogan 1964
Flemington, Balbriggan — Enclosure, field boundaries, drainage ditches, cereal-drying kiln, metalworking. Finds included E-ware pottery and a rotary quern stone	2005	Highly significant	05E0663	Margaret Gowen	Rescue	Residential development	Bolger 2009
Flemingtown — Cereal-drying kiln	2002	Uncertain	02E0296	Margaret Gowen	Rescue	Bord Gais pipeline to the west (Gormanston to Ballough Phase 6)	Byrnes 2002 (2002:0592); Monk and Kelleher 2005, 108; Grogan, O'Donnell and Johnston 2007, 219
Folkstown, Balbriggan — Enclosure	N/A	Significant	N/A	N/A	Rescue	N/A	Baker 2009, 100 (Colm Moriarty excavator)
Glebe South, Balrothery — Early medieval settlement landscape. Early medieval inhumation burials cut into 1 of 2 Iron Age ring-ditches with cremation pits. Late Iron Age/early medieval charcoal-rich oxidized figure-of-eight pit adjacent to ring ditch 2 as was possible inhumation burials. Two 11th–13th-century cereal-drying kilns lay in proximity to 11th–13th-century linear ditch	2004	Significant	04E0680	Judith Carroll	Rescue	Residential development	Carroll, Ryan and Wiggins 2008, 107–28

Site name	Site type and brief description	Year	Significance	Licence	Company	Excavation type	Reason for excavation	Reference
Gracedieu	Cemetery. 65 burials related to a probable enclosed cemetery. Artefacts included sherd of E-ware and scraps of ferrous and non-ferrous metal. Animal bone retrieved from ditch fills and gully.	1999	Highly significant	99E0217	Margaret Gowen	Rescue	Bord Gais Ballough–Kilshane pipeline	Conway 1999b (1999:248).
Gracedieu	As above.	1988	Highly significant	E000464	Margaret Gowen	Rescue	Bord Gais North-eastern pipeline	Gowen 1988a (1988:16), 1988b (1988:17)
Grange Industrial Park (Grange Castle), Kilmahuddrick, Clondalkin	Enclosure, pits, hearths. Terminus ante quem of 12th–13th century for two curving ditches. Worked lignite and decorated bone comb. Iron slag.	1997	Significant	97E0116	ADS	Testing	Development	O'Brien 1997 (1997:087).
Grange Industrial Park (Nangor Castle), Kilmahuddrick, Clondalkin	Enclosure. Possible ploughed-out rath. Early medieval pottery, slag, lignite core and slivers. 12th–13th-century activity	1996	Significant	96E273	ADS	Testing	Development	McConway 1996 (1996:068)
Grange Industrial Park (Nangor Castle), Kilmahuddrick, Clondalkin	Pits and ditches spanning the early medieval and medieval periods	2000	General	00E0754	Margaret Gowen	Rescue	Development	Doyle 2000b (2000:0226), 2005, 45
Grange Industrial Park, Kilmahuddrick, Clondalkin	Early medieval field systems enclosing a prehistoric ring-barrow.	2000	General	00E0448	Margaret Gowen	Rescue	Development	Doyle 2000a (2000:0225), 2005, 52
Grange, Baldoyle 10.2	Pit with heavy oxidization of edges. 04E0706 A charcoal sample returned a radiocarbon date of cal. AD49–545 (OxA–17448, 1432±27BP)	2004	General	04E0706	Archaeology Company	Rescue	Development	Elder 2004c (2004:0463); Stuart Elder, pers. comm.
Grange, Baldoyle 5.1	Pits produced radiocarbon dates ranging from 1000 to 934 cal. BC (OxA–17335, 2917±33BP) to cal. AD648–702 (OxA–17... 1275±27BP)	2003	General	03E1535	Archaeology Company	Rescue	Development	Elder 2004d (2004:0446); Stuart Elder, pers. comm.

Site name	Site type and brief description	Year	Significance	Licence	Company	Excavation type	Reason for excavation	Reference
Grange, Baldoyle 5.2	Pit (charcoal-rich) with a metalled base and intense *in-situ* burning produced radiocarbon dates of cal. AD537–593 (OxA–17404, 1385±28BP) and cal. AD679–751 (OxA–17405, 1245±26BP).	2004	General	04E0698	Archaeology Company	Rescue	Development	Elder 2004b (2004:0454); Stuart Elder, pers. comm.
Grange, Baldoyle 5.4	Pit (charcoal-rich) produced radiocarbon dates of cal. AD667–719 (OxA–17406, 1257±26BP) and cal. AD643–695 (OxA–17407, 1281±26BP).	2004	General	04E0699	Archaeology Company	Rescue	Development pers. comm.	Elder 2004e (2004:0455); Stuart Elder,
Grange, Baldoyle, 4.2	Pits (charcoal-rich) produced radiocarbon dates of cal. AD552–606 (OxA–17383, 1371±27BP) and cal. AD464–520 (OxA–17384, 1458±28BP).	2004	General	04E0697	Archaeology Company	Rescue	Development pers. comm.	Elder 2004f (2004:0451); Stuart Elder,
Grange, Baldoyle, 4.3	Pits (charcoal-rich), figure-of-eight shaped feature, two intercutting ditches and possible windbreaker. Site produced radiocarbon dates of 353–295 cal. BC (OxA–17385, 2274±29BP) and cal. AD389–445 (OxA–17386, 1533±28BP).	2004	General	04E0589	Archaeology Company	Rescue	Development	Elder 2004a (2004:0452); Stuart Elder, pers. comm.
Grange, Baldoyle, 4.4	Enclosure with internal metalled pathway, gate tower feature, rubbish pits and single post-hole. Find included a lignite bracelet, stick pin and socketed iron object. Lower fills of enclosure were radiocarbon dated to cal. AD566–622 (OxA–17386, 1356±28BP) and cal. AD699–751 (OxA–17387, 1235±26BP).	2004	General	04E0342	Archaeology Company	Rescue	Development	Elder 2004g (2004:0453); Stuart Elder, pers. comm.

Site name	Site type and brief description	Year	Significance	Licence	Company	Excavation type	Reason for excavation	Reference
Islandbridge	Scandinavian cemetery: 2 or possibly 3 furnished Viking burials aligned north–south together with a series of burials aligned east–west without grave-goods.	1933/1934	Highly significant	N/A	National Museum	Rescue	Development (War Memorial Park)	O'Brien 1995; O'Brien 1998 (Excavators: Adolf Mahr, S.P. Ó Ríordáin and Liam Gógan)
Islandbridge	Scandinavian furnished burial.	2009?	Significant	N/A	National Museum	Rescue	Development (War Memorial Park)	Sikora et al. (this volume)
Jordanstown (BGE 6/12/1)	Cereal-drying kilns, hearths and linear features.	2002	General	02E0684	Margaret Gowen	Rescue	Bord Gais pipeline to the west (Gormanston to Ballough Phase 6)	Tobin 2002 (2002:0604); Monk and Kelleher 2005, 109; Grogan, O'Donnell and Johnston 2007, 221–5
Kilshane	Cemetery. Unenclosed cemetery. Two agricultural ditches/drains. Plain blue glass bead was the only find.	1999	Highly significant	99E0220	Margaret Gowen	Monitoring	Bord Gais Ballough-Kilshane pipeline	Conway 1999a (1999:253)
Kilshane	As above.	1988	Highly significant	E000467	Margaret Gowen	Rescue	Bord Gais North-eastern pipeline	Gowen 1988a (1988:18)
Kingstown	Pit lined with a dense layer of twigs or brushwood and high charcoal content.	2000	Uncertain	00E0256	Valerie J. Keeley	Rescue	M50 South-eastern Motorway	Clinton 2000 (2000:0315)
Lambay Island (near church)	Burials. Part of one skeleton and fragments of another. The burial lay c.110m to the north-west of the church on the island.	1991	General	J00092	National Museum	Rescue	Coastal erosion	Ó Floinn and Cherry 1991 (1991:049); Cooney 1993, 27
Lambay Island (White House)	Cemetery. Stone-lined inhumations recovered while developing White House to the south of the harbour in the 1930s may represent early medieval cemetery.	1930s	General	N/A	National Museum	Rescue	Residential development	Cooney 1993, 27 (Excavator unidentified)

	description	year	significance		Company	Excavation type	Reason for excavation	Reference
Laughanstown/ Glebe (Site 42)	Cereal-drying kilns.	2000/ 2001/ 2002	Significant	00E0283	Valerie J. Keeley	Rescue	M50 South-eastern Motorway	Seaver 2004, 2005; Monk and Kelleher 2005, 109.
Laughanstown/ Glebe (Site 43)	Enclosure and field systems. A cluster of internal post-holes, hearth and pit within enclosure. Field ditches radiating from enclosure. Iron slag, smithing hearth, intercutting pits and possible internal posts for a wattle type structure. Artefacts included bone trial piece and bone pin.	2000/ 2001/ 2002	Highly significant	00E0758	Valerie J. Keeley	Rescue	M50 South-eastern Motorway	Seaver 2004, 2005
Lusk	Cereal-drying kiln.	2002	General	02E0794	Arch-Tech	Monitoring	Residential development	McCabe 2002a (2002:0623); O'Connell 2009, 57–8; Monk and Kelleher 2005, 109
Lusk	As above.	2002	General	02E1398	Arch-Tech	Rescue	Residential development	McCabe 2002b (2002:0628); O'Connell 2009, 57–8; Monk and Kelleher 2005, 109
Lusk, Dun Emer Estate	Enclosure with attached ancillary enclosures and field systems. Timber bridge over ditch. Internal oval or circular structures. A curvilinear cut feature that appeared to be associated with metalworking to north-east of the enclosure. Cereal-drying kiln. Ironworking waste.	2005	Highly significant	05E0848	Arch-Tech	Rescue	Residential development	Giacometti 2006, 2007
Margaretstown, Milverston	Burial. Slab-lined burial and V-sectioned ditch. Possibly associated with another burial site in adjacent townland at Baltrasna.	1991	Uncertain	N/A	OPW	Rescue	Residential development	Stout 1991 (1991:052)

Site name	Site type and brief description	Year	Significance	Licence	Company	Excavation type	Reason for excavation	Reference
Maynetown	Enclosure. One section of ditch excavated. Decorated bone bead uncovered.	2000	General	00E0732	Margaret Gowen	Testing	Uncertain	Wallace 2000 (2000:0328)
Mooretown North/ Oldtown, Swords	Ecclesiastical (?) enclosures and field systems. Post- and stake-holes, pits. Possible Souterrain Ware, animal bone and several other artefacts. Skeletal remains of at least 20 people.	2004	Significant	04E0543	Arch-Tech	Testing	Development	Halliday 2004 (2004:0651); Baker 2004; Baker 2010, 9–13.
Mooretown North/ Oldtown, Swords	As above	2003	Significant	03E1080 03ER095	Margaret Gowen	Testing	Development	Halliday 2004 (2004:0651); Baker 2004; Baker 2010, 9–13.
Mount Offaly, Cabinteely 'Graves' Moat'	Settlement/cemetery. Multi-phase enclosed cemetery. Burial ground contained 1,553 burials, also disarticulated remains and charnel pits. Settlement evident by numerous dress items, functional objects, imported pottery, butchered animal bone and areas of cobbling. Evidence for industry included a furnace and associated hearth. Undated but the site possibly originated during the late Iron Age and may then have been taken over by the church.	1998/ 1999	Highly significant	98E0035	Margaret Gowen	Rescue	Development	Conway 1999d
Mount Offaly, Cabinteely 'Graves' Moat'	As above	1995	Highly significant	95E131	Margaret Gowen	Testing	Development	Conway 1999d
Mount Offaly, Cabinteely 'Graves' Moat'	As above	1998	Highly significant	98E0582	Freelance	Testing	Residential development	Conway 1999d

Site name	Site type and brief description	Year	Significance	Licence	Company	Excavation type	Reason for excavation	Reference
Mount Offaly, Cabinteely 'Graves' Moat'	Stone cist grave. Other human remains have been reported from the general area.	1957	Highly significant	N/A	National Museum	Rescue	Uncertain	Ó Floinn 1991 (1991:050); Gowen 1995 (1995:103); Conway 1999d (Nell Prendergast excavator)
Mount Offaly, Cabinteely 'Graves' Moat'	Burial. Single skeleton beside 1957 stone cist. Worked antler burr identified.	1991	Highly significant	J000201	National Museum	Rescue	Uncertain Conway 1999d	Ó Floinn 1991 (1991:050);
Murphystown, Carmanhall, Leopardstown	Cemetery. Probable unenclosed cemetery of 7 wholly or partly intact skeletons, along with 13 isolated bones or groups of bone. Burials were extended inhumations without grave-goods, oriented east–west.	2002	Uncertain	02E0153	Valerie J. Keeley	Testing	M50 South-eastern Motorway	Breen 2002 (2002:0631).
Park West, Gallanstown	Cemetery. Enclosed cemetery located in proximity to a well of uncertain date and pits, all of which contained cereal remains.	2000	Significant	00E0267	Margaret Gowen	Rescue	Development	Purcell 2000 (2000:0299)
Park West, Gallanstown	As above.	1999	Significant	99E0108	Margaret Gowen	Testing	Development	Purcell 1999 (1999:246)
Pelletstown East, Castleknock	Cemetery. Small unenclosed cemetery of approximately 5 burials. Radiocarbon dates for 3 burials indicate a 6th–8th-century date-range for the cemetery.	2003	Significant	03E1823	Margaret Gowen	Rescue	Development	Frazer 2003 (2003:467); Denise Keating, pers. comm.
Phrompstown 1	Enclosure. Excavation of two sections of ditch. No finds.	2002	General	02E1020	Freelance	Testing	Golf course (2002:0643)	Byrne 2002a
Phrompstown 2	Enclosure. Enclosure ditches, possible field boundaries, pit.	2002	General	02E1022	Freelance	Testing	Golf course	Byrne 2002b (2002:0644)

Site name	Site type and brief description	Year	Significance	Licence	Company	Excavation type	Reason for excavation	Reference
Porterstown	Enclosure. Enclosure ditch. No finds. Possible Bronze Age feature within.	1990	Uncertain	N/A	National Museum	Rescue	Development (1990:039)	Cotter 1990b
Rosepark, Balrothery	Hilltop multi-phase enclosure complex spanning approximately the late Iron Age to the 8th/9th centuries AD. Unenclosed habitation, of 7 souterrains, potentially succeeded the hilltop settlement but was abandoned prior to the arrival of the Anglo-Normans. Small number of disarticulated burials on summit of hill. 11 cereal-drying kilns. Variety of domestic and functional artefacts. Also E-ware. Animal bone from enclosure ditches.	1999	Highly significant	99E0155 & ext.	Arch-Tech; Judith Carroll	Rescue	Development	Carroll 2008
Scholarstown	Enclosure. Internal D-shaped structure and hearth. Post- and stake-holes present. Finds included flints, an iron knife and a stone loom-weight.	1985	General	E000303	Valerie J. Keeley	Rescue	M50 Southern Cross Route Motorway	Keeley 1985 (1985:26)
St Assam, Raheny	Ecclesiastical site. Possible enclosure ditch. No finds.	1996	Uncertain	96E0183	Judith Carroll	Testing	Development	Carroll 1996 (1996:136)
St Assam, Raheny	Ecclesiastical site. Possible enclosure ditch.	1970	Uncertain	N/A	?	Rescue	Unidentified road development	Carroll 1996 (1996:136) (Leo Swan excavator)
St Brendan, Coolock	Ecclesiastical site. Enclosure ditch and bank. Unstratified finds included 2 brooches, a lead ingot and worked antler.	1990	Significant	E000570	OPW	Rescue	Development	Swan 1990b (1990:033)
St Canice, Finglas	Ecclesiastical site. Possible early medieval/medieval agricultural pits, gullies and ditches.	2003	Significant	03E0224	Archaeological Projects	Testing	Development	Hayden 2003 (2003:0602)
St Canice,	Ecclesiastical site. Possible	1994	Significant	94E010	ADS	Rescue	N2 Finglas Bypass	Halpin 1994b (1994:093)

	description	year	significance	licence	company	Excavation type	Reason for excavation	Reference
St Canice, Finglas	As above.	1993	Significant	93E193	ADS	Testing	N2 Finglas Bypass	Halpin 1994a (1994:092)
St Canice, Finglas	Ecclesiastical site. Possible enclosure ditch, Viking burial, medieval rubbish pits and iron slag.	2004	Significant	04E0900	National Archaeological Services, Ard Solas	Rescue	Residential development	Kavanagh 2004 (2004:0599); Wallace 2004b
St Columcille, Swords	Ecclesiastical site. Extensively quarried. Possible early medieval quarrying for nearby round tower. Shell layer, area of paving. Medieval hearths and other features.	1998/2000	General	98E0082	CRDS	Testing/monitoring	Development 2000 (2000:0347)	O'Carroll 1998 (1998:218),
St Columcille, Swords	Ecclesiastical Site. Pre-17th-century burials.	1997	General	97E0272	Freelance	Testing	Residential development	Dunne 1997 (1997:186)
St Cronan Mochua, Clondalkin	Ecclesiastical site. Excavation at church. Brooch discovered.	1964	Significant	N/A	National Museum	Rescue	Residential development	Rynne 1967
St Doulagh's, Kinsealy, Balgriffin	Ecclesiastical site. Possible enclosure ditch identified and early medieval glass bead discovered.	2004	General	04E1371	IAC	Testing	Residential development	McLoughlin 2004 (2004:0513)
St Doulagh's, Kinsealy, Balgriffin	Ecclesiastical site. Excavation of church. Possible enclosure ditch. Burials. Medieval activity.	1989/1990	General	N/A	OPW	Conservation	Conservation 1990a (1990:031)	Swan 1989 (1989:021).
St Gobban, Kilgobbin, Stepaside	Ecclesiastical site. Multi-phase evidence for settlement, agriculture and industry related to the ecclesiastical site.	2004	Highly significant	04E0777	Arch-Tech	Monitoring	Residential development	Larsson 2004b (2004:0645)
St Gobban, Kilgobbin, Stepaside	As above.	2004	Highly significant	04E0981	Arch-Tech	Rescue	Residential development	Larsson 2004c (2004:0646)
St Gobban, Kilgobbin, Stepaside	As above.	2004	Highly significant	04E1373	Margaret Gowen	Rescue	Residential development	Bolger 2004 (2004:0647)
St Gobban, Kilgobbin, Stepaside	As above.	2004	Highly significant	04E0501	Arch-Tech	Testing	Residential development	Larsson 2004a (2004:0644)

Site name	Site type and brief description	Year	Significance	Licence	Company	Excavation type	Reason for excavation	Reference
St Laurence, Chapelizod?	Ecclesiastical site? 10th–11th-century millrace, field ditches, slag, furnace bases and smithing hearths.	2002	Significant	00E0878	Freelance	Testing	Development	Walsh 2002 (2002:0492)
St Mac Cuillin, Lusk	Ecclesiastical site. Possible enclosure ditch. Linear ditches, gullies, charcoal-rich deposits and a stake-hole. Finds included a bone spindle-whorl and an iron blade.	2001/2002	Significant	01E0872 & ext.	Arch-Tech	Testing	Development	Moore 2001 (2001:448); Baker 2001 (2001:449), 2002 (2002:0621)
St Mac Cuillin, Lusk	Ecclesiastical site. Charcoal-rich burnt pit and hearth (undated) within ecclesiastical enclosure.	2002	Significant	02E1031	Arch-Tech	Rescue	Residential development	McCabe 2002c (2002:0627)
St Mac Cuillin, Lusk	Ecclesiastical site. Enclosure ditch, souterrain, burials.	2005	Significant	N/A	ACS	Rescue	Road scheme	O'Connell 2009, 51–63
St Mac Cuillin, Lusk	Ecclesiastical site. At least five inhumations possibly related to the medieval monastery, 150m to the east. The burials lie within the bounds of the original monastery as suggested by the curving route of Church Road and Treen Lane.	2005	Significant	05E0161	ACS	Testing	Road scheme	Clarke 2005 (2005:504)
St Maelruain, Tallaght	Ecclesiastical site. Enclosure ditch.	1994	Significant	94E0135	ADS	Rescue	Development	McConway 1994 (1994:102)
St Maelruain, Tallaght	As above.	1997	Significant	96E0188	Archaeological Projects	Rescue	Development	Walsh 1997 (1997:187)
St Maelruain, Tallaght	Ecclesiastical site. Possible enclosure ditch and pit.	1990	Significant	N/A	ADS	Testing	Development	Newman 1990 (1990:045)
St Maelruain, Tallaght	Ecclesiastical site. Enclosure ditch.	1995	Significant	95E155	ADS	Testing	Development	McConway 1995 (1995:111)

Site name	Site type and brief description	Year	Significance	Licence	Company	Excavation type	Reason for excavation	Reference
St Maelruain, Tallaght	Ecclesiastical site. Enclosure ditch contained charcoal, iron slag and animal bone. Animal bone from the ditch was radiocarbon dated to cal. AD654–998 (1210±100BP, GrN-18244).	1990	Significant	N/A	Margaret Gowen	Testing	Development	O'Brien 1990 (1990:043)
St Maelruain, Tallaght	Ecclesiastical Site. Identification of enclosure ditches.	1991	Significant	N/A	Margaret Gowen	Testing	Development	Gowen 1991 (1991:053)
St Nahi, Churchtown Upper, Taney, Dundrum	Ecclesiastical site. Possible enclosure ditch.	2005	General	05E0847	Margaret Gowen	Testing	Development	Bolger 2005 (2005:404); Harkin 2005, 171–86
St Peter's Church, Balrothery	Ecclesiastical site. Bullaun stone from topsoil.	2004	General	04E0671	ACS	Monitoring	Cemetery extension	Stevens 2004 (2004:0470)
St Peter's Church, Balrothery	Ecclesiastical site. Fragmentary burials and Souterrain Ware were discovered.	2002	General	02E1316	ACS	Testing	Cemetery extension	Murphy 2002 (2002:0472)
St Sillan, Glen Munire, Ballyman	Ecclesiastical site. Cereal-drying kiln radiocarbon dated to the 5th century earliest feature on site. Finds related to settlement and industry included terminal of bronze zoomorphic penannular brooch (dating to 6th/7th century), ring portion of similar brooch, clay mould sherd. Animal bone present. Cobbled surface with evidence for ironworking post-dated settlement activity.	1979/1980/1981/1982/1983/1984/1985/1986	Significant	E000182	Rathmichael Historical Society	Research	None	O'Brien 1977–79 (1977–79:0036), 1985a, 1985b (1985:22), 1986 (1986:21); O'Brien 2005, 293–302; Monk and Kelleher 2005, 109

Site name	Site type and brief description	Year	Significance	Licence	Company	Excavation type	Reason for excavation	Reference
Stephenstown, Balrothery	Unenclosed habitation site. Hearth and 3 post-holes from a possible structure.	2005	Uncertain	05E0098	Mary Henry	Monitoring	ESB development	Devine 2005 (2005:533)
Sutton	Burial. Cist. Skeleton extended west–east. No grave-goods. On top of gravel on a raised beach.	1930s?	Uncertain	N/A	National Museum	Rescue	Coastal erosion	Raftery 1941, 303 (E. O'Mahony excavator)
Taylorsgrange, Brehon's Chair	Cereal-drying kilns.	1998	General	96E0091	IAC	Rescue	Residential development	Lynch 1998 (1998:222); Monk and Kelleher 2005, 107
Tibradden	Metal/Iron working. Bowl furnace, furnace bottoms and slag, copper fragment.	1998	Uncertain	98E0206	Valerie J. Keeley	Monitoring	M50 Southern Cross Route Motorway	Gracie 1998 (1998:121)
Tully Church, Laughanstown	Ecclesiastical site. Cross-slab. Deeply buried in an upright position 1m to the south-west of the chancel.	1982	General	N/A	OPW	Rescue	Uncertain	Ó hÉailidhe 1982
Westereave	Cemetery. 57 burials. No evidence for enclosure. Small iron buckle and fragment of bronze only finds.	1988	Highly significant	E000466	Margaret Gowen	Rescue	Bord Gais North-eastern pipeline	Gowen 1988d (1988:21)
Woodside	Metal/iron working. Undated pit.	2002	Uncertain	02E1584	Arch-Tech	Monitoring	Residential development	McCabe 2002d (2002:0698)

BIBLIOGRAPHY

Baker, C. 2001 (2001:449) Lusk, Co. Dublin: early medieval settlement. www.excavations.ie.
Baker, C. 2002 (2002:0621) Lusk, Co. Dublin: early medieval settlement. www.excavations.ie.
Baker, C. 2004 A lost ecclesiastical site in Finglas. *Archaeology Ireland* 18:3, 14–17.
Baker, C. (ed.) 2009 *Axes, warriors and windmills: recent archaeological discoveries in north Fingal*. Dublin.
Baker, C. 2009 Fingal's past in the present: an overview. In Baker (ed.) 2009, 88–103
Baker, C. 2010 Occam's Duck: three early medieval settlement cemeteries or ecclesiastical sites? In C. Corlett and M. Potterton (eds) *Death and burial in early medieval Ireland in the light of recent archaeological excavations*, 1–21. Dublin.
Ball, F.A. 1902–20 *A history of the County Dublin*. 6 vols. Dublin.
Brady, N. 2006 Mills in medieval Ireland: looking beyond design. In S. Walton (ed.) *Wind and water in the Middle Ages: fluid technologies from Antiquity to the Renaissance*, 39–68. Pennsylvania.
Bolger, T. 2004 (2004:0647) Kilgobbin, Stepaside, Co. Dublin: environs of early ecclesiastical site. www.excavations.ie.
Bolger, T. 2005 (2005:404) Churchtown Upper: environs of ecclesiastical site. www.excavations.ie.
Bolger, T. 2009 Organising the landscape: archaeological excavations at Flemington, Balbriggan. In Baker (ed.) 2009, 23–35.
Breen, T. 2002 (2002:0631) Murphystown Site 6, Murphystown/Carmanhall and Leopardstown, Co. Dublin: cemetery, destroyed fulacht fiadh, hearths etc. www.excavations.ie.
Byrne, M. 2002 (2002:0643) Phrompstown 1, Co. Dublin: ringfort. www.excavations.ie.
Byrne, M. 2002 (2002:0644) Phrompstown 2, Co. Dublin: ringfort (site) and linear cropmarks. www.excavations.ie.
Byrnes, E. 2002 (2002:0592) Flemingtown, Co. Dublin: grain-drying kiln. www.excavations.ie.
Byrnes, E. 2007 Flemingtown. In Grogan, E., O'Donnell, L. and Johnston, P. (ed.) *The Bronze Age landscapes of the Pipeline to the west: an integrated archaeological and environmental assessment*, 219. Bray.
Carroll, J. 1996 (1996:136) Cahill Motors Ltd, Raheny, Co. Dublin: ecclesiastical settlement. www.excavations.ie.
Carroll, J. 1997 (1997:184) The Old Orchard Inn, Butterfield Avenue, Rathfarnham: medieval occupation and burials. www.excavations.ie.
Carroll, J. 2001a (2001:339) Corcagh Demesne, Clondalkin, Co. Dublin: monitoring. www.excavations.ie.
Carroll, J. 2001b (2001:340) Corcagh Demesne, Clondalkin, Co. Dublin: human burial, corn-drying kilns. www.excavations.ie.
Carroll, J. 2004 (2004:0495) Darcytown/Glebe South, Co. Dublin: monitoring. www.excavations.ie.
Carroll, J. 2005 (2005:519) Old Orchard Twin Restaurants, Butterfield Avenue, Rathfarnham, Co. Dublin: no archaeological significance. www.excavations.ie.
Carroll, J. 2008. *Archaeological excavations at Rosepark, Balrothery, Co. Dublin. Vol. 1: Balrothery excavations*. Dublin.
Carroll, J., Ryan, F. and Wiggins, K. 2008 *Archaeological excavations at Glebe South and Darcystown, Balrothery, Co. Dublin. Vol. 2: Balrothery excavations*. Dublin.
Clarke, L. 2005 (2005:504) Church Road, Lusk, Co. Dublin: early medieval burial site. www.excavations.ie.
Clinton, M. 1998 The souterrains of County Dublin. In C. Manning (ed.) *Dublin and beyond the Pale: studies in honour of Patrick Healy*, 117–28. Bray.
Clinton, M. 2000 (2000:0315) Kingstown, Co. Dublin: isolated pit. www.excavations.ie.

Clinton, M. 2001a *The souterrains of Ireland*. Bray.

Clinton, M. 2001b (2001:335) Carrickmines Great, Co. Dublin: medieval castle/manorial centre/prehistoric landscape. www.excavations.ie.

Clinton, M. 2002 (2002:0479) Carrickmines Castle, Carrickmines Great, Co. Dublin: prehistoric/medieval castle and landscape/post-medieval. www.excavations.ie.

Cochrane, R. 1893 The ecclesiastical antiquities in the parish of Howth, County of Dublin. Part I. *Journal of the Royal Society of Antiquaries of Ireland* 23, 386–407.

Collins, T. and Coyne, F. 2007 Shape-shifting: enclosures in the archaeological landscape. In C. Manning (ed.) *From ringforts to fortified houses: studies on castles and other monuments in honour of David Sweetman*, 21–32. Bray.

Conway, M. 1997 (1997:079) Ballymount Great, Co. Dublin: 17th-century manorial complex and earlier ditched enclosure. www.excavations.ie.

Conway, M. 1999a (1999:253) Kilshane, Co. Dublin: unenclosed cemetery. www.excavations.ie.

Conway, M. 1999b (1999:248) Gracedieu, Co. Dublin: early Christian cemetery. www.excavations.ie.

Conway, M. 1999c (1999:278) Westereave, Co. Dublin: early Christian cemetery. www.excavations.ie.

Conway, M. 1999d *Director's first findings from excavations at Cabinteely*. Transactions vol. 1. Dublin.

Cooney, G. 1993 Lambay: an island on the horizon. *Archaeology Ireland* 7:4, 24–8.

Corcoran, E. 2009 Multi-period excavations at Barnageeragh, Skerries, Co. Dublin. In Baker (ed.) 2009, 36–50.

Cotter, C. 1990a (1990:030) 'St Olaf's Church', Balally, Co. Dublin: church site (environs of). www.excavations.ie.

Cotter, C. 1990b (1990:039) Porterstown, Co. Dublin: Bronze Age/?early Christian. www.excavations.ie.

Coyne, F. 2006 Excavation of an early medieval 'plectrum-shaped' enclosure at Newtown, Co. Limerick. In J. O'Sullivan and M. Stanley (eds) *Settlement, industry and ritual: proceedings of a public seminar on archaeological discoveries on national road schemes, September 2005*, 63–72. Bray.

Coyne, F. and Collins, T. 2003 Plectrum shaped enclosures-a new site type at Newtown, Co. Limerick. *Archaeology Ireland* 17:4, 17–19.

Desmond, S. 2001 (2001:322) Balally, Co. Dublin: urban medieval. www.excavations.ie.

Devine, E. 2005 (2005:533) Stephenstown, Co. Dublin: possible circular structure. www.excavations.ie.

Doyle, I.W. 1998 The early medieval activity at Dalkey Island, Co. Dublin: a reassessment. *Journal of Irish Archaeology* 9, 89–103.

Doyle, I.W. 2000a (2000:0225) Kilmahuddrick (Grange Castle International Business Park), Clondalkin, Co. Dublin: ring barrow. www.excavations.ie.

Doyle, I.W. 2000b (2000:0226) Nangor (Grange Castle International Business Park), Clondalkin, Co. Dublin: medieval field complex. www.excavations.ie.

Doyle, I.W. 2000c (2000:0213) Brownsbarn-Kilshane, Bord Gáis Éireann Pipeline, Co. Dublin: various. www.excavations.ie.

Doyle, I.W. 2005 Excavation of a prehistoric ring-barrow at Kilmahuddrick, Clondalkin, Dublin 22. *Journal of Irish Archaeology* 14, 43–75.

Duffy, S. 2005 A reconsideration of the site of Dublin's Viking *Thing-mót*. In T. Condit and C. Corlett (eds) *Above and beyond: essays in memory of Leo Swan*, 351–60. Bray.

Dunne, G. 1997 (1997:186) The Old Vicarage, Swords, Co. Dublin: burials. www.excavations.ie.

Elder, S. 2004a (2004:0452) Site 4:3, Grange, Baldoyle, Co. Dublin: complex of pit features. www.excavations.ie.

Elder, S. 2004b (2004:0454) Site 5:2, Grange, Baldoyle, Co. Dublin: pit. www.excavations.ie.

Elder, S. 2004c (2004:0463) Site 10:2, Grange, Baldoyle, Co. Dublin: pit. www.excavations.ie.

Elder, S. 2004d (2004:0446) Grange, Baldoyle, Co. Dublin: testing. www.excavations.ie.

Elder, S. 2004e (2004:0455) Site 5:4, Grange, Baldoyle, Co. Dublin: pit. www.excavations.ie.

Elder, S. 2004f (2004:0451) Site 4:2, Grange, Baldoyle, Co. Dublin: pits. www.excavations.ie.

Elder, S. 2004g (2004:0453) Site 4:4, Grange, Baldoyle, Co. Dublin: enclosure. www. excavations.ie.

Elliott, R. 2001 (2001:338) Corkagh Demesne, Clondalkin, Co. Dublin: pit furnace. www.excavations.ie.

Eogan, G. 1968 Excavations at Knowth, Co. Meath, 1962–1965. *Proceedings of the Royal Irish Academy* 66C, 299–382.

Eogan, G. 1974 Report on the excavation of some passage graves, unprotected inhumation burials and a settlement site at Knowth. *Proceedings of the Royal Irish Academy* 74C, 11–112.

Eogan, G. 1977 The Iron Age–early Christian settlement at Knowth, Co. Meath, Ireland. In V. Markotic (ed.) *Ancient Europe and the Mediterranean: studies presented in honour of Hugh Hencken*, 69–76. Warminster, Wilts.

Evans, E.E. 1968 Archaeology in Ulster since 1920. *Ulster Journal of Archaeology* 31, 3–8

Fitzgerald, M. 2006 Archaeological discoveries on a new section of the N2 in Counties Meath and Dublin. In J. O'Sullivan and M. Stanley (eds) *Settlement, industry and ritual: proceedings of a public seminar on archaeological discoveries on national road schemes, September 2005*, 29–42. Bray.

Fitzpatrick, E. 2009 Native enclosed settlement and the problem of the Irish 'ring-fort'. *Medieval Archaeology* 53, 271–307.

Frazer, W. 2003 (2003:467) Pelletstown and Cabragh, Castleknock, Co. Dublin: three unenclosed burials. www.excavations.ie.

Gerritsen, F. 2003 *Local identities: landscape and community in the late prehistoric Meuse Demesr-Scheldt region*. Amsterdam.

Getty, E. 1855a Notices of the round towers of Ulster. *Ulster Journal of Archaeology* 3, 14–32.

Getty, E. 1855b Notices of the round towers of Ulster (continued). *Ulster Journal of Archaeology* 3, 110–16.

Getty, E. 1855c The round towers of Ulster (continued): Trummery, County Antrim. *Ulster Journal of Archaeology* 3, 292–300.

Giacometti, A. 2006 Living in the landscape. *Archaeology Ireland* 20:2, 36–9.

Giacometti, A. 2007 Excavation report: site of residential development. Development Phase 6, Dun Emer Estate, Lusk, Co. Dublin. Unpublished report prepared for Arch-Tech Ltd. Available at www.arch-tech.ie.

Gowen, M. 1988a (1988:18) Kilshane, Co. Dublin: Christian cemetery. www.excavations.ie.

Gowen, M. 1988b (1988:16) Gracedieu, Co. Dublin: early Christian cemetery, enclosure. www.excavations.ie.

Gowen, M. 1988c (1988:17) Gracedieu, Co. Dublin: medieval, post-medieval structures. www.excavations.ie.

Gowen, M. 1988d (1988:21) Westereave, Co. Dublin: Christian cemetery. www.excavations.ie.

Gowen, M. 1991 (1991:053) Site bounded by St Maelruan's Church and Graveyard, Belgard Road and Main St., Tallaght, Co. Dublin: medieval. www.excavations.ie.

Gowen, M. 1995 (1995:103) Esso, Cabinteely (Mount Offaly): medieval urban. www.excavations.ie.

Gracie, C. 1998 (1998:121) Southern Cross Motorway Route, Balrothery/Firhouse/Scholars-town/Ballycullen/Newtown/Edmondstown/Tibradden/Marley Grange/Taylor's Grange, Co. Dublin: hearth, fulacht fiadh, bowl furnace. www.excavations.ie.

Grogan, E., O'Donnell, L. and Johnston, P. 2007 *The Bronze Age landscapes of the Pipeline to the west: an integrated archaeological and environmental assessment.* Bray.

Halliday, S. 2004 (2004:0651) Mooretown North, Swords, Co. Dublin: early medieval enclosure. www.excavations.ie.

Halpin, A. 2005 Development phases in Hiberno-Norse Dublin: a tale of two cities. In S. Duffy (ed.) *Medieval Dublin VI*, 94–113. Dublin.

Halpin, E. 1994a (1994:092) Finglas bypass, Finglas: possible ecclesiastical enclosure. www.excavations.ie.

Halpin, E. 1994b (1994:093) Finglas bypass, Finglas: possible ecclesiastical enclosure. www.excavations.ie.

Harbison, P. (ed.) 1998 *Beranger's antique buildings of Ireland.* Dublin.

Harrison, S.H. 2001 Viking graves and grave-goods in Ireland. In A.C. Larsen (ed.) *The Vikings in Ireland*, 61–75. Roskilde.

Harkin, M. 2005 St Naithi's Church and graveyard, Dundrum, Co. Dublin. In T. Condit and C. Corlett (eds) *Above and beyond: essays in memory of Leo Swan*, 171–86. Bray.

Hartnett, P.J. and Eogan, G. 1964 Feltrim Hill, Co. Dublin: A Neolithic and early Christian site. *Journal of the Royal Society of Antiquaries of Ireland* 94, 1–38.

Hayden, A. 1998 (1998:130) 1–7 (Rear of) St Agnes Road, Crumlin, Co. Dublin: medieval ditches and fields. www.excavations.ie.

Hayden, A. 2003 (2003:0602) Church Road, Finglas: early medieval. www.excavations.ie.

Hencken, H. 1938 Cahercommaun: a stone fort in County Clare. *Journal of the Royal Society of Antiquaries of Ireland* 68, 1–82.

Hencken, H. 1950 Lagore crannog: an Irish royal residence from the seventh to tenth centuries (contributions by Liam Price and Laura E. Start). *Proceedings of the Royal Irish Academy* 53C, 1–247.

Herity, M. 2001 *Ordnance Survey letters Dublin: letters containing information relative to the antiquities of the county of Dublin collected during the progress of the Ordnance Survey in 1837.* Dublin.

Kavanagh, J. 2004 (2004:0599) 4–8 Church Street, Finglas: Viking/medieval/post-medieval. www.excavations.ie.

Keeley, V. 1985 (1985:26) Scholarstown, Co. Dublin: ringfort. www.excavations.ie.

Kerr, T., Harney, L., Kinsella, J., O'Sullivan, A. and McCormick, F. 2009 Early medieval dwellings and settlements in Ireland, AD400–1100. Vol. 2: gazetteer of site descriptions. Submitted for Irish National Strategic Archaeological Research (INSTAR) programme 2009. Available at www.emap.ie.

Kinsella, J. 2010 A new Irish early medieval site type? Exploring the 'recent' archaeological evidence for non-circular enclosed settlement and burial sites. *Proceedings of the Royal Irish Academy* 110C, 89–132.

Larsson, E. 2002a (2002:0639) Ballycullen, Oldcourt, Co. Dublin: monitoring. www.excavations.ie.

Larsson, E. 2002b (2002:0640) Site 1, Ballycullen, Oldcourt, Co. Dublin: possible habitation site.www.excavations.ie.

Larsson, E. 2004a (2004:0644) Kilgobbin Lane/Enniskerry Road, Stepaside, Co. Dublin: early medieval. www.excavations.ie.

Larsson, E. 2004b (2004:0645) Kilgobbin Lane/Enniskerry Road, Stepaside, Co. Dublin: early medieval. www.excavations.ie.

Larsson, E. 2004c (2004:0646) Kilgobbin Lane/Enniskerry Road, Stepaside, Co. Dublin: early historic settlement/fulacht fiadh. www.excavations.ie.

Lawlor, H.C. 1925 *The monastery of Saint Mochaoi of Nendrum Belfast.* Belfast.

Ledwich, E. 1790 *Antiquities of Ireland.* Dublin.

Liversage, G.D. 1968 Excavations at Dalkey Island, Co. Dublin, 1956–1959. *Proceedings of the Royal Irish Academy* 66C, 53–233.

Lynch, P. 2002 (2002:0473) Bellinstown, Co. Dublin: Iron Age ring-barrow. www.excavations.ie.

Lynch, R. 1998 (1998:222) 'The Brehon's Chair', Taylorsgrange, Co. Dublin: multi-period. www.excavations.ie.

Tobin, R. 2002 (2002:0604) Jordanstown (BGE 6/12/1): cereal-drying kilns. www.excavations.ie.

McCabe, S. 2002a (2002:0623) Lusk, Co. Dublin, monitoring: prehistoric burial-pit, pit and kiln. www.excavations.ie.

McCabe, S. 2002b (2002:0628) Lusk, Co. Dublin: prehistoric burial-pit, pit and kiln. www.excavations.ie.

McCabe, S. 2002c (2002:0627) Lusk, Co. Dublin: hearth and possible cremation pit. www.excavations.ie.

McCabe, S. 2002d (2002:0698) Woodside, Co. Dublin: metal waste pit, Bronze Age hut and 18th-century stone structure. www.excavations.ie.

McCarthy, C. 2009 Final excavation report, vol. 1. Residential development. Ballynakelly, Newcastle, Co. Dublin. Unpublished report prepared for Arch-Tech Ltd. Available at www.arch-tech.ie.

McConway, C. 1994 (1994:102) St Maelruan's, Tallaght, Co. Dublin: early Christian enclosure. www.excavations.ie.

McConway, C. 1995 (1995:111) St Maelruan's, Tallaght, Co. Dublin: medieval. www.excavations.ie.

McConway, C. 1996 (1996:068) Nangor Castle, Clondalkin, Co. Dublin: medieval. www.excavations.ie.

McGowan, L. 2004 (2004:0483) Cheeryhound, Co. Dublin: early medieval corn-drying kiln. www.excavations.

McLoughlin, G. 2004 (2004:0513) Balgriffin Park, Co. Dublin: ditch, possibly enclosing church site. www.excavations.ie.

Monk, M.A. and Kelleher, E. 2005 An assessment of the archaeological evidence for Irish corn-drying kilns in the light of the results of archaeological experiments and archaeobotanical studies. *Journal of Irish Archaeology* 14, 77–114.

Moore, E. 2001 (2001:448) Lusk, Co. Dublin: early ecclesiastical enclosure ditch. www.excavations.ie.

Moriarty, C. 2005 (2005:419) Drinan/Nevinstown East, Co. Dublin: prehistoric and early medieval. www.excavations.ie.

Mount, C. 1990 (1990:029). 'Cross Church of Moreen', Balally, Co. Dublin: church site within enclosure. www.excavations.ie.

Mount, C. and Keeley, V. 1990 An early medieval strap-tag from Balally, County Dublin. *Journal of the Royal Society of Antiquaries of Ireland* 120, 120–5.

Murphy, D. 1999 (1999:173) 1–7 St Agnes Rd, Crumlin, Co. Dublin: medieval church enclosure. www.excavations.ie.

Murphy, D. 2002 (2002:0472) St Peter's Church, Balrothery, Co. Dublin: early medieval. www.excavations.ie.

Newman, C. 1990 (1990:045) St Maelruan's Church, Tallaght, Co. Dublin: early Christian site. www.excavations.ie.

O'Brien, E. 1977–9 (1977–9:0036) Ballyman, Co. Dublin: habitation site. www.excavations.ie.

O'Brien, E. 1984 Ballyman, Co. Dublin. *Medieval Archaeology* 28, 255–6.

O'Brien, E. 1985a Ballyman, Co. Dublin. *Medieval Archaeology* 29, 214.

O'Brien, E. 1985b (1985:022) Ballyman, Co. Dublin. www.excavations.ie.

O'Brien, E. 1986 (1986:021) 'Glen Munire', Ballyman, Co. Dublin. www.excavations.ie.

O'Brien, E. 1990 (1990:043) Old Bawn Road, Tallaght, Co. Dublin: early Christian (?) ditch. www.excavations.ie.

O'Brien, E. 1995 A tale of two cemeteries. *Archaeology Ireland* 9:3, 13–15.

O'Brien, E. 1998 The location and context of Viking burials at Kilmainham and Islandbridge. In H.B. Clarke, M. Ní Mhaonaigh and R. Ó Floinn (eds) *Ireland and Scandinavia in the early Viking Age*, 203–21. Dublin.

O'Brien, E. 2005 An early medieval fulacht fiadh at Ballyman, Co. Dublin. In T. Condit and C. Corlett (eds) *Above and beyond: essays in memory of Leo Swan*, 293–302. Bray.

O'Brien, R. 1997 (1997:087) Grange Castle Business Park, Kilmahuddrick, Clondalkin, Co. Dublin: medieval. www.excavations.ie.

O'Carroll, F. 1998 (1998:218) Church Lane, Swords, Co. Dublin: urban medieval. www.excavations.ie.

O'Carroll, F. 2000 (2000:0347) Church Lane, Swords, Co. Dublin: urban medieval. www.excavations.ie.

O'Connell, A. 2009 Excavations at Church Road and the early monastic foundation at Lusk, Co. Dublin. In Baker (ed.) 2009, 51–63.

O'Donnchadha, B. 2003 (2003:455) Balally, Co. Dublin: early Christian enclosure. www.excavations.ie.

O'Donovan, E. 2008 The Irish, the Vikings and the English: new archaeological evidence from excavations at Golden Lane, Dublin. In S. Duffy (ed.) *Medieval Dublin VIII*, 36–130. Dublin.

O'Donovan, E. and Geber, J. 2009 Archaeological excavations on Mount Gamble Hill: stories from the first Christians in Swords. In Baker (ed.) 2009, 64–74.

O'Donovan, E. and Geber, J. 2010 Excavations on Mount Gamble Hill, Swords, Co. Dublin. In C. Corlett and M. Potterton (eds) *Death and burial in early medieval Ireland in the light of recent archaeological excavations*, 227–38. Dublin.

Ó Floinn, R. 1991 (1991:050) 'Graves' Moat', Loughlinstown: early medieval cemetery. www.excavations.ie.

Ó Floinn, R. 1998. The archaeology of the early Viking age in Ireland. In H.B. Clarke, M. Ní Mhaonaigh and R. Ó Floinn (eds) *Ireland and Scandinavia in the early Viking Age*, 131–65. Dublin.

Ó Floinn, R. and Cherry, S. 1991 (1991:049) Lambay Island, Co. Dublin: burial. www.excavations.ie.

Ó hÉailidhe, P. 1982 Three unrecorded early grave-slabs in County Dublin. *Journal of the Royal Society of Antiquaries of Ireland* 112, 139–41.

O'Kelly, M.J. 1958 Church Island near Valencia, Co. Kerry. *Proceedings of the Royal Irish Academy* 59C, 57–136.

O'Kelly, M.J. 1967 Knockea, Co. Limerick. In E. Rynne (ed.) *North Munster studies: essays in commemoration of Monsignor Michael Moloney*, 72–101. Limerick.

Ó Néill, J. 2000a (2000:0205) Ballymount Castle, Ballymount Great, Co. Dublin: Iron Age(?), medieval and post-medieval. www.excavations.ie.

Ó Néill, J. 2002b (2002:0462) Ballymount, Ballymount Great, Co. Dublin: multi-period site. www.excavations.ie.

Ó Néill, J. 2006 Excavation of pre-Norman structures on the site of an enclosed early Christian cemetery at Cherrywood, County Dublin. In S. Duffy (ed.) *Medieval Dublin VII*, 66–88. Dublin.

Ó Néill, J. and Coughlan, J. 2010 An enclosed early medieval cemetery at Cherrywood, Co. Dublin. In C. Corlett and M. Potterton (eds) *Death and burial in early medieval Ireland in the light of recent archaeological excavations*, 239–50. Dublin.

O'Reilly, P.J. 1901a The Christian sepulchral leacs and free-standing crosses of the half-barony of Rathdown. Part I. *Journal of the Royal Society of Antiquaries of Ireland* 31, 134–61.

O'Reilly, P.J. 1901b The Christian sepulchral leacs and free-standing crosses of the half-barony of Rathdown. Part II. *Journal of the Royal Society of Antiquaries of Ireland* 31, 246–58.

O'Reilly, P.J. 1901c The Christian sepulchral leacs and free-standing crosses of the half-barony of Rathdown. Part III. *Journal of the Royal Society of Antiquaries of Ireland* 31, 385–403.

Ó Ríordáin, B. 1971 Excavations at High Street and Winetavern Street, Dublin. *Medieval Archaeology* 15, 73–85.

Ó Ríordáin, B. 1976 The High Street excavations. In B. Almqvist and D. Greene (eds) *Proceedings of the seventh Viking congress, Dublin, 15–21 August 1973*, 135–40. London.

Ó Riordáin, S.P. 1942 The excavation of a large earthen ring-fort at Garranes, Co. Cork. *Proceedings of the Royal Irish Academy* 47C, 77–150.

O'Sullivan, A. 2003 The Harvard Archaeological Mission and the politics of the Irish Free State. *Archaeology Ireland* 17:1, 20–3.

O'Sullivan, A. 2008 Early medieval houses in Ireland: social identity and dwelling places. *Peritia* 20, 226–56.

O'Sullivan, J. 1998 Nationalists, archaeologists and the myth of the Golden Age. In M.A. Monk and J. Sheehan (eds) *Early medieval Munster: archaeology, history and society*, 178–89. Cork.

Opie, H. 2001 (2001:344) Coldwinter, Co. Dublin: Iron Age. www.excavations.ie.

Phelan, S. 2003 (2003:457) Baldonnell Lower, Co. Dublin: corn-drying kiln. www.excavations.ie.

Prunty, J. 2009. Nineteenth-century antiquarian accounts of medieval and early modern Dublin. In J. Bradley, A.J. Fletcher and A. Simms (eds) *Dublin in the medieval world: studies in honour of Howard B. Clarke*, 473–504. Dublin.

Purcell, A. 1999 (1999:246) Parkwest, Gallanstown, Co. Dublin: early Christian cemetery. www.excavations.ie.

Purcell, A. 2000 (2000:0299) Parkwest, Gallanstown, Co. Dublin: vicinity of cemetery. www.excavations.ie.

Raftery, J. 1941 Long stone cists of the early Iron Age. *Proceedings of the Royal Irish Academy* 46C, 299–315.

Rynne, E. 1967 Excavation of a church-site at Clondalkin, Co. Dublin. *Journal of the Royal Society of Antiquaries of Ireland* 97, 29–37.

Seaver, M. 2004 From mountain to sea: excavations at Laughanstown/Glebe. *Archaeology Ireland* 18:1, 8–12.

Seaver, M. 2005 From mountain to sea: excavations in the townlands of Glebe and Laughanstown, County Dublin. In J. O'Sullivan and M. Stanley (eds) *Recent archaeological discoveries on National Road Schemes 2004: proceedings of a seminar for the public, Dublin, September 2004*, 51–64. Bray.

Sikora, M. et al. 2011 *Preliminary report on a Viking warrior grave at War Memorial Gardens, Islandbridge*. In S. Duffy (ed.) *Medieval Dublin XI*, 170–84. Dublin.

Simpson, L. 2000 Forty years a-digging: a preliminary synthesis of archaeological investigations in medieval Dublin. In S. Duffy (ed.) *Medieval Dublin I*, 11–68. Dublin.

Simpson, L. 2005 Viking warrior burials in Dublin: is this the *longphort*? In S. Duffy (ed.) *Medieval Dublin VI*, 11–63. Dublin.

Sleeman J. and Hurley, M. 1987 Brownsbarn, Co. Dublin. In Cleary, R.M., Hurley, M.F and Shee-Twohig, E. (eds) *Archaeological excavations on the Cork-Dublin pipeline*, 71–3. Cork. University College Cork.

Stevens, P. 2004 (2004:0470) St Peter's Church, Balrothery, Co. Dublin: medieval. www.excavations.ie.

Stout, G. 1982 The archaeology of Ballymount Great, Co. Dublin. In C. Manning (ed.) *Dublin and beyond the Pale: studies in honour of Patrick Healy*, 145–54. Bray.

Stout, G. 1991 (1991:052) Margaretstown, Co. Dublin: slab-lined grave. www.excavations.ie.

Stout, G. and Stout, M. 1992 Patterns in the past: County Dublin 5000BC–1000AD. In F.H.A. Aalen and K. Whelan (eds) *Dublin city and county: from prehistory to present*, 5–14. Dublin.

Stout, G. and Stout, M. 2008. *Excavation of a secular cemetery at Knowth Site M, County Meath, and related sites in north-east Leinster*. Dublin.

Stout, M. 1997 *The Irish ringfort*. Dublin.

Swan, D.L. 1989 (1989:021) 'St Doulagh's', Balgriffin, Co. Dublin: early Christian site with medieval and modern church, baptistry and holy well. www.excavations.ie.

Swan, D.L. 1990a (1990:031) 'St Doulagh's', Balgriffin, Co. Dublin: early Christian site with medieval and modern church, baptistry and holy well. www.excavations.ie.

Swan, D.L. 1990b (1990:033) 'Church of St John the Evangelist', Coolock: early Christian and later site. www.excavations.ie.

Tierney, M. 1998 Theory and politics in early medieval Irish archaeology. In M.A. Monk and J. Sheehan (eds) *Early medieval Munster: archaeology, history and society*, 190–9. Cork.

Tobin, R. 2002 (2002:0604) Jordanstown (BGE 6/12/1), Co. Dublin: cereal-drying kilns. www.excavations.ie.

Tobin, R. 2007 Jordanstown. In Grogan, E., O'Donnell, L. and Johnston, P. 2007. *The Bronze Age landscapes of the Pipeline to the west: an integrated archaeological and environmental assessment*, 221–5. Bray.

Van de Noort, R. and O'Sullivan, A. 2006 *Rethinking wetland archaeology*. London.

Wakeman, W.F. 1848 *Archaeologica hibernica: a hand-book of Irish antiquities, pagan and Christian: especially of such as are easy of access from the Irish metropolis*. Dublin.

Wakeman, W.F. 1890–1 Primitive churches in County Dublin. *Journal of the Royal Society of Antiquaries of Ireland* 21, 697–702.

Wakeman, W.F. 1892 Ante-Norman churches in the County of Dublin. *Journal of the Royal Society of Antiquaries of Ireland* 22, 101–6.

Wallace, A. 2000 (2000:0328) Maynetown: enclosure (site of). www.excavations.ie.

Wallace, P. 1984 A reappraisal of the archaeological significance of Wood Quay. In J. Bradley (ed.) *Viking Dublin exposed*, 112–33. Dublin.

Wallace, P. 1985 The archaeology of Viking Dublin. In H. Clarke and A. Simms (eds) *The comparative history of urban origins in non-Roman Europe: Ireland, Wales, Denmark, Germany, Poland and Russia from the ninth to the thirteenth century*, 103–45. Oxford.

Westropp, T.J. 1922 The promontory forts and adjoining remains in Leinster. Part I, Co. Dublin. *Journal of the Royal Society of Antiquaries of Ireland* 52, 52–76.

Defining the 'Pill': the contribution of excavations at Ormond Quay Upper to the interpretation of the original topography of the Liffey foreshore

TERESA BOLGER

INTRODUCTION

Archaeological investigations were undertaken at a development site on the north bank of the Liffey; the site extended across a plot defined by Ormond Quay Upper, Ormond Place, Charles Street West and Ormond Square, Dublin 7 (fig. 3.1). The investigations identified evidence for late prehistoric activity on the Liffey foreshore as well as seventeenth-century land reclamation activity and subsequent post-medieval development and aplottment of the site.

Despite the location of the site within the medieval transpontine suburb of Oxmantown and its position directly facing the medieval town on the south bank of the Liffey, no evidence for medieval activity was uncovered at the site. However, the site does provide important evidence about the topography of this section of the Liffey foreshore, which would be relevant to understanding and reconstructing the medieval topography of the north side of the Liffey.

SUMMARY OF THE EXCAVATION FINDINGS

The archaeological investigations at 31–36 Ormond Quay Upper have produced evidence for four significant phases of activity, stretching from modern times back as far as the Iron Age. Phases I and II were focused in the south of the site and associated with activities on the foreshore – a timber-laced embankment and brushwood surface.

The Phase I embankment (fig. 3.2) is most likely to have acted as a flood bank, decreasing the flow of the Liffey onto the mudflats to its north, rather than as a revetment or quay. The hurdle pathway on the landward side of the embankment suggests that it also provided a routeway to access the foreshore, possibly to undertake fishing or similar activities. Prior to the construction of the Phase I embankment, the environmental evidence indicates that the area was a dynamic river's edge environment with low-lying mud-flats subject to frequent flooding, with carr woodland and freshwater pools present (Allen 2008; Reilly 2008). However, with the construction of first the embankment

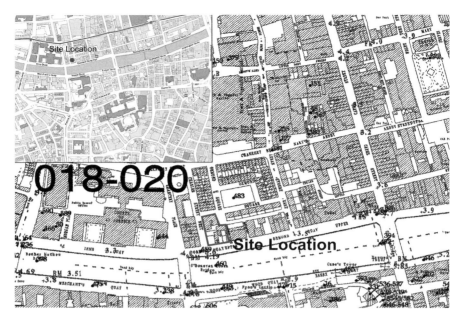

3.1 Site location.

and later the brushwood surface, the profile of the environmental data changes with an increase in the evidence for animal activity and for standing or pooling water (indicative of less frequent flooding or tidal activity). The Phase II brushwood surface was a much simpler and less complex structure than the earlier embankment. While it may have served as a platform within the mudflats, it seems most likely to have functioned as a pathway. Analysis of the carbon-14 determinations obtained from both structures indicates that they were constructed in the Developed Iron Age, probably in very close sequence, during the period *c.*170–50BC.

An interesting facet of the site is the almost complete absence of evidence for any activity between the Iron Age and the commencement of land reclamation activity in the seventeenth century. Historical analyses of the development of the medieval suburb at Oxmantown (for example, Purcell 2003) suggest that there was extensive medieval activity in the environs of the site, with St Mary's Cistercian abbey located on the east side of the Pill and St Saviour's Dominican priory to the west (immediately adjacent to the medieval bridge). A network of medieval streets was located directly to the north (radiating from the east–west oriented Pill Lane, now modern Chancery Street) and the Pill itself was the focus of fishing and boating activities. However, only four sherds of medieval ceramic were retrieved from the site, all of which appear to be stray finds washed in by river activity; no *in situ* deposits of medieval material were identified.

3.2 Plan of the Phase I timber-laced embankment.

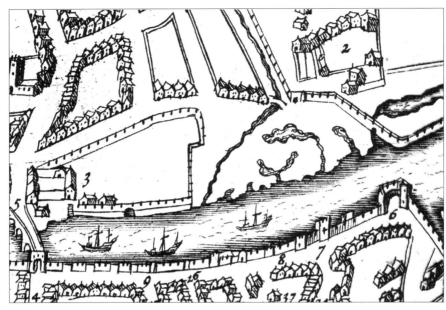

3.3 Extract from Speed's map of Dublin, 1610.

Phase III was characterized by land reclamation associated with the early modern development of the site. This phase can be closely associated with the career of Humphrey Jervis and his developments on the north side of the Liffey and is likely to have centred on the period *c.*1676–80. Phase IV was characterized by post-medieval (eighteenth to early nineteenth century) structural remains. The layout and organization of the structures recorded in the south of the site corresponds closely to the first-edition Ordnance Survey as well as Rocque's earlier plan (1756). 31–36 Ormond Quay Upper and 1–2 Charles Street can be clearly distinguished. The latest activity at the site, Phase V, was most clearly evident in the northern half, where concrete foundations and basements had largely removed any evidence for earlier eighteenth-/nineteenth-century structures as well as truncating the shallow land reclamation deposits on that part of the site.

'THE PILL BEYOND THE WATER'

The site is located on the foreshore at the western edge of the confluence of the Liffey and one of its main tributaries, the Bradogue, in an area referred to during the medieval and early post-medieval period as 'the Pill beyond the water' or, more simply, 'the Pill'. The area appears to have been a broad delta at the mouth of the Bradogue, generally comprising a series of mudflats and

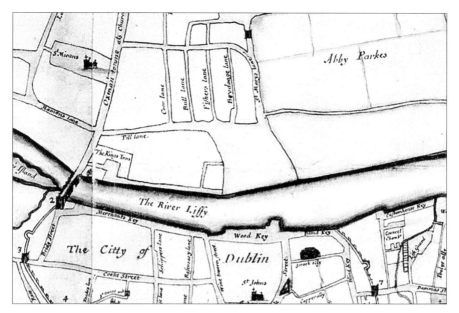

3.4 Extract from de Gomme's map of Dublin, 1673.

sandbars, interspersed with narrow river channels; certainly this is how it appears on the earliest surviving cartographic record of the area – Speed's map of Dublin, 1610 (fig. 3.3). De Courcy (2000, 129) has argued that it may, in earlier times, have been a 'bay', effectively inundated at high tide to create a single body of water, rather than a delta of narrow channels and sandbars depicted on the early seventeenth-century map.

THE TOPOGRAPHY OF THE 'PILL'

Most of our information on the precise location and the topography of the Pill derives from historical sources and maps. Speed's map of Dublin (1610; fig. 3.3) shows the Pill as a series of inlets and streams bounded to the east by St Mary's Abbey and to the west by the walled lands of 'The Innes'. To the north, Pill Lane (corresponding to modern Chancery Street) connects Oxmanstown Street to the walled lands of St Mary's Abbey. The Bradogue extends north, directly outside the west wall of the abbey lands. De Gomme's map of Dublin (1673) shows some realignment of the northern bank of the Liffey (fig. 3.4); the islets and inlets of the Pill, illustrated by Speed, do not appear, nor does the Bradogue. However, the area of the Pill is still clearly distinguishable and appears undeveloped.

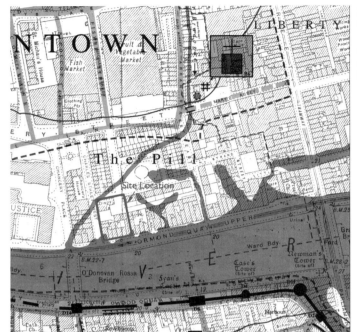

3.5 Extract from the *Irish Historic Towns Atlas*, map 4: Dublin, *c*.840–*c*.1540 (Clarke 2002).

Modern interpretations and cartographic reconstructions of the topography of the Pill (drawing primarily on these two source maps) have indicated that the arc of the Pill extended from Chancery Place in the west to Capel Street on the east, with the main channel of the Bradogue curving to the north of the excavation site at 31–36 Ormond Quay Upper, and entering the Liffey at a point between Chancery Place and Charles Street (fig. 3.5). The Pill appears not to have extended north of the line formed by Chancery Street and St Mary's Abbey, while there are suggestions of at least one channel extending eastwards from it, parallel to the Liffey, following the line of the present Strand Street Great.

Archaeological investigations on the north shore of the Liffey have been less extensive than those undertaken on the south shore (particularly within the footprint of the medieval city). However, a preliminary assessment of the available results indicates that the eastern extent of the Pill, as suggested by the analysis of historic mapping, is potentially accurate. Investigations at 52–56 Strand Street Great (Walsh 2004) identified a medieval waterfront revetment on an alignment consistent with the possible inlet channel, which is shown extending east from the Pill on Speed's map. A thirteenth-century waterfront revetment was identified during excavations at St Mary's Abbey/Strand Street Little, Dublin (Kehoe 2007); while precise mapping for this structure has not been consulted, the general location corresponds to the suggested eastern limit of the Pill.

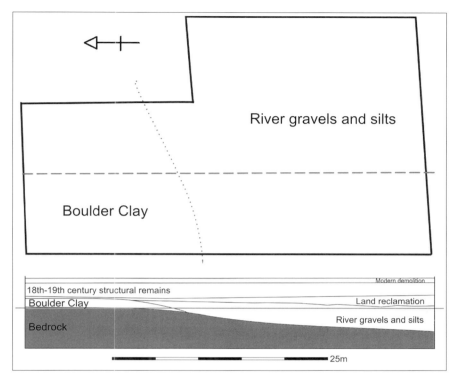

3.6 Reconstructed cross-section of the key stratigraphy at the site.

Modern cartographic reconstructions suggest that the 31–36 Ormond Quay Upper site should lie entirely within the mudflats of the Pill. However, the results of the investigations at the site conflict with this interpretation; the evidence from the excavation places the site squarely on the western edge of the mudflats with the northern half of the site clearly on dry land. While natural riverine deposits were present across a substantial portion of the site footprint, the northern half of the site was characterized by the presence of boulder clay. The interface between the boulder clay and the river gravels was between 30m and 35m north of the Ormond Quay frontage (fig. 3.6).

The post-medieval basements and concrete foundations in the northern part of the site were cut through into the boulder clay; only a very thin deposit of seventeenth-century land reclamation material was found in this part of the site (less than 50cm deep). It does not appear that this section of the site ever lay within the river channel. This was supported by the levels recorded for the occurrence of bedrock at the site; bedrock at the north of the site was *c.*+0.3m OD, dropping to *c.*-0.95m OD in the centre of the site and *c.*-2.4m OD in the south (fig. 3.6).

The location of the interface between boulder clay and riverine deposits within the site would suggest the western limit of the Pill was close to Charles Street West (rather than extending to Chancery Place). Of equal importance, it appears unlikely that the main channel of the Bradogue could have passed to the west of the site (as suggested by modern reconstructions of the topography) – it is far more likely that it was located to the east. This point becomes important when considering the orientation and construction of the Phase I embankment. The embankment curved very gently from north-east to south-west, suggesting that rather than running entirely parallel to the Liffey, it was curving north-east into the Pill. The east end of the structure was also considerably thicker than the west end and had been deliberately reinforced. Despite this, this end of the structure had accumulated the most debris and become the more disorganized, which would suggest that the eastern end of the structure had been more exposed to dynamic riverine activity. It is possible (though difficult to substantiate definitively on the present evidence) that the slight curvature to the Phase I structure reflected a location adjacent to the main channel of the Bradogue and that, in curving to the north-east, the structure was moving from a parallel course to the Liffey, to follow the alignment of the Bradogue. If this is the case then it would indicate that the main channel of the Bradogue was originally located immediately east of the excavation site.

CONCLUSIONS

While the excavations at 31–36 Ormond Quay Upper have shed little light on the medieval activity along the riverfront, they have shed important light on the original topography and early development of the north shore of the River Liffey. The investigations have produced definite evidence for the location of the original shoreline of the Liffey and the western edge of the Pill, as well as the evolution and development of that shoreline.

A more accurate understanding of the original topography can contribute not only to improving our reconstruction and understanding of the historic riverfront, but also to the more accurate prediction of the location of archaeologically sensitive material. The evidence from this investigation indicates that the western edge of the Pill and the main channel of the River Bradogue lie further east than previously predicted. It indicates that this confluence of the two rivers was the focus of potentially complex settlement activity in later prehistory, during the Developed Iron Age. The Phase I structure is a clear attempt to actively manage the river frontage; the environmental evidence from the investigations clearly indicates that the structure had a significant and altering impact on the local environment. The scope of this intervention along the river frontage suggests that a substantial (though perhaps short-lived) Iron Age settlement was located in the immediate environs of the site.

The absence of medieval deposits at the site suggests that, despite its seemingly prime location, medieval activity was focused in other areas of the Pill. It is likely that, at least partially as a result of the Iron Age interventions at the site, the main shoreline of the river could have been located further to the south and east by the medieval period.

ACKNOWLEDGMENTS

The investigations at this site were funded by John Paul Construction Ltd. I would also like to thank the staff of Margaret Gowen and Co. Ltd, and those who worked on the investigations at the site, at various stages – Kevin McInerney, Michael Moran, Antoine Arekian, Gary Devlin, Ciara Griffin, Stefan Bueck, Peter Kerins, Kevin Weldon and Riona Doolin; in particular thanks are due to Ingela Ericson (site supervisor) and Gary Devlin (surveyor). Specialist analysis of finds and samples from the sites was undertaken by Lorna O'Donnell (wood), Ryan Allen (macrofossil plant remains), Dr Eileen Reilly (beetles), Jonny Geber (human and faunal remains) and Siobhan Scully (ceramics and small finds).

BIBLIOGRAPHY

Allen, Ryan 2008 Assessment of the macrofossil plant remains from 31–36 Ormond Quay Upper/Ormond Place/Charles Street West/Ormond Square, Dublin 7. Unpublished report.

Clarke, H.B. (ed.) 2002 *Dublin Part 1, to 1610: Irish historic town atlas no. 11.* Dublin.

De Courcy, J.W. 2000 Bluffs, bays and pools in the medieval Liffey at Dublin. In *Irish Geography* 33:2, 117–33.

Hayden, Alan 2004 Excavation of the medieval river frontage at Arran Quay, Dublin. In Seán Duffy (ed.) *Medieval Dublin V*, 149–242. Dublin.

Kehoe, Helen 2007 St Mary's Abbey/Strand Street Little, Dublin. In Isabel Bennett (ed.) *Excavations 2004.* Bray.

Purcell, Emer 2003 Land-use in medieval Oxmantown. In Seán Duffy (ed.) *Medieval Dublin IV*, 193–228. Dublin.

Reilly, Eileen 2008 Insect remains analysis from the excavations at 31–36 Ormond Quay Upper/ Ormond Place/Charles Street West/Ormond Square, Dublin 7. Unpublished report.

Walsh, Claire 2004 52–56 Strand Street Great, Dublin. In Isabel Bennett (ed.) *Excavations 2002.* Bray.

Preliminary report on a Viking warrior grave at War Memorial Park, Islandbridge

MAEVE SIKORA, BARRA Ó DONNABHÁIN
AND NIAMH DALY

ABSTRACT

The discovery of a Viking sword and spearhead was reported to the National Museum of Ireland in 2007. The artefacts were found accidentally when a trench for electrical cables was being dug at the War Memorial Park in Islandbridge, Dublin. A rescue excavation was undertaken in order to recover any other artefacts that may have been damaged during the ground works. A disturbed inhumation and three copper-alloy objects were found in the course of the excavation. This report is a preliminary summary of the findings of the excavation. An analysis of the skeletal remains and the results of isotopic analysis of bone and tooth enamel suggest a younger male who may have grown up in Scandinavia. It is suggested that the finds together represent the grave of a Scandinavian warrior.

BACKGROUND

The discovery of an iron sword and spearhead was reported to the National Museum of Ireland in October 2007. The artefacts had been found in 2004, by Mr Liam Byrne, a contractor laying electrical cables in the War Memorial Park at Islandbridge, Dublin.[1]

The site of the discovery was in the garden of a lodge immediately inside the entrance to the War Memorial Park off South Circular Road.[2] The park, which occupies an area approximately 1km from east to west, was laid out in the early 1930s as a memorial to those Irish who died fighting in the First

[1] Mr Byrne had made a number of attempts to report the find. The 2007 report was initially made to Tom Condit, Archaeologist, National Monuments Section of the Department of the Environment, Heritage and Local Government, through Denis O'Sullivan, head gardener at the War Memorial Park in Islandbridge. Thanks are due to Margaret Gormley, Hugh Bonar, Denis O'Sullivan and all the Office of Public Works staff at the War Memorial Gardens who assisted on the excavation. Thanks are also due to Carol Smith and Fiona Reilly for assistance on the excavation. Isotopic analysis was conducted in Arizona State University under the direction of Dr Kelly Knudson at the Archaeological Chemistry Laboratory. [2] IGR 312592 234167.

World War. It is situated on the south side of the Liffey, west of South Circular Road and north of Con Colbert Road. On the first edition of the Ordnance Survey 6-inch-to-one-mile map, it is marked as the townland of Inchicore North. The land slopes downward from the ridge at Inchicore to the river at Islandbridge. As Clarke notes, the highest point to which the tide now flows is the weir at Islandbridge, which may have been built in the early 1300s by the Knights Hospitaller of the nearby priory of Kilmainham (Clarke 2002). The underlying rock of the area is calp limestone and overlying the bedrock are deposits of boulder clay (Clarke 2002).[3]

The site where the artefacts were discovered is located on the edge of what was known as 'the great pit', a gravel pit that was in use in the 1860s. A number of Scandinavian furnished burials were discovered through gravel extraction at that time (Wilde 1866). This area is described by Sir William Wilde as being 'in the fields sloping down from the ridge of Inchicore to the Liffey, and to the south-west of the village of Islandbridge, outside the municipal boundary of the city of Dublin' (Wilde 1866, 13). The first edition (1844) Ordnance Survey map shows a long, narrow pit extending from the backs of houses fronting onto South Circular Road, almost to the eastern edge of the Memorial Garden. A larger-scale map published in 1868 (from an 1867 survey) shows a gravel pit having extended northwards all the way along behind the row of houses on South Circular Road.[4] Wilde notes how the burials were found resting on the gravel, which underlay dark alluvial soil varying from 'eighteen inches to two feet in depth' (Wilde 1866, 14).

The gate lodge beside the north-eastern corner of the War Memorial Park was built in the 1930s, when the park was laid out. The northern boundary of the front garden of the lodge appears to have been changed in the mid-1990s or early 2000s to allow for a new footpath and road to the north. The size of the garden appears to have been reduced and a new boundary wall was built, running north-west/south-east. The foundation of this wall appears to have disturbed the burial discussed below.

THE 2004 DISCOVERY

When found, the sword was lying flat, and the spearhead was discovered in the spoil heap. The finder also mentioned seeing human remains in the trench, which he thought had remained in the ground when the trench was backfilled. He suggested that the remains had been under or beside the boundary wall of the Memorial Park. The National Parks and Wildlife Service commissioned a geophysical survey of the area but, while a few areas of archaeological potential

3 See also O'Brien 1998 for a map of the area showing the contours.   4 We are grateful to Stephen Harrison for drawing our attention to this map.

were noted to the west of the site, nothing was found in the immediate area where the burial was discovered.[5] No distinctive anomalies suggesting the existence of further burials were noted (Nicholl 2008).

In late 2008, the National Museum of Ireland conducted a small rescue excavation in order to recover any other associated artefacts that might have been disturbed in the course of the digging of the cable trench. The potential recovery of any human remains, albeit disturbed, was particularly important given the fact that so few were retained from Viking graves discovered in the nineteenth century.[6] Estimation of sex in Viking graves in Ireland has therefore been largely dependent on the nature of the grave-goods and while for the most part this is reliable (Harrison 2001, 66), the examination of associated human remains is clearly preferable.

ARTEFACTS FOUND IN 2004

Iron sword (2007:215): The sword found by Liam Byrne is a large, single-edged iron sword. It can be classed as a Rygh type 491 (R491) sword, or a Petersen Type C sword (Rygh 1885, 28; Petersen 1919, 66–70). The tip of the blade is broken. The extant blade measures 68.5cm long by 5.5cm wide at the guard, tapering to 4cm at the broken tip. The grip and pommel were apparently intact when found but were broken by the time they were taken into the National Museum. The sword would have measured 85.5cm in total length when found. No traces of other metal were found when the sword was x-rayed, but traces of wood and leather, probably from the scabbard, have been noticed on the surface of the blade.[7]

This type of sword is distinguished by its very heavy weight and appearance. The pommel is five-sided, and its shape has been compared to a cocked hat (Walsh 1998, 226). It is generally considered to be an early type: Petersen suggests that it developed from an earlier Migration-period weapon, and considers it to be a Norwegian type that was in use up to the mid-ninth century. Petersen lists more than one hundred examples from Norway. The type has a wide distribution across the country (Petersen 1919, 66–70). Both single- and double-edged swords of this type are known, but the majority of examples in Norway are single-edged, and these are generally considered to be the earlier form (Graham-Campbell 1980, 67).

5 08R174, undertaken by John Nicholl. The geophysical survey did show areas of potentially significant anomalies in the part of the park closest to the river; however, without excavation it is not possible to state whether these features are archaeological, modern or natural (Nicholl 2008).   6 Apart from recent excavations carried out by Simpson at Ship Street Great and South Great George's Street (Simpson 2002, 2003, 2004) and O'Donovan's work at Golden Lane (O'Donovan 2007), human remains are lacking for a large proportion of furnished Viking graves in Dublin.   7 We are grateful to Carol Smith and Jennifer Mulrooney of the Conservation Department in the National Museum of Ireland for the

In his 1998 article, Aidan Walsh counted eight examples of this type known from Ireland (Walsh 1998, 226). Six of the type C swords found in Ireland are single-edged, and only two are double-edged. Six come from the Kilmainham/ Islandbridge grave-fields, one was found at a crannog in Moynalty Lough, in the townland of Moynaltyduff, Co. Monaghan, and one is unprovenanced (Walsh 1998, 226–7). The vast majority, therefore, come from graves in Dublin. Within the Dublin provenance, Harrison and Ó Floinn note that single-edged swords have a limited distribution, and have only been found in the Kilmainham/Islandbridge complex (Harrison and Ó Floinn forthcoming).

Iron spearhead (2007:216): The spearhead found in 2004 is also of iron and an x-ray has shown that it has seven copper-alloy rivets in the socket. Five of the rivets pierce the socket from one side to the other, while the lowermost piercing is actually formed of two rivets, which meet in the centre of the socket. The tip of the blade appears to have been deliberately bent backwards on itself in antiquity. It is an exceptionally long example, measuring approximately 57cm in total length. The blade measures 4cm in maximum width and the socket is 16cm long. The spearhead is of a similar type to a number discovered at Kilmainham/Islandbridge in the nineteenth century (Bøe 1940, 62–4) and which Harrison and Ó Floinn now term 'Dublin type' (Harrison and Ó Floinn, forthcoming).[8] The blade is slender and does not have a prominent mid-rib like the Scandinavian types. In his catalogue, Bøe (1940, 26) notes that several examples of this type of spearhead were found at Kilmainham/Islandbridge, as well as in other localities in Ireland, but that the type is very rarely found in the Scandinavian North. Bøe comments that the slender shape of the blade and the socket and the sloping transition from blade to socket are characteristic of this type (ibid., 26). This type is also characterized by the lack of a prominent mid-rib and the presence of one to four copper-alloy rivets in the socket. Bøe compares the type to Rygh's R529 but he notes that in the Irish examples the sockets were shorter in comparison with the length of the blade (ibid., 26). He suggests some local influence in their manufacture, and refers to them as an Insular type.

The example found in 2004 conforms broadly to this so-called Insular type, even though some differences are also apparent: it has a higher number of rivets than average – seven – and at 16cm the socket is longer than the average. One example of Bøe's Insular type, from Strokestown, Co. Roscommon, is of similar length to the 2004 find, being 42.5cm long (Bøe 1940, 88).[9] Another

analysis of the sword during conservation.   8 Harrison and Ó Floinn point out that this type of spearhead is largely confined to Dublin. The only exception is an example from a burial at Larne (Harrison and Ó Floinn forthcoming). Interestingly, the Larne burial also contained a ringed pin, a rare grave-find in the corpus of Viking graves outside of Dublin also.   9 NMI Wk4. This was incorrectly provenanced to the River Shannon by Bøe (Ó Floinn 1998, 148).

example found at Islandbridge, and on display in the National Museum of Ireland (Bøe 1940, 64), measures 51.6cm in length, but this seems unusual, and most are around 30cm in overall length.

THE 2008 EXCAVATION

Electricity Supply Board (ESB) maps of the location of the electrical cable showed that the trench had been dug across the front lawn of the lodge, dipped to go under the concrete wall bounding the property and came out the other side. An area measuring *c*.4m by *c*.1.8m was opened around this trench.

The ESB trench had cut through redeposited garden soil, which contained large quantities ceramic sherds, glass sherds, modern iron nails, modern plastic wrappings, painted wood and animal bone at all levels. The fill of the trench consisted of tarmac and modern debris. Disarticulated human and animal bone was also found scattered throughout the fill of the trench. All of the human bone found in the fill was disturbed and most showed evidence of recent breaks suggesting that portions of a skeleton had been disturbed during the excavation of the trench.

In situ human remains (08E0693:001) were discovered at a depth of 80–90cm below ground level in a triangle of undisturbed ground between the ESB cable trench and the boundary wall. Portions of the right scapula and clavicle, fragments of seven right ribs, unsided fragments of radius and ulna, and fragments of vertebra remains were found and have been identified by Ó Donnabháin (see Appendix 4.1) as those of a young adult male. The burial extended *c*.20cm underneath the wall foundation, and some portions of ribs had adhered to the base of the concrete foundation, which had been placed directly on the bones.[10] These remains were lying on gravel and exposed bedrock. The bones were in poor condition, exhibited recent breaks and were probably disturbed by at least two separate events: the construction of the wall and the digging of the cable trench. Two fragments of a right mandible were also found underneath the wall foundation, in a disturbed context.

It appears that the individual was lying in a supine position and, based on the position of the *in situ* vertebrae, was oriented approximately north–south, with the head at the north. The left hip appears to have been slightly flexed, as indicated by the portion of the left femur, which was *in situ*. The upper and lower sections of the body had been disturbed and removed or displaced when the wall was constructed.

As was probably the case with the other graves discovered here (Wilde 1866), there was no evidence for stone protection around the grave, but the burial respected a small rock outcrop to the south.

---

10 All visible bone was excavated. The left side of the body and the skull were probably disturbed and displaced during previous groundworks.

ARTEFACTS FROM THE 2008 EXCAVATION

Teeth were recovered in the area of the ribs, indicating that the human remains were badly disturbed, and the associated grave-goods may have been slightly displaced, although organics were fortuitously preserved on some of the copper-alloy objects. Copper staining on some rib bones suggests that the artefacts were originally lying on the torso.

A copper-alloy ringed pin was found lying in the area of the rib bones, and portions of a copper-alloy dish, perhaps a pan for a balance scales, were also found in this area. All of these artefacts were lying underneath the wall foundation and were therefore excavated in section. The ringed pin was parallel to the long axis of the burial, with the ring of the pin at the north. A third object, a flat piece of copper-alloy, was also found in this area.

Copper-alloy ringed pin (08E0693:002): The ringed pin is of Fanning's plain-ringed loop-headed variety. The shank of the pin measures 11.6cm in length and it is decorated with incised parallel and crossed lines on the lower shank of the pin. The lower portion of the shank is bent, indicating that it had been used prior to its deposition. The ring is circular with narrowed terminals which meet under the loop on the pin. The pin is rectangular in cross-section, while the ring has a round section. Fanning describes this type of ringed pin as the simplest of all, and the most popular type in the Viking period. It is also the most common type outside of Ireland, in the Scottish Isles and the Isle of Man. A small number of pins of probable Irish manufacture are known from Norway, but the majority found in Scandinavia were probably made locally (Fanning 1994, 21–3).

Most ringed pins found in Viking graves in Ireland have been found in Dublin (Wilde 1866, 20; Coffey and Armstrong 1910, 121; Bøe 1940, 88; Harrison and Ó Floinn, forthcoming). Outside Dublin, ringed pins are known from a Viking grave at Larne, Co. Antrim (Bøe 1940; Ó Floinn 1998, Fanning 1970), and from Woodstown, Co. Waterford (O'Brien et al. 2005, 35). Both of these were male interments accompanied by weapons.

Copper-alloy balance pan (?) (08E0693:003): This object is similar in form and size to a balance pan, but is unusual in that the edge of the pan does not appear to be perforated as would be expected if it were to function as part of a balance scales.[11] It is a dished circular object made of copper-alloy and measuring 4.3cm in diameter, somewhat smaller than the other scale pans found at Islandbridge (see Bøe 1940, 49–50). It was originally convex but was dented in

11 There is some damage to the edge where one perforation may have been, but the lack of perforations around the remainder of the circumference would seem to indicate that this pan was not perforated.

antiquity, apparently by force applied to the convex side. Traces of possible fur have been noted on the inside of the bowl while traces of other organics – leather or wood – have been identified on the outside.[12]

The convex face is decorated with faintly incised compass-drawn concentric rings and arcs, forming a marigold pattern. This decoration has been noted on other scale pans, such as a pair from Fishamble Street, Dublin (NMI E190:7673), although in this case the decoration is on the inside of the pan. There is no evidence for tinning on this pan, unlike some of the others from Kilmainham/Islandbridge (Bøe 1940, 50).

If the pan is to be interpreted as part of a balance, it was either unfinished or never intended to be used. Traces of textile indicate that it was either placed near clothing on the body of the interred, or perhaps wrapped in textile.

Fragment of a copper-alloy object (08E0693:004): This object is also of copper-alloy. It is a flat strip of copper-alloy tapering at one end to a rounded point, and broken at the wide end. It was found directly underneath the wall foundation. Its function is not clear, but it was part of a larger object, the remainder of which may have been removed or disturbed when the wall foundation was laid. Given the presence of a possible scale pan, it is tempting to consider this to be part of a balance, such as a pointer; however, it is much broader and the point is less tapered than most similar examples (see Bøe 1940, 51; Shetelig 1940, 155–66). It measures 55.87mm in length and is 8.5mm wide at the wide end. An incised longitudinal line is visible on one face. If this object was intended to be part of a balance, it was not likely to be the same object to which the pan was intended to belong, as it is proportionally larger than other pointers known, while the pan is relatively small.

Bøe (1940, 50) lists four separate finds of scales from the Kilmainham/ Islandbridge complex and Harrison and Ó Floinn have been able to ascribe some of these finds to more exact acquisition groups, and, consequently, locations (Harrison and Ó Floinn forthcoming). One balance from an 1866 acquisition group comprises a beam and pans, which have a diameter of 6.5cm (R2402). Another fine example comes from another acquisition group, R2395, which Harrison and Ó Floinn state were almost certainly found with the six weights having a diameter of 7.9cm (Harrison and Ó Floinn, forthcoming; see also Bøe 1940, 49–50). Bøe compares all these scales to Rygh's R476, the only type of balance illustrated in his text.

These do not appear to have find associations and so it is not possible to speculate on whether they come from female or from male interments. In

---

12 If the damage to the pan occurred recently, one would expect the organics to have disintegrated and the pan to fracture completely. We are grateful to Carol Smith, Conservation Department, National Museum of Ireland, for identification of the fur and leather on the surface of the pan.

Scandinavia, weights and scales are found in both male and female interments, though they are mainly associated with males. In his 1940 survey of Insular material found in Norway, Shetelig lists forty-four examples of sets of scales, the vast majority of which come from male graves (Shetelig 1940, 155–66; Harrison 2001, 71). Graham-Campbell disputed the idea that all of these scales are Insular in origin, indicating that there is little evidence to support or deny this (Graham-Campbell 1980). Wamers has pointed out that only a few found in Scandinavia can be definitively said to be Insular in origin (Wamers 1998, 41). Scales remain a rare find in Insular Viking graves and, significantly, are not found in a burial context outside of Dublin, again reinforcing the importance of Dublin even in this early period.[13]

THE GRAVE IN ITS CONTEXT

Although it will never be possible to definitively associate the sword and spearhead found in 2004 with the human remains, copper-alloy objects and ringed pin excavated in 2008, it seems likely that these objects represent one and the same grave. The collection appears to represent the grave of a young male warrior of high social status.

The main body of comparable material for this grave is that found in the Islandbridge/Kilmainham/Inchicore area (Wilde 1866; Coffey and Armstrong 1910; Bøe 1940). Graves from this area, the largest cemetery in the Viking west, have produced a rich array of artefacts with an impressive collection of weapons and trading material, among other objects.[14] Finds are recorded as early as the eighteenth century, and during the nineteenth-century construction of the railway, and gravel extraction uncovered further burials. More recently, in the 1930s, a group of burials was found during the laying out of the War Memorial Park at Islandbridge (Wilde 1866; Coffey and Armstrong 1910; Bøe 1940; O'Brien 1998; Ó Floinn 1998; Harrison and Ó Floinn, forthcoming).

The burial discussed here is in Harrison and Ó Floinn's western zone of the burial complex, which has so far produced fifteen burials (Harrison and Ó Floinn, forthcoming).[15] The majority of these came from the 'great gravel pit' already mentioned, many of which were published by Wilde in 1866. The 2004 and 2008 material which is discussed here is thought to represent another burial in this grave-field.

---

13 One pair of similar scales (1989:22A-B) and three decorated weights (2003:35–7) were found at a crannog at Coolure Demesne in Lough Derravarragh, Co. Westmeath (O'Sullivan et al. 2007, 34). **14** Confusion has arisen as to the provenance of many artefacts, and there has been much discussion of how the grave-fields at Kilmainham and Islandbridge should be understood spatially (see O'Brien 1998; Ó Floinn 1998). The author follows Harrison and Ó Floinn's model of a Kilmainham/Islandbridge complex divided into various zones (Harrison and Ó Floinn, forthcoming). **15** It should be noted that this

Although disturbed, the grave and grave-goods reinforce the existing evidence of the social make-up of Scandinavian colonists in early Viking Age Dublin. It has already been noted that Viking graves from various locations in Dublin speak of a substantial population of warrior elite engaged in commercial activity, with a male:female ratio of about 10:1 (Ó Floinn 1998, 142). Weapons are the commonest artefact from male graves (the combination of sword and spearhead being most frequent), while a very significant amount of trading equipment has also been found (Bøe 1940; Ó Floinn 1998, 138; Harrison and Ó Floinn, forthcoming). The results of isotope analysis on bone and tooth enamel from the excavation suggest that this individual is non-local, and perhaps spent his early years in the Scandinavian region.[16]

Bent or mutilated weapons have traditionally been considered to represent cremation burial, with good reason, like the burial from Hesket-in-the Forest in Cumbria, for example (Graham-Campbell 1998, 113), but there is no evidence to support a cremation burial in this case. There may be some other evidence for non-cremation related weapon mutilation – such as at Woodstown, Co. Waterford, where the sword had been broken and the broken pieces were subsequently wrapped in cloth, and deposited in the burial (O'Brien et al. 2005, 35; Harrison and Ó Floinn, forthcoming). An example is also known from a grave discovered in 1934 during the laying out of the War Memorial Park, where the sword was broken and replaced in position (see Bøe 1940, 60, fig. 39). Again, assuming that the sword and spearhead were associated with the inhumation burial discovered here, it suggests that some ritual activity was carried out before interment, which involved making the spearhead effectively useless. It may also be significant that the copper-alloy dish, if it is a scale pan, was not functional either, and in fact seems to have been damaged in antiquity.

CONCLUSIONS

Altogether, this can be considered to be a well-furnished grave, and corresponds with the rich character of Viking graves previously found in this area. The early type of sword also fits with others known from this burial complex, and corroborates the ninth-century date that others have suggested for this complex as a whole.[17]

does not include the five burials found in the 1930s in the War Memorial Park.   **16** Because the teeth were disturbed, it is not possible to definitively associate them with the sword and spearhead, or with the *in situ* remains, though the authors suggest that these are likely to represent the same burial.   **17** In the course of the excavation in 2008, Mr John Connolly of South Circular Road informed us that as a child, some thirty years ago, he had discovered an iron sword while digging for worms to the west of the gate lodge. His description of the sword suggests that it was a large iron Viking-type sword. Unfortunately, Mr Connolly discarded the sword soon after discovery. This probably represents a further warrior burial.

APPENDIX 4.1: THE HUMAN REMAINS FROM THE VIKING AGE
BURIAL RECOVERED FROM ISLANDBRIDGE, DUBLIN (08E693)

Barra Ó Donnabháin

Introduction: An articulated skeleton was found in the grounds of the lodge at the entrance to the War Memorial Park, Islandbridge, Dublin. The skeleton had been cut in recent years by an Electricity Supply Board (ESB) service trench and by the digging of a wall foundation. A number of artefacts were recovered by the workmen who dug the service trench and it was the notification of these finds that brought the burial to the attention of the National Museum of Ireland (NMI). The articulated remains were found in a small triangle of undisturbed soil between the service trench and the wall foundation. The *in situ* remains extended under the concrete that had been poured into the trench dug for the wall foundation. Some of the bones were practically touching the base of the concrete and must have been exposed when the foundation was dug. Most of the remaining human bones were recovered from the backfill of the ESB trench and one of these fragments could be matched with the undisturbed bones. Many animal bones were recovered from the upper levels at the site. Some were also found at the level of the skeleton but none was directly related to the burial. While the skull of this individual was not found, a fragment of mandible was discovered in the disturbed material immediately adjacent to the burial and may be derived from this individual. The bones were in a fragmentary state but were moderately well preserved.

The *in situ* remains: The following remains were found in articulation: fragments of the right scapula and clavicle; fragments of seven right ribs; unsided fragments of the midshafts of a radius and an ulna; the left capitate and lunate; fragments of the sacrum and lumbar vertebrae; the left hip bone; and the proximal end of the left femur. One rib fragment has evidence of copper staining. The body was placed in the grave on its back with the head to the north. The left hip was slightly flexed. It was not possible to determine the positions of the hands.

Age-at-death: The morphology of the pubic symphysis suggests that this individual was in late adolescence or in young adulthood. The epiphysis of the left ischial tuberosity had fused not long before death. This normally fuses between the ages of 16 and 18 years. The epiphyseal plates of the vertebrae were also in the process of fusing at the time of death. This normally occurs between the ages of 20 and 25 (Albert et al. 2010). There is a pronounced epiphyseal line on the left femur, indicating that the head of the femur had fused to the shaft not long before death. Based on these factors, an age-at-death estimate of 18 to 20 years seems most likely.

Sex: The morphology of the sciatic notch of the left hip bone suggests that this was a male. This is also indicated by the maximum diameter of the head of the left femur. It was not possible to estimate the living stature of this individual.

The *ex situ* remains: Some human bones were also found in disturbed contexts, mostly to the south-west of the ESB service trench. The break on one fragment of the femur shaft matches with the *in situ* fragment of that bone. The human remains that had been disturbed have an MNI of one and it seems likely that they are all from the individual represented by the articulated remains. The bones that had been disturbed include: the right hip bone; the right second, third and fourth metatarsals; the left second or third metatarsal; one foot phalanx; and one hand phalanx.

Two fragments of a right mandible were recovered from the area under the wall foundation. One of these is a fragment of a right ramus, while the other is a portion of alveolar bone, also from a right mandible. The following teeth were present in this fragment (the teeth in italics were missing post-mortem):

48	47	46	45	*44*

There was minimal wear on the premolar and second molar, while attrition was more marked on the first molar, where patches of secondary dentine had been exposed. The socket for the third molar suggests that the roots of this tooth were complete. The third molar usually erupts between 17 and 21 years, while the roots are usually complete between 18 and 25, so it is possible that this fragment of mandible was from the same individual as the articulated remains. One loose tooth was also recovered: this was an upper right central incisor.

Pathology: There is what appears to be a small cut-mark on the portion of mandible. The cut area is just 6mm long and is located on the buccal surface of the bone. It is at an oblique angle and is obscured at both ends by postmortem breakage. It has the appearance of perimortem sharp-force trauma, but given that the fragment is small and the cut surface even smaller, damage incurred when the remains were disturbed in recent years cannot be ruled out.

Other than the possible cut-mark described above, the only pathological change noted in the remains occurs in one of the lumbar vertebrae, L5, that was found *in situ*. This has a crescent-shaped lesion at the right anterior superior margin of the centrum, which has an irregular surface and protrudes anteriorly. This type of lesion has received little attention from clinical medicine but has been noted in the palaeo-pathological literature. It may be an early manifestation of an intervertebral osteochon-drosis (Kelly 1982), a degenerative change in the bone that, if the individual had lived, would have been superseded by more typical and symptomatic degenerative changes. More recently, Maat and Mastwijk (2000) have described similar lesions and suggested that they represent avulsion injuries to the vertebral endplate. An avulsion injury occurs when a piece of bone is torn from the main mass of the bone as a result of trauma. Each of these interpretations of the lesions is compatible with the other in that both suggest that physical stress of some kind as the cause of the lesions. It seems likely that apart from minor backache, these lesions are relatively asymptomatic, which is why they have received little attention in the clinical literature. Mays (2007) has recently reported that similar lesions can occur in the vertebrae of people infected with brucellosis. This is a zoonosis that can pass to humans as a result of ingesting the milk or meat of infected animals. The disease will persist for months if untreated but is rarely fatal. However, Mays has further argued that these lesions are more likely to be traumatic in origin unless other skeletal lesions are also present or the remains have been tested for the presence of brucella bacteria DNA. Given the absence of other lesions in this case (though it should be remembered that little of the skeleton has been recovered), it is safer to suggest that the lesion is related to physical stress to the lower back in the form of a traumatic incident or to strenuous physical activity.

APPENDIX 4.2: ISOTOPE RESULTS

Niamh Daly

The isotopic and elemental data from the archaeological human remains from Islandbridge, Dublin, are presented in Table 4.1 and Table 4.2. In this study, we observe from the major, minor and trace element concentrations of the elements calcium (C), phosphorous (P), strontium (Sr) and barium (Ba) that little diagenetic contamination was observed in either the bone or tooth enamel samples analyzed. Therefore, we can suggest that little diagenetic activity is observable in this burial. Thus, these elemental results are crucial with regard to establishing a unique parameter on which to base all the isotopic results.

Palaeodietary analysis

This study produced isotopic values of $\delta^{13}C_{carbonate\ (V\text{-}PDB)} = -25.4‰$ in relation to the tooth enamel sample and $\delta^{13}C_{carbonate\ (V\text{-}PDB)} = -24.2‰$ for the bone sample respectively. In addition, the mean $\delta^{13}C_{collagen\ (V\text{-}PDB)} = -20.2‰±0.0‰$ and mean $\delta^{15}N_{collagen\ (AIR)} = +11.6‰±0.2‰$. The $\delta^{13}C$ data for both the apatite and collagen analysis would be consistent with the consumption of a diet rich in C^3 plants. As C^3 plants demonstrate $\delta^{13}C$ values that range from -20 to $-35‰$, we can suggest that this individual consumed a diet rich in plants that photosynthesized using a C^3 pathway; for example, wheat (*Triticum*), barley (*Hordeum*), and oats (*Avena sativa*). Therefore, this information would correlate perfectly with the fact that Northern Europe is located in a temperate region where the majority of plants are photosynthesized using a C^3 pathway.

Furthermore, terrestrial mammals and birds have a mean bone collagen $\delta^{15}N$ value of $+5.9‰$, whereas marine mammals have an average value of $+15.6‰$ (Schoeninger et al. 1983). In relation to the mean $\delta^{15}N$ values from the collagen analysis, we can suggest that this individual consumed a diet rich in terrestrial mammals. This information correlates with the dietary information documented in the early historical sources from Scandinavia and Ireland as well as the environmental archaeological evidence from previously excavated Viking sites in Dublin. In general, the relatively recent social perception of the Vikings is one of a seafaring people relying on marine sources for both subsistence and trade; however, this assumption was not traceable in the dietary intake of this individual. Therefore, based on this dietary analysis, we can suggest that there appears to be no homogeneous 'Viking diet' recorded from this individual.

Paleomobility

In relation to the received oxygen isotopic data from this sample, the data from the tooth enamel provides a value of $\delta^{18}O_{carbonate\ (V\text{-}PDB)} = -8.9$ and a value of $\delta^{18}O_{carbonate}$

(V-PDB) = −8.4 for the rib bone sample. In order to convert the observed oxygen isotope values into drinking water values, the oxygen isotope data referenced above were converted to a common scale. In this regard, the tooth enamel and bone $\delta^{18}O$ $_{carbonate}$ (V-PDB) values (Vienna Pee Dee Belemnite Formation) were re-referenced to the V-SMOW (Vienna Standard Mean Ocean Water) standard according to Coplen et al. (1983). Therefore, by converting the data via a series of formulas, the tooth enamel sample (-8.9) converts to a value of $\delta^{18}O$ $_{dw\ ‰}$ VSMOW = −14.96±0.01 and the bone sample (-8.4) converts to a value of $\delta^{18}O$ $_{dw\ ‰}$ VSMOW = −14.164±0.04.

According to the International Atomic Energy Agency (IAEA), the oxygen isotope signatures from Ireland range from (-5 to -8‰), and the Scandinavian oxygen isotopic signatures range from (–8 to –11‰). We observe from the stable oxygen isotope analysis that the drinking water levels both in the tooth enamel and bone samples from this Early Viking Age individual are significantly higher than the expected oxygen isotope signatures or values in relation to Ireland (−5 to –8‰), as stated by the IAEA. Furthermore, we can observe that the drinking water levels in both the tooth enamel and the bone samples from this individual are significantly closer to the Scandinavian oxygen isotopic signatures. However, although the stable oxygen isotope values from the Early Viking Age individual are slightly higher, we suggest that this difference in values can be noted from different contributing factors, such as the possibility that the water may have been derived from numerous sources. Climatic variation or the storage and heating of water may also affect isotopic signatures that may affect the results (Knudson 2009). Therefore, these factors must be taken into account when analyzing the oxygen isotope data from this particular individual.

Ultimately, although the oxygen isotope signatures display slightly higher values as stated by the IAEA Scandinavian levels, we suggest that this individual may have originated from a geographic region similar to the Scandinavia oxygen isotope values. We propose that the individual central to this study is non-local to Dublin and spent most of his early life in some region of Scandinavia before coming to Ireland.

Finally, in relation to the radiogenic strontium isotopic ratios, the enamel strontium isotope values are 87Sr/86Sr = 0.71882 and the rib bone strontium isotope values are 87Sr/86Sr = 0.71043. Based on these observations, we suggest that the Early Viking Age individual central to this study originated from an area with older bedrock; that is, different in composition to the available recorded strontium values known for Irish bedrock. Notably, there are differences in radiogenic strontium isotope values of both the tooth enamel and bone samples from this individual. In this regard, the radiogenic strontium isotope value for the tooth enamel is higher than the radiogenic isotope value from both the rib sample and the local signature derived from an archaeological faunal sample from the region. As tooth enamel undergoes little change after it is formed in childhood, we propose that this individual may have moved residence in the later years of his life. In addition, the radiogenic isotope value from the rib sample falls just outside the local signature derived from the Dublin faunal sample. Thus, we suggest that based on this information, this individual moved to Ireland in the period leading up to his death. Therefore, based on the radiogenic strontium isotope values, we can suggest that this individual spent his early years in Scandinavia, and subsequently moved to Ireland in the period leading up to his death.

Table 4.1: Summary of elemental and isotopic analysis, Early Viking Age burial, Islandbridge, Dublin.

Lab Number	Specimen Number	Material	Ca/P	Ba/Sr	$^{87}Sr/^{86}Sr$	Standard deviation	$\delta^{13}C_{c(V-PDB)}$	Standard deviation	$\delta^{8}O_{c(V-PDB)}$	Standard deviation
ACL-2791	DUBL-08E693	LRM2	2.1	0.09	0.71882	0.00667	-25.4	0.04	-8.9	0.01
ACL-2792	DUBL-08E693	rib	2.2	0.11	0.71043	0.00343	-24.2	0.05	-8.4	0.04

Table 4.2: Carbon and nitrogen isotopic data, Early Viking Age burial, Islandbridge, Dublin.

Lab Number	Specimen Number	Material	Mean $\delta^{13}C_{collagen}$ (V-PDB) (‰)	SD	Mean $\delta^{15}N_{collagen}$ (AIR) (‰)	SD	C:N	% C	% N	% collagen
ISB1	DUBL-08E693	Mandible/ Rib	-20.2	0.0	11.6	0.1	3.2	27.6	9.9	3.7

BIBLIOGRAPHY

Bøe, J. 1940 *Part III: Norse antiquities in Ireland*. In H. Shetelig (ed.) *Viking antiquities in Great Britain and Ireland*. Oslo.

Clarke, H.B. 2002 *Dublin Part 1, to 1610: Irish historic town atlas no. 11*. Dublin.

Coffey, G. and Armstrong, E.C.R. 1910 Scandinavian objects found at Islandbridge and Kilmainham. *Proceedings of the Royal Irish Academy* 28C, 107–22.

Coplen, T.B., Kendall, C., Hopple, J. 1983 Comparison of stable isotope reference samples. *Nature* 302, 236–8.

Fanning, T. 1970 The Viking grave-goods discovered near Larne, Co. Antrim in 1840. *Journal of the Royal Society of Antiquaries of Ireland* 100, 71–8.

Fanning, T. 1994 *Viking Age ringed pins from Dublin*. Dublin.

Graham-Campbell, J. 1890 *Viking artefacts: a select catalogue*. London.

Harrison, S.H. 2001 Viking graves and grave-goods in Ireland. In A.C. Larsen (ed.) *The Vikings in Ireland*. Roskilde.

Harrison, S.H. and Ó Floinn, R. (forthcoming) *Viking graves and grave-goods in Ireland*.

Kelly, M.A. 1982 Intervertebral osteochondrosis in ancient and modern populations. *American Journal of Physical Anthropology* 59, 271–9.

Knudson, K.J. 2009 Oxygen isotope analysis in a land of environmental extremes: the complexities of isotopic work in the Andes. *International Journal of Archaeological Science* 24, 417–29.

Maat, G.J.R. and Mastwijk, R.W. 2000 Avulsion injuries of vertebral endplates. *International Journal of Osteoarchaeology* 10, 142–52.

Mays, S.A. 2007 Lysis at the anterior vertebral body margin: evidence for brucellar spondylitis? *International Journal of Osteoarchaeology* 17, 107–18.

Nicholl, J. 2008 Geophysical survey report: War Memorial Gardens, Islandbridge, Dublin (licence 08R174), report submitted to the Department of Environment, Heritage and Local Government.

O'Brien, E. 1998 The location and context of Viking burials at Kilmainham and Islandbridge, Dublin. In H.B. Clarke, M. Ní Mhaonaigh and R. Ó Floinn (eds) *Ireland and Scandinavia in the early Viking Age*, 222–35. Dublin.

O'Brien, R., Quinney, P., and Russell, I. 2005 Preliminary report on the archaeological excavation at finds retrieval strategy of the Hiberno-Scandinaivan site of Woodstown 6, County Waterford. *Decies: Journal of the Waterford Archaeological and Historical Society* 61, 13–122.

O'Donovan, E. 2007 The Irish, the Vikings and the English: new archaeological evidence from excavations at Golden Lane, Dublin. In S. Duffy (ed.) *Medieval Dublin VIII*, 36–130. Dublin.

Ó Floinn, R. 1998 The archaeology of the early Viking Age in Ireland. In H.B. Clarke, M. Ní Mhaonaigh and R. Ó Floinn (eds) *Ireland and Scandinavia in the early Viking Age*, 131–65. Dublin.

O'Sullivan, A., Sands, R. and Kelly, E.P. 2007 *Coolure Demesne crannog, Lough Derravaragh: an introduction to its archaeology and landscapes*. Bray.

Petersen, J. 1919 *De norske vikingesverd: en typologisk-kronologisk studie over vikingetidens vaaben*. Kristiania.

Rygh, O. 1885 *Norske Oldsager*. Christania.

Schoeninger, M.J., Deniro, M.J. and Tauber, H. 1983 Stable nitrogen isotope ratios of bone collagen reflect marine and terrestrial components of prehistoric human diet. *Science* 220, 1381–3.

Shetelig, H. 1940 *Viking antiquities in Great Britain and Ireland. Part V: British antiquities of the Viking period, found in Norway*. Oslo.

Simpson, L. 2002 *Excavations at Ship Street Great* (licence 01E0722) lodged with the former Dúchas: the Heritage Services, latterly Department of Environment, Heritage and Local Government, National Monuments Section.

Simpson, L. 2003 59–64 Great George's Street South. In I. Bennett (ed.) *Excavations 2001*, 382. Bray.

Simpson, L. 2005 Viking warrior burials in Dublin: is this the Longphort? In S. Duffy (ed.) *Medieval Dublin VI*, 11–62. Dublin.

Walsh, A. 1998 Viking Age swords in Ireland. In H.B. Clarke, M. Ní Mhaonaigh and R. Ó Floinn (eds) *Ireland and Scandinavia in the early Viking Age*, 222–35. Dublin.

Wilde, W. 1866 On the Scandinavian antiquities lately discovered at Islandbridge, near Dublin. *Proceedings of the Royal Irish Academy* 10, 13–22.

Viking identities in Ireland: it's not all black and white[1]

CLARE DOWNHAM

There has been recent debate about the meaning of the labels *Finn* ('white/fair') and *Dub* ('black/dark') assigned to different viking groups in ninth- and tenth-century Ireland. In the mid-1970s Alfred Smyth argued that these terms could be appropriately translated as 'old' and 'new', in contrast to previous scholarship where the contrasting colours of viking groups had been linked with their physical appearance (for example, hair, weaponry or dress).[2] Smyth favoured the received view that *Dub* described Danes and that *Finn* described Norwegians. Nevertheless, his exploration of the origin of these terms was significant for analyses which followed. David Dumville has argued in an earlier volume in this series that these labels did not identify separate Danish and Norwegian groups active in Ireland, but linked them to 'new' and 'old' groups that ruled Dublin in the ninth century.[3] Colmán Etchingham has recently put forward a counter-argument favouring the translation of *Dubgaill* as Danes and *Finngaill* as Norwegians.[4] This paper is written to reconsider the case that the label 'dark foreigners' can be equated with the followers and descendants of Ólafr and Ívarr who ruled at Dublin from the mid-ninth century.

Terms describing 'dark' vikings can be found in Irish and Welsh chronicles. The use of colour terms to describe viking groups is, however, restricted to the description of a small number of events. There are fourteen events recorded in Irish chronicles (Annals of Ulster; *Chronicon Scotorum*; Annals of Clonmacnoise and Annals of the Four Masters) where these terms are used.[5] In Welsh chronicles

1 I should like to thank Finn Rindahl for reading and commenting on a draft of this paper. The term viking means different things to different people. Advocates of 'Viking' as an ethnic label consistently use upper-case 'V' and that has been the prevailing usage in popular culture. Those who treat 'viking' as an occupational term (translated into medieval Latin as *pirata*, 'pirate') use a lower-case initial. In this article I use 'viking' as a cultural label. Vikings participated in a cultural phenomenon linked with Scandinavia, but they were not members of a single ethnic group. The choice to avoid a capital 'v' merely signals a rejection of 'Viking' as an ethnic category. 2 Alfred Smyth, 'The *Black* foreigners of York and the *White* foreigners of Dublin', *Saga-book of the Viking Society*, 19 (1974–77), 101–17. 3 David Dumville, 'Old Dubliners and New Dubliners in Ireland and Britain: a Viking Age story' in Seán Duffy (ed.), *Medieval Dublin VI* (Dublin, 2005), pp 78–93. 4 Colmán Etchingham, 'Laithlinn, "Fair Foreigners" and "Dark Foreigners": the identity and provenance of Vikings in ninth-century Ireland' in John Sheehan and Donnchadh Ó Corráin (eds), *The Viking Age: Ireland and the West. Proceedings of the Fifteenth Viking Congress* (Dublin, 2010), pp 80–9. 5 Corresponding to the years 851, 852, 856, 867, 870, 875, 877x2, 893, 917, 918, 921, 927 and 940.

(conventionally labelled *Annales Cambriae*, *Brenhinedd y Saesson* and *Brut y Tywysogyon*), the term 'dark' is used to describe vikings on five occasions and 'fair' vikings do not appear at all.[6] It is therefore difficult to use these colour terms as a basis for defining a wide range of groups or individuals as 'Danish' or 'Norwegian', despite the efforts of a number of commentators to do so. The desire to define groups according to national categories appears to reflect anachronistic national concerns, not the preoccupation of chroniclers in the ninth and early tenth centuries.

The argument has been presented elsewhere that national distinctions of 'Danes' and 'Norwegians' held little significance in describing vikings in the ninth century.[7] The first record of the names Denmark ('the borderland/ march of the Danes') and Norway ('the North way') is found in the English translation of the history of Orosius, dating to the 890s.[8] Kings of Denmark, Norway and Sweden in the ninth century did not rule areas coextensive with the late medieval states, and parts of Scandinavia lay outside their direct control. Perhaps the most centralized kingdom of Scandinavia in this period was Denmark; however, the historical evidence suggests that division rather than unity prevailed there from the mid-ninth century until the reign of Haraldr Blátönn.[9] Unification in Scandinavia, as elsewhere, was more of a process than an event.[10] Recent work on material culture by Johan Callmer, Fredrik Svanberg and Søren Sindbæk has indicated that within Scandinavia local identities would have been adhered to more strongly than any sense of national identity.[11] It is therefore doubtful that vikings would have primarily identified themselves as being Danes, Norwegians or Swedes. Furthermore, the attested coalescence and division of viking armies in England and the Continent suggests that vikings from different areas allied together for campaign purposes. This would have complicated any attempt to divide vikings into groups of different national origin outside Scandinavia.[12] Nevertheless, the terms *dub* and *finn* have been used by historians to evaluate events in ninth-

6 Corresponding to the years 853, 867, 892, 987 and 989.   7 Janet Nelson, 'The Frankish Empire' in Peter Sawyer (ed.), *The Oxford illustrated history of the Vikings* (Oxford, 1997), pp 19–47 at pp 20, 23, 35; Clare Downham, '"Hiberno-Norwegians" and "Anglo-Danes": anachronistic ethnicities and Viking Age England', *Medieval Scandinavia*, 19 (2009), 139–69. 8 Janet Bately (ed.), *The Old English Orosius*, Early English Texts Society (Oxford, 1980), pp 13–16.   9 Else Roesdahl, 'The emergence of Denmark and the reign of Harald Bluetooth' in S. Brink and N. Price (eds), *The Viking world* (London, 2008), pp 652–4.   10 T.L. Thurston, 'Historians, prehistorians and the tyranny of the historical record: Danish state formation through documents and archaeological data', *Journal of Archaeological Method and Theory*, 4 (1997), 239–63.   11 J. Callmer, 'Territory and dominion in the Late Iron Age in southern Scandinavia' in K. Jennbert et al. (eds), *Regions and reflections in honour of Märta Strömberg* (Lund, 1991), pp 257–73; S.M. Sindbæk, 'The lands of *Denemearce*: cultural differences and social networks of the Viking Age in South Scandinavia', *Viking and Medieval Scandinavia*, 4 (2008), 169–208; F. Svanberg, *Decolonizing the Viking Age*, 2 vols (Lund, 2003).   12 Nelson, 'Frankish Empire', pp 35–6.

and early tenth-century Ireland as a battleground between Danish and Norwegian factions.

The concern of historians to assign the viking colonization of different areas of Europe to different Scandinavian national groups has been a widespread phenomenon. So, for example, the migration to Russia has been perceived as a Swedish venture and the English 'Danelaw' is linked to Danes. This pattern in historiography developed with the growth of national consciousness, and a concern to categorize the achievement and heritage of different peoples. In areas where two Scandinavian national groups were perceived as being active, their mutual exclusivity was emphasized with political tensions and even outright hostility being assumed between them. Yet this paradigm of national segregation can be questioned as an oversimplification of patterns of migration and political allegiance.[13]

In Ireland, the ninth-century rivalry between *Finngaill* (fair foreigners) and *Dubgaill* (dark foreigners) has been interpreted as the clash of two Scandinavian nations. Nevertheless, ambiguities and contradictions in the evidence mean that historians have not been in agreement as to which national group prevailed. In 1891, Heinrich Zimmer argued that it was the Danes.[14] Alexander Bugge responded in 1900, arguing that the vikings in Ireland and their kings were Norwegians.[15] Bugge's view has prevailed as most scholars have regarded the vikings of Ireland as being of Norwegian stock. Nevertheless, debates about the origin of Dublin's royal dynasty have continued. Alfred Smyth argued that after a brief period of warfare, Norwegians seized Dublin in 853, but after the death of their leader Ólafr, the descendants of Ívarr (whom Smyth identified as Danes) took control.[16] In contrast, Donnchadh Ó Corráin has argued that the royal dynasty came from Norway via the Scottish islands.[17]

It is worth noting that in the Middle Ages there were different traditions as to where leaders of vikings in Ireland came from. According to the twelfth century *Historia Gruffudd vab Kenan*, the royal dynasty of Dublin was descended from Haraldr hárfagri ('Finehair') of Norway.[18] In the eleventh-century saga embedded in 'The Fragmentary Annals of Ireland', Ívarr and Ólafr are presented as sons of a Norwegian king Guðrøðr.[19] Ívarr and Ólafr are

13 Svanberg, *Decolonizing the Viking Age*; Clare Downham, 'Viking identities: an overview of recent scholarship', *History Compass* (forthcoming). 14 H. Zimmer, 'Keltische Beiträge, III: Weitere nordgermanische Einflüsse in der ältesten Überlieferung der irischen Heldensage', *Zeitschrift für deutsches Alterthum*, 35 (1891), 1–176. 15 Alexander Bugge, *Contributions to the history of the Norsemen in Ireland*, Videnskabsselskabets Skrifter, II, Historisk-filosofisk Klasse, nos 4–6 (3 pts, Oslo 1900). 16 Alfred Smyth, *Scandinavian kings in the British Isles, 850–880* (Oxford, 1977). 17 Donnchadh Ó Corrain, 'The Vikings in Scotland and Ireland in the ninth century', *Peritia*, 12 (1998), 296–339. 18 Paul Russell (ed. and trans.), *Vita Griffini Filii Conani: The medieval Latin Life of Gruffudd ap Cynan* (Cardiff, 2005), §4, pp 54–5. 19 J.N. Radner (ed.), *Fragmentary annals of Ireland* (Dublin, 1978), §§ 239, 347, pp 94–7, 126–7. Íslendingabók and Landnámabók connected a king Óláf inn hvíti of Dublin with the Norwegian house of Vestfold. He is often linked with Óláfr who

again presented as brothers in a legendary account concerning the foundation
of viking towns recorded by Gerald of Wales.[20] The reference to an Ívarr son of
Rögnvaldr of Møre who travelled west with Haraldr hárfagri in the thirteenth
century *Orkneyinga Saga* may also present an origin legend for Ívarr whose
descendants ruled at Dublin.[21] In later accounts of the thirteenth and fourteenth
centuries, *Ragnars saga loðbrókar* and *Þáttr af Ragnarssona*, Ívarr was assigned
a Danish pedigree. Since the late nineteenth century, this identification has
found most favour with historians, despite the late and legendary nature of the
sources.[22] All of these genealogical claims may be viewed as dubious attempts
to fit Ívarr within a bigger historical scheme of Viking Age events.[23] This would
add lustre to the peoples from which he was allegedly descended, and to those
who claimed descent from him. In a comparable way, conflicting pedigrees
exist for other founder figures in viking colonies. For example, Rollo of
Normandy is identified as a Norwegian by the author of *Orkneyinga saga*, but
as a Dane by Dudo of St Quentin.[24]

   Since the eleventh century, commentators have sought to identify different
viking groups retrospectively according to their national origins. This move
was perhaps influenced by contemporary concerns as the kingdoms of Norway
and Denmark became more centralized and rivalries heightened between
them. However, the fact remains that in the ninth and early tenth centuries no
unambiguous national identifications of Dane or Norwegian are made in Irish
sources. The colour terms *dub* and *finn* could just as well refer to groups under
different political leadership. The earliest surviving source to interpret 'dark'
vikings as Danes and 'fair' vikings as Norwegians is the saga embedded in the
'Fragmentary Annals of Ireland'.[25] The saga has been dated to the second or
third quarter of the eleventh century.[26] In this text, the presentation of different
viking groups appears to have been manipulated to heighten the reputation of
a ninth-century king of Osraige, who is the hero of the narration. As relations

was active in Ireland 853–71. However, the chronology of this association is problematic:
Smyth, *Scandinavian kings*, pp 102–4; Ó Corráin, 'Vikings in Scotland', pp 297–9. **20** J.J.
O'Meara (ed.), 'Giraldus Cambrensis in Topographia Hiberniae: text of the first recension',
Proceedings of the Royal Irish Academy, 52C (1948–50), 113–79 at 175; J.J. O'Meara (trans.),
Gerald of Wales, The history and topography of Ireland (London, 1982), III.43, p. 122.
21 Finnbogi Guðmundsson (ed.), *Orkneyinga Saga*, Íslensk Fornrit 34 (Reykjavík, 1965), §4,
pp 7–8; Herman Pálsson and Paul Edwards (trans.), *Orkneyinga Saga: The history of the
earls of Orkney* (London, 1981), pp 26–7. **22** James Henthorn Todd (ed.), *Cogadh Gaedhel
re Gallaibh: The war of the Gaedhil with the Gaill*, Rolls Series (London, 1867), pp liii–lvi;
For source analysis, see Rory McTurk, *Studies in Ragnars saga loðbrókar and its major
Scandinavian analogues* (Oxford, 1991). **23** Elizabeth Ashman Rowe, 'Helpful Danes and
pagan Irishmen: saga fantasies of the Viking Age in the British Isles', *Viking and Medieval
Scandinavia*, 5 (2009), 1–21. **24** Guðmundsson (ed.), *Orkneyinga Saga*, §4, p. 7; Pálsson
and Edwards (trans.), *Orkneyinga Saga*, p. 26; Jules Lair (ed.), *De Moribus et actibus
primorum Normanniae ducum* (Caen, 1865), pp 141–2; Eric Christiansen (trans.), *Dudo of St
Quentin, History of the Normans* (Woodbridge, 1998), p. 26. **25** Radner (ed.), *Fragmentary
annals*, §§ 233–35, pp 88–94. **26** Radner (ed.), *Fragmentary annals*, pp xxii–xxvi.

between Denmark and Norway were strained at the time when the saga was composed, it may have seemed quite natural to identify rival viking groups as Norwegians and Danes.[27] These distinctions were used by some later commentators, but other descriptions contradict them. Thus, in Gaelic poetry of the sixteenth and seventeenth centuries, the term 'fair foreigner' is used of the 'Old' English and sometimes Hebrideans, rather than Norwegians; while 'dark foreigner' described the English brought to Ireland by the Tudor conquest, not the Danes.[28]

The interpretation advanced by Alfred Smyth that 'dark' refers to 'new' groups and 'fair' refers to 'old' is also attested in the seventeenth-century Annals of Clonmacnoise. Under the year 922 (for which the correct year is 927), the death of 'Sittrick o'Himer, prince of the new and old Danes' is recorded, where other chronicles record the death of 'Sigtryggr, king of the dark and fair foreigners'.[29] This definition is very late. Colmán Etchingham has challenged the notion that Irish *dub* can carry the meaning 'new'. However, the colour coding of old and new is found more widely, perhaps because older was considered to be more eminent.[30] Wherever viking groups came from in the ninth century, it appears that they are being identified in the use of colour terms, by their respective arrival in the Irish Sea, thus reflecting local concerns, not Scandinavian political labels.

27 Clare Downham, 'The good, the bad and the ugly: portrayals of vikings in "The Fragmentary Annals of Ireland"', *The Medieval Chronicle*, 3 (2005), 28–40. 'The Fragmentary Annals' survive in a single manuscript of the seventeenth century. The text is copied from a transcription of an earlier manuscript made by Dubhaltach Mac Fhirbhisigh. The same definition of dark and light foreigners as the 'Fragmentary Annals' was adopted in Mac Fhirbhisigh's *Leabhar Mór na nGenealach: The Great Book of Irish Genealogies*, ed. Nollaig Ó Muraíle, 5 vols (Dublin, 2003), § 1364.3, III.714–15. Cf. Nollaig Ó Muraíle, *The celebrated antiquary Dubhaltach mac Fhirbisigh (c.1600–1671). His lineage, life and learning* (Maynooth, 1996), pp 88–93. A lost version of the 'Fragmentary Annals' was used in the compilation of the Annals of the Four Masters, but the interpretation of *Dubgaill* as Danes and *Finngaill* as Norwegians did not carry over into that text. C. Downham, 'The career of Cearbhall of Osraighe', *Ossory, Laois and Leinster*, 1 (2004), 1–18. 28 Wilson McLeod, '*Rí Innsi Gall, Rí Fionnghall, Ceanas nan Gàidheal*: sovereignty and rhetoric in the late Medieval Hebrides', *Cambrian Medieval Celtic Studies*, 43 (2002), 25–48 at 37–9; M. Pía Coira, '"A kingdom apart by itself, like a little world ...": Geoffrey Keating and the construction of Irish national history', *Journal of Celtic Studies*, 5 (2011), 2. In post-twelfth-century manuscripts of *Cogadh Gaedhel re Galliabh*, the term 'azure' (*gormglas*) foreigners is substituted for 'Norwegians' (*Lochlannachaibh*): Todd (ed. and trans.), *Cogadh*, §1, pp 2–3. 29 Denis Murphy (ed.), *Annals of Clonmacnoise, being annals of Ireland from the earliest times to AD1408* (Dublin, 1896), *s.a.* 922 [=927]; Seán Mac Airt and Gearóid Mac Niocaill (eds), *Annals of Ulster* (Dublin, 1983), *s.a.* 927.2. 30 Coira, 'A kingdom apart', pp 17–25; Etchingham, 'Laithlinn', p. 85. Etchingham's suggestion that 'dark foreigners' were viewed as worse than 'fair foreigners' conflicts with their presentation in the Fragmentary Annals, where the identification with Danes and Norwegians is put forward (with 'Danes' being shown in a more positive light than 'Norwegians'). In other words, Etchingham is adopting part of the picture presented there, but rejecting the rest.

Colmán Etchingham has followed Alfred Smyth in asserting that vikings from *Laithlinn* (a word distinct from later *Lochlann* meaning Norway or Scandinavia) were the 'old/fair foreigners' in Ireland before the 'new/dark foreigners' arrived.[31] There has been some disagreement between scholars over the location of *Laithlinn*, which is sparsely recorded in Irish texts. Donnchadh Ó Corrain has linked *Laithlinn* with the Scottish islands, whereas Anders Ahlqvist has identified *Laithlinn* with Dublin.[32] Colmán Etchingham has followed a hypothesis put forward by Egon Wamers that *Laith* may be derived from Hlaðir in Norway.[33] Etchingham's further suggestion that the Irish word *linn* ('pool') might be used to describe the impressive 'waterway of Trondheim fjord' is questionable (*loch* would seem more appropriate).[34] Due to the lack of evidence, it is difficult to draw a conclusion on the whereabouts of *Laithlinn*. Nevertheless, references to *Laithlinn* in Irish chronicles are remarkable for their association with titles that demonstrate Irish knowledge of its political organization. Under the year 848, Tomrar is referred to as *erell* ('jarl') of *Laithlinn* (the first record of that title in Irish sources) and 'heir to the king of *Laithlinn*'. Under 853, Óláfr is called 'a son of the king' of *Laithlinn*. This suggests that wherever *Laithlinn* was deemed to be, it was a well-defined kingdom rather than a vague geographical area.

The equation of *Laithlinn* with *Finngaill* in ninth-century Ireland can be questioned. Vikings had been active in Ireland since the 790s, but the first reference to people from *Laithlinn* comes under the year 848. This begs the question whether vikings from *Laithlinn* were the 'new' or 'dark' arrivals in a mid-ninth-century context. The sequence of references to *Laithlinn* and dark/fair vikings in the Annals of Ulster for the years 848–53 is as follows:[35]

> AU 848.5 *Bellum re nOlcobur, ri Muman, & re Lorggan m. Cellaig co Laighniu for gennti ecc Sciaith Nechtain in quo ceciderunt Tomrair erell, tanise righ Laithlinne, & da cet dec imbi* ('A battle was won by Ólchobar king of Munster and Lorcán m. Cellaig with the Leinstermen against the heathens at Sciath Nechtain in which fell Þórir the earl (*jarl*), heir-designate of the king of *Laithlinn* and 1200 about him').

31 *Lochlann* can be identified as Norway. However, the meaning of the term could encompass all of Scandinavia in the late Middle Ages. Thus, Dubhaltach Mac Fhirbhisigh identified *Dubhlochlannaigh* as Danes: Ó Muraíle (ed.), *Leabhar Mór na nGenealach*, §1364.3, III.714–15.   32 Anders Ahlqvist, '*Is acher in gaíth ... úa Lothind*' in J.F. Nagy and L.E. Jones (eds), *Heroic poets and poetic heroes in the Celtic tradition: CSANA Yearbook 3–4* (Dublin, 2005), pp 19–27.   33 E. Wamers, 'Insular finds in Viking Age Scandinavia and the state formation of Norway' in H.B. Clarke et al. (eds), *Ireland and Scandinavia in the Early Viking Age* (Dublin, 1998), pp 37–72 at p. 66 n. 84.   34 Ó Corrain, 'Vikings in Scotland'; Colmán Etchingham, 'The location of historical *Laithlinn/Lochla(i)nn*: Scotland or Scandinavia?' in Micheál Ó Flaithearta (ed.), *Proceedings of the Seventh Symposium of Societas Celtalogica Nordica* (Uppsala, 2007), pp 11–31 at pp 27–8.   35 Mac Airt and Mac Niocaill (eds), *Annals of Ulster*.

AU 849.6 *Muirf[.]echt .uii.xx. long di muinntir righ Gall du thiachtain du tabairt greamma forsna Gaillu ro badur ara ciunn co commascsat hErinn n-uile iarum* ('A sea-going expedition of 140 ships of the people of the king of the Foreigners came to exercise authority over the Foreigners who were in Ireland before them and they upset all Ireland afterwards').

AU 851.3 *Tetact Dubgennti du Ath Cliath co ralsat ár mór du Fhinngallaibh 7 coro [sh]latsat in longport eitir doine 7 moine. Slat do Dubhgenntib oc Lind Duachail 7 ar mor diib* ('The Dark Heathens came to Áth Cliath, and inflicted a great slaughter on the Fair Foreigners, and they pillaged the base, both people and possessions. An attack by the Dark Heathens on Linn Duachaill and a great slaughter of them').

AU 852.3 *Lucht ocht .xxit long di Fhindgentibh do-roachtadur du cath fri Dubgennti do Shnamh Aighnech; .iii. laa 7 .iii. aithchi oc cathugud doaib act is re nDuibhgennti ro mmeabaidh co farggabsat a ceile a llonga leu. Stain fugitiuus euasit 7 Iercne decollatus iacuit* ('The crew of eight score ships of Fair Heathens came to battle against Dark Heathens at Snám Eidhneach; they battled for three days and three nights but the Dark Foreigners prevailed, and the others left their ships to them. Steinn escaped fleeing, and Iarnkné lay beheaded').

AU 853.2 *Amhlaim m. righ Laithlinde do tuidhecht a nErinn coro giallsat Gaill Erenn dó & cis o Goidhelaib* ('Óláfr son of the king of *Laithlind* came to Ireland and the Foreigners of Ireland gave him hostages and he got tribute from the Irish').

One can read the Irish chronicles from 848–53 two ways; firstly, that the people of *Laithlinn* were the first vikings in Ireland, then the *Dubgaill* come along, then the people of *Laithlinn* reasserted themselves. This is the view favoured by Etchingham and Smyth. Or secondly, if we identify people of *Laithlinn* with *Dubgaill* then we have an account of the *Dubgaill*/people of *Laithlinn* progressively asserting themselves over vikings who were in Ireland before them. This would be a simpler reading of the evidence.

ÍVARR AND HIS ASSOCIATES

There has been a tendency in the historiography to analyze the deeds of vikings in Ireland and Britain in isolation; nevertheless, vikings could easily pass across the seaways between the islands. There has been some debate as to whether some of the figures who appear in Irish sources in the ninth century are the same as individuals who appear in a British context, in particular King

Ívarr and his associates Óláfr, Ásl and Hálfdan. It is relevant in this respect to note that the label 'dark' foreigner was used to describe some vikings active in Britain as well as in Ireland. The identification of Ívarr and his close associates is key to any interpretation of the terms 'fair' and 'dark' as applied to different viking groups.

At Ívarr's death in 873, he is commemorated as 'king of the Northmen of all Ireland and Britain' in Irish chronicles.[36] His career in Ireland can be traced from chronicles between 857 and 863 and then there is a gap until 870.[37] It cannot be proven that he was the same Ívarr who assisted in the capture of York in 867.[38] Nevertheless, the Annals of Ulster demonstrate Irish interest in the event, reporting that a battle was won by the 'dark' foreigners there.[39] In England, Ívarr was held responsible for the martyrdom of Edmund of East Anglia in 869 and the 'Chronicle of Aethelweard' attributes his death to the same year.[40] However, Ívarr's disappearance from England and assumptions about the nature of divine retribution may have led to a mistaken conclusion being drawn. Ívarr appears leading a viking army in Strathclyde in 870, which arrived in Dublin in 871.[41] The interlocking chronology of Ívarr's deeds in Britain and Ireland and the title assigned to him at his death provide a strong case that we are dealing with the same individual.

Ívarr's ally Óláfr is mentioned in Irish chronicles from 853 to 871. He is called the 'son of the king of *Laithlinn*'.[42] Colmán Etchingham has tentatively identified him as a brother of Ívarr and as a 'fair foreigner'.[43] The claim of fraternity rests on evidence dating from the eleventh century, and is not secure.[44] Óláfr is not explicitly identified as either a *Finngall* or a *Dubgall* in contemporary Irish sources. Óláfr campaigned in Ireland with Ívarr between 857 and 863 and later sailed to Pictland, returning to Ireland in 867. He joined Ívarr for the sack of Dumbarton Rock in Strathclyde in 870. Once Ívarr had returned to Dublin in 871, Óláfr sailed back to Pictland, where he was killed in 874. His death is recorded in the 'Chronicle of the kings of Alba'.[45] Óláfr is closely linked with Ásl, who campaigned with Ívarr in 863 and who travelled to Pictland with Óláfr in 866. Ásl did not achieve the fame of Ívarr or Óláfr and was murdered 'by his brothers' in 867.[46] During the period of Óláfr's hegemony in Ireland, the continued activity of 'dark foreigners' is witnessed in

36 Ibid., *s.a.* 873.3.   **37** Downham, *Viking kings*, pp 257–9.   **38** Dorothy Whitelock et al. (trans.), *Anglo-Saxon chronicle* (London, 1961), *s.a.* 866.   **39** Mac Airt and Mac Niocaill (eds), *Annals of Ulster*, *s.a.* 867.7.   **40** Alistair Campbell (ed. and trans.), *Chronicon Æthelweardi. The chronicle of Æthelweard* (Edinburgh, 1962), IV.2, pp 36–7.   **41** Mac Airt and Mac Niocaill (eds), *Annals of Ulster*, *s.aa.* 870.6, 871.2.   **42** Downham, *Viking kings*, pp 238–40.   **43** Etchingham, 'Laithlinn', p. 86. Alex Woolf, *From Pictland to Alba* (Edinburgh, 2007), pp 107–8, has put forward an interesting interpretation that Óláfr's arrival led to a reconciliation between two groups, who then worked together.   **44** Radner (ed.), *Fragmentary annals*, §§239, 347, pp 94–7, 126–7.   **45** Benjamin T. Hudson (ed. and trans.), 'The Scottish chronicle', *Scottish Historical Review*, 77 (1998), 129–61 at 148, 154; Downham, *Viking kings*, p. 142.   **46** Mac Airt and Mac Niocaill (eds), *Annals of Ulster*, *s.a.*

870 when Máel Sechnaill son of Niall, a king of Southern Brega, was treacherously killed by Ulfr, a 'dark foreigner'.[47] This Ulfr does not appear in English sources and he may have been one of Óláfr's deputies in Ireland while he waged war in Strathclyde.

The 'Anglo-Saxon Chronicle' identified a man called Hálfdan as a brother of Ívarr. Hálfdan first appears as a participant in the battle of Ashdown in 871. His career in Britain lasted until 876, when he shared out lands in Northumbria among his followers.[48] In 874/5, Hálfdan was based on the River Tyne, from where he led a campaign against Pictland and Strathclyde. A battle between the dark foreigners and the Picts is recorded in Irish chronicles for the year 875. Irish sources also record that Hálfdan killed Eysteinn son of Óláfr in the same year. Hálfdan fell in battle at Strangford Lough in 877, and the Annals of Ulster refer to him as a leader of the 'dark foreigners'.[49] Surviving contemporary sources are not explicit in linking the Hálfdan active in North Britain with the Hálfdan of Ireland. However, given the location of Strangford Lough across the North Channel of the Irish Sea, and the timing of Hálfdan's activities as recorded in English and Irish sources, this identification seems likely.[50]

Colmán Etchingham, in his recent article, accepts the identification of Hálfdan, a leader of 'dark foreigners', as a brother of Ívarr. He further identified Ívarr's close political ally and possible brother Óláfr as leader of 'fair foreigners'. Etchingham's definition of 'fair' as 'Norwegian' and 'dark' as 'Danish' relies on the premise that vikings active in Ireland are Norwegians while those in English-speaking areas are Danes, with little mixing between the two groups. However, due to the campaigns of Ívarr, Hálfdan and Óláfr, this would mean that 'Danes' and 'Norwegians' fought in Pictland and Strathclyde, and that they allied together at the siege of Dumbarton Rock. Furthermore, as Ívarr was active in Britain and Ireland, his core retinue would presumably, according to Etchingham's definition, have been acting as 'Norwegians' in Ireland but as 'Danes' in Britain. This does not match easily with theories of rivalry inherent in the interpretation of 'fair' and 'dark' groups.

Etchingham has provided a counter-argument to David Dumville's view that Ívarr's associates and his descendants at Dublin were 'dark' or 'newer' foreigners. According to Etchingham, the twelfth-century saga *Cogad Gáedel re Gallaib*, when describing the battle at Strangford Lough in 877, 'plausibly identifies the Findgenti leader as Barith, who is elsewhere identified as Barith son of Ivarr'.[51] This identification is not convincing. The link with Barðr son of Ívarr (d. 881) is indirect and *Cogad* is not reliable on the matter as a twelfth-century saga which contains an admixture of information drawn from chronicles. No reference is made to Barðr's presence at the battle in contemporary

867.6.   **47** Ibid., *s.a.* 870.7.   **48** Whitelock et al. (trans.), *Anglo-Saxon chronicle, s.a.* 876. **49** Mac Airt and Mac Niocaill (eds), *Annals of Ulster, s.a.* 877.5.   **50** Etchingham, 'Laithlinn', p. 87.   **51** Ibid., p. 87.

accounts.[52] It may be that the claim of Barðr's leadership of the 'fair' heathens was invented in *Cogad* to create a narrative link with the plundering of the caves of Kerry by Barðr, which is mentioned in the same section of the text.[53] The cavalier approach of the author of *Cogad* to historical accuracy for the sake of linking events to make a good story can be seen elsewhere.[54] The account of the battle is framed by accounts which cast doubt on its reliability. It is preceded by the tale of deceitful murder at a feast and followed by the account of an earthquake which swallowed the army of the king of Alba; both motifs owe more to literature than history.[55] The chronology at this point in the text is also out of sequence.

Cogad Gáedel re Gallaib states that the 'dark foreigners' left Ireland after the battle, and having passed into North Britain, killed Causantín king of the Picts.[56] However, this record can be rejected, as the battle was fought in 877 and the king died in 876. Causantín's death must have taken place prior to the battle at Strangford Lough. Etchingham has interpreted *Cogad*'s claim that Hálfdan's forces were expelled as marking the long-term removal of 'dark foreigners' from Ireland, but this is unwarranted. *Cogad* also claims that this expulsion was followed by a forty-year rest in viking activity in Ireland, an assertion which is flatly contradicted by contemporary sources.[57] Ó Corráin has made the convincing case that the topos of the forty-year rest was inspired by biblical narrative.[58] Although *Cogad* contains a rich body of narrative, it should not be considered as more important or equally important to the surviving contemporary sources.

AFTER THE BATTLE OF STRANGFORD LOUGH

The battle of Strangford Lough was an important engagement that failed to secure the supremacy of dark foreigners in the north-east of Ireland. After the engagement, Ívarr's family (whom I interpret as being leaders of the 'new' or dark foreigners) focused their efforts on the development of Dublin and their

---

52 *Cogad* claims that the leader of the dark foreigners was someone called Rögnvaldr's son who is not mentioned in contemporary sources. It is doubtful that Rögnvaldr's son can be identified with Hálfdan (who was there). In the earliest surviving manuscript of *Cogad*, it was written that Rögnvaldr's son died at the battle, but according to the other manuscripts he was murdered at a banquet in Dublin afterwards: Todd (ed. and trans.), *Cogadh*, §25, pp 26–7, 232.   53 Seán Mac Airt (ed. and trans.), *Annals of Inisfallen* (Dublin, 1951), *s.a.* 873; Todd (ed. and trans.), *Cogadh*, § 25, pp 24–7.   54 For example, Todd (ed. and trans.), *Cogadh*, §§ 11–14, pp 12–15; Downham, 'The chronology of Cogadh Gaedhel re Galliabh' (forthcoming).   55 Todd (ed. and trans.), *Cogadh*, §25, pp 26–7.   56 Ibid.   57 Emer Purcell, 'Ninth-century Viking entries in the Irish Annals: no "forty years' rest"' in John Sheehan and Donnchadh Ó Corráin (eds), *The Viking Age: Ireland and the West. Proceedings of the 15th Viking Congress* (Dublin, 2010), pp 322–37.   58 Donnchadh Ó Corrain, 'Vikings

ambitions overseas. In 893, the Annals of Ulster record that 'dark foreigners' suffered a major defeat at the hands of the English.[59] This is probably a reference to the battle of Buttington, which was fought in that year.[60] A departure of vikings from Dublin is recorded in the same year and a contingent from Dublin may have fought there alongside the Northumbrians.[61] Jarl Sigfrøðr, who led one of the contingents from Dublin, has been tentatively identified with Sigfrøðr, leader of a Northumbrian fleet that attacked Wessex in the same year.[62] Whether or not this identification is correct, the coincidence in affairs of 893 indicates that viking ambitions in England and Ireland were intertwined.

'Dark foreigners' are not named again in Irish chronicles until 917. This year was marked by a great battle between the forces of Leinster and the grandsons of Ívarr, who had returned to Ireland following their expulsion in 902. After taking control of Waterford, the family had set their sights on regaining Dublin. In the battle at Ceann Fuait, Rögnvaldr, grandson of Ívarr, is called 'king of dark foreigners' by the Annals of Ulster.[63] This is significant because Rögnvaldr at this time was not king of York.[64] This identification flies in the face of theories that the title 'king of the dark foreigners' may be interpreted as 'king of the Danes of York' and that 'king of the fair foreigners' means 'king of the Norwegians of Dublin'. It was not until the following year that Rögnvaldr would add York to his domain. After the battle, Dublin was taken and brought under the control of Rögnvaldr's brother or cousin Sigtryggr. This was presumably so that Rögnvaldr, the senior partner, could pursue his career in England. It appears that Rögnvaldr never ruled in Dublin. The title 'king of the dark foreigners', if accurately recorded in 917, would seem to apply to the chief member of the family of Ívarr. The term 'dark' could refer to the family and its adherents, successors of the 'new' vikings who had arrived in Ireland in the mid-ninth century.

Rögnvaldr continued to hold the title 'king of the dark foreigners' when he led his men from Waterford to York in 918.[65] On his death in 921, Rögnvaldr is called 'king of the fair foreigners and the dark foreigners' in Irish chronicles.[66] His brother or cousin Sigtryggr is assigned the same title on his death in 927.[67] The label suggests that both kings had won recognition as leaders of the dynasty of Ívarr and overlordship of the 'old' foreigners of Ireland who may have remained in the island while Ívarr's family had been in exile. It is

I: "Forty years' rest"', *Peritia*, 10 (1996), 224.   **59** Mac Airt and Mac Niocaill (eds), *Annals of Ulster*, s.a. 893.3.   **60** Whitelock et al. (trans.), *Anglo-Saxon chronicle*, s.a. 893.   **61** F.M. Stenton, *Anglo-Saxon England*, 3rd ed. (Oxford, 1971), p. 267.   **62** Smyth, *Scandinavian York*, I, p. 34; W.S. Angus, 'Christianity as a political force in Northumbria in the Danish and Norse Periods' in Alan Small (ed.), *The Fourth Viking Congress, York* (Edinburgh, 1965), p. 147.   **63** Mac Airt and Mac Niocaill (eds), *Annals of Ulster*, s.a. 917.3.   **64** Alex Woolf, *From Pictland to Alba* (Edinburgh, 2007), pp 142–4; Downham, *Viking kings*, pp 92–5.   **65** Mac Airt and Mac Niocaill (eds), *Annals of Ulster*, s.a. 918.4.   **66** Ibid., *s.a.* 921.4.   **67** Ibid., *s.a.* 927.2.

tempting to identify the 'fair foreigners' with vikings based in Limerick. There is no record of vikings being expelled from Limerick in 902 and only the seizure of Waterford and Dublin is recorded in 914 and 917 by grandsons of Ívarr. The family of Ívarr suffered a major blow when King Æthelstan seized York in 927. This may have promoted greater competition for resources in Ireland. Tensions heightened between leaders of Limerick and Dublin from 927. After some years of strategic manoeuvring, matters came to a climax in 937 when Óláfr son of Guðrøðr, king of Dublin, captured Óláfr 'Scabby head', king of Limerick, on Lough Ree and destroyed all his ships. Óláfr son of Guðrøðr is the last king who bore the title 'king of fair and dark foreigners' in Ireland.[68] I would suggest that this is because, after his reign, the 'old' or 'fair' foreigners of Ireland were securely under the thumb of the dynasty of Ívarr and so were no longer a force to be reckoned with. It can be argued that the terms *Finngaill* and *Dubgaill* were coined in Ireland to describe affairs in Ireland, rather than the politics of distant territories.

WELSH EVIDENCE

The concept of 'dark' foreigners arises in Welsh chronicles and was probably borrowed from Ireland. In a comparable way, Welsh *llongborth* was derived from the Irish *longphort*, or 'ship camp'. As in Irish sources, the usage of colour terminology to describe viking groups in Wales appears infrequently albeit across a wider timespan. In Welsh chronicles, 'dark' foreigners are referred to in the years 853, 867, 892, 987 and 989. The terms used vary from Latin *gentilibus nigris* to Welsh *Dub gint*, *Llu Du* and *Nordmannieit Duon*. There is no reference to 'fair foreigners', suggesting that this concept was not meaningful in a Welsh context.

If Colmán Etchingham is correct in seeing the Irish Sea as a theatre of contact between separate spheres of 'Danish' and 'Norwegian' activity, the absence of reference to 'fair' vikings (or 'Norwegians' as he has defined them) in Welsh sources would be hard to explain. However, if we reject the identification of 'fair' foreigners with 'Norwegians', it could simply be that the 'old' vikings of Ireland lost significance from a Welsh perspective, once they had lost Dublin. It is only from the 850s that vikings play an important part in Welsh politics. The 'dark' terms referred to in Welsh sources may be consistently interpreted as armies under the leadership of the dynasty of Ívarr, who were active at Dublin and elsewhere.

In 853, according to Welsh chronicles, the 'dark' vikings ravaged Anglesey.[69] This is a year after Irish chronicles record a victory of 'dark' foreigners over

68 W.M. Hennessy (ed. and trans.), *Chronicum Scotorum* (London, 1866), *s.a.* 940 [=941].
69 David Dumville (ed. and trans.), *Annales Cambriae, AD682–954: texts A–C in Parallel*

their 'fair' rivals at Strangford Lough, and three years before Irish chronicles record the death of Ormr, a leader of the 'dark' foreigners at the hands of Rhodri son of Merfyn, king of Gwynedd.[70] This could be interpreted as the 'dark foreigners' seeking to extend their influence in Britain following their success in Ireland.[71] Welsh chronicles then identify 'dark foreigners' as the ravagers of York in records for the year 867. The event is referred to as 'Cat Dubgynt' or the 'Battle of the Black army'. Curiously, one version of *Annales Cambriae* (identified as the 'C' text or 'The Chronicle of St David's') erroneously renders this 'Cat Dulin' or 'Battle of Dublin', which may be an error of transcription or show confusion on the part of the scribe.[72] 'Dark' foreigners next appear in Welsh chronicles for the year 890/2 in an attack apparently aimed against Gwynedd.[73] The north-west coast of Wales was within the sphere of influence of the vikings of Dublin, as represented in later events including the migration of Ingimundr to Anglesey in 902, as well as archaeological finds including the settlement at Llanbedrgoch.[74] It is credible that Dubliners (or more broadly, followers of the dynasty of Ívarr) were the 'dark Northmen' (*Nordmannieit Duon*) referred to on this occasion.

'Dark' foreigners are not referred to again in Welsh chronicles until the 980s. In the year 987, according to *Annales Cambriae* and *Brut y Tywysogyon*, Guðrøðr son of Haraldr, king of Man and the Hebrides, led a contingent of 'dark' vikings to ravage Anglesey and took a large number of captives.[75] In the same year, the Annals of Ulster report that the son of Haraldr allied with *Danair* ('Danes') and won a battle on the Isle of Man.[76] This evidence is a key part of Etchingham's case that 'dark' foreigners may be equated with 'Danes'. Nevertheless, Guðrøðr was himself a likely descendant of Ívarr and thus a 'dark foreigner'.[77] Furthermore, as Scandinavian fleets operating in the Irish Sea at this time appear to have been allied with Dublin, Guðrøðr may have also been working with both *Danair* and Dubliners in 987, deploying one group in Man, and the other in Anglesey.

The arrival of fleets from Scandinavia can be shown to cause a shift in patterns of allegiance in the Irish Sea. In 984, prior to the appearance of

(Cambridge, 2002), *s.a.* 853.   **70** Mac Airt and Mac Niocaill (eds), *Annals of Ulster, s.aa.* 852.3, 856.6.   **71** Rhodri was to be chased from his patrimony by dark foreigners in 877 and sought refuge in Ireland: Mac Airt and Mac Niocaill (eds), *Annals of Ulster, s.a.* 877.3. **72** Dumville (ed. and trans.), *Annales Cambriae, s.a.* 867.   **73** The event is not recorded in *Annales Cambriae*. According to the Peniarth 20 manuscript of *Brut y Tywysogyon*, 'Black Northmen', came to Gwynedd. *Brenhinedd y Saesson* records that the 'Black Northmen' came to Gwyn. Thomas Jones interpreted this as a contraction for Gwynedd. The Red Book of Hergest text of *Brut y Tywysogyon* anachronistically links the attack to Baldwin's Castle: Thomas Jones (trans.), *Brut y Tywysogyon of The Chronicle of the princes – Peniarth MS 20 Version* (Cardiff, 1952), p. 138 n. 5.28.   **74** Downham, *Viking kings*, pp 206–8. **75** Dumville (ed. and trans.), *Annales Cambriae, s.a.* 987; Jones (trans.), *Brut y Tywysogyon*, pp 145–6, n. 10.1–2.   **76** Mac Airt and Mac Niocaill (eds), *Annals of Ulster, s.a.* 987.1 **77** Downham, *Viking kings*, pp 186–91.

Danair on the Irish political scene, we see hostility between the Manx vikings and Dubliners. This was represented by an alliance between the Islesmen (led by the sons of Haraldr) and the Irish king Brian Bóruma, in a planned attack on Dublin.[78] When fleets of *Danair* appear in Irish sources two years later, they sacked Iona and the Isles.[79] They seized Máel Chiaráin, the abbot, and he was martyred in Dublin.[80] It appears that Danish fleets were cooperating with the political elite of Dublin and treating the Islesmen as common enemies. However in the following year, Guðrøðr son of Haraldr, king of the Isles, won a battle on the Isle of Man allied with *Danair*.[81] Thus Guðrøðr and the Scandinavians had been brought together against an unnamed enemy. This may reflect internal rivalry within the kingdom of the Isles, for, in the same year, many *Danair* were killed in a battle that was interpreted as revenge for their sack of Iona.[82] A continued alliance between the *Danair* and the Dubliners is suggested as the two groups campaigned together in eastern Ireland in 990.[83]

The 'dark' army who allied with Guðrøðr in 987 reappear in Welsh records two years later. In 989, the Welsh king Maredudd ab Owain paid a ransom to the 'dark' foreigners to release the captives who had been seized from Anglesey in their earlier attack.[84] We may get an insight into the circumstances behind this deal by comparing other events of the year. It may be significant that both Guðrøðr son of Haraldr, king of the Isles and Glúniarn son of Ólafr, king of Dublin died in 989.[85] The arrival of new leaders in the Hebrides and at Dublin may have opened possibilities for negotiation. Also in 989, a heavy tax was imposed on the people of Dublin by the Irish king Máel Sechnaill mac Domnaill.[86] Presumably the people seized from Anglesey were being held in Dublin (a notorious slave market). The 'dark' army may have chosen to ransom the captives as a quick method of raising cash to pay off their royal tax collector.

To conclude, there is nothing in Welsh chronicles that conflicts with the interpretation of *Dubgaill* as armies under the leadership of the dynasty of Ívarr. The Scandinavian fleets arriving in the Irish Sea must have appeared somewhat different in cultural terms to the vikings whose families had long settled in Ireland. A new term *Danair*, meaning 'Danes', was coined for them

78 Mac Airt (ed. and trans.), *Annals of Inisfallen*, *s.a.* 984.   **79** Mac Airt (ed. and trans.), *Annals of Inisfallen*, *s.a.* 986; Mac Airt and Mac Niocaill (eds), *Annals of Ulster*, *s.a.* 986.2, 986.3. Three ships of the *Danair* also landed on the coast of Dál Riata, where 140 people are reported to have been executed and others sold.   **80** John O'Donovan (ed. and trans.), *Annala rioghachta Eireann. Annals of the kingdom of Ireland by the Four Masters*, 2nd ed., 7 vols (Dublin, 1856), *s.a.* 985 [=986]; Hennessy (ed. and trans.), *Chronicum Scotorum*, *s.a.* 986.   **81** Mac Airt and Mac Niocaill (eds), *Annals of Ulster*, *s.a.* 987.1.   **82** O'Donovan (ed. and trans.), *Annals of the Four Masters*, *s.a.* 986 [=987]; Mac Airt and Mac Niocaill (eds), *Annals of Ulster*, *s.a.* 987.3   **83** O'Donovan (ed. and trans.), *Annals of the Four Masters*, *s.a.* 989 [=990].   **84** Dumville (ed. and trans.), *Annales Cambriae*, *s.a.* 986; Jones (trans.), *Brut y Tywysogyon*, *s.a.* 987 [=989].   **85** Hennessy (ed. and trans.), *Chronicum Scotorum*, *s.a.* 989. **86** Ibid., *s.a.* 989.

in the 980s. This indicates that from an Irish perspective *Danair* were regarded as separate from *Dubgaill*.

ONOMASTIC EVIDENCE

Colmán Etchingham has argued that 'dark foreigners' had little influence in Dublin affairs, appearing in 851–2 and very sporadically thereafter.[87] However, their onomastic legacy in Ireland could suggest otherwise. In 1013 we find the personal name *Dubgall* appearing within the royal Dublin dynasty.[88] At least two members of in the Northern Uí Néill dynasty that intermarried with the vikings of Dublin bore this name in the tenth century.[89] It is also worth noting that the name *Lochlann* appears in this family, suggesting their alliance with vikings.[90] *Dubgall* also appears as a name among the Gailenga of Brega, an area where Dublin wielded economic influence.[91] These naming patterns seem to indicate a connection between the people of Dublin and the 'dark foreigners'.

The impact of 'dark foreigners' is also seen in place-names. A bridge near Dublin was called in Irish *Droichet-Dubhghaill*, 'the bridge of the dark foreigners', as referred to in the Annals of the Four Masters under the year 1112.[92] *Baile Dubhghaill* (Baldoyle) in Co. Dublin may also refer to 'dark foreigners'.[93] Similar place-names include Baldoyle (Co. Meath); Ballindoyle (Co. Wicklow); Ballydoyle (Co. Cork); Ballydoyle (Co. Tipperary); Ballydoyle (Co. Wexford). Undoubtedly, a more thorough investigation would reveal other locations incorporating the name *Dubgaill*. For example, it has been suggested that Cooladoyle (Co. Wicklow) incorporates the term *Dubgaill* under the influence of Scandinavian settlement.[94] It is likely that some place-names include the Leinster surname Doyle, derived from *Dubgall*, rather than being a direct reference to vikings.[95] However, the onomastic evidence indicates that 'dark foreigners' of the Viking Age left their mark in Ireland, and were less insignificant than Etchingham has suggested.

87 Etchingham, 'Laithlinn', p. 87. 88 Mac Airt (ed. and trans.), *Annals of Inisfallen, s.a.* 1013; Mac Airt and Mac Niocaill (eds), *Annals of Ulster, s.aa.* 1013.8, 1014.2. 89 M.A. O'Brien (ed.), *Corpus genealogiarum Hiberniae* (Dublin, 1962), §140 a 33, p. 135; O'Donovan (ed. and trans.), *Annals of the Four Masters, s.a.* 912, 923, 978. 90 O'Donovan (ed. and trans.), *Annals of the Four Masters, s.a.* 1023; T.W. Moody et al., ed., *A new history of Ireland, IX: maps, genealogies, lists* (Oxford, 1984), p. 128. 91 O'Brien (ed.), *Corpus genealogiarum,* §154a17, p. 247. 92 O'Donovan (ed. and trans.), *Annals of the Four Masters, s.a.* 1112. 93 Richard Butler (ed.), *Registrum prioratus omnium sanctorum juxta Dublin* (Dublin, 1845), p. Ii. 94 M. Murphy and M. Potterton, *The Dublin region in the Middle Ages: settlement, land-use and economy* (Dublin, 2010), p. 64. 95 A.J. Hughes, 'Irish place-names: some perspectives, pitfalls, procedures and potential', *Seanchas Ardmhacha,* 14:2 (1991), 116–48 at 139.

CONCLUSION

Retrospective interpretations of the Viking Age through a nationalist framework have held a dominant place in modern historiography. However, the paradigm of national segregation among viking settlers risks promoting an over-simplified picture of the past. It seems debatable that vikings operated as unmixed groups of Norwegians or Danes in the mid-ninth century and that they could be identified as such by outsiders. In reality, the ethnic and cultural make-up of vikings in the ninth and tenth centuries was multi-faceted. Arguably, the seas lying between the islands of Britain and Ireland acted as highways for maritime entrepreneurs to travel and mix, rather than serving as ethnic moats with Danes concentrated on one side and Norwegians on the other. Furthermore, as vikings assimilated elements of local culture and intermarried, they developed new hybrid identities that may have affected the categories that the first vikings carried with them. Nevertheless, the received wisdom has been that if a 'Dane' arrived on the Irish coast in the ninth century, his or her descendants remained 'Danish' six or more generations later.[96] The terms *finngaill* and *dubgaill* were arguably coined in reference to local circumstances, not in reference to Scandinavian national identities. They were dubbed by the Irish rather than by the Scandinavians. Although scholars have been keen to identify invaders, settlers and leaders as either Norwegians or Danes, this was not a principal interest for people in ninth-century Ireland.[97] Indeed, it has been argued that that there was no word for 'Norway' in Irish until the eleventh century.[98] For these reasons, reinterpretations of events freed from overarching categories of Dane and Norwegian in early Viking-Age Ireland seem desirable.

   Scholars have struggled for years as to whether to identify particular vikings in Ireland as Danes or Norwegians. Fundamentally, this is because the conventional translation of *Finngaill* as 'Norwegian', and *Dubgaill* as 'Dane', does not fit easily with the primary sources. The case presented by Etchingham is far from conclusive. An alternative view sits better with the ninth- and tenth-century evidence; namely that *Dubgaill* were the associates and descendants of Ívarr, and *Finngaill* were the dominant viking group in Ireland before their arrival. Nevertheless, this argument does require an acceptance that retrospective interpretations were imposed on the labels *Finn* and *Dub* from the eleventh century due to changing political circumstances. This is an assertion

---

96 Etchingham, 'Laithlinn', p. 85.   **97** In the late nineteenth century, the heritage of vikings in Scotland and Ireland came under greater scrutiny with the resulting emphasis that they were Norwegians, not Danes as in England. This seems partly inspired by the desire to define Irish and Scottish national heritage as distinct from England. A. Newby and L. Andersson Burnett, 'Between empire and "the North": Scottish identity in the nineteenth century' in Henrik Meinander (ed.), *Parting the mists: views on Scotland as part of Britain and Europe* (Helsinki, 2008), pp 37–53.   **98** Ahlqvist, '*Is acher in gaíth*', p. 26 n.

not all scholars will be comfortable with, for it undermines the value of later historical evidence.[99] Nevertheless, in other contexts it has been accepted that that shifting patterns of political allegiance and perspective caused history to be reinterpreted and reworded throughout the Middle Ages, and it is a fascinating aspect of the literature which has survived.[100] Because of the limitations of the surviving sources, the matter of identifying *Finngaill* and *Dubgaill* is not all black and white. However, the debate is important for our understanding of viking identities in the Insular world of the ninth and tenth centuries.

40; Ó Corráin, 'Vikings in Scotland', p. 306.   **99** Downham, 'The good'.   **100** Ruth Morse, *Truth and convention in the Middle Ages* (Cambridge, 1991).

Chieftains, betaghs and burghers: the Irish on the royal manors of medieval Dublin

ÁINE FOLEY

In an article written at the end of the nineteenth century, James Mills concluded that in spite of the colonization of the hinterland of Dublin by a substantial group of settlers, the Gaelic Irish still made up a considerable proportion of the population.[1] The documentary evidence appears to support this; on the manor of Lucan, for example, the bulk of the revenue generated there came from rents of betaghs, tenants who were Irish in origin.[2] The aim of this essay is to investigate Mills' conclusion and to see if it applies to the royal manors of Co. Dublin, namely Crumlin, Esker, Newcastle Lyons and Saggart, and to explore the relationships between the English and Irish living in this locality.

The attacks by the Irish from the mountains, which became acute from the latter part of the thirteenth century, may leave us with the impression that interactions between the English and Irish were primarily negative. This conflict between the races is seen most tangibly in the petitions sent by beleaguered tenants of the royal manors. At least one of these petitions emanating from Saggart, however, was sent by both the English *and* the Irish tenants.[3] Though it is certainly true that the difficult conditions that defined the fourteenth century were exacerbated by the Irish of the mountains, it is also important to bear in mind that the bulk of the population living on the royal manors was probably Irish. This is particularly true of the manors of Saggart and Newcastle Lyons, which were closer to the mountains. Many tenants were betaghs who were tied to the land but whose rights were often defended even to the detriment of their fellow English tenants. Other tenants of Irish extraction bought English law – or assumed an English identity – and as a result became almost indistinguishable from their English counterparts on the manors.

THE MEIC GILLA MO-CHOLMÓC

In the aftermath of the invasion, the English king took, among other choice pickings, Dublin and its subordinate territory into his own hands and retained

1 James Mills, 'The Norman settlement in Leinster: the cantreds near Dublin', *Journal of the Royal Society of Antiquaries of Ireland*, 24 (1894), 174. 2 F.E. Ball, *A history of the County Dublin* (Dublin, 1906), p. 36. 3 G.O. Sayles (ed.), *Documents on the affairs of Ireland*

it as royal demesne. Nonetheless, the original Gaelic ruling elite of this territory, the Meic Gilla Mo-Cholmóc (the lineal descendants of the Uí Dúnchada), held on to much of their old property, though now held of the king, for at least another generation. In 1207, the 'cantred of Lynhim' was granted by King John to Diarmait Mac Gilla Mo-Cholmóc.[4] This was probably a confirmation of an earlier grant and represented the lands of Newcastle Lyons in south-west Dublin. The use of the word cantred, however, implies a larger geographical area than that of the manor of Newcastle Lyons[5] and may also have incorporated the lands of some of the other royal manors, particularly nearby Saggart. Their property in Kilmactalway was resumed by the crown in 1215 in order to enlarge the newly formed royal manor of Newcastle Lyons.

The Mac Gilla Mo-Cholmóc family, in their desire to integrate into the new order, quickly abandoned their ancestral surname and are generally known by anglicized forms such as FitzDermot. A pipe roll entry for 1262 reveals that John FitzDermot held lands in Rowlagh in Esker,[6] as well as lands in Lucan and Palmerstown.[7] An ancestor of his, who was also called John, held lands on the royal manor of Esker, for which he paid rent of two otter skins in 1227.[8] It is likely that these lands originally belonged to Domnall Mac Gilla Mo-Cholmóc because he and his wife Derbforgaill, who was a daughter of Diarmait Mac Murchada, granted property in Rowlagh to the hospital of St John the Baptist around 1190.[9] Domnall and Derbforgaill also confirmed a grant of lands held by Lifled to the church of Clondalkin sometime before 1190 and, though this manor belonged to the archbishop of Dublin, it appears that they had interests here too.[10] It has also been suggested that this family held Ballyfermot.[11] The continued presence of this family in the area may well have ensured that its colonization by the English was a less unsettling process than it otherwise might have been. This was important, as there was probably limited displacement of a large section of the local population, particularly those at the lower end of the social scale, namely the betagh class, which will be discussed more fully below.

The Meic Gilla Mo-Cholmóc were not the only prominent Gaelic family in this area at the time of the invasion. The Uí Amalgada, descendants of the Uí Chellaig Chualann, who were driven into the mountains by the Uí Dúnlainge

before the king's council (Dublin, 1979), §41.   **4** Paul MacCotter, *Medieval Ireland, territorial, political and economic divisions* (Dublin, 2008), p. 163.   **5** Ball, *County Dublin*, iv, p. 64. **6** Rowlagh is now in Clondalkin, but during the medieval period it was part of the manor of Esker. Even as late as the beginning of the twentieth century this townland was in the parish of Esker: Ball, *County Dublin*, iv, p. 75.   **7** 46 Hen. III, *Report of the Deputy Keeper of the Public Records in Ireland* (Dublin, 1869–) [hereafter *RDKPRI*], xxxv, p. 44.   **8** John Gilbert, *History of the city of Dublin* (Dublin 1854), p. 233.   **9** Eric St John Brooks (ed.), *Register of the hospital of S. John the Baptist without the New Gate* (Dublin, 1936), §363; Marie Therese Flanagan, *Irish royal charters: texts and contexts* (Oxford, 2005), p. 276.   **10** N.B. White (ed.), *The 'Dignitas decani' of St Patrick's Cathedral, Dublin* (Dublin, 1957), §111.

(ancestors of the Meic Gilla Mo-Cholmóc), were overlords here in the twelfth century. Mills assumed that the lands of the Uí Chellaig Chualann were south of Tallaght, but, based on place-name and documentary evidence, Nicholls established that this territory not only took in these lands but stretched further east as far as Ballinteer and Balally.[12] A Hamon Hohauelgan is mentioned in the pipe roll of 1225 as owning land on the mountainous royal manor of Okelly and his name would suggest that he was a descendant of the Uí Amalgada. Balally, or Ballyhawyl as it was known in governmental records of the post-invasion period, was called after this family and Hamon himself seems to have given Edmondstown its name.[13] Just like the Mac Gilla Mo-Cholmóc family, the Uí Amalgada adapted to each subsequent wave of settlement and remained landowners in the area at least until the late thirteenth century. When the royal manor of Okelly vanished from the records, much of its territory was lost to the Irish but some areas like Ballinteer became outer granges of the royal manor of Saggart.

BETAGHS ON THE ROYAL MANORS

The Gaelic Irish are not always easy to identify, but the group that we can certainly recognize as being Irish on the royal manors are the betaghs. Edmund Curtis believed that the betagh class existed before 1170 and Mac Niocaill and others have further advanced our understanding of what was meant by the term betagh in pre-Anglo-Norman Ireland.[14] However, the betagh class of the post-invasion period bear little similarity to their pre-invasion counterparts.

---

11 The evidence that this family owned this manor is based on the erroneous assumption that Ballyfermot means Dermot's town (see Ball, *County Dublin*, iv, p. 101). Indeed, in some documents dating from the late thirteenth century it is called Ballydermot, but it is more commonly styled Balitormod (see, for example, H.S. Sweetman and G.F. Handcock (eds), *Calendar of documents relating to Ireland* [hereafter *CDI*], 1171–1307, 5 vols (London, 1875–86); *1293–1301*, §§280, 587). Þormundr (Thormod) is an Old Norse personal name, but the *baile* component is entirely Irish (see Magne Oftedal, 'Scandinavian place-names in Ireland' in Bo Almqvist and David Greene (eds), *Proceedings of the Seventh Viking Congress* (Dublin, 1976), p. 127). The name Ballyfermot probably dates to no earlier than the middle of the twelfth century, as there is scant evidence that *baile* was used before this date (Liam Price, 'A note on the use of the word *baile* in place-names', *Celtica* 6 (1963), 119–26). Therefore, though it is possible that the FitzDermots were the owners of these lands at the time of the invasion, it is more likely that their owner was an Ostman.   12 Mills, 'The Norman settlement in Leinster', 170; K.W. Nicholls, 'Three topographical notes', *Peritia* 5 (1986), 411. Ballinteer was an outer grange of the royal manor of Saggart in the fourteenth century, Pipe roll 11 Ed. III, *RDKPRI*, xlv, p. 56.   13 K.W. Nicholls, 'Medieval Leinster dynasties and families: three topographical notes', *Peritia* 5 (1986), 409–15 at 412.   14 Edmund Curtis, 'Rental of the manor of Lisronagh, 1333, and notes on "betagh" tenure in medieval Ireland', *Proceedings of the Royal Irish Academy*, 43C3 (1936), 41–76; Liam Price, 'The origin of the word betagius', *Ériu* 20 (1966), 185–90; Gearóid Mac Niocaill, 'The origins of the betagh', *Irish Jurist* n.s. 1 (1966), 292–8.

This word appears to have been used very loosely by the English colonists and it is likely that often it meant little more to them than tenant or client. Gradually, the term betagh became associated with the Irish who had remained in the conquered areas after the invasion, and this group, by and large, was comprised of the native peasantry. The betaghs on the royal manor of Okelly, as well as the royal manors of Othee and Obrun in modern-day Co. Wicklow, are mentioned in the pipe roll of 1228: they paid £8 10s. 4d. in rent and also gave food at Christmas.[15]

Though betaghs could still be found on the manors belonging to the archbishop of Dublin during the late sixteenth century, the court rolls for Esker and Crumlin, which also date from this period, reveal that betaghs had long since disappeared from these royal manors.[16] Nevertheless, they were undoubtedly an important element of society on the royal manors in an earlier period. In fact, a family by the name of Betagh can be found on the royal manor of Esker in the early-modern period and they may possibly be descendants of Adam and Ralph Betagh who appear in the sources three hundred years earlier.[17] Unfortunately, it cannot be established where Adam and Ralph Betagh had lands except that they came from Dublin. However, they had to pay substantial fines into the exchequer of up to five marks on more than one occasion as surety to keep the peace and therefore they appear to have been persons of some means.

In 1307, Henry Kissok was granted forty-five acres of land in Esker that had previously belonged to an Irishman named Maurice Moleran, who was a betagh of the king.[18] Kissok also held lands in Bothercolyn, which was part of Saggart, at this time and he may have acquired this mountainous property from an Irishman too.[19] An inquisition established that Moleran had no goods with which to pay the rent of 8½d. per acre owed for this land. He had also sold his house here and had concealed another five acres he held on this manor to avoid paying rent on it. This confiscation of land clearly had more to do with Moleran's irresponsibility as a tenant than his ethnic origins.

In fact, the evidence would suggest that it was the exception rather than the rule to remove betaghs from their land and grant them to Englishmen, and therefore this might imply that the Kissok family were Irish in origin. They either took their name from Kissoge in Esker or gave the area this name. It is entirely possible that they were a Gaelic Irish family who had acquired English law. As will be seen below, the rights of Irish tenants on the king's lands were

15 Pipe roll 13 Hen. III, *RDKPRI*, xxxv, p. 21; see Linzi Simpson, 'Anglo-Norman settlement in Uí Briúin Cualann, 1169–1350' in Ken Hannigan and William Nolan (eds), *Wicklow: history and society* (Dublin, 1994), pp 191–236 esp. pp 202–6.   **16** Edmund Curtis, 'The court book of Esker and Crumlin, 1592–1600', *Journal of the Royal Society of Antiquaries of Ireland*, 20 (1930), 143.   **17** Edmund Curtis, 'Court book', 19 (1929), p. 48; *CDI, 1285–92*, §§965, 1078, 1148; *CDI, 1293–1301*, §§206.   **18** National Archives of Ireland [NAI] EX 2/1, 193–4.   **19** *CDI, 1293–1301*, §391.

protected by the royal courts. This was probably because the Irish, the majority of whom were probably unfree tenants, had more tenurial obligations than their English counterparts and it was to the crown's advantage to protect these rights. The Kissoge family, who are unlikely to have been betagh in origin, will be discussed below.

The policy of protecting the rights of the betaghs is illustrated in a case dating from 1310. In this year, David Otrescan complained that he had been illegally ousted from lands in Saggart that had originally belonged to his father Nicholas who was a betagh.[20] The new occupant of the lands was an Englishman called John Fangoner who claimed rights of this land through his wife Ostina, who appeared to be Nicholas' granddaughter as the lands had previously passed from Nicholas to his son John, David's brother. This case shows an example of intermarriage between the Irish and the English which would have otherwise gone unrecorded if not for the dispute over these lands. John Fangoner argued that Ostina held these lands as her inheritance at the time he married her. The court did not dispute this, but nonetheless David the Irishman was given seisin of these lands. The court ruled in his favour because he was a 'true betagh of the king' and had the means to pay the rent and services for this land. They feared that John Fangoner, as an Englishman (and free), could not be compelled to carry out the customary obligations associated with this holding. Moreover, he could move away at any time and take his goods with him, while David as a betagh was tied to the lands. In short, the court decided in David Otrescan's favour because, in this case, it was more advantageous to the king to have a betagh as a tenant rather than an Englishman. David Otrescan's holding was nine acres and while this would be considered a small plot of land by modern standards it was more than enough to sustain a family at that time. In England, large peasant holdings varied between twelve and eighty acres and thus Otrescan's holding was modest but bigger than the average holding of a small-holder, which was about five acres.[21] What is more, Otrescan's landholding was probably larger than that of cottagers living on the same manor. It is important to differentiate between cottagers and betaghs because, though betaghs were also tied to the land and could hold similar-sized plots of land, some of them could also be very substantial landholders.

When Clement Ocathyl, one of the king's betaghs, was slain at Cruagh in the Dublin Mountains in 1303 he left behind a large amount of property.[22] At the time of his death he possessed four cows with calves, one ox, three horses, thirty sheep and a pig. Aside from the livestock, he also had a substantial amount of grain and other foodstuff in his possession and among his personal property was a brass pot worth half a mark and a chest. John le Archer, Richard Rikeman, Augustine Ocolan and Godfrey de Brotham stood security

---

20 NAI EX 2/3, pp 488–9.   **21** Robert Bartlett, *England under the Norman and Angevin kings, 1075–1225* (Oxford, 2000), pp 319–20.   **22** NAI EX 2/1, p. 60.

to pay his heriot, the death duty owed to the king. These men, who appear to be both English and Irish in ethnic origin, also undertook to keep these goods in safekeeping until Ocathyl's sons came of age. Although no landholding is mentioned, this memoranda–roll entry does specify that these sons would inhabit the demesne lands of the king, and therefore Ocathyl probably lived on one of the royal manors, quite possibly one of the outer granges of the manor of Saggart. Again, this particular case confirms that the tenurial rights of the Irish tenants on the royal manors were protected.

In 1306 eight crannocks of oats belonging to Conor O'Hanley, who was also a betagh of the king, were found in the house of William Fetting in New Street near St Patrick's.[23] In the same year Gregory de Bree and John de Colchester acknowledged that they had goods worth in excess of 10*s*. that had belonged to another king's betagh named William Oharchur. Moreover, John le Tanner of the Coombe admitted that he had in his possession three crannocks and two bushels of barley that had once belonged to the same William. Why they had the property of these two men is unknown, but since William Oharchur appears to have died in violent circumstances they may have had some involvement in this crime too. The circumstances of William's death are not explained, but it is unlikely that his ethnicity was a particular motivation. While John de Colchester was almost certainly of English blood, it is possible that Gregory de Bree was an Irishman.[24]

LAND USAGE AS EVIDENCE OF THE SOCIAL STATUS OF THE BETAGH CLASS

What is clear is that both the above betaghs had a fairly large amount of cereal in their possession at the time of their death and this may indicate that they were involved in arable farming. Land usage can be an indicator of social status and the extent of the lands and chattels an individual possessed obviously offer clues as to their place in society. If O'Hanley and Oharchur did grow cereal it would indicate that they probably held fertile, low-lying lands, and were reasonably prosperous. In the medieval period, wealth was normally assessed by the amount of land a person possessed. Mary Lyons observed that land usage among the tenants of the royal manors was linked to the size of their holding.[25] The larger the holding the more likely it was that its owner would be involved in tillage farming. Moreover, it follows that the greater the involvement in tillage farming the higher up the social scale that person was likely to be and, indeed, the less likely it was that he was Irish.

---

23 Ibid., p. 160.　24 He was possibly related to Robert le Bree, prominent merchant and mayor of Dublin who bought English law, *CDI, 1285–92*, §748.　25 M.C. Lyons, 'Manorial administration and the manorial economy of Ireland, *c.*1200–1377' (PhD, U. Dublin, 1984),

Those lower down the social scale were more likely to be involved in raising livestock. In 1295 John O'Tire, an Irishman who held lands in Ballinteer, which formed part of the manor of Saggart, received hens as rent from the betaghs on his land.[26] Moreover, when, in 1319, a group of smallholders on the manor of Crumlin went into arrears, the sheriff seized their sheep; this seizure occurred at harvest time, but there is no mention of the sheriff taking any crops from them. This is probably because this particular group of tenants did not grow cereal on a significant scale.[27] While these few examples cannot definitively prove that social status was linked to different forms of farming practice, it does seem reasonable that this was the case. This changed somewhat as the fourteenth century progressed when there was a general shift from tillage to pastoral farming. The unsettled conditions of the colony were part of the reason for this shift in farming practices. Judging by the rents they paid, the betaghs living on John O'Tire's lands probably only held small amounts of land. However, betaghs like Clement Ocathyl left a substantial amount of belongings behind when they died, indicating that it is not possible to pigeon-hole betaghs into a particular economic group. While some may have held little more land than a cottager, others – at the very least – could count themselves among the most prosperous tenants on the manors.

COMPARISON BETWEEN THE BETAGH CLASS OF IRELAND AND THE VILLEIN CLASS OF ENGLAND

Many writers in the early to mid-twentieth century, like Curtis and Otway-Ruthven, made parallels between the betagh class to be found in Ireland and the villein class of England. When the Normans invaded England in the eleventh century, much of the native population was pressed into this servile class, and a sharp distinction developed between the villeins, who were tied to the land, and freemen.[28] The question is whether the betagh class in Ireland was inspired by the villeinage system in England, or whether they developed independently of each other. The conditions of servitude for the betaghs may well have been similar to those of villeins across the Irish Sea,[29] but this does not necessarily mean that they shared a common origin.

In terms of legal status, the betaghs of the royal manors appear to have had many similarities with villeins living on the royal demesne in England. Though English villeins could not appeal to royal courts, these courts would often intervene and investigate if their rights as tenants on the king's lands were infringed.[30] In Dublin, this is echoed in the case already mentioned involving the Irishman David Otrescan, whose rights as a king's betagh were upheld

p. 35. **26** *CDI, 1293–1301*, §259. **27** NAI RC 8/12, 94–5. **28** Mac Niocaill, 'Origins of the betagh', 298. **29** Price, 'Origin of the word betagius', 185. **30** R.S. Hoyt, *The royal*

against the claims of the Englishman John Fangoner over the same parcel of land. The crown did not do this because it was particularly enlightened or fair with regard to the rights of its betaghs; it simply made more sense to protect the rights of a legally unfree tenant because of the customary obligations they were compelled to perform.[31] Moreover, these unfree men could not leave their property without their lord's permission. A freeman, on the other hand, could come and go as he pleased and was not obliged to perform the same duties as a villein or betagh. Ensuring that tenants were compelled to remain on their lands was even more important in Dublin than England because an empty parcel of land here made the whole locality vulnerable. Lands that were waste could fall into the hands of the Irish in the nearby mountains, or English outlaws, which resulted in the rents and profits being forever lost to the crown.

While the inhabitants of the royal demesne in England enjoyed certain freedoms, those individuals living on the ancient demesne were a particularly 'privileged species'. Even those of villein status felt the benefits of living on the ancient demesne. Technically, as legally unfree men, they could not appeal to the royal courts but the royal justices were willing to intervene on their behalf and investigate any complaints or concerns they may have had. A villein would legally become a freeman if he lived on the ancient demesne for more than a year and a day and could not be removed by his previous lord. The same privileges extended to Ireland and a villein living on the king's rural demesnes or within one of the royal towns, including Dublin, could claim freedom from his former lord if he lived there for more than a year and a day.

Interestingly, there is evidence that betaghs, the native Irish peasantry, who resided on the king's rural lands, enjoyed the same royal protection and could not be taken back by their former lords. In 1283 William le Deveneys, who was keeper of the king's demesne lands in Dublin, was granted three carucates and forty-five acres of land in the tenement of Brownstown, adjacent to the royal manor of Newcastle Lyons, for seven pounds of silver. He also held lands in Balitened, which is modern-day Powerscourt in Co. Wicklow. He paid a much reduced rent for his land because extensive areas of it remained waste due to war with the Irish. The proximity of these lands to the mountains undoubtedly explains why he received them so cheaply. William stressed in a petition dating from 1290 that he had restored these lands to the peace. The petition states that the betaghs who had previously occupied these lands had fled at the time that they were in a state of war and he sought permission to recover these tenants. He requested the right to erect a gallows and the power to judge the Irish, the king's rebels, and traitors who broke the peace on his land. This privilege was denied him. Evidently he thought the gallows would serve as a

demesne in English constitutional history, 1066–1272 (New York, 1950), p. 196. **31** See R.H. Hilton, *A medieval society* (Cambridge, 1983), p. 129, for some of the obligations associated with villeinage in England.

deterrent if they considered absconding again. He was, however, given permission to seek out and recover his betaghs with one stipulation; if they were living elsewhere on the king's demesne they were to be left unmolested.

This would suggest that legally they were considered to be of similar status to the villeins of England and that they were under the king's protection. In England, this concession does not appear to have been extended to villeins who lived in all parts of the royal demesne and may have been reserved to those resident on the ancient demesne. It is possible that this order to Deveneys was referring to betaghs residing on the ancient demesne lands in Dublin.

The Irish may not have had the same recourse to the law as those among their English neighbours who belonged to the emerging gentry class. Nevertheless, they must have had a lot in common with the peasantry of English extraction living on the manors, as they would not have had the same access to justice as their wealthier neighbours. Some of the petitions sent from the royal manors mention both the English and Irish tenants and while they are visible as a group separately they do not feature prominently in the sources. Most of the sources relied on for the royal manors are administrative in nature and they tend to offer a distorted view of the social make-up of the locality.

THE IRISH AND GRANTS OF ENGLISH LAW

The Irish were technically outside the law and did not serve in local administrative office or did not appear in the panels of jurors. Therefore, most are invisible within these sources. However, some Irishmen do turn up in these administrative documents, particularly those individuals who purchased English law. The Irish often had names that do not appear to be obviously Irish and sometimes the only evidence we have of their ethnic origins is the fact that they were granted English law. Consequently, there could potentially be a lot of Irishmen featured in the sources who cannot be identified as such. One famous example that can be identified, however, is Robert de Bree (or Bray) who served as mayor of Dublin in 1292–4, but there is also evidence of ambitious men of his ilk on the royal manors.[32]

In 1292 William, son of Donald le Clerk, and his children were granted the use of English law.[33] William came from the royal manor of Newcastle Lyons and this patent letter is the only indicator of his ethnic origins. Donald is probably an anglicized version of Domhnall, but he gave his son an English name. His surname may suggest that he was a cleric or it may simply have

---

32 *CDI, 1285–92*, §748; J.T. Gilbert (ed.), *Historic and municipal documents of Ireland, 1172–1320* (London, 1870), pp xxx–xxxi; H.F. Berry, 'Catalogue of mayors, provosts and bailiffs of Dublin City, AD1229 to 1447' in Howard Clarke (ed.), *Medieval Dublin, the living city* (Dublin, 1990), p. 158.   33 *CDI, 1285–92*, §1096.

indicated that he was able to write. If he had an education he may have worked in an administrative position which would imply that not every person of Irish origin living on the manors was necessarily a betagh. It would at least suggest that not all Irishmen living in Dublin worked on the land and that they could have other occupations. He may have given his son an English name because he wanted his family to smoothly assimilate into English society.

In about 1285 an Irishman from Saggart called Richard Pudding petitioned for and was granted English law.[34] Richard was described as a burgher in this petition, and therefore even before he applied for English law he was already enjoying some of the benefits associated with being a freeman. Saggart was a borough and this meant that it possessed a basic municipal corporation and special privileges conferred by royal charter. Boroughs were towns in the legal sense of the word but many in Ireland never developed into anything more than rural settlements. These boroughs with their special privileges were established to attract colonists from England.[35] The benefits of creating a borough in Saggart are clear. It was closer to the mountains and more at risk from Irish raids than other areas of Dublin, and therefore these privileges gave potential tenants an extra incentive to settle here. An Irishman may have been accepted as a burgher because it was difficult to find enough suitable Englishmen to put down roots in the area. Moreover, Saggart was part of the ancient demesne, with all the privileges that entailed. His status as a tenant living on the king's ancient demesne would have set Richard Pudding apart from other tenants living on the king's lands – Irish or English. It is likely that Richard, though he was not of English extraction, applied for English law in order to continue enjoying the privileges that he already had as a freeman on this manor. In 1292 Pudding was in debt for £8 to the king,[36] which may have been connected to his purchase of English law. It is likely that he paid a substantial amount of money to obtain this privilege. Richard was allowed to pay off his debts in instalments of 20*s.* a year; hence, even though he could not afford to pay off the whole sum at once, he must have been relatively prosperous if he was capable of paying off this amount each year. Pudding appears to have frequently got into legal difficulties. He was fined 15*s.* in 1288 and 40*d.* in 1292 for unspecified trespasses.[37] In 1294 Pudding was paying the farm of the royal manor of Saggart into the exchequer and it is possible that he held the office of reeve at this time as it was usually this individual who was responsible for collecting the rent of the manor and delivering it to the

---

34 The National Archives [TNA], SC 8/331/15677.   35 For medieval rural boroughs, see John Bradley, 'Rural boroughs in medieval Ireland: nucleated or dispersed settlements?' in Jan Klápšte (ed.), *Ruralia III* (Prague, 2000), pp 288–93, and for Co. Dublin boroughs, see John Bradley, 'The medieval boroughs of Dublin' in Conleth Manning (ed.), *Dublin and beyond the Pale: studies in honour of Patrick Healy* (Bray, 1998), pp 129–44.   36 *CDI, 1285–92*, §§1108, 1109; *Calendar fine rolls, 1272–1307*, p. 311.   37 *CDI, 1285–92*, §§371, 1148.

exchequer each year.[38] Four years later he was paying the rent on the mills of this manor.[39] The tenement containing the mill was usually the most desirable and lucrative holding on the manor, particularly as often the other tenants were obliged to grind their corn here too. Richard Pudding must have been dead by 1302, because by this date his wife Margery was responsible for paying the rent on these mills.[40]

TREATMENT OF THE IRISH WITHIN THE JUDICIAL SYSTEM

It is likely that there were many Irishmen living on the royal manors who purchased English law, or who assimilated themselves into English society to such an extent that no one remembered that they were Irish anymore. These few examples of Irishmen willing to assume the identity of Englishmen should not be taken as typical, however. There is evidence that the Irish did see themselves as being separate and distinct from their English neighbours, and it is also true in many cases that they were treated differently because of their ethnic origins. The clearest proof of this can be found in how they were dealt with by the courts. Sources like the justiciary rolls, for example, are very informative as to the kinds of punishments handed out to the various different ethnic groups. Ciaran Parker observed that in Co. Waterford an Irishman was no more likely to be convicted than an Englishman, but if found guilty was more likely to be hanged.[41] This seems to be the case in Co. Dublin too, but it appears that these Irish were also likely to be among the poorest members of society. Cormok de Carrickbrenan, who was undoubtedly an Irishman, was hanged for the murder of Jordan le Waleys,[42] who was most probably of Welsh extraction. The justiciary roll entry reveals that Cormok had no chattels, and thus perhaps social status, as well as ethnicity, played a part in how some of the Irish were treated by the courts.

An Irishman who was executed even though he had the ways and means to pay his fine was likely to have been a particularly notorious individual, or a repeat offender. For example, Milo Mcbridyn of Cruagh, hanged in 1305, must have been reasonably well off because his wife Raghenilda paid 60s. for the return of his chattels after his execution.[43] Among the ten men who served as her pledges was Reginald de Barnewell, who was one of the most prominent landowners in Dublin, and William Corbaly, who probably came from Corbally in Saggart; they and the rest of the pledges were all Englishmen. Incidentally, Reginald de Barnewell was also one of the jurors who decided her husband's

38 *CDI, 1293–1301*, §139.   39 Ibid., §§550, 587, 637.   40 *CDI, 1302–7*, §72.   41 Ciaran Parker, 'The politics and society of County Waterford in the thirteenth and fourteenth Centuries' (PhD, U. Dublin, 1992), p. 334.   42 James Mills et al. (eds), *Calendar of the justiciary rolls of Ireland* [hereafter *CJRI*], 3 vols (Dublin, 1906–56), ii, p. 498.   43 Ibid., p. 485.

fate.[44] McBridyn was charged with killing Henry Golygthly and burying his body so secretly that it could not be found. The entry also mentions that he was assisted by his son Luke, who is not mentioned elsewhere in the rolls, and it is possible he was pardoned; perhaps if prominent members of the gentry were standing as pledges for his mother they may have assisted him in gaining a pardon too.

In 1305 the community of the royal manor of Saggart showed a solidarity that transcended ethnic divisions. Kevin of Saggart, who is likely to have been an Irishman, was charged with receiving his son Martin, a common burglar and robber; however, the jury found him not guilty. The same jury found Andrew le Deveneys and his wife Grathagh not guilty of receiving Kelt, a man of David McKilecoul O'Toole. Grathagh was an O'Toole herself but had married an Englishman; it is possible that they were the parents of John le Deveneys, who was employed by William le Long of Saggart as his squire. Some years later William and John were charged with stealing a stallion belonging to Robert Darditz in the liberty of Trim and driving it into Dublin.[45] William was the son of Martin le Long who served on the jury that acquitted Andrew le Deveneys and his Irish wife. As tenants on the same manor, they would have known each other well, and obviously it would have been difficult to convict someone with whom one was on personal terms. Kevin of Saggart may have even named his son after his fellow tenant, Martin le Long; this Christian name was certainly not common in Ireland at this time. Other members of the jury were certainly locals; Reginald de Barnewell held the manors of Ballyfermot, Drimnagh and Terenure, John Owen was a major tenant on the royal manors of Esker and Saggart. Furthermore, John Marshal may have had landed interests in nearby Rathcoole and was possibly related to the Marshals of Newcastle Lyons. The jurors not only acquitted Grathagh but described how she often went up into the mountains and assisted in the recovery of cattle stolen by her kinsmen. In later years Grathagh again got into trouble for her close association with the O'Tooles when she was accused of spying on the men of Saggart on behalf of the Irish in the mountains. The jurors were not willing to give Grathagh the benefit of the doubt on this occasion and she was found guilty of spying and executed.[46] This shift in attitude may have had much to do with the general deteriorating conditions of the colony at this time. The great European famine of 1315–17 would have been tumultuous enough in itself, but it also led to increased raids from the Irish of the mountains. Moreover, the unrest created by the Bruce invasion at exactly the same time may also have motivated the Irish to raid the manors closest to the mountains. Grathagh may have posed a genuine threat to the security of this manor, however, and there is no evidence that she was in any

44 Ibid., pp 478–9.   **45** Ibid., iii, p. 163.   **46** James Lydon, 'Medieval Wicklow: "a land of war"' in Hannigan and Nolan (eds), *Wicklow: history and society*, p. 14.

way typical of the Irish living here; or even that the punishment meted out to her by her fellow tenants was in any way representative of how they normally treated their Irish neighbours. Some of the petitions emanating from the royal manors were sent on behalf of both the king's Irish and English tenants. Therefore, it would appear that, by and large, the Irish tenants were as concerned by these raids as their English counterparts.[47]

Consequently, the evidence would suggest that the Irish living on the royal manors and their environs were just as beleaguered by the Irish living in the mountains as the rest of the community. In 1306 an Irishman named Oconyl was forced to move from Kilmesantan to Tathmothan, both of which were located on the manor of Tallaght, to avoid providing the O'Tooles with food and drink. The jurors in his case included tenants on all four of the royal manors, namely Martin le Long of Saggart, Adam Jordan and W. le White of Newcastle Lyons, John Kissok of Esker and John de Crumlin. They vouched for him and confirmed that Oconyl never gave the O'Tooles food and drink except when they were in the king's peace and they stressed that even then he only did so under duress.[48] In spite of their support, he was fined 100s. Here was an example of communal unity that crossed not only ethnic but possibly social divisions too. Moreover, not only did the jury accept that Oconyl was an unwilling receiver, but two other local men who were probably of English extraction, Hugh Canoun and Simon le Bailiff of Clondalkin, stood as his pledges.

While acknowledging that evidence for solidarity between both races living on the royal manors can be found, it is important also to acknowledge that the courts had a tendency to mete out different punishments depending on the ethnic origins of the defendant. Certainly, Englishmen accused of the same crime that led to Grathagh le Deveney's conviction and execution were treated far more leniently. In 1306 John Jordan, a brother of Adam Jordan of Newcastle Lyons, was fined £20 for being a spy for the Irish and for receiving them and other malefactors. One assumes these malefactors were English outlaws and perhaps even the Tyrels of nearby Lyons, a notorious gang roaming the locality as this time.[49] In his case, there is no evidence that the jury thought him innocent of these crimes – in fact the heavy fine would suggest otherwise. Also in 1306 a monk of St Mary's Abbey, Dublin, was charged with receiving Cormok de Carrickbrenan and though only a fragment of his name survives it

---

47 For an example of a petition from both English and Irish tenants, see Sayles (ed.), *Affairs of Ireland*, §41.   48 Adam Jordan, a king's serjeant, appears to have held lands in the manor of Newcastle Lyons, because in 1309 John Lympit who was provost of this manor forgave him part of his rent because Adam did not make the tenants of Newcastle Lyons serve on inquisitions and juries while he was in office, NAI, EX 2/3 pp 475–8.   49 For an account of this criminal gang, see Áine Foley, 'Violent crime in medieval County Dublin: a symptom of degeneracy?' in Seán Duffy (ed.), *Medieval Dublin X* (Dublin, 2010), pp 226–40.

is likely that he was English. He was found not guilty, but the fact that he was charged in the first place would suggest an association between these two men. The evidence in the justiciary rolls proves that there was a great deal of interaction between both races even in an area as heavily colonized as south Co. Dublin, and – what is even more remarkable considering the type of source – much of this interaction was positive.

The justiciary rolls yield other examples of interactions between the different ethnic groups within Co. Dublin; for example, in 1308 William Bernard, probably an Englishman, was accidentally stabbed by John McCorcan, who was almost certainly Irish, during a game of ball involving men from the town of Newcastle Lyons.[50] The entry makes it clear that both men were 'fast friends' both in the past and at the time of the event and after he paid William damages of 5*s*. John was pardoned. Clearly both ethnic groups within the manor of Newcastle Lyons interacted with each other; they shared common pastimes and acknowledged bonds of friendship. John accidently stabbed his friend while running for a ball – evidently there was no ill feeling there. Unfortunately, court records often highlight the animosity between both ethnic groups and not the bonds that frequently held them together. Though the statutes passed at the parliament in Kilkenny in 1297 admonished Englishmen for wearing Irish dress, for example, there is no hint here that the administration was promoting the kind of segregation found in later statutes and the evidence suggests close ties and integration between both ethnic groups, even in an area of the colony as heavily settled with English as Dublin. In fact, most of the evidence for violence and crime was among the English themselves. Moreover, when the Irish committed crimes against those of their own race they were usually just fined; for example, a group of men including Dermot McBride were fined 40*s*. for robbing Finyn the clerk of Bryaneston,[51] who was a follower of John de Balygodman; both Dermot and Finyn appear to be Irish, but many Irishmen would have adopted English names and it is not always easy to recognize them in the sources, and therefore it is possible that others received similar leniency from the courts. In most cases where men who were clearly Irish were involved in acts of violence it was as followers of more powerful members of the English gentry. Certainly, the 1297 statutes would suggest that a high degree of interaction and, indeed, assimilation was occurring between the two races. It would also indicate that the administration was uncomfortable about this interaction. This acculturation was seen in its most tangible form when Englishmen adopted the dress of Irishmen and began sporting a distinctive Irish hairstyle known as the *cúlán*.[52] This led to many

50 *CJRI*, iii, p. 103, note that the source refers to Newcastle Lyons as a town; this may signify its borough status. 51 *CJRI*, ii, p. 484. 52 H.F. Berry (ed.), *Statutes and ordinances and acts of the parliament of Ireland, King John to Henry V* (Dublin, 1907), p. 211; Philomena Connolly, 'The enactments of the Dublin Parliament of 1297' in James Lydon

unfortunate incidences where Englishmen were murdered on the mistaken assumption that they were Irish!

IRISH MANORIAL ADMINISTRATORS?

Many of the reeves and provosts serving on the royal manors may have been Irish in origin. Names like Kissok, Beg, Schynnagh,[53] Heyne and Bretnagh at least suggest the possibility that the native population played a part in the administration of the manors. The Kissok family, who have already been mentioned, were possibly Gaelic Irish in origin. They came from Kissoge on the manor of Esker and, as noted above, either got their name from this area or gave the place its name. At the beginning of the fourteenth century Henry Kissok held lands on the royal manors of Esker and Newcastle Lyons.[54] Other members of this family also held lands on the royal manor of Saggart.[55] Maurice Kissok held land on the archiepiscopal manor of Clondalkin, and while his fellow tenants were freeholders he appears to have been a burgher, which may imply that he was of higher social status.[56] The Kissok family held lands on the same manors as the Meic Gilla Mo-Cholmóc a century earlier. This may be no more than a coincidence but it is at least plausible that the Kissok family were their descendants. The Meic Gilla Mo-Cholmóc transformed themselves into the FitzDermots in the early thirteenth century, but John FitzDermot's son Ralph appears to have left no male heirs because Albert de Kenley, who married his widow Joan, acquired an interest in at least some of his lands after his death.[57] Though the main line might have died out, it is more than likely that cadet branches of this family remained in this area and assimilated into English society. Dermot of Ballydowd, who also appears in the records at the beginning of the fourteenth century, may be another descendant of this family.[58]

   Those who held the offices of reeve and receiver usually came from the locality of the royal manors and since a substantial proportion of those tenants were Irish it is reasonable to assume that some of them served in these offices. Certainly members of the Kissok family served in manorial administration.[59] Another family whose name suggests they were Irish in origin were the Begs of Saggart.[60] In 1306 Richard Beg was provost of Saggart and his family already

---

(ed.), *Law and disorder in thirteenth-century Ireland: the Dublin parliament of 1297* (Dublin, 1997), p. 159.   **53** Pipe roll, 18 Ed. II, *RDKPRI*, xlii, pp 54–5. Schynnagh may be derived from Sionnach, the Irish word for fox, and there was a family of this name living on the royal manors during the medieval period.   **54** NAI, RC 8/4, p. 474; RC 8/6, pp 282–4. **55** See, for example, *CDI, 1293–1301*, §637.   **56** Charles McNeill (ed.), *Calendar of Archbishop Alen's Register* (Dublin, 1950), pp 185–9.   **57** *CDI, 1285–92*, §1122; St John Brooks (ed.), *Register of St John*, §365.   **58** *CDI, 1293–1301*, §289.   **59** NAI, EX 2/1, pp 181, 218.   **60** From the Irish word *beag* (small, little).

had a long history on this manor.[61] John Beg may also have served as provost of Saggart, because in 1281 he along with Robert le Deveneys, John Reynald, Simon de Camera, Richard Gerveys and William Comyn paid into the exchequer the farm of Saggart for the previous three years.[62] In Easter term 1286 and on several subsequent occasions John paid the farm of the same manor.[63] Sometime before 1328 another John Beg served as provost of Esker and he may have been the older John's son.[64] From 1296 Richard Beg was paying rent for lands in Saggart.[65] John Beg was still occasionally paying rent on this manor and it is likely that Richard was his son.[66] Richard appears to have been an important individual within his community and he served as provost on more than one occasion.[67] He also served as a juror on inquisitions.[68] The family's interests extended beyond Saggart and they also held lands in Clondalkin at the end of the thirteenth century and they may have had property in Esker, as Thomas Beg served as a pledge for William Kissok of Esker in 1306.[69] He also stood in as a pledge for Henry Kissok who was serjeant of Saggart in the same year.[70] It is possible that he was their kinsman. Sometime before 1318 he was provost of the manor of Crumlin and subsequently he held the office of provost of Esker.[71] Additionally, at some point before 1313 Nicholas Beg served as provost of Crumlin.[72] In the 1350s Adam Beg was paid £1 for capturing John O'Toole and bringing his head before the king's council and he also received £1 13s. 4d. for burning the dwellings of the O'Tooles and the O'Byrnes.[73] However, even though the Beg family seem to have had interests on several royal manors and appear to continue to reside in the vicinity well into the middle of the fourteenth century, there is no evidence that they were major landholders. No member of the family appears to have held any administrative office above manorial level and they did not enjoy the same success as the Kissok family outside the royal manors. Consequently, it is likely that this family were peasants, albeit very prosperous ones.

Another family that appears with some regularity in the records during the fourteenth century is the Dyers of Saggart. In 1332–3 William le Dyer served as the external reeve of Saggart.[74] A decade later Richard Dyer was provost of this manor and in 1364 another William Dyer served as reeve.[75] The Gaelic

---

61 NAI, EX 2/1, p. 159.   62 Pipe roll 10 Ed. I, *RDKPRI*, xxxvi, p. 67.   63 *CDI, 1285–92*, §§215, 271, 1078, 1148; *CDI, 1293–1301*, §§4, 21, 41.   64 Pipe roll 2 Ed. III, *RDKPRI*, xliii, p. 29.   65 *CDI, 1293–1301*, §§329, 363, 408, 550; *CDI, 1302–7*, §72.   66 *CDI, 1293–1301*, §§363, 587.   67 Pipe roll 8 Ed. II, *RDKPRI*, xxxix, p. 56. He was provost of Saggart again in 1313–14.   68 NAI, EX 2/1, pp 258–9; P. Dryburgh and B. Smith (eds), *Inquisitions and extents of medieval Ireland* (London, 2007), §160, p. 87.   69 An inquisition from 1293 names Robert Beg as coming from Clondalkin (*CDI, 1293–1301*, §106). He was responsible for paying the issues of the see of Dublin into the exchequer at the end of the thirteenth century (ibid., §658).   70 NAI, EX 2/1, p. 153.   71 Pipe roll 12 Ed. II, *RDKPRI*, xlii, p. 27; Pipe roll 15 Ed. II *RDKPRI*, xlii, p. 30.   72 Pipe roll 7 Ed. II, *RDKPRI*, xxxix, p. 50. 73 Philomena Connolly (ed.), *Irish exchequer payments, 1270–1446* (Dublin, 1998), p. 483. 74 Pipe roll 6 Ed. III, *RDKPRI*, xliii, p. 61.   75 NAI, RC 8/23, p. 474; NAI, RC 8/28, p. 393.

Irish living in English areas often assumed occupational surnames, and indeed there is compelling evidence that the Dyers were in fact Irish. In 1384–5 Richard Dyer of Saggart was described as a *nativus* of the king.[76] While the term *nativus* may just indicate that Dyer was a serf, it is much more likely that he was a betagh, or at least held land by betagh tenure. As has been demonstrated already, a betagh of the king had legal rights that often exceeded those of a freeman and it is possible that Richard Dyer would have long forgotten his Irish roots if not for the legal benefits he enjoyed as a *nativus* of the king.

CONCLUSION

The evidence would suggest that certainly in the thirteenth and early fourteenth centuries the English lived more or less in harmony with their Irish neighbours on the royal manors. There is proof that they intermarried, though to what degree is difficult to ascertain. Moreover, some of the Irish who had the means acquired English law in order to enjoy the same legal benefits and privileges as their English neighbours. The case of Grathagh le Deveneys may display a hardening in attitudes towards the Irish that grew more acute as the fourteenth century progressed. As the raids by the O'Tooles and O'Byrnes intensified, it is possible that the Irish living on the manors became negatively and erroneously associated with these raiders. Two incidences at Newcastle in 1370 highlight this negative attitude. Thomas de Snitterby captured the Irishman Richard McAoohye and his two sons on this manor on St Patrick's Day.[77] Likewise, another Irishman, Lorcan O'Bouye, was beheaded in Newcastle at around the same time.[78] Nonetheless, an examination of the court rolls of Esker and Crumlin dating from the late sixteenth century confirms that a large proportion of the population of these manors was still Irish. This would suggest that, in spite of the difficulties and ethnic tensions, the Irish were not driven away from the manors. In fact, it would appear that they had eventually lost the taint of betaghry and were now on a more level footing with their English neighbours.[79]

76 NAI, Ferguson Coll., vol. 2, p. 32.   77 NAI RC 8/8, pp 664–5.   78 J.S. Brewer and W. Bullen (eds), *Calendar of the Carew Manuscripts preserved in the archiepiscopal library at Lambeth, 1515–74 [The Book of Howth]* (London, 1867), p. 169.   79 Curtis, 'Court book', 20, p. 143.

Patricians in medieval Dublin: the career of the Sargent family

CHARLES SMITH

INTRODUCTION

Medieval cities and towns were invariably controlled by a small group of wealthy merchant families. They are known variously as *prudhommes*, *seniores* or patricians. Dublin was no exception. The Sargents were among the leading families in the city and played an active role in civic life for over two hundred years. This paper describes their career. It shows how they interacted with others of their class in their business dealings, in the government of the city and in intermarriage. Finally, it describes how they moved successfully into the landed gentry by marriage to the heiress of the lordship of Castleknock, Co. Dublin.

The original meaning of 'sargent 'or 'sergeant' was servant. Later it denoted an officer of the courts. It could mean also a holder of land below the rank of knight.[1] The seal of Thomas Seriaunt, of whom more anon, shows three batons, testimony to the antiquity of this symbol of a sergeant's authority.[2] The name appears in the records in various forms, for example, le Seriaunt, le Sergaunt, Sargent, Sergeant and Serjaunt; I have adopted the form 'sargent', unless the context makes it preferable to use the form in the particular record. Early references suggest an occupation, as in Walter le Seriant; two of that name were admitted to the Dublin guild merchant before 1222. A Radulphus le Sergant of Drogheda was admitted in 1234–5.[3] Many non-residents were admitted to the guild, so one cannot say whether any of these were progenitors of the later Dublin family. Furthermore, there may have been more than one family of the name active in the city. For much of the period, a direct relationship cannot be proved. I think all the Sargents in this account were related, but different branches may have been to the fore at different times.

Ralph, Richard and Roger Serjaunt witnessed grants of land in *Kylmellan* to the monastery of All Hallows, Dublin.[4] Another Serjaunt, Reginald, already

1 Basil Cottle, *Dictionary of surnames* (London, 1967, 2nd ed., 1978), p. 331. 2 J.L. Robinson, 'On the ancient deeds of the parish of St John, Dublin', *Proceedings of the Royal Irish Academy*, 33C7 (1916), p. 223 and pl. xxix. 3 Philomena Connolly and Geoffrey Martin (eds), *The Dublin guild merchant roll, c.1190–1265* (Dublin, 1992), pp 32, 39, 68. 4 Richard Butler (ed.), *Registrum prioratus Omnium Sanctorum juxta Dublin* (Dublin, 1845), pp 58–61.

had property in the same place.[5] *Kyllmellan* has not been identified, but it was in the Kilmainham/Castleknock area.[6] Hugh Tyrrell, lord of Castleknock, confirmed at least one of the grants; the witnesses included Richard and Ralph. These grants were made no later than the 1280s and may have been as early as the 1240s.

FAMILY PROSPERS IN DUBLIN

It is impossible to establish the relationship between Ralph, Richard, Roger and Reginald, but there can be little doubt that they were related. Indeed, in later years one finds these forenames recurring frequently among the Sargents. Another who may have belonged to this family was Alan; he witnessed a grant to St John the Baptist's hospital in the 1250s of 10*s.* from rents from property in Bridge Street. He himself had property near Newgate in 1264–5.[7] There was also a Hugo, who was a provost of the city in 1277–8.[8] There were two provosts, elected officials who assisted the mayor in the discharge of his duties. The Sargents were moving up the social ladder. Further evidence of this is to be found in the career of Walter Sargent. In 1297, he was said to have served the king 'manfully' in Scotland, to such effect that he was pardoned for the death of one Richard de Neusom.[9] But of greater significance is the fact that in 1290 Walter was one of the witnesses to a grant of land in the parish of St James to a John Sargent.[10]

John may have been a son of Hugo, mentioned earlier, given the tendency for civic offices to run in families. He appeared in the records about 1289–90 as a city bailiff.[11] In that capacity, he witnessed the grant of a messuage in Bridge Street, a property that belonged ultimately to Christ Church.[12] In the same year, he accounted for the fee farm of the city.[13] He was a witness with the mayor, his fellow bailiff and other distinguished citizens to a grant of land in Oxmantown to St Mary's Abbey. It appears that quarrying was significant in

5 Ibid., p. 61.   **6** Four saints named Mellán are noted in Whitley Stokes (ed.), *Martyrology of Oengus*, p. 434. Mellán of Inis maccu Cuinn was said to be St Fursa's soul friend. Fursa visited St Maighnenn of Kilmainham (Stokes (ed.), *Martyrology of Oengus*, p. 44). Colm Kenny also has this story in his *Kilmainham* (Dublin, 1995), p. 94.   **7** Eric St John Brooks (ed.), *Register of the hospital of St John the Baptist without the Newgate, Dublin* (Dublin, 1936), pp 20, 31.   **8** Butler (ed.), *Registrum prioratus Omnium Sanctorum*, pp 21–2. He witnessed a grant of land in St George's parish to All Hallows.   **9** H.S. Sweetman and G.F. Handcock (eds), *Calendar of documents relating to Ireland, 1171–1307* [hereafter *CDI*], 5 vols (London, 1875–86), iv (1293–1301), no. 380, pp 175–6.   **10** St John Brooks (ed.), *Register of St John*, p. 3. One cannot be absolutely certain that this Walter and the man who served in Scotland three years earlier are the same.   **11** The title 'provost' was replaced by 'bailiff' towards the end of the thirteenth century.   **12** M.J. McEnery and Raymond Refaussé (eds), *Christ Church deeds* (Dublin, 2001), no. 142, p. 60. This entry is almost certainly incorrect. John Seriaunt and Nicholas the clerk never served as joint bailiffs but Seriaunt was mayor in 1300–1 when Nicholas was a bailiff.   **13** *Report of the deputy keeper of the public records in*

the area, because the northern boundary of the plot was said to be the king's quarry.[14] John was acting in his official capacity, but the family would go on to acquire substantial interests in Oxmantown. At this time, however, John was acquiring property in the parish of St James near Newgate outside the city walls. The deed witnessed by Walter was only one of several.

John Sargent became mayor of Dublin in 1294. He was elected again in 1299 and was re-elected in 1300 and probably in 1301.[15] The city was taken into the king's hands, however, in 1301–2 and during that period he served as a bailiff.[16] He was mayor again in 1304–5, 1306–7 and 1310–11.[17] He witnessed numerous grants and leases as mayor. For example, in 1304 he witnessed a grant of 10s. of rent from a tenement in High Street inside Newgate towards the upkeep of the fabric of St Audoen's Church and the maintenance of a light in the chapel.[18] The family was closely associated with the guild of St Anne in St Audoen's in later years.

John also witnessed several grants in Oxmantown, including one in 1301 in association with a William Sargent, who already had land in the area.[19] He was almost certainly a relative of John, perhaps a brother or a son. He was a city bailiff himself in 1311–12 and in that capacity he was a witness to the transfer of land in Oxmantown by Robert de Nottingham to his nephew, John.[20] Robert was a prominent citizen. He served as mayor on eight occasions between 1309 and 1322. It was he who gave the order to burn the suburbs in the face of the advancing army of the Bruces in 1317. It is clear that the Sargents were now one of the city's leading families.

John found himself in some difficulties during his time as mayor. He had to deal with the problems arising from the arrest of Geoffrey de Morton, a merchant and former mayor. Geoffrey was accused of various offences and was detained for a time in the Tower of London. He had given the keys of the civic chest, in which the city seal was kept, to his wife and John had the task of reclaiming them.[21] More seriously, he had to answer an enquiry in 1304 into his conduct as a bailiff when the city was in the king's hands. He could not produce the records to show that all moneys due to the crown had been paid. He pleaded that his house in Bridge Street, where he kept the rolls, had been destroyed in a great fire that had consumed much of the city. The jury accepted his plea and he was discharged.[22]

Ireland (Dublin, 1869–) [henceforth *RDKPRI*], pp 37, 30.   **14** J.T. Gilbert (ed.), *Chartularies of St Mary's Abbey, Dublin and annals of Ireland, 1162–1370*, 2 vols (London, 1884–6), i, p. 501.   **15** T.W. Moody, F.X. Martin, F.J. Byrne (eds), *A new history of Ireland* (Oxford, 1984, repr. 2002) [henceforth *New history*], ix, p. 549.   **16** *CDI*, v, p. 6.   **17** *New history*, ix, p. 549.   **18** H.F. Berry, 'History of the religious gild of S Anne, in S Audoen's church, Dublin, 1437–1740', *Proceedings of the Royal Irish Academy*, 25C3 (1904), no. 58, p. 64.   **19** Robinson, 'On the ancient deeds', no. 5, p. 180.   **20** Ibid., no. 23, p. 183.   **21** J.T. Gilbert (ed.), *Historic and municipal documents of Ireland, 1172–1320* (London, 1870), p. 229.   **22** Ibid., p. 522.

The mayor also dispensed justice within the city. John found himself sitting in judgment on John Tyrrell, who was charged with stealing food and other goods from many poor people. He committed him to gaol but he seized an axe and escaped by force. He was recaptured and imprisoned again. He appealed to the justiciar but the mayor's judgment was upheld.[23]

John's son, also called John, followed in his father's footsteps.[24] He was a city bailiff in 1330, when he witnessed a property grant in High Street (the premises lay between the messuage of a Richard Rabo on the east and that of John, son of Robert de Moenes on the west; Rabo or Roebuck is in the south of the county and it was held by the le Brun family).[25] He followed his father into the mayoralty in 1341. He continued in the office until the summer of 1347, when he was succeeded by Geoffrey Crompe, followed by Kenewrek Sherman and Crompe again. Sargent was mayor again in 1349–50. In fact, from 1339 to 1350 the office of mayor was held exclusively by these three, Crompe, Sherman and Sargant.[26] This shows the extent to which the city was controlled by a small clique of wealthy individuals, because one had to be wealthy to bear the costs of office. That Sargent was in a position to hold office for seven years in a row testifies to the family's wealth and, possibly, to the potential rewards of office, which made it worthwhile.

One of the tasks John had to undertake as mayor was the prevention of a duel. He was ordered by the king in 1346 to 'take into the king's hands the quarrel between Robert Drake and Alexander de Cretyng', who were about to fight a duel in the field next to St Mary's Abbey.[27]

In 1349, while he was still mayor, he suffered significant loss at the hands of Robert de Emeldon, treasurer of Ireland. The latter was accused of many crimes, ranging from corruption to robbery, rape and murder. One of the charges was that he wrecked the house of the mayor and robbed him of a Flanders chest, a cupboard or dresser, a wooden granary, timber and other goods, all to a total value of 40s.[28] At his trial, de Emeldon claimed benefit of clergy. He was handed over to the archbishop, who freed him after a year.

John was a substantial landholder in Oxmantown. He had a messuage next to St Michan's churchyard at a rent of 8s. a year to the cathedral of the Holy Trinity or Christ Church. He also had land in the manor of Grangegorman 'in the field of the prior' at an annual rent of 43s. 6d.[29] As the rent of an acre was said to be 1s., John must have had over forty-three acres. He survived the Black

23 James Mills et al. (eds), *Calendar of the justiciary rolls of Ireland*, 3 vols (Dublin, 1906–56), i, p. 23.   24 Edward Tresham (ed.), *Rotulorum patentium et clausorum cancellariae Hiberniae calendarium* (Dublin, 1828) [henceforth *RPH*], p. 42.   25 McEnery and Refaussé (eds), *Christ Church deeds*, no. 579, p. 146.   26 *New history*, ix, pp 549–50.   27 *RPH*, p. 57. De Cretyng seems to have been a royal official. He was constable of Cashel castle in the 1350s. Philomena Connolly (ed.), *Irish exchequer payments, 1270–1446*, 2 vols (Dublin, 1998), ii, pp 479, 486, 491, 497.   28 G.O. Sayles (ed.), *Documents on the affairs of Ireland before the king's council* (Dublin, 1979), pp 198–9.   29 McEnery and Refaussé (eds), *Christ Church deeds*, no. 570, pp 144–5; James Mills (ed.), *Account roll of the priory of the Holy*

Death, possibly by withdrawing to his Grangegorman estate. He was still alive in 1353, when he witnessed, with others, the release by Maurice, earl of Kildare, of the rectory and vicarage of Kilcullen to Christ Church. He was named in the witness list as 'Seriaunt senior', obviously to distinguish him from his son, John junior.[30]

John junior, the third of the name, was mayor by 1353 and continued to hold office through 1356. He was a witness to various transactions, many, no doubt, by virtue of his office. But the pattern indicates continuity with the family's known interests and connections. Thus he was a witness to grants relating to Christ Church and to leases in Oxmantown.[31] In 1354, he was involved in graver matters touching the defence of the colony. He was called on by the justiciar to come to his assistance with archers in the war against the O'Byrnes in Wicklow. He was paid £6 13s. 4d. from the exchequer for losses sustained in the conflict and for wages. It is worth quoting the record in full:

> John Serjaunt junior, who, because of deficiency of the number of archers which the justiciar needed in furtherance of the war recently begun against the Obrynnes, was asked by the justiciar to choose an equivalent number of strong and powerful archers in the city of Dublin and the neighbouring parts and bring them without delay to the justiciar at Wicklow where he was then with his army, and John, well arrayed for war with these archers and also certain hobelars, came to the justiciar at the said place, and in various conflicts and encounters with the said enemies bravely placed himself and his said archers and hobelars almost in the front of the army and fought valiantly, so that he lost certain men and a large horse and certain other horses of great price, arms and other things in the aforesaid encounters, granted to him by the justiciar and others of the council to assist him in the payment of wages and losses: £6 13s. 4d.[32]

Two years later, he was sent on royal service again. The justiciar and other ministers were arrested in Waterford. John was ordered by the council to go there to explain 'certain important business of the king to James le Botiller, earl of Ormond, concerning the safety of the land of Ireland and to expedite these matters'.[33]

There is evidence of links between the Sargents and another prominent Dublin family, the Passavaunts, around this time. John acted as attorney for Peter Harold of Templeogue in 1361 in connection with the transfer of a

Trinity, 1337–1346 (Dublin, 1890–1, repr. 1996), p. 192.   **30** McEnery and Refaussé (eds), *Christ Church deeds*, no. 242, p. 82; Hugh Jackson, 'A calendar of the *Liber Niger* and *Liber Albus* of Christ Church, Dublin', *Proceedings of the Royal Irish Academy*, 26C1 (1908), no. 18, p. 18.   **31** McEnery and Refaussé (eds), *Christ Church deeds*, no. 648, p. 158; no. 662, p. 160; Robinson, 'On the ancient deeds', no. 48, p. 189.   **32** Philomena Connolly (ed.), *Irish exchequer payments, 1270–1446* (Dublin, 1998), ii, p. 461.   **33** Ibid., ii, p. 486.

messuage and forty acres in Templeogue to John Passavaunt.[34] That is the last
record of a John Sargent for twenty years. There is, however, reason to believe
that he was married to Joan (or Joanna) Tyrrell, one of the co-heiresses to the
manor of Castleknock, possibly a second marriage. If so, he was certainly dead
no later than 1374, when Joan is on record as being married to William de
Bolthame.[35] The baton passed to a Nicholas and a William Sargent. Nicholas
was mayor in 1374–5 and again between 1376 and 1378.[36] His origins are
unknown, but he was probably related in some way to John senior and junior.
In 1378, Nicholas and others granted six shops outside Newgate to Walter
Passavaunt.[37] He himself obtained a shop in High Street in 1382, which John
Passavaunt had held.[38] He also had an inn, probably in the general area of St
Audoen's.[39] He was married to Alice Gallane, a member of a prominent merchant
family, two of whom served as mayor.[40] He seems to have died between 1382
and 1392. He is remembered in the *obits* of Christ Church on 3 March. He left
a mark for the maintenance of the church and half a mark to the canons.[41]

The shop that Nicholas obtained in 1382 was released by, among others,
William, Robert and John Sargent. William was the son of an otherwise
unknown Henry.[42] He had property in St Audoen's Lane.[43] He may be the
same William Serjaunt of Rathmore (now Co. Kildare but Co. Dublin in the
Middle Ages), who was appointed a custodian of the pleas of the crown in Co.
Dublin in 1375–6.[44] He acted as deputy escheator in 1381–2 while the
escheator was in England.[45] He was pardoned of outlawry in 1389.[46] He was
probably dead by 1397.

As regards Robert, a deed of 1414, by which date he was deceased, shows
that he had a shop and a tavern in the general area of High Street and Newgate
in St Audoen's parish.[47] Since Nicholas had property, including a tavern, in the
same area, it is possible that he and Robert were related. D'Alton's statement
that he was the husband of Joan or Joanna Tyrrell, co-heiress of the manor of
Castleknock, is not supported by the evidence and must be rejected.[48]

Finally, John may be the person called John Seriaunt, bastard, in the
documents. He had a shop in High Street next to that of Nicholas.[49] He seems
to have been dead by 1415. Equally, he could be the John who was active about
this time in the north of the county. He was granted custody of lands in

34 J.G. Smylie, 'Old deeds in the library of Trinity College, Dublin', *Hermathena*, 66 (1945)
–74 (1949), 69, no. 76, p. 34.   35 *RPH*, 88.   36 *New history*, ix, p. 550.   37 Smylie, 'Old
deeds in the library of Trinity College', *Hermathena* 69, no. 96, p. 43.   38 Berry, 'History of
the religious gild of S Anne', no. 62, p. 66.   39 Ibid., no. 20, p. 47: 'The cripple who lies
opposite Nicholas Seriaunt's inn'.   40 Ibid., no. 63, p. 66.   41 J.C. Crosthwaite and J.H.
Todd (eds), *The book of the obits and martyrology of the cathedral church of the Holy Trinity
commonly called Christ Church, Dublin* (Dublin, 1844), p. 14.   42 Berry, 'History of the
religious gild of S Anne', no. 64, p. 66.   43 Ibid., no. 115, p. 79.   44 *RPH*, 97.   45 *RPH*,
114.   46 *RPH*, 140.   47 Berry, 'History of the religious gild of S Anne', no. 65, p. 66.
48 John D'Alton, *The history of County Dublin* (Dublin, 1838, repr. 1976), p. 557.
49 Berry, 'History of the religious gild of S Anne', no. 66, p. 67.

Lispopple, Co. Dublin, by the crown in 1381 but otherwise nothing is known about him.[50]

ACQUISITION OF CASTLEKNOCK

Over the years, the Sargents had shown an inclination to acquire land. There was the farm in Grangegorman, mentioned earlier. In 1360, John the third leased the manor of Dundrum in south Co. Dublin for twenty-four years.[51] But they were still primarily merchants, dealing in urban property and participating in the government of the city with others of their class. As the fourteenth century waned, however, an event took place that put them firmly among the landed gentry of the Pale. Robert Tyrrell, the seventh and last baron of Castleknock in the direct Tyrrell line, died without issue in 1370.[52] His sisters, Joan or Joanna and Maud, also known as Matilda, were his co-heiresses. The elder, Joan, was married to John Sargent, as mentioned earlier.[53] The marriage must have taken place around 1360, because her son, Thomas Sargent, was of full age in 1382, when he was in England (he appointed Nicholas and Robert Sargent as his attorneys, strong evidence of a family connection).[54] Joan died in 1404, but her second husband, William de Bolthame, continued to enjoy her estate until his own death in 1407.[55] An inquisition in May 1408 found that Thomas Sargent was the son and heir of Joan. He paid 13s. 4d. for his homage, but he must have died very soon after because a second inquisition in September 1408 found that he was dead and that his son and heir was John Sargent.[56]

During his lifetime, Thomas engaged in the activities expected of a country landholder. He served as a justice of the peace for Co. Dublin in 1402 and as a guardian and supervisor of the peace in 1403. He must have been still serving in 1405, because in that year he was pardoned a fine of 100s. imposed on him because of the escape from custody of two felons.[57] Also in 1403, he was one of the three mandated to convene the magnates of the county and afterwards to raise the levy of forty marks granted by them for the defence of the marches.[58] He is recorded in the *obits* of Christ Church under 11 September, where he was called lord of Castleknock. He left a shop in High Street near the cross to the cathedral and another in 'vico estemanorum' near the cemetery of St

50 *RPH*, 110.   **51** *Calendar of ancient deeds and muniments in the Pembroke Estate Office* (Dublin, 1891), no. 49, pp 18–19. I owe this reference to Dr Martin Holland, who noted it in his book *Clonskeagh: place in history* (Dublin, 2007), p. 27.   **52** Gilbert (ed.), *Chartularies of St Mary's Abbey*, ii, p. 397.   **53** Mem. roll 13 Hen. VI (i) as noted by F.E. Ball in his notes, held in the Royal Society of Antiquaries of Ireland. The inquisition is late, 1434–5, and is garbled but seems to be correct on this point.   **54** *Calendar of the patent rolls, 1381–5*, i, p. 161.   **55** Eric St John Brooks, 'The grant of Castleknock to Hugh Tyrrel', *Journal of the Royal Society of Antiquaries of Ireland*, 63 (1933), 219.   **56** *RPH*, 187–8.   **57** Ibid., 160, 178, 181.   **58** Ibid., 166, 178.

Michan's Church (in Oxmantown). For these donations he was granted nine lessons.[59] The continuing close connection with Christ Church will be noted.

John followed in his father's footsteps. In June 1409, he and others were ordered by the king to arrest malefactors (allegedly of the retinue of the lord lieutenant, Thomas of Lancaster) who were alleged to have stolen forty-two cattle from Wolfram Eustace. In the same year he was appointed a justice of the peace for Co. Kildare.[60] He was a justice of the peace for Co. Dublin in 1415.[61] He completed the release of shops in Oxmantown in 1408 in succession to his late father. The record shows that he still had the lands in Oxmantown that his father had held and that seem to be the same lands that were held by the earlier John in the 1340s. He leased property in Francis Street to a Philip Hamound, a butcher. He granted him the same property in 1417, on which occasion he used his father's seal and the title 'baron of Castleknock'.[62] He was called a knight in a document of 1432, by which date he seems to have been dead.[63]

Sir John appears to have had a son, also John. There is a reference in a royal grant of 1423 to a John Serjaunt junior, but he is referred to as the former or late renter of the lands in question.[64] He may be the 'John Seriaunt, son and heir of Margaret, daughter and heiress of Roger Passavaunt' who released a tenement within Newgate in December 1433.[65] It is not clear, however, that he ever succeeded his father as lord of Castleknock. There is a record in the *obits* of Christ Church of a Robert Seriaunt, son of John Seriaunt and lord of Castleknock.[66] It is impossible to say if he was the son of Sir John or of John junior. He must have been dead by 1436, because his widow was granted her dower in the manor of Castleknock in 1436–7.[67] He must have died without issue, because he was succeeded by Ismay, the daughter and heiress of John Seriaunt.[68] She was the last of the Sargents of Castleknock and Oxmantown.

She was most likely Robert's sister although, like him, it is impossible to say which John Sargent was her father. She was married to Nicholas Barnewall of Crickstown. The two of them were granted a royal pardon in 1432 'for all intrusions into the half of the manor of Castleknock that was formerly John Serjaunt's, Knt.'[69] The Barnewalls were a legal family and Nicholas served as chief justice of the common pleas from 1461 to 1464, when he probably died.[70] Ismay then married Sir Robert Bold, baron of Ratoath, Co. Meath.[71] She

59 Crosthwaite and Todd (eds), *Christ Church obits*, p. 41.   **60** *RPH*, 193.   **61** Ibid., 213. **62** Robinson, 'On the ancient deeds', no. 94, p. 195; no. 101, p. 196.   **63** *RPH*, 255, the reference was to 'the half of the manor of Castleknock that was formerly John Serjaunt's, Kt'.   **64** *RPH*, 227.   **65** Berry, 'History of the religious gild of S Anne', no. 98, p. 73. **66** Crosthwaite and Todd (eds), *Christ Church obits*, p. 50.   **67** *RPH*, 407.   **68** Colm Lennon and James Murray (eds), *The Dublin city franchise roll, 1468–1512* (Dublin, 1998), p. 49. Ball has two family trees that suggest she was the daughter of Robert Serjaunt but his source is not given. Ball, notes in RSAI, 25.   **69** *RPH*, 255.   **70** S.S. Barnwell, 'The family of Barnewall (de Berneval) during the middle ages', *Irish Genealogist* 3:4 (July 1959), 124–35 at 131. J.T. Hughes (ed.), *Patentee officers in Ireland, 1173–1826* (Dublin, 1960), p. 7. **71** Robert Bold was created lord of Ratoath in 1468. He was admitted to the Dublin city

probably died in the 1470s. She is remembered in the Christ Church *obits* under 23 July.[72]

An entry in the Christ Church deeds for 1481 refers to land 'late belonging to Ismay Serjaunt' (which suggests she was dead) situate on the west side of St Michan's and to the north of the churchyard.[73] This appears to be the land in Oxmantown that was held by the Sargent family since at least the early fourteenth century. It passed to the Barnewalls on the death of Ismay when her eldest son by Nicholas Barnewall, Christopher, succeeded to Crickstown and to his mother's estates in Castleknock and Oxmantown. There is a reference to Christopher Barnewall of Crickstown holding land in Oxmantown on the west side in 1486.[74] While one cannot be certain, this looks like the former Sargent property. It was called the land of Christopher Barnewall as late as 1661.[75]

THE LAST SARGENT

There was one more Sargent, another John. His place in the family is unknown, but he was not accorded the Castleknock title or a knighthood in the surviving records. He was called merchant and citizen in 1478 when he obtained a lease of a shop and chamber in High Street from the guild of St Anne.[76] He was closely associated with the guild and served as master in 1489.[77] There is no record of a connection with Oxmantown apart from the events of 1493 (see next paragraph). As a merchant, he took several apprentices; four of them were admitted to the franchise between 1481 and 1498, including a woman, Jenet Galmole.[78]

John was a city bailiff in 1480 and 1481.[79] He became mayor in 1485 and was elected again in 1490 and in 1492.[80] But disaster struck in 1493. He was deposed, arrested and detained in Dublin Castle from 8 May until 19 July.[81] He had been caught up in the dispute between the Geraldine and Ormond factions. Serious disorder broke out in the city in June 1492 following the removal of Gearóid Mór, earl of Kildare, as lord deputy.[82] His supporters were also removed, accused of serious crimes and ordered to surrender themselves at Dublin Castle. The list included John.[83] Fighting between the followers of Kildare and Ormond reached a peak in July 1493 when a murderous encounter

franchise in 1469 by special grace. H.G. Richardson and G.O. Sayles (eds), *The Irish parliament in the middle ages* (London, 1952), p. 177 n. 208; Lennon and Murray (eds), *Dublin city franchise roll*, p. 49. **72** Crosthwaite and Todd (eds), *Christ Church obits*, p. 33. **73** McEnery and Refaussé (eds), *Christ Church deeds*, no. 1032, pp 211–12. **74** Ibid., no. 1074, p. 217. **75** Ibid., no. 1764, 382. **76** Berry, 'History of the religious gild of S Anne', no. 81, p. 69. **77** Ibid., no. 102, p. 76. **78** Lennon and Murray (eds), *Dublin city franchise roll*, pp 15, 19, 24, 34. **79** Ibid., pp 14–15. **80** *New History*, ix, p. 553. **81** Lennon and Murray (eds), *Dublin city franchise roll*, p. 80 and n. 3. **82** A.J. Otway-Ruthven, *A history of medieval Ireland* (London, 1968), p. 407. **83** Philomena Connolly (ed.), *Statute rolls of the Irish parliament, Richard III–Henry VIII* (Dublin, 2002), p. 123 (8 Henry VII, c.21).

on Oxmantown Green on St Margaret's Day led to the deaths of a former mayor, William Tue, and two others.[84] The feast of St Margaret, virgin and martyr, fell on 20 July. Was Sargent's release on 19 July a cause of the affray or was it an attempt to calm the situation? In any event, he survived the conflict and continued to operate his business as a merchant. One of his apprentices was admitted to the franchise in 1498.[85]

CONCLUSION

Thereafter, the Sargents disappear from history. But they were not entirely forgotten. In a lease by the master of St Anne's guild in 1594 of property in Bridge Street, a house on the boundary of the property was referred to as 'sometime Seriante's inheritance'.[86] The Sargents were part of the small group, who, united by ties of business and marriage, controlled Dublin for over two hundred years. That was not the limit of their achievement. They realized the ambition of many a successful merchant when they became lords of Castleknock and joined the gentry of the Pale.[87]

84 'The register of the mayors of Dublin and other memorable observations', p. 4, no. 85, in *Memorandum rolls of the city of Dublin from 26 Henry VI (1447) to 24 Elizabeth (1582)*, transcribed in 1868 for J.T. Gilbert, i, pt. 1, Dublin city archives.   85 Lennon and Murray (eds), *Dublin city franchise roll*, p. 34.   86 Berry, 'History of the religious gild of S Anne', no. 34, pp 54–5.   87 This paper was prompted by an article entitled 'Medieval building survival' by Giles Dawkes, which appeared in *Archaeology Ireland* 21:4 (winter 2007). In it, he reported on the excavation of a medieval granary near St Michan's Church in Dublin. He mentioned that the plot had been held continuously by the Sargent family and subsequently by the Barnewalls.

The medieval vill of Portmarnock

COLM MORIARTY

INTRODUCTION

This paper details the results of an excavation (Licence 08E0376) that was carried out at Portmarnock, Co. Dublin, between September and December 2009 (fig. 8.1). It was undertaken in advance of a large-scale residential development, which has since been put on hold, and was located in an area locally referred to as 'Old Portmarnock'. The excavation revealed the remains of a late medieval village in the northern part of the development site adjacent to Station Road and to the west of Portmarnock Railway Station. The village consisted of six well-defined properties that were separated by internal divisions into toft (front) and croft (back) areas. The plots measured between 16m and 22m wide and were up to 65m long, with the majority of settlement activity taking place in the toft areas where the remains of at least five

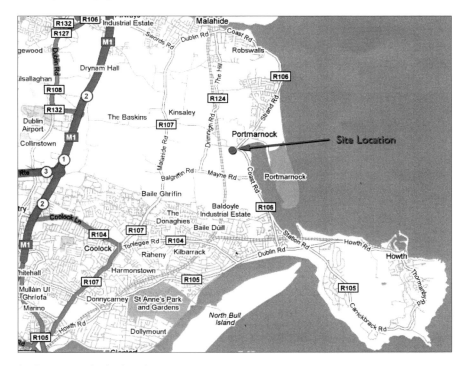

8.1 Portmarnock: site location.

truncated buildings were identified. Yard areas defined by metalled surfaces were identified to the front of the tofts and in some instances these had been terraced into the natural slope. Each plot also contained at least one large well and these were sometimes accessed by metalled pathways. Numerous small gullies, ditches and rubbish pits were also excavated, and these indicate that the plots were intensively occupied over a considerable length of time.

This site corresponds to the vill of Portmarnock, a possession of St Mary's Abbey, Dublin, which on the dissolution of the monastery in 1539 contained ten cottages.[1] The medieval vill was distinct from the modern village of Portmarnock, which is a largely nineteenth-/twentieth-century development *c*.700m to the north-east of the site. Prior to the excavation, no upstanding remains of the medieval village survived and this was probably due to deep ploughing as the site was located in an area of intensive tillage farming. Further truncation had also been caused by Station Road, which was a nineteenth-century thorough-fare constructed to facilitate the new Dublin–Belfast railway line. This road bounded the northern part of the site and had severely damaged the front of the village plots.

HISTORICAL BACKGROUND

Early medieval
Although the earliest reference to the church at Portmarnock dates to AD1185, when it was granted to St Mary's Abbey, Dublin, by the future King John,[2] its origins appear to be considerably earlier. This is suggested by its proximity to a holy well, the former presence of an ogham stone at the site and the church's dedication to St Marnock, who was an early religious figure. A contemporary of St Columba, St Marnock is also associated with Scotland, where Kilmarnock bears his name. His relics were kept at Portmarnock until the late fifteenth century, when they were moved to St Mary's Abbey, Dublin.[3] The holy well adjacent to the church was venerated annually on 15 July,[4] and was an important pilgrimage site well into the seventeenth century.[5] There is a second holy well, known as Tobermaclaney, at the northern end of the Velvet Strand, while an early church site (DU015:012) is also located to the south-east of the proposed development at Balgriffin. This church was dedicated to St Samson, a Welsh abbot who is said to have come to Ireland in around AD516. In 1949, when a bungalow was constructed at the church site, the owner uncovered

1 J.T. Gilbert (ed.), *Chartularies of St Mary's Abbey, Dublin: with the register of its house at Dunbrody, and annals of Ireland*, 2 vols (London, 1884), ii, pp 68–70. 2 Ibid., i, p. 85. 3 Ibid., ii, p. xxiii.
4 John Murphy, *The life of St Patrick, Apostle of Ireland* (Dublin, 1863), p. 128. 5 Raymond Gillespie, *Devoted people: belief and religion in early modern Ireland* (Manchester, 1997), p. 91.

numerous bones and pieces of masonry, including part of a stone cross, which is now in the National Museum of Ireland (1958:50). Politically, during the earlier medieval period, Portmarnock lay within the kingdom of Gailenga Becca (Lesser Gailenga), the ruling lineage of which traced its descent from the eponymous Cormac Gaileng, a supposed son of the legendary Tadc son of Cian.[6] This minor kingdom, which included St Mo-Bí's foundation of Glas Naíden (Glasnevin) and apparently also Finn Glas (Finglas), most likely extended from the Tolka to the Broad Meadow, and was one of several túatha making up the regional kingdom of Brega.[7] By the late eighth century the political scene had changed somewhat, with the territory of Gailenga Becca now largely controlled by the Síl nÁeda Sláine, a branch of the Southern Uí Néill. However, their tenure as overlords was relatively short-lived as, during the ninth and tenth centuries, the territory increasingly fell under the sway of the Dublin Norse. Indeed, Viking influence over north Co. Dublin was such that this area was soon referred to as Fine Gall (Fingal), or 'territory of the foreigners', that is, the Vikings.

High medieval to Dissolution
The Viking hegemony over Fingal was to end in 1170 when Dublin fell to the Anglo-Normans. These new arrivals quickly set about securing the city and its hinterland and the Hiberno-Norse aristocracy were largely dispossessed. In Fingal, the Anglo-Normans granted large tracts of land to the church, Portmarnock becoming an estate of St Mary's Abbey, Dublin. The earliest recorded grants date to sometime shortly after 1170, when Strongbow ceded lands to St Mary's at Muniakon and Lisloan, which had formerly belonged to the Hiberno-Norse MacTorcaill family.[8] Although the exact location of these properties remains uncertain, they are described as being within the 'tenement of Portmarnock'.[9] The townland of Portmarnock was certainly held by the St Mary's monks by at least 1172, when it is mentioned in a survey carried out by William Fitz Audelin at the behest of Henry II.[10] Portmarnock was subsequently confirmed to St Mary's Abbey by royal charter, firstly by Henry II in 1174 and then by John, lord of Ireland, in 1185.[11] Further grants occurred in the late twelfth century, when Richard de Talbot, of Malahide, and his son Reginald ceded land at 'Portmyrnoch and Muachydebeg'.[12] By this stage, it appears that the monks' possessions corresponded with the parish boundaries, as shown on the Down Survey map, and included the townlands of Portmarnock, Robswall, Carrickhill, Conneyborough and Portmarnock Grange (fig. 8.2).

6 Ailbhe MacShamhráin, 'Swords and district: the political and ecclesiastical background fifth to twelfth centuries AD' (Dublin, 2005). Unpublished report for Margaret Gowen and Co. Ltd.   7 Ibid.   8 Gilbert (ed.), *Chartularies of St Mary's Abbey*, i, p. 83.   9 Ibid., p. 83.   10 Ibid., p. 138.   11 Ibid., pp 81–5.   12 Ibid., pp 130–4.

8.2 Down Survey
map (1652).

These extensive land grants, however, did not go unchallenged and a
dispute soon arose between the abbot of St Mary's and Helias Comyn of
Kinsealy. Although this was finally resolved by arbitration in 1206,[13] bad blood
continued to exist between the two sides, culminating in 1277 with the killing
of John Comyn, lord of Kinsaley, by a number of monks residing at the
Grange.[14] The main perpetrator, John Unred, a lay brother, was arrested and
convicted of murder by the justiciar (chief governor) of Ireland, who handed
him over to the abbot of St Mary's, Phillip Troy, for punishment. Unred was
incarcerated in the abbey's prison, where he remained until his death fourteen
years later. In 1305, the Portmarnock monks were once more in trouble with
the authorities when a number of brothers, led by a William de Baa, were
accused of stealing goods, including pitch, wax, tin and steel, from a stranded
ship.[15] In this instance, however, the monks were acquitted after protesting that
the goods had been taken for safekeeping and would be returned to their
rightful owners. These roles were reversed in December 1465 when the sheriff
of Co. Dublin, James Blackney, recovered eight barrels of Spanish wine that
had washed ashore at Portmarnock.[16] As flotsam, the wine rightfully belonged to

13 Ibid., p. 183.   14 Colmcille Ó Conbhuí, 'The lands of St Mary's Abbey, Dublin', *Proceedings of the
Royal Irish Academy*, 62C3 (1962), 21–84 at 44.   15 James Mills (ed.), *Calendar of the justicary rolls, or
proceedings in the court of the justicar of Ireland, Edward I* (London, 1914), p. 509.   16 Gilbert (ed.),
Chartularies of St Mary's Abbey, ii, p. xv.

the monks and the abbot of St Mary's, John Hanncock, successfully demanded its return.

Portmarnock is also mentioned in a document dating from 1318, which describes sales of livestock and crops to settle a debt owed by St Mary's Abbey to a William de la Rivere.[17] As part of this settlement, Portmarnock had to provide sixteen afers (draught horses), worth 40*d*. each, as well as eight oxen, which were slightly more expensive at 6*s*. 8*d*. each. In addition, the monks had to provide over two hundred crannocs of wheat and oats,[18] as well as sixty sheep, with each crannoc being worth 4*s*. and each sheep 7*d*. Although not specifically mentioned in this document, cows were also reared at Portmarnock as, in 1305, sixteen of their number were stolen from the Grange by a Simon Bek and his brothers.[19]

Portmarnock was to remain in the possession of St Mary's until the Dissolution of the monasteries by Henry VIII in the late 1530s. St Mary's survived the initial wave of closures in 1537, which saw the Cistercian houses of Bective, Baltinglass, Duiske, Dunbrody and Tintern dissolved. With the spectre of dissolution hanging over them, many of the monastic communities, including St Mary's, began to lease out large swathes of their property in an attempt to prevent financial ruin.[20] At Portmarnock, for example, leases were granted to Patrick Gygen of 'the hall ferme that is Pormarnoke', with the stipulation that the houses and buildings were kept 'styff and stanche'.[21] Similarly, the mills and rabbit warren were granted to Lord Leonard Grey, who was the lord deputy of Ireland. Grey's tenure at Portmarnock, however, was to be short, as in 1541 he was found guilty of treason and executed at the Tower of London.

Despite much protestation by the abbot, William Laundie, St Mary's finally succumbed in 1539 and its lands and possessions were transferred to the state. On inquisition, it was found to have a total income of £537, which made it by far the richest monastery of the Cistercian order in Ireland.[22] As part of these investigations, a detailed survey was carried out at Portmarnock,[23] which revealed, unsurprisingly, that the best land, worth £12 annually, was situated at the Grange, where the monks' farm would have been based. It contained 240 acres of arable land, ten acres of meadow and twelve acres of pasture, as well as three messuages or plots, held by Walter Goldynge, Hugo White and Bartholomew Enos respectively. The aforementioned Goldynge was an important member of the Pale gentry, holding the position of the summonister

17 Gilbert (ed.), *Chartularies of St Mary's Abbey*, i, pp 260–3. 18 A crannoc was a unit of dry measurement, generally equating to eight bushels. 19 Mills (ed.), *Calendar of justiciary rolls*, p. 483. 20 Brendan Scott, 'The religious houses of Tudor Dublin: their communities and resistance to the Dissolution, 1537–41' in Seán Duffy (ed.), *Medieval Dublin VII* (Dublin, 2006), p. 215. 21 J.F. Ainsworth, *National Library report on private collections*, no. 161 (Plunkett papers), p. 1541. 22 http://cistercians.shef.ac.uk/abbeys/dublin-st_mary_php. 23 Gilbert (ed.), *Chartularies of St Mary's Abbey*, ii, pp 68–70.

of the exchequer,[24] and being an unofficial advisor to Lord Deputy Grey.[25] The townland of Robswall, in contrast to the Grange, was considerably smaller and less productive, containing just a single messuage, owned by Patrick Gygen (see also below), along with sixty acres of arable land, seventeen acres of furze and pasture and three acres of meadow, with an annual return of £4 13s.

The most densely populated part of the former monastic estate was in Portmarnock townland, where a small village containing ten cottages and nine messuages was located. A number of the village residents are named in the survey, including Patrick Gygen (also of Robswall), Peter Mansfeld, John Taylor, Robert Benane, Thomas Kelly, John Gyles, John Rowe, Patrick Hogge and John Proydforde. These tenants paid an annual rent of twelve cart days, twelve plough days, twelve hook days, twenty-three hens and for every horse pasturing on the moor, a goose. The village, together with the rest of the townland, which consisted of 220 acres of arable land, five acres of meadow, one headland, a stang of pasture and one hundred acres of communal pasture, had a value of £11 17s. There were also two watermills to the north of the village along the Sluice River, which the villagers had to maintain as part of their annual rent, and a rabbit warren, which was situated on the sandy isthmus now occupied by Portmarnock Golf Course. The village tithe, which was collected by a Johnny Ryan and a Johnny Pacoke, was worth £4 10s. annually.

Early modern
The monastic lands, which were forfeited to the state during the Dissolution, were granted, subject to rent charges, to prominent laymen, or sold, according to the king's wish 'to men of honesty and good disposition to civility'.[26] At Portmarnock, the former possessions of St Mary's Abbey were divided up between two powerful landowners, Patrick Barnewall of Turvey and Walter Peppard of Kilkea. Barnewall, who had made the dissolved nunnery at Grace Dieu his home, received the lands of 'Robbokswalls near Malahide, the mills in Portmarnock and the Grange of Portmarnock',[27] while the village and townland of Portmarnock were granted to Walter Peppard.

Peppard, who was a gentleman of the king's chamber, had done extremely well out of the monastic confiscations, mainly due to his friendship with the king's vice-treasurer, William Brabazon. He had gained significant tracts of land, often for well below their market value, in Cos Dublin, Kildare and Kilkenny.[28] His lease for Portmarnock was renewed in 1552 and in 1560 he

24 James Morrin (ed.), *Calendar of the patent and close rolls of the chancery in Ireland of the reigns of Henry VIII, Edward VI, Mary and Elizabeth* (Dublin, 1861), pp 41, 140, 216.   25 F. Elrington Ball, *Judges in Ireland, 1221–1921*, vol. i (London, 2005), p. 200.   26 G.A. Hayes-McCoy, 'The royal supremacy and ecclesiastical revolution, 1534–47' in T.W. Moody, F.X Martin and F.J. Byrne (eds), *A new history of Ireland III: early modern Ireland, 1534–1691* (Oxford, 2006), p. 63.   27 Ó Conbhuí, 'St Mary's Abbey', p. 45.   28 See Ciaran Brady, *The chief governors: the rise and fall of the reform government in Tudor Ireland, 1536–1588* (Dublin, 2002), p. 37.

sub-let the lands and town of Portmarnock 'with the cottiers of the same' to David Fluddie of 'Drynshocke' for twenty-one years at a rent of £13 10s. along with six 'good and lawful cartloads of hay'.[29] This lease also states that John Taylor and Patrick Giggen (Gygen above) should 'occupy the farms lately held by Hugh Whight and Patrick Pruteforde'. The aforementioned Patrick Giggen was obviously a man of some importance, at least at a local level, as he held property at both Robswall and Portmarnock (see above) and it is possible that he is the same Patrick Giggen who was sheriff of Dublin in 1555.[30]

In 1574, Queen Elizabeth demised the lands formerly owned by Walter Peppard (now deceased) to her cousin and loyal follower Sir Thomas Butler, earl of Ormond,[31] who, in the following year, assigned the 'town of Portmarnocke' to Jacques Wingfield for 'a certain sum of money'.[32] Wingfield, who was originally from Middlesex in England, arrived in Ireland in 1556 and was appointed master of the ordnance in 1558. A former seneschal of the O'Byrne Country (south Co. Dublin and Wicklow), he is best remembered for a number of disastrous military encounters with the Irish. These included an ill-fated skirmish with Shane O'Neill in 1561, which saw Wingfield accused of cowardice, and a disastrous campaign, under the command of Lord Grey of Wilton, against Fiach McHugh O'Byrne in 1581.

After Wingfield's death in 1587, Portmarnock passed to his son, Thomas, a cousin and namesake of Sir Thomas Maria Wingfield, who in 1589 commanded the English retreat from the Battle of Yellow Ford. Thomas' title to Portmarnock was confirmed by royal grant in 1602, when the town is described as 'containing nine messuages, ten cottages, 220 acres arable, etc.', to which the 'the tenants pay yearly, twelve cart days, twelve plough days and certain other customs'.[33] This royal lease also mentions a tenant called Patrick Giggen and this is a family name that is seen on documents relating to Portmarnock dating from 1538, 1540 and 1560. In 1611, Wingfield leased the town of Portmarnock to Thomas Addies of Dublin at a rent of £13 17s.[34] However, this arrangement did not last long, as Thomas Addies' health soon failed and in the autumn of 1616 he died and was buried at St James' Church, Dublin.

After Thomas Addies' death, a complex interchange of land deeds took place. In December 1616, Portmarnock was granted by James I to Sir Adam Loftus of Rathfarnham and to Sir John King of Baggotrath.[35] Immediately following this grant, Sir John King, who had been a close friend of Thomas Addies and an executor of his will,[36] renounced his claim and the following day

29 Ainsworth, *Private collections*, no. 161 (Plunkett papers), p. 1542. **30** See Walter Harris, *The history of the antiquities of the city of Dublin, from the earliest accounts* (Dublin, 1766), p. 504. **31** Kenneth Nicholls (ed.), *The Irish fiants of the Tudor sovereigns during the reigns of Henry VII to Elizabeth I* (Dublin, 1994), pp 347, 353, 366. **32** Ainsworth, *Private collections*, no. 161 (Plunkett papers), p. 1543. **33** J. Moran (ed.), *Calendar of the patent and close rolls of the chancery in Ireland from the eighteenth to the forty-fifth of Queen Elizabeth* I (London, 1864), p. 605. **34** Ainsworth, *Private collections*, no. 161 (Plunkett papers), p. 1544. **35** Ó Conbhuí, 'St Mary's Abbey', p. 45. **36** Ainsworth, *Private*

Sir Adam Loftus conveyed the lands of Portmarnock to William Hilton. Hilton, who appears to have been a lawyer, then transferred the 'land and tenements; except for the mill and precinct called the coniger (warren) lately granted to Patrick Barnewall' to Ambrose St Lawernce for £300.[37] St Lawrence had recently married Thomas Addies' widow, Anne,[38] and this complex system of title transfer appears to have been designed to ensure that she retained ownership of her former husband's lands. Ambrose St Lawrence, who was a son of the 22nd earl of Howth, died without issue in 1625 and shortly afterwards Portmarnock passed into the hands of Luke Plunkett.

After the multiple owners of the preceding century, stability of tenure had finally arrived and the Plunkett family was to remain at Portmarnock for the next three hundred years. The Plunkett residence became known as 'Portmarnock House' and was located just outside the development site on the northern side of Station Road. In the Civil Survey of 1654–6, the Plunkett abode is described as containing two houses, one slated and the other tiled, along with several thatched outhouses and a malt house.[39] There was an adjoining village of ten thatched cottages as well as two small orchards and three gardens. The other main landowners in the parish during this period were Walter Plunkett, who owned the Grange, and Nicholas Barnewall, who possessed Robswall and Connyborough.

EXCAVATION SUMMARY

The site under discussion was located in a very large arable field that had been subjected to intensive farming practices since at least the 1970s. It was situated near the base of a gradual north-east-facing slope and overlooked the Sluice river floodplain to the north. The area of excavation was sub-rectangular in plan and measured 120m east–west by between 45m and 65m north–south. Within this, the remains of six well-defined property plots were identified and these are described individually as Plots 1–6 below (fig. 8.3). The site had clearly been damaged by deep ploughing and this had caused considerable truncation to the underlying archaeological deposits.

Plot 1 (fig. 8.4)
Plot 1, which was the most easterly plot identified at the site, was defined by a series of shallow inter-cutting ditches that enclosed an area measuring between 16m and 17m wide (east–west) by at least 64m long. This was not its full extent, however, as the very northern end of the plot was truncated by Station

collections, no. 161 (Plunkett papers), p. 1545.   **37** Ibid., p. 1546.   **38** Mervyn Archdall and John Lodge (eds), *The peerage of Ireland; or, A genealogical history of the nobility of that kingdom*, vol. iii (Dublin, 1789), p. 199.   **39** Robert Simington (ed.), *The Civil Survey: 1654–1656* (Dublin, 1961), p. 174.

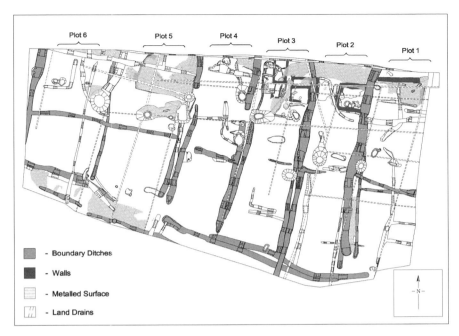

8.3 Site plan.

Road. The front (north) of the plot contained the truncated remains of a building (Structure C) with a metalled yard area to the rear, as well as a number of rubbish pits and a well, while the rear of the plot contained a metalled pathway, a hearth and a series of ditches.

The toft: The toft area, or the front/northern end of the plot, measured approximately 36m north–south by 16m east–west and contained the partial remains of a building (Structure C), an associated yard area, along with a number of pits, gullies and a well.

Structure C: The highly truncated remains of a rectangular building, measuring at least 15m long (east–west) were identified at the very front (northern end) of the toft. Its extent was only partially exposed during the excavation as the majority of the building had been truncated by Station Road as well as by a series of post-medieval ditches and land drains. Only the very southern side of the building survived relatively intact and this was defined by the remains of a stone wall, which had been largely robbed out in antiquity. Evidence for a doorway survived along this southern wall in the form of a 2m gap, which had been paved over with closely packed cobbles. Internally, the building contained a packed clay floor, the truncated remains of a hearth and

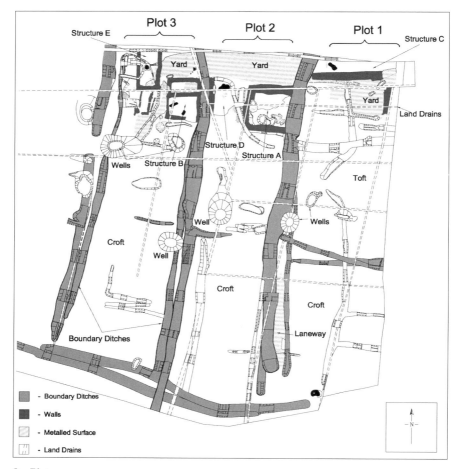

8.4 Plots 1–3.

the foundations for a lightweight partition wall. The southern wall was defined by a shallow foundation cut that measured at least 15m long by 1m wide by between 5cm and 25cm deep. The wall foundations had been severely truncated by a seventeenth-century robber trench, leaving only a small number of *in situ* stones. These were mainly found pressed into the northern edge of the foundation cut and consisted of mud-bonded, limestone boulders measuring on average 40cm by 28cm by 16cm. Finds recovered from these *in situ* wall deposits included marine shell, cattle bone and medieval pottery, while finds recovered from the robber trench included seventeenth-century pottery, a knife-blade and an Elizabethan coin (dated 1601). The floor of the building consisted of a compact yellow clay that measured between 4cm and 10cm in depth and which contained occasional inclusions of charcoal and animal bone

8.5 Stone-lined
drain, Plot 1.

(mainly sheep and cattle) as well as sherds of medieval pottery (Dublin-type wares) and ferrous objects (a blade and nails). A small area of *in situ* burning, possibly representing the remains of a highly truncated hearth, was identified in the western part of the building. It consisted of a thin, patchy, layer of charcoal (2cm deep) overlying an area of burnt clay measuring 80cm in length by 67cm in width. In addition, the remains of what may have been an internal partition were also identified in the western part of the building. It consisted of a short line of stones, laid in single file, set into the clay floor. They ran for a distance of 1.22m before being truncated by a post-medieval gully. It seems probable that these stones represented the foundations of an internal dividing wall, possibly made of a lightweight material such as wicker.

Yard area to the rear (south) of Structure C: A small rectangular yard, measuring approximately 14m east–west by 6m north–south, was located immediately to the south of Structure C. It was partially covered in a compacted metalled surface and was defined to the east by the remains of a low, mud-bonded, stone wall, to the north by a shallow gully and to the west by the plot boundary ditch. Features located within the yard included a stone-lined drain and three small pits, which appear to have been used to discard rubbish. Most of the yard, with the exception of its western extent, was covered in a tightly packed metalled surface, which was composed of small

(4cm by 3cm by 2cm) water-rolled pebbles sitting in a thin layer of grey silty clay. Finds associated with the surface included frequent inclusions of marine shell, animal bone (mainly cattle but also cat), medieval pottery (mainly Dublin-type wares and Leinster Cooking Ware) and ferrous objects (a cauldron fragment, a spur, a point, two whittle-tang knives and nails). The rubbish pits within the yard area were filled by similar charcoal-rich silty clays that contained frequent inclusions of animal bone (cattle, sheep, pig, horse and rabbit) and marine shell (oyster, mussels cockle, periwinkle, razorfish and whelks), while charred grains of oat, barley and wheat were also identified in one of the pits. Artefacts recovered from these features included a ferrous knife-blade with a decorative shoulder plate, small amounts of medieval pottery and a double-sided bone comb. A stone-lined drain was also identified in the northern part of the yard area, running parallel with the southern wall of Structure C (fig. 8.5). It was orientated east–west and measured 8.5m in length by a maximum of 67cm in width and was defined by two parallel lines of small sub-rectangular stones set within a shallow concave cut that measured between 8cm and 14cm in depth. This feature appears to have been designed to protect the southern wall of Structure C from water running down the hill.

Features to the south of the yard area: A number of features, including a short section of ditch, a deep well and two inter-cutting rubbish pits were identified immediately to the south of the yard area. The ditch appears to have been related to agricultural activities, while the well consisted of large sub-circular pit that measured 3.1m long (north–south) by 1.8m wide by 1.9m deep. It had steeply sloping sides, a roughly concave base and was filled by a series of waterlogged deposits. Finds recovered from these fills included organic material such as twigs and grass as well as infrequent inclusions of medieval pottery (Dublin-type wares). The two inter-cutting pits, which measured between 50cm and 56cm deep, were identified approximately 4.5m east of the well and appear to have been used to discard household waste. The later of the two pits was filled by a series of especially charcoal-rich deposits, one of which was radiocarbon-dated to AD1450–1631 (2 sigma). Large amounts of pottery, including a substantially complete Leinster Cooking Ware pot, were recovered from this feature along with a ferrous knife and nails. Analysis of the plant remains from the pit identified a large number of charred seeds, including bread wheat, barley, oats, indeterminate cereal, garden pea and both small and large seeded legumes, while the animal bone included species such as cattle, sheep and pig.

The croft: The croft area of Plot 1 measured approximately 25m north–south by *c.*17m to 18m wide and was separated from the toft by a shallow U-shaped ditch. It contained a metalled pathway along its western side, while a small stone-lined hearth was located adjacent to its southern boundary. An internal division defined by a north–south ditch and a series of associated gullies were also identified within the croft and these may have defined small garden areas. The metalled pathway was orientated north–south and was composed of tightly packed water-rolled pebbles (4cm by 3cm by 3cm), which covered an area measuring 18m long by a maximum of 2m wide. It had been severely truncated along its western side by a seventeenth-century ditch, while further truncation had been caused by deep ploughing. Finds in association with the surface included medieval pottery (Dublin-type wares and Leinster Cooking Wares), animal bone (mainly cattle) and a ferrous nail.

Seventeenth-century activity: A number of features dating to the seventeenth century were also identified in Plot 1, including four ditches, two of which redefined the eastern and western plot boundaries, as well as a large well. These features are not discussed in this paper.

Plot 2 (fig. 8.4)
Plot 2 was located immediately to the west of Plot 1 and measured between 14m and 16m wide by at least 65m long. The very northern end of the property was truncated by Station Road and it was defined by a series of shallow ditches, some of which were inter-cutting. The partial remains of two buildings and an associated yard area were identified to the front of the toft, while the croft was largely devoid of features. As with most of the other plots, two distinct phases of activity were identified, late medieval/early modern and seventeenth century.

The toft: The toft area in Plot 2 measured approximately 32m north–south by between 14m and 16m east–west and it contained the partial remains of two highly truncated rectangular buildings (Structures C and D), an associated yard area, and a number of pits and gullies.

Structure A (fig. 8.6): The more complete of the two buildings, Structure A, was defined by a series of shallow foundation cuts (8–20cm deep by 50–150cm wide), which enclosed a sub-rectangular area measuring approximately 6m north–south by at least 7m east–west. It had been severely truncated along its eastern side by a seventeenth-century ditch, while further truncation had been caused by modern land drains and deep ploughing. Despite this disturbance, a number of *in situ* wall stones survived along the course of the foundation trenches. These consisted of unhewn limestone boulders that were held together with a mud bond and which varied from 10cm by 10cm by 20cm to 20cm by 20cm by 30cm. Finds recovered from the wall foundations included large quantities of medieval pottery (Dublin-type wares, Leinster Cooking

8.6 Structure A.

Ware and Chester-type ware) and animal bone (sheep, pig and goose). Internally, the structure contained the partial remains of a packed clay floor (F88) along with a charcoal spread (F80). The clay floor was confined to the northern half of the building where it covered an area *c.*6m east–west by 3.8m north–south. Its depth varied from 3cm to 13cm depending on the level of the underlying subsoil and it contained infrequent inclusions of marine shell and charcoal. The spread of charcoal-rich material (F80) was identified near the south-east corner of the building and this appeared to represent hearth waste that accumulated in a natural hollow. Two pits were also located within the structure, but both pre-dated the building.

Structure D: The remnants of what may have been a second building were identified approximately 1.5m the west of Structure A. It was in a very poor state of preservation and had been severely truncated by a later gully to the

8.7 Horse skulls within Structure D.

north and east and by a seventeenth-century ditch to the west, while further damage had been caused by deep ploughing. The building remains survived as an area of clay flooring, with an associated hearth and were defined to the west by a very shallow wall cut. The floor surface consisted of a compact yellow clay, 10cm deep, that covered an area measuring 5.4m long by 3.5m wide. Finds recovered from this deposit included a ferrous blade, medieval pottery (Dublin-type wares and Leinster Cooking Ware) and the remains of eight horse skulls. The horse skulls were closely packed together and had been deliberately placed within the floor when it was thrown down (fig. 8.7). A large hearth (2.14m by 1.06m by 3cm deep) defined by an area of fire reddened clay and charcoal partially sealed the clay floor, while a highly-truncated wall defined its western extent. The wall was contained within a very shallow, north–south orientated, foundation cut that measured *c.*5m long by 74cm wide by just 3cm deep. Only a small number of stones survived *in situ*, the rest having being robbed out in antiquity. The stones appeared to represent the remains of an inner and outer wall face and survived best along the southern and middle parts of the wall cut. They were mainly limestone boulders, averaging 30cm by 25cm by 20cm, that were held together with a mud bond.

Yard area: A yard area, measuring *c.*16m east–west by at least 5m north–south, was located directly to the north of Structures A and D. It was defined by a metalled surface composed of tightly-packed water-rolled pebbles that measured on average 4cm by 3cm by 3cm. The metalling had been severely truncated by deep ploughing and a number of modern land drains, giving it an overall patchy appearance. Finds from the surface included medieval pottery sherds (Leinster Cooking Ware and Dublin-type wares), animal bone (sheep and cattle) and ferrous objects (nails, staples, bars, wall hooks and a chisel).

Additional toft features: A number of features including five pits, a shallow gully and a series of medieval furrows were identified within the toft area. The pits were largely small, shallow cuts and were probably used to discard rubbish as they contained inclusions suggestive of domestic waste such as medieval pottery sherds (Dublin-type wares, Leinster Cooking Ware and Saintonge), animal bone (cattle, pig, goose and sheep), marine shell and charcoal. The furrows and gully, in contrast, were probably related to agricultural activities.

The croft: The croft area measured *c.*30m north–south by 14m–16m east–west and was separated from the toft by a pair of shallow ditches. A roughly 2m-wide gap between these ditches appeared to have defined an entrance, which allowed access between the toft and croft areas. Only two features, a ditch and a furrow, were identified within the croft and these were both probably agricultural.

Seventeenth-century features: A number of features dating to the seventeenth century were identified in Plot 2. These included two ditches, which redefined earlier property boundaries, as well as a large well, a small pit and a short gully. These features are not discussed further in this paper.

Plot 3 (fig. 8.4)
Plot 3 measured approximately 14m–16m wide by 60m long, although its full extent could not be properly assessed as its northern end was truncated by Station Road. It was defined by a series of shallow ditches and was separated into toft and croft areas by an internal division. The toft contained at least two rectangular structures along with a series of associated pits, gullies and wells, while the croft area contained another well and a number of gullies.

The toft: The toft area of Plot 3 measured approximately 14m wide (east–west) by 32m long (north–south) and continued on beyond the northern limit of excavation (beneath Station Road). The truncated remains of at least two buildings (Structures B and E), along with a number of surfaces and walls were identified to the front of the toft, while two wells and a series of pits were found to the rear.

Structure B (fig. 8.8): The truncated remains of a rectangular building, measuring approximately 8.5m by 6m (externally), were uncovered at the front

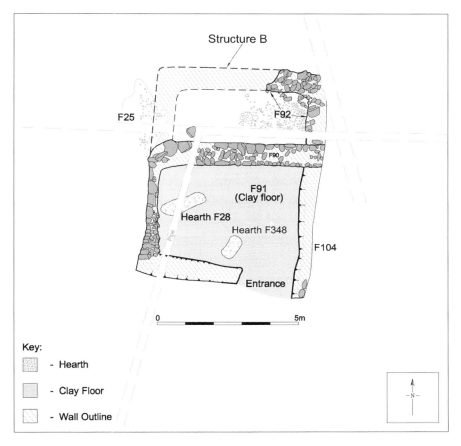

8.8 Structure B.

of the toft (fig. 8.9). It was divided into separate rooms (Rooms 1 and 2) by an internal partition, while a simple gap (2m wide) in the southern wall appeared to define an entrance. The southern room of the building (Room 1) measured 5m (east–west) by 4m internally and was defined by low foundation walls to the west and north and by robbed-out wall cuts to the south and east. Internally, it contained a packed clay floor, and two areas of *in situ* burning (F28 and F348) possibly represented the truncated remains of hearths. The presence of a second room or annex (Room 2) was indicated by an L-shaped wall (F92) that abutted the northern side of Room 1. The wall had been severely truncated by a combination of modern land drains and deep ploughing and originally may have defined a small chamber with internal dimensions of approximately 2m north–south by 4.8m east–west. The surviving walls of Structure 1 measured between 75cm and 87cm wide and consisted of unhewn limestone blocks held together with a mud bond. They were sitting in shallow foundation cuts and

8.9 Pre–excavation shot of Structure B.

8.10 Horse skull
within floor of
Structure B.

did not survive beyond one course in height. Internally Room 1 was covered in a compact clay floor, 10–15cm deep, that contained numerous lenses of charcoal and burnt clay, as well as animal bone (sheep, pig and fowl), medieval pottery (Dublin-type wares and Leinster Cooking Ware) and a horse skull (F103). Interestingly, the skull had been placed near the centre of the building (fig. 8.10), reminiscent of the horse skulls found in Structure D. The charcoal inclusions from the floor deposit included fragments of blackthorn and oak, while analysis of the plant remains identified a wide range of species, including barley, wheat, oat, garden pea, small seeded legumes and indeterminate wild seeds. A sample of oak charcoal from the floor was radiocarbon-dated to *c.*AD1491–1641 (2 sigma), which suggests that the building was probably constructed in the sixteenth century. Room 2, in contrast, was partially covered in a metalled surface from which no finds were recovered. The only other internal features identified were two patches of *in situ* burning (F28 and F348), possibly representing highly truncated hearths, which were located within Room 1. They both consisted of sub-circular areas of reddish orange, fire-reddened clay that directly overlay the floor surface.

Structure E (fig. 8.11): The remains of a second rectangular building (Structure E) were identified *c.*70cm to the north-west of Structure B. The building was severely truncated, especially along its northern and western extent, making its true dimensions difficult to discern. The surviving structure measured 5m wide (east–west) by at least 5.5m long (north–south) and contained a well-defined hearth (F24), which was probably originally located at the centre of the building. If this was the case, then the building may have had a true length of approximately 8.5m north–south. The structure was defined by a low, mud-bonded, wall (F170) and the presence of a spud stone suggested that it had contained an east-facing entrance. The building wall, which survived to just one course in height, measured between 50cm and 70cm wide and was built out of irregularly shaped limestone blocks that measured on average 20cm by 30cm by 20cm. The southern gable wall of the structure was the most complete, measuring *c.*5m in length, which represented the full width of the building. The western wall, in contrast, was highly truncated, extending for just 1m northwards from the southern gable wall. The eastern building wall, although very disturbed, was considerably longer, extending for *c.*5m before being totally truncated, while the northern gable wall did not survive. The interior of the structure contained the partial remains of a metalled surface, as well as a central hearth (F24), which consisted of an area of oxidized clay and charcoal surrounded by a loose setting of stones (fig. 8.12). Finds recovered from the hearth included sherds of medieval pottery (Leinster Cooking Ware), animal bone (rabbit, sheep, pig and fish) and cereal grains (wheat and barley), while charcoal analysis indicated that a variety of woods

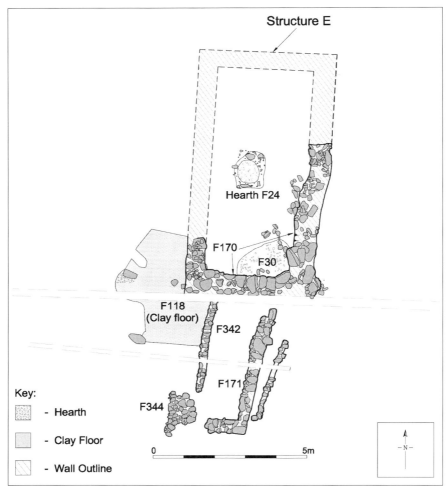

8.11 Structure E.

were used as fuel, including oak, cherry, pomaceous fruitwood and hazel. The interior of the building was sealed by blackish brown silty clay that probably represented accumulated domestic waste. This deposit contained frequent inclusions of food remains in the form of marine shell (cockle, mussel, razor-shell, oyster and periwinkle) and butchered animal bone (cattle, pig, sheep, dog, cat, rabbit, horse, fowl and goose), as well as large quantities of artefacts including medieval pottery (mainly Leinster Cooking Ware and Dublin-type wares), metal objects (nails and knives), a medieval roof-tile and a glass bead.

Additional structural remains: A series of stone walls along with the remains of a clay floor were identified immediately to the south of Structure E.

8.12 Hearth within
Structure E.

They did not form any coherent structural plan, but indicated the former presence of a building, which appears to have pre-dated Structure E. The first wall (F171) extended for *c* 4.5m from the southern side of Structure E in a roughly north–south direction before turning at a right angle and continuing west for a further 95cm. It was constructed out of unhewn limestone and sandstone blocks, held together with a mud bond. The wall was truncated along its northern extent by a modern field drain, which made its relationship with Structure E difficult to discern. A second, narrower stone wall (F342) was identified approximately 1.5m to the west of wall F171. It was also orientated north–south and comprised of a single course of unhewn limestone blocks averaging 25cm by 20cm by 15cm. It measured 3.12m long by 27cm wide and the narrow dimensions of this feature suggest that it may represent the foundations for a lightweight wall, possibly made out of material such as wicker. A similar stone footing, representing an internal division, was also identified in Structure C (see Plot 1). A sub-rectangular setting of stones (F344), possibly representing a foundation pad for a roof support or else a very truncated wall, was located to the west of wall F171 and was probably related. It measured 1.55m long (north–south) by 90cm wide and was built from unhewn limestone blocks. In addition, a compact yellow clay (F18/F118), probably representing a floor surface, was found in association with these wall remains and together these features suggest the former presence of a building.

Ancillary toft features: As well as the structural remains described above, a large number of ancillary features were identified within the toft area and these are indicative of intensive habitation. These included two wells, a series of gullies, a pathway and a number of pits as well as a metalworking area.

Wells: Two very large and deep pits, probably representing wells, were identified to the rear of Structures B and E. One of the wells was accessed by a metalled pathway, while both cuts were filled by a series of waterlogged deposits that had good organic preservation. The first well was identified 3m to the south of Structure B. It was sub-circular and measured 3.5m long, 2.5m wide and 1.8m deep. The sides of the cut sloped steeply to a concave base and it was filled by three distinct deposits, the lowest of which was waterlogged. Finds recovered from the well included leather shoe fragments, medieval pottery (Dublin-type wares and Leinster Cooking Ware) and animal bone (cattle, sheep, pig, horse, dog, fowl and hooded crow). Two small steps cutting natural boulder clay were identified along the north-western side of the well and these may have been used to get in and out of the cut as required. The second well was accessed by a metalled pathway, 12m long by 2m wide, which led away from its north-eastern edge towards Structures B and E. The well was oval in plan and measured 6.5m long (east–west) by 4.2m wide by 2m deep. The sides sloped steeply, with the exception of the eastern side, which had more gradual break of slope, probably for access purposes. The pit narrowed at the base, which was relatively flat, to approximately 1.8m in diameter. It was filled by two distinct deposits, both of which were waterlogged. Finds recovered from these fills included medieval pottery, animal bone and a scale-tang knife.

Metalworking area: What appear to have been the remains of a metalworking area were identified immediately to the south of Structure C and to the east of Structure E. It was defined by an irregular stone surface that contained a number of associated post-holes as well as an area of *in situ* burning. The stone surface covered an area measuring approximately 4.45m by 4.2m and was composed of small (5cm by 6cm by 7cm) and medium-sized (10cm by 10cm by 12cm) stones that were sealed by blackish brown silty clay. The finds recovered from the overlying layer included large quantities of ferrous slag (10.4kg) as well as animal bone (cattle, sheep, pig, dog, cat, fowl, duck, geese, rabbit and possibly wolf), medieval pottery (Leinster Cooking Ware, Dublin-type wares and Chester-type ware), ferrous objects (knives, nails, corroded objects and a flesh hook) and a hone stone. Virtually all the slag recovered during excavation was found in association with this surface, suggesting that this was a metalworking area. A number of post-holes were found in association with the stone surface and these may have been related to some form of lean-to structure abutting the northern wall of Structure C.

8.13 Well within Plot 3.

Pits and gullies: Six pits and four gullies were also identified within the toft area. The pits varied in size and shape, the majority containing material suggestive of dumped domestic waste, such as marine shell, animal bone (cattle, sheep, horse, dog), medieval pottery (Dublin-type wares, Leinster Cooking Ware, Bristol-Redcliffe ware and Low Countries redware) and ferrous artefacts (a blade, a fishing hook and nails). The gullies, meanwhile, were generally shallow, U-shaped, cuts that were probably related to drainage or agricultural activities.

The croft: The croft area, which measured approximately 15m east–west by 27m north–south, was separated from the toft by a shallow east–west gully. It contained the remains of a deep well and three closely spaced gullies that may have defined a garden area. The well was located immediately to the south of the toft/croft boundary gully and consisted of a deep sub-circular pit that measured 4.3m long (east–west) by 3.14m wide by 2.13m deep (fig. 8.13). The sides of the cut sloped steeply to a flat base which measured approximately 1.6m in diameter and was filled by three distinct deposits. The primary fill was waterlogged in nature and contained occasional inclusions of organic matter such as decayed grass and twigs, while the remaining fills appeared to represent backfill deposits.

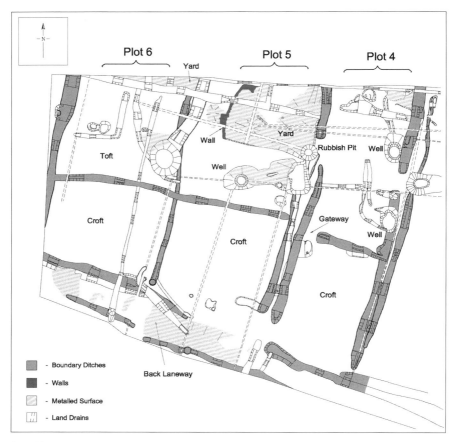

8.14 Plots 4–6.

Seventeenth-century features: A small number of seventeenth-century features were identified in Plot 3. These included re-cuts of the eastern and western boundary ditches, along with a small pit located at the very southern end of the plot. These features are not discussed any further in this paper.

Plot 4 (fig. 8.14)
Plot 4 measured approximately 15m wide by 55m long and was defined by a series of shallow inter-cutting ditches. Despite the presence of wells and rubbish pits, which are suggestive of domestic occupation, no structures were identified within Plot 4. However, it remains possible that associated buildings may have been located beyond the northern limit of excavation. As with the other plots, two distinct phases of activity were identified, late medieval/early modern and seventeenth century.

The toft area: The toft area measured approximately 3m north–south by 15m east–west and contained the remains of two wells, three rubbish pits, a small area of metalled surfacing and a number of gullies.

Metalled surface: A small area of metalled surface, probably representing the remains of a truncated yard, was identified in the very north-eastern part of the toft. It was located within a shallow depression (8cm deep) and was partially sealed by a layer of seventeenth-century stone infill. The metalled surface was composed of closely packed water-rolled pebbles (average dimensions 5cm by 2cm by 2cm) that covered an area measuring 5m (east–west) by 3m. Finds recovered from the surface include marine shell, medieval pottery (Dublin-type wares and Leinster Cooking Ware) and a ferrous rivet.

Wells: Two very large and deep wells were also identified within the toft. They contained waterlogged deposits suggesting the former presence of standing water and one of the cuts was radiocarbon-dated to AD1491–1642 (2 sigma). The first well-pit was identified towards the front of the toft and was partially truncated along its eastern side by a seventeenth-century ditch, while a medieval gully, possibly intended as an overflow channel, led away from its southern edge. The well was sub-circular in plan and measured 5.4m long (north–south) by 3m wide by 2m deep. The sides sloped steeply, with the exception of the northern side, which had a more gradual break of slope. The northern side also contained the remnants of a metalled surface, suggesting that the pit was accessed from this edge. The well narrowed at the base, which was relatively flat, to roughly 1.9m in diameter, and it was filled by two deposits. The primary fill was waterlogged black clayey silt that measured 1.2m deep and contained frequent inclusions of grass and twigs (mainly oak and hazel) as well as leather shoe fragments and parts of a wooden bowl. The plant remains recovered from this deposit included two hemp seeds as well as a number of species associated with cultivated land including goosefoot, broadleaved dock and nettle. Hazel charcoal from the primary fill was radiocarbon-dated to AD1491–1642 (2 sigma), which suggests that the well was broadly sixteenth-century in date. The secondary fill was yellowish grey silty clay that appears to represent a backfill deposit that accumulated after the well went out of use. A second well pit was also identified within the toft, approximately 8m to the south of the first well. The pit was sub-circular and measured 3.4m long (north–south) by 3.2m wide by 2m deep. The sides sloped steeply to a flat base, which measured roughly 1.8m long by 1.2m wide. The primary fill was waterlogged grey/black silty clay that was 30cm deep and was quite organic in nature, containing frequent inclusions of grass and twigs. The secondary fill was yellowish brown silty clay that measured 1.7m in depth and contained infrequent inclusions of charcoal and seashell. This fill appears to represent a backfill deposit that accumulated after the well went out of use.

Possible rubbish pits: Three cuts, possibly representing rubbish pits, were identified within the toft area. The first pit was located at the very front of the toft, while the remaining two cuts were closely spaced to the rear of the toft. Finds recovered from the pits included marine shell, sherds of medieval pottery (Leinster Cooking Ware, Dublin-type wares, Chester-type ware and Saintonge green-glazed ware), animal bone (sheep, cattle and pig) and ferrous objects (a key, heckle teeth, blades and nails).

The croft: The croft area, which measured *c.*15m east–west by 23m north–south, was separated from the toft by a shallow east–west ditch (1m wide by 44cm deep). This cut terminated 2m short of the western plot boundary ditch and this gap may have defined a gateway allowing access between the toft and croft areas. The only feature identified in the croft was a shallow pit (2.8m long by 2.6m wide by 18cm deep), which was filled by charcoal-rich silty clay that contained infrequent inclusions of animal bone (mainly cattle) and medieval pottery (Leinster Cooking Ware and Dublin-type ware).

Seventeenth-century features: A number of seventeenth-century features were identified in Plot 4. These included re-cuts of the eastern and western boundary ditches, along with an east–west ditch, a stone dump and a large pit, all of which were located within the toft area. These features are not discussed further in this paper.

Plot 5 (fig. 8.14)
Plot 5 measured approximately 21m wide by 48m long and, as with the previous properties, was defined by a series of shallow ditches. The very front of the plot was truncated by Station Road, while internally it was separated into toft and croft areas by an east–west orientated ditch. The front of the toft was dominated by a large terraced yard area, while the croft contained a scatter of pits and a large metalled laneway to the rear. Two distinct phases of activity were identified within the plot, late medieval/early modern and seventeenth century.

The toft: The toft area of Plot 5 measured approximately 21m wide (east–west) by 22m long (north–south) and continued on beyond the northern limit of excavation (beneath Station Road). The northern end of the toft was dominated by a large terraced yard area, which was defined by an area of metalled surface and a low wall. A large well, accessed via a metalled pathway, was located to the south of the yard along with three pits, while a second much smaller area of metalled surface was identified immediately to the west of the yard area.

8.15 Yard area at the front of Plot 5.

Yard area: To provide a level area for the yard at the front of the toft, the natural north–south slope had been scarped to form a large rectangular terrace (fig. 8.15). This measured approximately 16m east–west by 12m north–south and was revetted along its western side by a low stone wall, which was a maximum of three courses high and was mud-bonded. The surface of the yard was covered in tightly packed pebbles (3cm by 3cm by 1cm), interspersed with slightly larger water-rolled stones (10cm by 10cm by 3cm). Finds found in association with the surface included medieval pottery (Dublin-type wares and Leinster Cooking Ware), a bone spindle whorl, iron objects (a door key, a horseshoe fragment, a heckle tooth, a chisel, a saw and two blades) and animal bone (pig, fowl and sheep).

Metalled surface: A second, much smaller, area of metalled surface was identified immediately to the west of the yard area described above. It measured 4.5m north–south by 3.45m east–west and was sitting directly over natural boulder clay. The surface was composed of tightly packed water-rolled pebbles, which measured between 2cm by 1cm by 1cm and 7cm by 6cm by 5cm. Finds found in association with the surface included seashell (muscles, cockles and razorshell), animal bone (pig, sheep and fowl), a ferrous point and medieval pottery (Dublin-type ware and Leinster Cooking Ware).

8.16 Back laneway being exposed.

Well and associated pathway: A very deep pit, probably representing a well, was identified *c*.5m to the south of the yard area. It contained waterlogged deposits and was originally accessed via a metalled pathway, which led away from its north-eastern edge and measured 9m long by 3m wide. The well-pit was sub-circular in plan and measured 3m long (north–south) by 2m wide by 1.9m deep. The sides sloped steeply to a flat base, which measured approximately 1.5m in diameter. Finds recovered from the well included marine shell (mainly cockle and mussel) and decayed grass as well a single sherd of Dublin-type fine ware.

Pits: Three pits were identified within the toft area and these were probably used for dumping rubbish as the finds recovered from them, such as medieval pottery (Dublin-type wares and Leinster Cooking Wares), marine shell (cockles, razorshell and mussels) and animal bone (fish, sheep, pig, horse and dog) were suggestive of waste disposal.

The croft: The croft area measured approximately 21m east–west by 23m north–south and was separated from the toft by an east–west orientated ditch (1.3m wide by 60cm deep), which had been re-cut during the seventeenth century. The remains of a metalled laneway were identified at the very back of the croft along with four small pits.

Laneway: The partial remains of a laneway, running roughly north-east-south-west, were identified to the rear of Plot 5 (fig. 8.16). This feature, which also continued to the rear of Plot 6, consisted of a closely packed metalled surface, formed by small (3cm by 3cm by 2cm) and medium-sized (7cm by 4cm by 3cm) pebbles. These were sitting in a blackish brown sandy clay matrix that contained frequent inclusions of charcoal and marine shell. The surface was linear in plan, measuring 5m in width and extending for 25m before becoming much more patchy and truncated and finally stopping after about 43m. Finds found in association with the surface included animal bone (cattle, sheep, pig, horse, cat and dog), medieval pottery (Dublin-type wares and Bristol Redcliff ware) and a large number of metal artefacts (a lace chape, a ferrous Jews harp, a ferrous spur, nails and twelve horseshoes). It is possible that prior to truncation by deep ploughing this laneway was more extensive and allowed access to all of the plots. It was certainly large and durable enough to be used by carts as a number of wheel ruts were clearly visible on its surface.

Pits: Four relatively shallow pits (10–40cm deep) were identified to the rear of the croft. Three of the cuts were filled by very similar charcoal-rich deposits, while the fourth was filled by grey silty clay. Only a few sherds of medieval pottery were recovered from these cuts.

Seventeenth-century features: A number of features dating to the seventeenth century were identified in Plot 5. These included six ditches, some of which redefined earlier medieval boundaries, as well as a large pit, which truncated the medieval yard area. These features are not discussed further in this paper.

Plot 6 (fig. 8.6)

Plot 6 measured approximately 20–22m wide (east–west) by 38m long, with the very front of the plot extending on beneath Station Road to the north. It was defined by a series of shallow ditches and was separated into toft and croft areas by an internal division. Internally, the toft contained a small area of metalled surface, as well as a series of gullies and pits, while the croft contained the partial remains of a metalled laneway to the rear. As with the other plots, two distinct phases of activity were identified, late medieval/early modern and seventeenth century.

The toft: The toft area of Plot 6 measured approximately 20m wide (east–west) by 20m long (north–south) and continued beyond the northern limit of excavation (beneath Station Road). Medieval activity within the toft was quite limited, being restricted to a metalled surface, two ditches and a pit. This paucity of features may indicate that the plot was less intensively settled than the other properties or, more likely, that the majority of medieval activity occurred towards the front of the toft, which was beyond the northern limit of excavation.

Possible yard area: An area of metalled surface was identified at the very northern limit of the toft, where it extended beyond the limit of excavation. It was composed of closely packed water-rolled pebbles, averaging 5cm by 4cm by 2cm, which covered an area measuring 8m east–west by 2.5m north–south. The pebbles were sitting directly on natural subsoil and had been truncated by three seventeenth-century ditches. Finds recovered from the surface included animal bone (sheep, pig and fowl), marine shell, medieval pottery (Leinster Cooking Ware, Dublin-type wares and Saintonge green-glazed ware), and ferrous objects (an awl, a large sewing needle, a nail, a buckle, a bar and a whittle-tang knife).

Ditches: Two shallow ditches were identified immediately to the south of the yard area and these may have defined small gardens or vegetables patches. The first was a curvilinear ditch, orientated broadly north–south-east, in the eastern part of the toft. This ditch, in combination with the eastern plot boundary, enclosed an irregularly shaped parcel of land measuring a maximum of 15m north–south by 8m east–west. The second ditch was an L-shaped cut directly to the west of the curvilinear ditch. In combination with the western plot boundary, it enclosed a rectangular area of land, which measured 8m east–west by 9m north–south and was open to the north.

Rubbish pit: A large figure-of-eight-shaped pit was identified within the area enclosed by the L-shaped ditch. The pit, which had a total length of 4.2m, consisted of two concave bowls that measured 45cm and 23cm deep respectively. The bowls were filled by homogeneous light brown sandy silt that contained occasional inclusions of marine shell, charcoal and animal bone (cattle, sheep, pig and horse) as well as medieval pottery (Dublin-type ware and Leinster Cooking Ware) and a large hone stone.

The croft: The croft area measured *c.*16m north–south by 22m east–west and was separated from the toft by a an east–west oriented ditch (1.3m wide by 60cm deep) that also continued into Plot 5. The croft contained a large laneway to the rear (described previously under Plot 5) as well as an oblong pit. The latter feature was probably a rubbish pit as it contained occasional inclusions of animal bone (sheep and dog) and medieval pottery (Dublin-type ware, Leinster Cooking Ware and Iberian coarse ware).

Seventeenth-century features: A number of seventeenth-century features were identified within Plot 6. These included five ditches, three of which extended into Plot 6 from Plot 5, as well as a very large pit and an associated area of metalled surface. These features are not discussed further in this paper.

DISCUSSION

During the medieval period, Portmarnock formed part of a large monastic grange belonging to the Cistercian monks of St Mary's Abbey, Dublin. It had originally been granted to the monks by royal charter in 1174,[40] and the estate's boundaries seem to have corresponded nearly exactly to the modern parish of Portmarnock. It included the townlands of the Grange, Carrickhill, Portmarnock, Conneyburrough and Robswall, with the medieval village being located in the townland of Portmarnock (fig. 8.2). Granges such as Portmarnock were large independent farms worked by lay brothers and were often the model farms of their day. Their nucleus typically comprised a refectory and dorter, an oratory, a granary and other necessary farm buildings.[41] At Duleek, Co. Meath, for example, the buildings 'lay about a single great courtyard flanked by buildings. On the east … the domestic quarters of the grange occupied the whole of one side … a variety of agricultural buildings and two substantial gatehouses occupied the remaining three sides of the court'.[42] These buildings included a granary, a thatched pig-sty and ox-house, a sheep house and a stable. Outside the court were gardens, a dovecote and a watermill. At Portmarnock, the exact location of the grange buildings remains uncertain, but is likely to have been somewhere within Grange townland, which was to the north of the medieval village (fig. 8.2).

Although Portmarnock is recorded in a number of documents dating from the medieval period, the first specific mention of the village is not until 1539, when it is described as containing ten cottages and nine messuages (property plots).[43] A number of the village inhabitants are named in this survey, including Patrick Gygen, Peter Mansfeld, John Taylor, Robert Benane, Thomas Kelly, John Gyles, John Rowe, Patrick Hogge and John Proydforde. Patrick Gygen appears to be a man of some importance as he also held land at Robbswalls,[44] and in an earlier document his holding is described as a hall-ferme.[45] This is a term used to describe larger farms, which were often manorial centres and could indicate that a more substantial residence formed part of the village core. The exact location of this hall-ferme is unknown, but it is possible that it was

40 Gilbert (ed.), *Chartularies of St Mary's Abbey*, i, p. 83. **41** D.H. Williams, *The Welsh Cistercians* (Bodmin, 2001), p. 192. **42** B.J. Graham (ed.), *Medieval Irish settlement: a review* (Norwich, 1980), p. 27. **43** Gilbert (ed.), *Chartularies of St Mary's Abbey*, ii, pp 68–70. **44** Ibid. **45** Ainsworth, *Private collections*, no. 161 (Plunkett papers), p. 1541.

located at the site of the future Portmarnock House. In the neighbouring
townland of Grange, the property of Walter Golding, who was a prominent
member of the local elite,[46] is also referred to as a hall-ferme, suggesting that
during the late medieval period a number of large farms and associated
buildings were to be found within the parish bounds. It is possible that these
hall-fermes were originally grange farms, which were leased out to members of
the local gentry as the monastic communities declined in the later Middle
Ages. The village continues to be mentioned in a number of sixteenth- and
seventeenth-century documents, with the final specific reference to it occurring in Civil Survey of 1654–6.[47] It is normally described as containing ten
cottages, although the Civil Survey mentions the presence of a number of
additional houses and buildings, which formed part of the Plunkett residence
of Portmarnock House.

The village layout
The general layout of the village site, with its regular plots, sub-divided into
toft and croft areas, suggests that it was laid out as a single planned event,
probably under the jurisdiction of St Mary's Abbey. This form of village
mirrors contemporary sites in England, such as Wharram Percy,[48] Cowlam[49]
and Grienstein.[50] In the English examples, the villages were often aligned
along a central road with a row of property plots on either side, and a similar
layout may once have existed at Portmarnock. If this was the case then the
excavation may have exposed only one side of the village, with the remainder
occurring on the northern side of Station Road, in an area now occupied by a
modern residential complex. This possibility is reinforced by the fact that the
historical documents suggest that the medieval/early-modern village of
Portmarnock once contained at least nine plots, rather than the six uncovered.

The property boundaries at Portmarnock were defined by shallow inter-
cutting ditches, some of which continued to be redefined into the seventeenth
century. As well as demarking the extents of the individual properties, these
cuts would have channelled water run-off away from the buildings, which were
located at the bottom of a gradual north-east-facing slope. Internally, the plots,
which measured between 16m and 20m in width, were divided into toft and
croft areas by ditches. The toft (front of the plot) was where the majority of
settlement activity took place, while the croft (rear of the plot) was probably
used for keeping livestock as well as growing garden crops. The croft areas
appear to have been accessed by a large metalled laneway, which ran parallel to
the rear of the plots, and this is a feature often seen at medieval village sites in

46 Morrin (ed.), *Calendar of patent and close rolls of chancery in Ireland, Henry VIII to 18 Elizabeth*, pp 41, 140, 216.   **47** Simington (ed.), *Civil Survey: Dublin*, p. 174.   **48** M.W. Beresford and John Hurst, *Wharram Percy, deserted medieval village* (London, 1990), p. 49, fig. 34.   **49** M.W. Beresford and J.K. Sinclair St Joseph, *Medieval England: an aerial survey* (Cambridge, 1969), p. 125, fig. 48.   **50** Grenville Astill and Annie Grant, *The countryside of medieval England* (Oxford, 1992), p. 48, fig. 3.3.

England.[51] The laneway was obviously a well-used thoroughfare, as a large number of horse shoes were recovered from its fabric and a series of wheel ruts were clearly visible along its surface. In Ireland, similar medieval roadways have recently been excavated at Mullaghmast, Co. Kildare,[52] and Phoenixtown, Co. Meath.[53]

The village buildings

As already mentioned, the majority of settlement activity was identified in the toft areas and these included the partial remains of at least five structures. The buildings were all broadly rectangular, and varied in size, Structure C appearing to be the largest. This building, although highly truncated, measured at least 15m in length, which is comparable in size to a medieval building excavated at Bouchier's Castle, Co. Limerick[54] (14.5m by 7.6m), and also to medieval peasant houses from England such as Cropston Road, Leicestershire,[55] Meldon, Devon[56] and Wharram Percy, Yorkshire.[57] The remaining buildings at Portmarnock were smaller, with Structure A measuring 7–8m by 6m, Structure B measuring 8.5m by 6m and Structure E measuring 8.5m by 4m. These dimensions are paralleled at a number of excavated Irish medieval houses, including Structure II at Caherguillamore, Co. Limerick,[58] (8.4m by 3.8m, internally), Killeen Castle, Co. Meath,[59] (8.2m by 4.5m) and Howth, Co. Dublin,[60] (8.6m by 4.8m). Where discernible, the Portmarnock structures appear to have been defined by low stone walls, which were located within shallow foundation cuts. In many instances, the walls had been robbed out, leaving only the wall foundation cuts behind. Where the stone walls did survive, they were rather flimsy and do not appear to have extended beyond one course in height. This suggests that they were intended either as foundations for wooden base-plates to support an upper wall made of timbers and wattle, or, more likely, as a dry footing to support walls made from mud/earth. Mud-walled buildings were very popular in Fingal right up until the last century, and a number of small vernacular cottages containing mud walls survive in this part of Co. Dublin. Typically, the clay for these buildings was mixed with rushes, rye or oaten straw, with water

51 Beresford and St Joseph, *Medieval England*, p. 9.   52 Angus Stephenson, 'Wining and dining in a medieval village at Mullaghmast, Co. Kildare' in E. Danaher and James Eogan (eds), *Dining and dwelling: proceedings of a public seminar on archaeological discoveries on national road schemes, August 2008* (Dublin, 2009), pp 143–53.   53 Ed Lyne, 'Lives through time', *Archaeology Ireland*, 84 (summer 2008), pp 17–21.   54 R.M. Cleary, 'Excavations at Lough Gur, Co. Limerick: Part II', *Cork Archaeological and Historical Society Journal*, 87 (1982), 77–106.   55 Jennifer Browning and Tim Higgins, 'Excavations of a medieval toft and croft at Cropston Road, Anstey, Leicestershire', *Transactions of the Leicestershire Archaeological and Historical Society*, 77 (2003), 65–81.   56 Mark Gardiner, 'Vernacular buildings and the development of the later medieval domestic plan in England', *Journal of Medieval Archaeology*, 44 (2000), 178, fig. 6.   57 Beresford and Hurst, *Wharram Percy*.   58 S.P. Ó Ríordáin and J. Hunt, 'Medieval dwellings at Caherguillamore Co. Limerick', *Journal of the Royal Society of Antiquaries of Ireland*, 72 (Dublin, 1942), 37–63.   59 Christine Baker, *The archaeology of Killeen Castle, Co. Meath* (Bray, 2009), p. 63.   60 Alan Hayden, 'Excavation of a medieval house in the grounds of Howth House, Co. Dublin' in Seán Duffy (ed.), *Medieval Dublin VII* (Dublin, 2006), pp 103–12.

added and the whole lot pounded into a mortar-like mass by trampling. It was then cut into blocks and lifted into the position on the wall, while still plastic, and rammed down. It was a very widespread and efficient means of constructing walls and was used throughout Leinster, especially in areas that had been heavily colonized by the Anglo-Normans such as Cos Dublin, Meath and Wexford. Other examples of excavated medieval houses constructed in this method included Structure I, Jerpoint, Co. Kilkenny,[61] and Structure II, Bouchier's Castle, Co. Limerick.[62]

The roofs of the Portmarnock structures were probably thatched as they are described as such in the Civil Survey of 1654–6.[63] It is unclear what thatching material was used, although it may have been wheat straw as it was grown in the surrounding fields (see below) and was favoured by thatchers due to its long lifespan, uniform length and easiness to prepare. If wheat straw was not readily available, other materials such as oat straw, barley straw, rye straw, reeds, rushes, flax or even marram grass could have been used. A small number of medieval roof-tile fragments were also recovered during the excavation and these suggest that a more substantial, tiled, building existed somewhere in the vicinity. This structure may have been related to the monks' grange or possibly to a hall-ferme (see above), which was located close to the village.

Internally, the majority of buildings contained floors of packed clay and in two instances horse skulls were recovered from these deposits. This mirrors folklore accounts from the seventeenth and nineteenth centuries, which indicate that horse skulls were often buried in floors to provide luck for the inhabitants and also apparently to improve the acoustics of the buildings. In Armagh, for example, during the early nineteenth century, 'the frontal bones of a horse's head were regarded as being particularly "sonsie" (lucky), and were often buried in barn floors and under the threshold of dwelling houses for this reason'.[64] Similarly, in Wexford, 'when a horse died the head would be cut off and kept and whenever a person would be building the first thing to go down (in the floor) would be the head'.[65] In general, the clay floors appear to have been kept fairly clean as they contained hardly any evidence for habitation deposits. This parallels the treatment of English medieval houses, which appear to have been regularly cleaned out; for example, at Wharram Percy the buildings had been swept so many times that hollows had started to form in the floors.[66] The only exception to this rule at Portmarnock was Structure E, whose interior was covered in a thin, artefact-rich, layer of humus which

61 Claire Foley, 'Excavations at a medieval settlement site in Jerpoint Church Townland, Co. Kilkenny', *Proceedings of the Royal Irish Academy*, 89C (1989), 71–126.   62 R.M. Cleary, 'Excavations at Lough Gur, Co. Limerick: Part II', *Cork Archaeological and Historical Society Journal*, 87 (1982), 77–106.   63 Simington (ed.), *Civil Survey: Dublin*, p. 174.   64 J. Donaldson, *An historical and statistical account of the Barony of Upper Fews in the County of Armagh in 1838* (Dundalk, 1923), p. 77.   65 Seán Ó Súilleabháin, 'Foundation sacrifices', *Journal of the Royal Society of Antiquaries of Ireland*, 75 (1945), 47.   66 Beresford and Hurst, *Wharram Percy*, p. 41.

appeared to represent discarded waste. The reason that this building was dirtier than the other buildings remains unclear, although it could indicate that it had a specialized function such as a cook house, resulting in more waste being produced, or quite simply that the inhabitants were less concerned with cleanliness than their neighbours were.

Areas of *in situ* burning, possibly representing truncated hearths, were identified in Structures B to E. These consisted of small areas of fire-reddened clay and their definition as hearths remains tentative. The only certain example was a centrally placed stone-lined hearth from Structure E. This consisted of an area of fire-reddened clay that was sealed by a thick deposit of charcoal, analysis of which indicated that oak, cherry, pomaceous fruitwood and hazel had been used as fuel.[67] A number of charred fish and animal bones were recovered from the hearth, indicating that it was used for cooking, with an adjacent stake-hole probably forming part of a spit. The doorways into the buildings, where discernible, were defined by simple gaps in the walls, with the entrance to Structure A being further emphasized by the addition of a tightly packed cobbled surface. The entrance to Structure B was slightly unusual, as it was located at the corner of the building, which would appear less structurally sound than a centrally placed door, although it is paralleled in a medieval house from Howth, Co. Dublin.[68] The doors were probably made of wood and may have been hung on spud stones, an example of which was recorded at Structure E. The doors appear to have been secured by locks, as evidenced by the door keys recovered from Plots 2 and 3 and a barrel padlock key also from Plot 3. In addition, parts of a door-locking mechanism were recovered from one of the ditches defining the rear of Plot 5.

Thus, the evidence from the site suggests that the Portmarnock buildings were small mud-walled structures, with thatched roofs, internal floors of packed clay and wooden doors that could be locked. A number of seventeenth-century accounts of cottager cabins survive and these may reflect what the Portmarnock buildings originally looked like. For example, the French traveller to Ireland, M. de la Baillie le Goes, described a relatively humble dwelling in 1644

> The cabins are of another fashion. There are four walls the height of a man, supporting rafters over which they thatch with straw and leaves. They are without chimneys and make the fire in the middle of the hut, which greatly incommodes those who are not fond of smoke.[69]

---

67 Lorna O'Donnell, 'The charcoal report, Portmarnock, Co. Dublin (2009)'. Unpublished report for Margaret Gowen and Co. Ltd. 68 Hayden, 'Excavation of a medieval house in the grounds of Howth House', pp 103–12. 69 Edward MacLysaght, *Irish life in the seventeenth century: after Cromwell* (Cork, 1950), p. 106.

Meanwhile, an extract from the diary of John Stevens, *c.*1689, details a typical
Irish interior as follows:

> In the better sort of cabins, there is commonly one flock bed, seldom
> more, feathers being too costly. This serves the man and his wife. The
> rest all lie on straw, some with one sheet and blanket, only their clothes
> and blanket to cover them. The cabins seldom have any floor but the
> earth, or rarely so much as a loft. They say it is of late that chimneys are
> used, yet the house is never free from smoke.[70]

The internal layout of the plots
It is possible that some of the building layouts seen at Portmarnock represent
small courtyard farms, with the main domestic residence located at the front of
the plot, facing onto the road and ancillary structures to the rear. In England,
courtyard farms are generally a late medieval development and become the
dominant farm type by the sixteenth century. They typically consist of a
domestic residence, a yard and a number of ancillary structures, such as barns,
byres, bake-houses or kitchens. At Portmarnock, it is possible that Structure C,
which appears to have been the largest building at the site, may represent a
domestic residence, with a yard area to the rear. If this was the case, it suggests
that the main domestic residence belonging to Plots 2 to 6 did not survive due
to truncation caused by Station Road. The remaining buildings in these plots
could represent ancillary structures such as barns, outhouses or cook houses.

As well as building remains, each of the plots contained a least one large
well. These cuts measured up to 2m in depth and were filled by waterlogged
deposits that contained relatively few finds, suggesting that an effort had been
made to keep them clean. Some plots, for example Plots 1, 3 and 4, contained
more than one well, indicating that over time some of the wells may have
become polluted or dried up, necessitating the excavation of new waterholes.
In two instances, the wells were accessed by metalled pathways, while in
another case the well contained a series of crude steps. The large size of some
of the wells, which were up to 5m in diameter at the surface, may indicate that
they were originally used as quarries for gathering good quality clays for
constructing the mud-walled buildings. This reuse of quarry holes as wells has
been recorded at a number of deserted village sites in England, including
Brenig, Caldecote and Grienstein.[71]

Most of the plots also contained the remains of yards and these were
generally defined by areas of tightly packed metalled surfaces. These were
probably intended as dry surfaces for carrying out everyday farmyard
activities, while the larger examples seen in Plots 1, 2 and 4 may also have been

70 Andrew Browning, *English historical documents from 1660–1714* (London, 1996), p. 729.   **71** Grenville
Astill, 'Rural settlement: the toft and the croft' in Astill and Grant (eds), *Countryside of medieval
England*, p. 57.

used as 'crew yards' for over-wintering small numbers of livestock. One of the yards, however, appears to have been used for a more specialized function, as large quantities of ferrous slag were recovered from its surface. This was the only slag recovered during the excavation, suggesting that this yard was probably associated with metalworking. The yard, which was located at the front of Plot 3, appears to have been covered by a lean-to structure that abutted Structure B and was supported by a number of post- and stake-holes. A small, highly,truncated, hearth was also found in association with the yard and this, combined with the evidence already mentioned, suggests that this plot may have been inhabited by the village blacksmith.

Farming and diet

Specialist analysis of plant remains from the medieval village indicates that a wide range of crops were grown in the surrounding fields, including wheat, barley, oats, peas and other legumes.[72] Wheat, which was the dominant taxa present, could be used for making bread and other foodstuffs and was normally grown as an autumn crop. Barley and oats, in contrast, were grown as spring crops, with barley being used for bread, porridge and beer, while oats were predominantly a fodder crop. The peas and legumes would have played an important part of the three-crop rotation system as well as being used for the household pottage (stew) and as fodder for livestock. In medieval England, pulses represent about a tenth of the food mentioned in the maintenance agreements, which might be an indication of their importance in the diet of the ordinary people.[73] No quern-stones were identified during the excavation, which suggests that the villagers used the nearby mills for grinding their corn. In 1539, two mills were recorded to the north of the village (on the Sluice River), which the villagers had to maintain as part of their annual dues.[74] However, the earliest surviving reference to these sites dates from the late thirteenth century, when Americus de Nugent granted the monks of St Mary's land upon which to build a mill at the mouth of the Sluice River.[75] This estuarine location is significant, as the mill appears to have been partially powered by the sea and is described as a 'tyde water mill' in the Civil Survey.[76] In addition to the foodstuffs mentioned above, hemp was also grown, probably for its fibres, which could be used to make coarse cloth and rope. It was often planted within the croft areas and used as a cash crop to generate extra income for the household.

The villagers' livestock were probably kept in the croft areas behind the houses as well as on the communal pasture, which was one hundred acres.[77]

72 Ryan Allen, 'The plant remains from Portmarnock, Co. Dublin (2009)'. Unpublished report for Margaret Gowen and Co. Ltd. 73 Richard Smith, 'Human resources' in Astill and Grant (eds), *Countryside of medieval England*, p. 201. 74 Gilbert (ed.), *Chartularies of St Mary's Abbey*, ii, pp 68–70. 75 Gilbert (ed.), *Chartularies of St Mary's Abbey*, i, pp 330–1. 76 Simington (ed.), *Civil Survey: Dublin*, p. 174. 77 Gilbert (ed.), *Chartularies of St Mary's Abbey*, i, pp 260–3.

The animals may also have been allowed to graze on arable land after harvesting and during fallow periods, as their dung would have been an important fertilizer. Analysis of the animal bone recovered during the excavation revealed that cattle were the main domesticate present, with lesser amounts of sheep and pig also recorded.[78] The cattle bone was dominated by mature cows, which is suggestive of a dairying economy, although it is likely that some of these animals were also used for traction, as, in contemporary England, cows were often incorporated into plough teams when oxen or draught horses were unavailable.[79] The sheep bone was also mainly from mature animals, indicating that they were being kept for their wool rather than their meat. The pigs, in contrast, were primarily a meat-producing animal and the majority were killed within their first three years. All of the animals had evidence for butchery marks, which is not surprising, as, in England, even old cows and sheep were generally fattened up for eating towards the end of their lives.[80] The butchery marks indicate that the carcasses were first split axially and then divided up into smaller portions using axes and knives.

A large number of horse bones, mainly from medium-sized ponies, were also recovered during the excavation. These probably represent the remains of draught horses that were used for carrying out everyday farm work such as ploughing and haulage. In England, from the twelfth century onwards, horses increasingly took the place of oxen for haulage and both animals are mentioned in a fourteenth-century document relating to Portmarnock.[81] This describes sales of livestock and crops to settle a debt owed by St Mary's Abbey to a William de la Rivere, in which Portmarnock had to provide sixteen draught horses, worth 40*d.* each, as well as eight oxen, which were slightly more expensive at 6*s.* 8*d.* each. This difference in price mirrors English accounts, where draught horses tended to be less valuable beasts than oxen or cart horses.[82] Horses are also mentioned in a document relating to Portmarnock in 1539, which states that for every horse pasturing on the moor (the commonage), the villagers had to pay an annual rent of one goose.[83] Unsurprisingly then, geese bones were also recovered during the excavation, along with hen and duck remains, all of which would have been important providers of both eggs and meat.

The inhabitants' diet was probably also supplemented by wild animals. For example, a number of rabbit bones, some of which were charred from cooking, were recovered during the excavation. The rabbits may have come from the surrounding fields or from a warren belonging to St Mary's Abbey, which was

78 Johnny Geber, 'The animal bone from Portmarnock, Co. Dublin (2009)'. Unpublished report for Margaret Gowen and Co. Ltd.   79 Annie Grant, 'Animal resources' in Astill and Grant (eds), *Countryside of medieval England*, p. 156.   80 Ibid., p. 160.   81 Gilbert (ed.), *Chartularies of St Mary's Abbey*, i, pp 260–3.   82 John Langdon, *Horses, oxen and technological innovation: the use of draught animals in English farming from 1066–1500* (Cambridge, 2002), p. 294.   83 Gilbert (ed.), *Chartularies of*

located just a short distance away on the sandy isthmus now occupied by Portmarnock Golf Course. The warren, which was rented by the Lord Leonard Grey in 1539,[84] was obviously relatively substantial, as the townland it occupied became known as 'Coneyborough' (Coney being an old word for rabbit). The rabbits were probably hunted using a combination of nets and ferrets and, interestingly, ferret remains were also identified at the village.

In addition to wild and domesticated animals, the village's location beside the sea suggests that fishing may have played an important part in the local economy. This is reinforced by the faunal evidence from the site, which identified the presence of fish species such as ling, hake, cod and conger eel. These species generally prefer deeper water and were probably caught from small fishing vessels using nets or baited lines, an iron fishing hook from Plot 4 being evidence for the latter. Large quantities of shell fish, which would have been easily gathered from the nearby foreshore, were also recovered during the excavation and included species such as cockle, mussel, razorclam, oyster, whelk and periwinkle. Indeed, fish and shellfish probably played an important role in the diet of the medieval villagers, as religious custom forbade meat consumption during Lent and Advent and after Pentecost, as well as on holy days.

The finds from the excavation

A large number of finds were recovered during the course of the excavation and these give an indication of the wealth and lifestyle of the villagers. The assemblage includes a large collection of pottery[85] and metal objects[86] (figs 8.17, 8.18), along with much smaller quantities of stone,[87] bone,[88] wood,[89] leather[90] and glass artefacts.[91] In general, small personal items were relatively rare, which may be an indication of the relative poverty of the village inhabitants. They included a small bone comb of fourteenth- to seventeenth-century type, a glass bead, possibly from a set of rosary beads, as well as objects for fastening clothes, such as a ferrous stick-pin of fourteenth- to sixteenth-century type and two copper-alloy buckles, belonging to a shoe and belt respectively. Other personal items included two Jews harps and a copper-alloy Elizabethan penny dating from 1601. Evidence for craftwork at the site was slightly more forthcoming and included a number of objects associated with textile production, including a bone spindle-whorl from Plot 4, a ferrous needle from Plot 6 and a number of ferrous heckle-teeth from Plots 3 and 4. Leatherworking also appears to have been carried out at the village, as a

St Mary's Abbey, ii, pp 68–70. **84** Ibid. **85** Siobhan Scully, 'The pottery finds from Portmarnock, Co. Dublin (2009)'. Unpublished report for Margaret Gowen and Co. Ltd. **86** Colm Moriarty, 'The metal finds from Portmarnock, Co. Dublin (2009)'. Unpublished report for Margaret Gowen and Co. Ltd. **87** Siobhan Scully, 'The small finds from Portmarnock, Co. Dublin (2009)'. Unpublished report for Margaret Gowen and Co. Ltd. **88** Ibid. **89** Ibid. **90** Ibid. **91** Ibid.

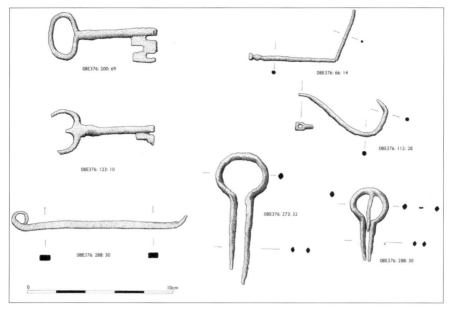

8.17 Selection of ferrous artefacts.

number of tools traditionally associated with this process such as awls, punches and points were recovered during the excavation. Similarly, woodworking was evidenced by the recovery of two chisels, a saw-blade fragment and in excess of 150 nails.

The inhabitants of the village were also obviously concerned about security, as indicated by the recovery of three keys and a mounted lock mechanism. The latter was probably from a casket or door, while the keys included a barrel padlock key and two door keys, with one of the door keys being of a type common from the fifteenth century onwards. A large quantity of horse equipment was also recovered from the village, demonstrating the importance of this animal to the local agrarian economy. The objects found included ferrous horseshoes (20), spurs (2), buckles (2), a possible snaffle bit ring (1) and bridal chain links (1), the majority of which were recovered from a laneway that traversed the rear of the plots. Where discernible, the horseshoes were of fourteenth- to sixteenth-century type, while the spurs were similar to those previously recovered from sixteenth-century contexts.[92] One of the more unusual finds recovered during the excavation was a small cannonball from one of the seventeenth-century ditches. The size and weight of this ferrous projectile suggest that it was fired by a falconet, which was a small cannon that was popular during the seventeenth century.

92 Moriarty, 'The metal finds from Portmarnock'.

8.18 Selection of knives.

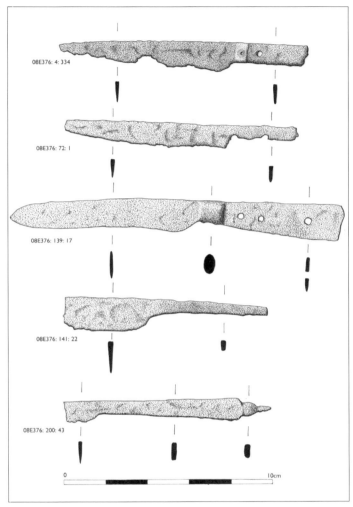

A number of objects associated with domestic activity were also identified during the excavation. These included artefacts relating to cooking, such as ferrous cauldron fragments and a flesh hook as well as domestic utensils such as wooden bowl fragments, twenty ferrous knife-blades and large quantities of broken pottery (see below). The wooden bowl fragments were all derived from shallow vessels that were made from ash wood, while the knives included ten whittle-tang knives, five scale-tang knives and five blade fragments. Two of the knives had decorative inlays in the form of copper-alloy shoulder plates and are probably post-fourteenth-century, while another knife had a decorated terminal/end cap and is similar to sixteenth-century examples from London. A maker's/cutler's mark was identified along the blade of another knife, in the

8.19 Leinster Cooking Ware pots.

form of a stylized rosette followed by a dot and a sideways chevron (facing left), while four of the remaining knives contained bolsters, which is generally seen as a sixteenth-century innovation.

The ceramic assemblage included over 2,500 sherds of pottery, 90 per cent of which were medieval. The medieval pottery was dominated by locally produced wares such as Leinster Cooking Ware and Dublin-type ware, which typically date from between the twelfth and the fourteenth century. The sherds were generally derived from large pots and jugs and in many instances had evidence for burning, which suggests that they were often used for cooking. Only a very small percentage (2.8 per cent) of imported wares was identified during the excavation and this may be a reflection of the relative poverty of the peasant inhabitants of the village. Although historical documents indicate that the village was inhabited throughout the sixteenth century, there is an apparent absence of pottery from this period at the site. This reflects the wider archaeological record, where late medieval pottery types are generally absent from excavations. A variety of reasons have been put forward for this apparent gap in the pottery record, including population decline following the Bruce invasion and Irish political revival, and the Black Death and subsequent plague recurrences, as well as a return to the use of wooden and leather vessels under native Irish influence.

At Portmarnock, however, the village appears to have survived these vicissitudes of war and plague, at least until the late seventeenth century. It seems unlikely then that a village on the outskirts of Dublin city and in the heart of the Pale would regress to such a state that pottery was no longer being produced or used. Instead, the paucity of pottery may be more apparent than real. This is suggested by the recovery of a nearly complete Leinster Cooking Ware pot (fig. 8.19) from a rubbish pit, which was radiocarbon-dated to *c*.1450–1631 (2 sigma). The largely intact nature of this pot indicates that it was discarded into the pit soon after breaking, suggesting that at Portmarnock this type of pottery was still being used well into the fifteenth and probably sixteenth century. Similarly sherds of Leinster Cooking Ware and Dublin-type ware were recovered from features (a well and a floor deposit), that were radiocarbon-dated to *c*.1490–1640 (2 sigma). This may indicate that, at Portmarnock, pottery styles such as Leinster Cooking Ware continued to be used throughout the late medieval period and were not replaced until the seventeenth century, when more elaborate imported wares became more accessible and fashionable. This extended date-range for ostensibly twelfth- to fourteenth-century pottery types has also been suggested for assemblages recovered from Ashbourne, Co. Meath,[93] and Thomas Street, Co. Dublin,[94] and would mirror the pottery record from Ulster, where medieval pottery, such as everted rim ware/Ulster coarse ware, was used well into the seventeenth century.

The origins of the village

The dating of the village remains problematic as the pottery evidence, which suggests a broadly twelfth- to fourteenth-century date for the site, is in conflict with the carbon-14 determinations, the historical research and the majority of the metal finds data, which is more indicative of a fourteenth- to seventeenth-century date for the site's primary use. However, as already discussed, some of the medieval pottery types traditionally assigned to the twelfth to fourteenth centuries may have had a much longer lifespan at Portmarnock, where their use possibly extended right up until the seventeenth century. If this was the case, then carbon-14 determinations may be a more accurate dating tool for the site. In total, three features were subjected to carbon-14 analysis, including a well from Plot 4 (AD1491–1642; 2 sigma), a primary floor surface from Structure B (AD1491–1641; 2 sigma), and rubbish pit from Plot 1 (AD1450–1631; 2 sigma). The date-range for all three features is broadly similar and is suggestive of a late fifteenth-/early seventeenth-century date for the main occupation of the village. This would mirror the surviving historical sources, as the earliest description of the village dates to 1541,[95] and the latest to 1654–6.[96]

93 W.O. Frazer, 'Final report for archaeological excavations at Lidl site, Ashbourne Town Centre Development, Killegland townland, Ashbourne, Co. Meath (2007)'. Unpublished report for Margaret Gowen and Co. Ltd. **94** Edmond O'Donovan, 'The growth and decline of a medieval suburb? Evidence from the excavations at Thomas Street, Dublin' in Seán Duffy (ed.), *Medieval Dublin IV* (Dublin, 2003), p. 167. **95** Gilbert (ed.), *Chartularies of St Mary's Abbey*, ii, pp 68–70. **96** Simington

Similarly, a number of the metal artefacts, including the only coin (dated 1601) recovered from the site, along with the horseshoes, keys, spurs and knives, are all broadly fourteenth to seventeenth century.

The reason for the growth of a village at Portmarnock during the late medieval period is uncertain, but it may be related to a general decline seen in monastic orders during the fifteenth century, which saw many foundations experiencing a paucity of recruits.[97] Cistercian granges, such as Portmarnock, were generally farmed by lay brothers, but as their numbers diminished during the fifteenth century the monastic authorities may have deemed it necessary to replace them with new lay tenants. During this period there would have been no shortage of replacement workers, as the area under English control in Ireland was contracting due to a Gaelic resurgence and many displaced people from the edges of the Pale were probably looking for new, more secure, homes near Dublin.

The abandonment of the village

The archaeological evidence from the site suggests that the village was abandoned sometime during the late seventeenth century, when a number of the structures and yard areas were truncated by ditches, probably defining new field systems. This seventeenth-century desertion of the site is paralleled at a number of other medieval villages, including Newtown Jerpoint, Co. Kilkenny, and Buolick, Kiltinan and Ardmayle in Co. Tipperary,[98] and may be related to the turbulent history of this period, which saw the country rocked by successive waves of conflict and famine.

Fingal was hit especially hard by the Confederate wars of the 1640s, when the majority of the local gentry rose up against the Dublin government. It was attacked on a number of occasions by government troops under the command of marquis of Ormonde, with Swords and the surrounding villages being burnt in 1641. This scorched-earth policy continued in 1642, when large tracts of Fingal were despoiled by government troops who 'pillaged all the Pale as far as to Drogheda ... burned all the lords' houses in the Pale and the gentlemen's, and fired all the Pale'.[99] The local populace suffered greatly during this warfare, a contemporary account describing how 'very many are dead lately, especially of the poorer sort, and the children die very thick of the measles and pox'.[100] In 1647, Fingal was once more devastated when Eoghan Roe O'Neill ravaged the country between Castleknock and Drogheda, 'then containing the

(ed.), *Civil Survey: Dublin*, p. 174.   **97** Ruth Dudley Edwards and Bridget Hourican (eds), *An atlas of Irish history* (Oxford, 2005), p. 109.   **98** T. Barry, '"The people of the country ... dwell scattered": the pattern of rural settlement in Ireland in the later middle ages' in John Bradley (ed.), *Settlement and society in medieval Ireland: studies presented to F.X. Martin OSA* (Kilkenny, 1988), p. 354.   **99** *April the first, 1642: a continuation of the triumphant and couragious proceedings of the protestant army in Ireland* (London, 1642), p. 1 (NLI, Lough Fea pamphlet no. 109).   **100** Máighréad Ní Mhurchadha, *Fingal, 1603–1660: contending neighbours in north Dublin* (Dublin, 2005), p. 269.

goodliest haggards of corn that were ever seen in those parts'.[101] This period of intermittent warfare was followed by a devastating plague, which lasted well into 1652, and at its height was killing up to 1,300 people a week in the city of Dublin alone.[102] Although the population of Fingal undoubtedly shrank significantly during this period, Portmarnock village appears to have survived, as the Civil Survey describes the presence of ten thatched cottages at the site in 1654–6.[103] Shortly afterwards, in 1659, the townland is recorded as having a population of thirty-two, the majority of whom presumably lived in the village.[104] In 1664, the Hearth Money Roll for Dublin records that Portmarnock townland had twelve buildings containing one hearth, a single building containing two hearths and a large structure with six chimneys.[105] The latter building is undoubtedly Portmarnock House, while some of the remaining single-hearth structures probably formed part of the adjoining village. Interestingly, some of the family names seen in the Hearth Money Roll correspond, with some variations in spelling, to village inhabitants named in the Dissolution Survey of 1539.[106]

Despite the fact that the village appears to have been extant in 1664, the archaeological evidence suggests that it was deserted soon afterwards. Exactly why this happened remains uncertain, but it may be related to the discovery of a small cannonball in one of the seventeenth-century ditches. It is tempting to suggest that this is evidence for a conflict at the site, which is not impossible, as the Plunkett family of Portmarnock were indicted of rebellion in both the Confederate wars of the 1640s,[107] and the Wars of the two Kings in the 1690s.[108] William Plunkett of Portmarnock fought at the Battle of the Boyne,[109] and it is possible that his home and the adjoining village were attacked in retaliation. Indeed, the victorious Williamite forces waged a widespread campaign of violence throughout the Dublin countryside in 1690,[110] and Portmarnock may have been a target of one of these attacks. However, this remains speculation and the only concrete evidence for the village's demise remains Rocque's map of 1760, which illustrates its former location as an ornamental garden and agricultural fields to the south of Portmarnock House.

101 Sir Maurice Eustace Ormond, 4 November 1647, in J.T. Gilbert (ed.), *History of the Irish confederation and the war in Ireland, 1641–3*, 7 vols (Dublin, 1882–91), vi, pp 206–7. **102** J.H. Ohlmeyer, *Ireland from independence to occupation, 1641–1660* (Cambridge, 2002), p. 178. **103** Simington (ed.), *Civil Survey: Dublin*, p. 174. **104** Séamus Pender and W.J. Smyth (eds), *A census of Ireland, circa 1659, with essential materials form the poll money ordinances of 1660–1661* (Dublin, 2002), p. 388. **105** 'Hearth Money Roll for County Dublin, 1664', *County Kildare Archaeological Society Journal*, 11 (1930–3), 389. **106** Gilbert (ed.), *Chartularies of St Mary's Abbey*, ii, pp 68–70. **107** Simington (ed.), *Civil Survey: Dublin*, p. 174. **108** John Dalton, *Illustrations, historical and genealogical of King James's Irish army list 1689* (Dublin, 1855), p. 202. **109** Ibid. **110** S.J. Connolly, *Divided kingdom: Ireland, 1630–1800* (Oxford, 2008), p. 191.

ACKNOWLEDGMENTS

The author would like to acknowledge the assistance and contribution of the hardworking excavation staff: Ciara Griffen (supervisor), Ciara Burke, Kevin McInerney, Michael Moran, Rachel O'Byrne, Finbar O'Dwyer, Ian O'Leary and Hannah Sheeran; the specialists who contributed to the original report: Jonny Geber (animal bone), Lorna O'Donnell (charcoal and wood), Ryan Allen (plant remains) and Siobhan Scully (finds analysis); and especially to Linzi Simpson for her thoughts and time. Thanks are also due to Michael McCarthy, Brian Clarke and Mary Murphy of Ballymore Residential Ltd for their invaluable help during the course of the excavation.

'Hys worthy seruice done in that vpror':[1] Sir John Whyte and the defence of Dublin during Silken Thomas' rebellion, 1534

RANDOLPH JONES

INTRODUCTION

On St Barnaby's Day, 11 June 1534, Thomas Fitzgerald, Lord Offaly, also known as 'Silken Thomas', son and heir of Gerald, earl of Kildare and the vice-lord deputy of Ireland in his father's absence in England, dramatically renounced his allegiance to Henry VIII in the chapter house of St Mary's Abbey, Dublin.[2] Thus began a train of events that was to lead eventually to Fitzgerald's execution at Tyburn, together with all of his uncles, in February 1537. One of the major highlights of Fitzgerald's subsequent revolt was the three-month siege of Dublin, both city and castle. It was in defence of the latter that one man came to the fore. His name was John Whyte.[3] Until now, his story has not been told, nor the reason why he chose to resist such a powerful enemy.

OPENING MOVES

Immediately after Fitzgerald's dramatic resignation, several members of the king's council sought refuge in Dublin Castle, in particular John Alen, the archbishop of Dublin, and Patrick Finglas, the chief justice of the king's bench.[4] However, Fitzgerald seems to have spent the time subsequently waiting for the king's reaction. It was not until late July that matters came to a head. Indeed, Thomas and many of his key confederates were deemed not to have committed treason until 25 July 1534, the date mentioned in their act of attainder passed in the Irish parliament.[5] It is not clear exactly what happened on that day,[6] but it was sufficient to cause the archbishop to flee. He did so two evenings later, embarking from Dame's Gate on a small ship. Whether by accident or by design, his vessel became stranded on the Clontarf sands and he

---

1 L. Miller and E. Power (eds), *Holinshed's Irish Chronicle: the historie of Irelande from the first inhabitation thereof unto the yeare 1509 collected by Raphaell Holinshed, and continued to the yeare 1547 by Richarde Stanyhurst* (Mountrath, 1979) [hereafter 'Holinshed'], p. 266.
2 Holinshed, pp 262–6. I have used White's own spelling.   3 There are many variant spellings of Whyte's surname in the contemporary records. I have used the one Whyte used

was forced to spend the night ashore in a gentleman's house at Artane waiting for a change in tide and wind. News of the archbishop's predicament soon reached the ears of Fitzgerald and he rode there in the early hours of the following morning with a small party. After unceremoniously hauling the archbishop from his bed, Fitzgerald's followers hacked him to death.[7] Upon hearing this dreadful news, the Dubliners secured the city's gates and manned the wickets within them.[8]

Fitzgerald subsequently ravaged the area around Howth and Malahide, before moving north with a force of two or three thousand men to attack Sir Walter Bellew of Roche in Co. Louth and to parley with O'Neill.[9] At this point, the O'Tooles took advantage of the mayhem and raided Fingal, the city's main food-producing area, previously untouched by Irish raiding parties. However, Fitzgerald probably encouraged them to do so, as they were joined by one of his adherents, a local landowner, John Burnell of Balgriffin. On 4 August, while conveying their spoil back to the Wicklow Mountains, the O'Tooles were intercepted by the Dubliners. A skirmish took place between Little Cabra and Salcock Wood, before the former could cross the Liffey at Kilmainham. Outnumbered and due to the lack of a suitable captain, the Dubliners were defeated. Nineteen of their men were killed, including Patrick Fitzsimon, kinsman of the mayor Walter Fitzsimon.[10]

Until now, Fitzgerald had not attacked the city itself, but decided to use this unexpected victory to frighten the inhabitants into submission. Because the Dubliners had impeded the movement of his followers through the Pale, he threatened to sack the city if they did not allow his men to enter it and besiege the castle from within, as Fitzgerald was anxious to secure the munitions thought to be stored inside. Discouraged by their defeat and weakened by the sickness that had taken hold of the city during the summer, the mayor and his citizens reluctantly agreed. Nevertheless, they delayed sending a response to Fitzgerald until they had dispatched Francis Herbert, merchant and former bailiff of the city, with letters to the king. The citizens also conveyed the news secretly to John Whyte, who was then ensconced in the castle. Unperturbed, Whyte agreed to defend it while the citizens came to a temporary accommodation with Fitzgerald. However, to ensure a successful defence, the

---

himself when signing off letters. **4** Holinshed, pp 265–6. **5** Philomena Connolly (ed.), *Statute rolls of the Irish parliament: Richard III–Henry VIII* (Dublin, 2002), p. 153. **6** It may have been the skirmish at Salcock Wood. This is described below as occurring on 4 August. Stanihurst's narrative is short on dates, but he places this event before the killing of Archbishop Alen. There is evidence elsewhere to show that the archbishop was murdered on 27 July. **7** Holinshed, pp 268–9. **8** A.J. Fletcher, 'The earliest extant recension of the Dublin Chronicle: an edition and commentary' in J. Bradley, A.J. Fletcher and A. Simms (eds), *Dublin and the medieval world: studies in honour of Howard B. Clarke* (Dublin, 2009), p. 405. **9** J.S. Brewer and W. Bullen (eds), *Calendar of the Carew Manuscripts preserved in the archiepiscopal library at Lambeth, 1515–74* (London, 1867), i, doc. 84. **10** Holinshed, pp 268–7. The date is given in the *Annals of Dudley Loftus*, Marsh Library MS 211 (Z4.2.7), fo. 410v.

citizens sent him supplies under cover of night. One, a former mayor, John Fitzsimon, personally provided twenty tons of wine, twenty-four tons of beer, two thousand dried ling and sixteen hogsheads of powdered beef. He also supplied an iron chain, newly forged in his own house for the castle's drawbridge, as well as twenty 'chambers'.[11] The abbot of St Mary's Abbey also claimed later that he and his house had provided the city 'with victuals and habiliments for their defence' during Fitzgerald's siege.[12]

'SERJEANT-AT-ARMS TO THE KING'S GOOD GRACE'[13]

Contrary to what is stated in Stanihurst's account in Holinshed's famous chronicles, John Whyte was not the constable of Dublin Castle at the time of the siege, but the king's serjeant-at-arms. He was granted this office for life on 6 July 1528, with a fee of ten pounds per annum, to be drawn from the issues of Crumlin manor.[14] His duty was to 'wait sometimes upon our deputy or chief governor of our said realm of Ireland and sometimes upon our chancellor', probably in command of a small bodyguard.[15] This dual responsibility could sometimes lead to problems, particularly if relations between the two officials were poor, as Whyte's successor found to his cost at Christmas 1538. On this occasion, the chancellor John Alen (not the aforementioned archbishop) insisted on the serjeant-at-arms accompanying him to Kilkenny when the latter was already attending Lord Grey, the lord deputy, who was entertaining a number of Irish chieftains at Maynooth Castle. Although it was conceded by all that the lord deputy's needs took precedence, Grey good-naturedly allowed the serjeant-at-arms to accompany the chancellor, despite the potential threat to his own security.[16] Indeed, this possible conflict of interests had been considered earlier in the same year, with a request made for Robert Casy, former servant of the duke of Norfolk, to be appointed 'serjeant-at-arms attendant', with a fee of five marks per annum.[17]

Whyte's qualification for the office of serjeant-at-arms is not known, but he clearly had some military experience, as demonstrated by his subsequent defence of the castle. It is perhaps noteworthy that Lewis Busshe, one of his predecessors, had been a yeoman of the guard, a professional body of soldiers first raised by Henry VII in England. Busshe was probably one of the two hundred such men brought to Ireland in 1520 by the lord lieutenant, the earl of Surrey.[18] Indeed, the first mention of Whyte occurs during Surrey's

11 Holinshed, p. 268.   12 *State papers published under the authority of His Majesty's commission: King Henry the Eighth* (London, 1834), iii, p. 143.   13 National Archives of Ireland, RC 10/4.   14 'Calendar to fiants of King Henry VIII' in *The seventh report of the deputy keeper of the public records in Ireland* (Dublin, 1875), appendix x, no. 24.   15 Rowley Lascelles, *Liber Munerum Publicorum Hibernicae* (London, 1852), i, pt ii, p. 86.   16 *State papers*, iii, pp 158–9.   17 *State papers*, iii, p. 68.   18 'Fiants Henry VIII', no. 7.

lieutenancy and suggests that he may have come to Ireland with that noble-man. It is clear from evidence considered later, that his family had some previous connection with the country.

Whyte's appointment as serjeant-at-arms also came at a moment of crisis. Less than a month before (12 May 1528), Lord Delvin, vice-deputy for the absent earl of Kildare, had been taken prisoner by O'Connor Faly during a parley in which many of Delvin's men were killed or taken prisoner.[19] One of the former was probably Edward Lense or Lencey, Whyte's immediate predecessor as serjeant-at-arms, who was said to have been dead by the time of Whyte's appointment. Lense had only held the office for less than a year.[20]

After Delvin's capture, the Irish council had decided by 15 May to appoint Thomas Fitzgerald, brother of the earl of Kildare and uncle of Silken Thomas, as 'captain of Ireland'.[21] Therefore, it may have been a connection with this branch of the Fitzgerald family that resulted in Whyte being appointed serjeant-at-arms. Also, the fact that Whyte had been granted the office for life, rather than for a term of years or for the duration of the king's pleasure, indicates perhaps that Whyte had performed some useful service already, his abilities were such as to warrant such a permanent appointment immediately, or it was the price to keep him quiet because he was not satisfied on some other matter.

Whyte's duties as the king's serjeant-at-arms would have brought him into contact with everyone of importance in the Pale and beyond. As such, he would have served and been in close proximity to successive lord deputies, namely Piers Butler, earl of Ossory, Sir William Skeffington and Gerald Fitzgerald, earl of Kildare, as well as the chancellors, John Alen, archbishop of Dublin and George Cromer, archbishop of Armagh.[22] Whyte would have been present at many of the major events that occurred prior to the revolt, including, no doubt, the council meeting in which Silken Thomas renounced his allegiance to the king on 11 June 1534. Through his unique position of observation, Whyte would have been acutely aware of the intense rivalries that drove the relationships between all of these men, including their families, friends, servants and enemies. In the forthcoming events, he would play his cards accordingly, based on the first-hand knowledge and experience he had gained over the preceding few years.

DUBLIN CASTLE

Whyte's first mention in connection with Dublin Castle is in an account com-piled in 1531 by John Alen, archbishop of Dublin, who was then chancellor.

19 *State papers*, ii, p. 127.   20 'Fiants Henry VIII', nos 16, 24.   21 *State papers*, ii, p. 128.
22 S.G. Ellis, *Ireland in the age of the Tudors, 1447–1603: English expansion and the end of*

Whyte was paid £20 11s. 1½d. for repairs to the castle itself, as well as the court of chancery within.[23] Despite these repairs, the castle was probably in a dilapidated state in 1534 and for several years afterwards. Indeed, up until the very moment of the siege itself, it was probably impossible to raise the drawbridge until John Fitzsimon had it provided with a newly forged chain! The castle may have suffered further structural damage in June 1534, when an earthquake shook Dublin between four and five o'clock in the morning.[24] A similar earthquake is known to have struck Chester at five o'clock in the morning on 15 September, in the very same year. An eyewitness, writing to London from Chester Castle, said that the rock on which it stood 'rocked like a cradle'.[25] In 1540, we are also told that all the stones, tiles and timbers from the demolished St Mary de Hogges' Abbey, were stored in Dublin Castle for the purpose of its repair.[26]

It is not clear whether Whyte was in charge of the security of the castle at the time he made the repairs in 1531, but it would seem feasible that he was. If not the actual constable, Whyte may have been the incumbent's deputy or lieutenant. If so, Whyte was responsible for a major dereliction of duty one night in 1533, when the castle was entered by Edmund O'Byrne and his men, who took away prisoners, cattle and goods valued at £2,000.[27] On the other hand, Whyte may only have been given full responsibility as a direct result of this event. In the under-treasurer's accounts ending Michaelmas 1537, Whyte was paid £53 6s. 8d., the equivalent of four years' salary as constable of Dublin Castle, even though he was not formally appointed to that office until 28 August 1535, in addition to his normal pay as serjeant-at-arms.[28] Who was actually constable at this time is not clear, if there was one at all. According to an act of the Irish parliament passed in 1494–5, the constable of Dublin and a number of other royal castles in Ireland was supposed to be 'one born in the realm of England'.[29] This qualification was reiterated in a list of royal castles in Ireland compiled in 1537.

This same list also recommended that Dublin Castle should have an establishment of one constable, one lieutenant, one chief porter, two second porters and eighteen wardens, six of whom were to guard the castle gate during the day, and two by night. The constable could not leave his charge, unless it was with the special licence of the lord deputy. Even then, his absence could not exceed twelve days.[30] Whether this establishment was in place in 1534 is

Gaelic rule (London, 1998), pp 129–36, 367, 370.   **23** J. Gairdner (ed.), *Letters and papers, foreign and domestic, Henry VIII* (London, 1880–) , v, p. 398.   **24** Fletcher, 'Dublin Chronicle', p. 405.   **25** *Letters and papers*, vii, p. 452   **26** N.B. White (ed.), *Extents of Irish monastic possessions, 1540–41* (Dublin, 1943), p. 69.   **27** *Letters and papers*, vi, p. 1587.   **28** *Letters and papers*, xii, p. 1319 ii (1); TNA SP65/1/2; J. Morrin (ed.), *Calendar of patent and close rolls of chancery in Ireland, Henry VIII to 18 Elizabeth* (Dublin, 1861), i, p. 25, no. 14; 'Fiants Henry VIII', no. 47.   **29** *The Statutes at large, passed in the parliaments held in Ireland* (Dublin, 1786), i. p. 51.   **30** Dublin City Archive, Gilbert MS 82, *State papers*

doubtful. Ellis states that there were fifty hand-gunners in the castle during the siege.[31] His source for this statement was the under-treasurer's accounts ending Michaelmas 1537.[32] Although two groups of fifty gunners are mentioned in this account (although they are probably one and the same group), there is nothing to indicate, in the calendared version at least, that they were actually in the castle at the time of the 1534 siege. It is probable that they were part of the army brought to Ireland by Sir William Skeffington in the autumn and that they manned his accompanying artillery train.[33]

We do know the names of two of the garrison in 1534, however. One was John Browne, whom Whyte later recommended to the king's secretary, Thomas Cromwell, for services rendered when Dublin Castle was besieged. Whyte stated in his letter that he 'trusted Browne as his own son in watch and ward'.[34] Anthony Mores and seventeen of the prior of Kilmainham's servants also formed part of the garrison during the twelve-week siege and were reported to have performed 'good service'.[35] Their English-born master had previously fled Ireland as soon as the rebellion started and Fitzgerald seems to have used Kilmainham as his base during the siege.[36]

ORDNANCE

Dublin Castle was also the usual repository for the king's ordnance and munitions in Ireland. As well as artillery, this included more mundane items such as demi-lances, black-bills, bows, bowstring, arrows, gunpowder and shot.[37] In 1533, however, the earl of Kildare was said to have removed all of these munitions and placed them in his own castles and fortifications around the country.[38]

Nevertheless, it is clear from Stanihurst's account that the castle contained at least one 'demi-cannon' during Fitzgerald's siege. Indeed, 'oon gret gonne of brasse' was said to have been lying in the castle, when the earl of Kildare was appointed deputy lieutenant of Ireland in 1532.[39] A demi- or half-cannon was a mighty piece of artillery. Although standardization was still a long way off, it probably weighed seven thousand pounds and required seven teams of horses or oxen to move. It also shot a massive twenty-five-pound ball and was

relating to the city of Dublin, 1524–99, transcribed by Robert Lennon and Henry Hamilton, fo. 3. *Letters and papers*, xii, pt 2, doc. 1097. The details of the Dublin Castle garrison are missing from the calendared version.   31 S.G. Ellis, 'The Tudors and the origins of the modern Irish states: a standing army' in T. Bartlett and K. Jeffery (eds), *A military history of Ireland* (Cambridge, 1996), p. 129.   32 TNA SP61/1/1.   33 *Letters and papers*, xi, p. 934 ii.   34 *Letters and papers*, xi, p. 847; xii, pt 1, p. 1098.   35 *Letters and papers*, viii, p. 695. 36 *State papers*, ii, pp 201–2.   37 S.G. Ellis, 'An indenture concerning the king's munitions in Ireland, 1532', *Irish Sword*, 14 (1980–1), 101–2.   38 *Letters and papers*, vi, p. 1072. *Statute rolls*, p. 150.   39 B. Trainor, 'Extracts from Irish ordnance accounts, 1537–1539', *Irish Sword*, 1 (1949–53), 324.

therefore more suitable for demolishing fortifications rather than defending them.[40] If Stanihurst's demi-cannon was the same 'gret gonne of brasse' mentioned earlier, its relative immovability and unsuitability for use in the field may have been sufficient reason for the earl of Kildare to leave it behind. Indeed, this seems to be supported by a list compiled in 1536, of all the king's ordnance said to be still held in the earl of Kildare's castles, in which only 'fawcons, hagbusshes and rede peaces' are mentioned.[41] Stanihurst also tells us that during the siege, the Dublin Castle demi-cannon was placed immediately behind the main gate. It was probably the only place in which it could be positioned usefully, to repulse any potential breakthrough at this most vulnerable point in the castle's defensive perimeter.[42]

This was probably not the only piece of ordnance in the castle in 1534. The provision of twenty 'chambers' by John Fitzsimon suggests that there were also a number of light, breech-loading guns known as 'serpentynes' held inside.[43] As the name suggests, these firearms had elongated barrels. They were also known as 'reed' pieces, probably for the same reason. An example of the interchangeable nature of the nomenclature is given in 1532, when it was recorded that there were '18 rede peces called serpentines of yron with 25 chambres and 400 pellets of leed for the same' stored in Drogheda. In the same year, it was also reported that there were seven carriages for rede pieces stored in Dublin Castle.[44]

Although none of the sources mention it, it is possible that some of this lighter ordnance was provided by the city – either by individuals or by the administration itself. In 1537–9, eight and fourteen handguns were purchased from James Hancock and Simon Lutterell respectively, both prominent citizens of Dublin.[45] It is perhaps noteworthy that the Trinity guild of merchants in Dublin, which included all of the city's prominent citizens, had a monopoly on the supply of iron in the city, and that this probably extended to items manufactured from this substance too.[46] Also, by 1541, the Dublin administration had its own arsenal of firearms, the more portable of which were kept in the tholsel. Nevertheless, if one had existed before this date, even the city's ordnance might not have been available to the castle garrison in 1534. An addendum made later to a list of the city's ordnance compiled in 1541 records that one 'great pott gunne of irne' was 'borrowed' by the earl of Kildare at some unspecified time previously. The earl in question could only have been the one who died in 1534, Silken Thomas' father. Therefore, the gun was probably removed from the city in 1533, at the same time as the king's

40 T. Arnold, *The Renaissance at war* (London, 2002), pp 38, 44.   **41** *Letters and papers*, x, p. 937 ii.   **42** Holinshed, p. 272.   **43** Holinshed, p. 270.   **44** S.G. Ellis, 'Indenture', p. 102. **45** Trainor, 'Ordnance accounts', p. 333; J.T. Gilbert (ed.), *Calendar of the ancient records of Dublin* [henceforth *CARD*] (Dublin, 1889), i, pp 395, 405.   **46** H.F. Berry, 'The records of the Dublin gild of merchants, known as the Gild of the Holy Trinity, 1438–1671', *Journal of the Royal Society of Antiquaries of Ireland*, 10 (1900), 53.

ordnance was taken from Dublin Castle. We are told that the city's gun was taken to the unidentified 'Statryk' castle, in the north of Ireland, in the boat belonging to Richard Baker of Howth. It was subsequently returned to the city, because it was found later in Baker's house, which lay upon the quayside. It is also recorded that the gun was broken up and sold as scrap in 1549–50.[47]

CASTLE BESIEGED

Once the castle was sufficiently supplied with men, munitions and victuals, the citizens agreed to a truce with Fitzgerald lasting until Michaelmas.[48] A small force under the command of John Field of Lusk was permitted to enter the city, consisting of one hundred of Fitzgerald's men. They promptly set up a battery, protected by earthen ramparts and consisting of two or three 'falcons', near to Preston's Inns, immediately opposite the castle's main gate. Falcons were lighter pieces (1,500lbs) than demi-cannon. Firing only three-pound balls, they were totally unsuitable for demolishing fortifications. Indeed, the only damage caused was a single hole punched through the castle's main gate, after which the spent pellet fell into the mouth of the defenders' demi-cannon positioned behind. Nevertheless, the rebels in the battery were undoubtedly annoyed by missiles shot from the castle walls. To put an end to this, 'they threatned to take the youth of the Citie, and place them on the toppe of theyr trenches for maister constable to shoote at, as at a marke he would be loath to hitte'.[49]

It was perhaps at this stage of the siege that Patrick Finglas, the chief justice, who had initially fled to the castle in June with the ill-fated archbishop of Dublin, decided to leave. Without Whyte's knowledge, Finglas secretly compounded with Fitzgerald and stole away one night, taking his men and their 'abilementis of warr' with him.[50]

With the siege at an impasse and neither side able to gain the advantage, Fitzgerald summoned the Pale gentry to go a-hosting with him into Co. Kilkenny. Consequently taking a much larger force than the two to three thousand he had originally led north against Bellew, Fitzgerald attacked and burned the lands of the loyalist Butlers. However, while Fitzgerald was scoring notable successes against his family's arch-rivals in the south, Francis Herbert returned from England by ship, bringing with him letters from the king.[51] These enjoined the mayor and citizens, upon their allegiance, to hold the city against Fitzgerald and that an army was being sent from England to relieve them under the command of the recently appointed lord deputy, Sir William

47 National Library of Ireland, MS 855, *Account book of the city treasurer, 1534–1613*, transcribed by Sir J.T. Gilbert.   48 British Library, Sloane MS 1449, fo. 295.   49 Holinshed, p. 270.   50 *State papers*, ii, p. 270.

Skeffington. Similar letters were also sent to Serjeant Whyte in respect of the castle. After some debate in the city council, the citizens were persuaded by their eloquent recorder, Thomas Fitzsimon, to resist Fitzgerald. Taking heart, they armed themselves, locked the city gates and turned on Fitzgerald's men besieging the castle. Most of the latter were seized in their quarters and imprisoned, but some managed to escape by swimming the Liffey.[52]

HIATUS

For a while, the pressure on Dublin seems to have relaxed. So much so that Serjeant Whyte and Janet his wife found time on 20 August 1534 to sign and seal an indenture with the prior of All Hallows, Walter Hancock, whose convent stood outside the city walls. This indenture was for the farm of the tithes and altarages of 'Clontork' parish. The prior and convent granted these to the Whyte and his wife for the term of their lives, in return for 26s. 8d. per annum payable at Michaelmas. Whyte was also obliged to find a curate for the parish during the lifetime of the prior.[53]

Upon hearing the disturbing news from Dublin, Fitzgerald left the Butlers to lick their wounds in Cos Kilkenny and Waterford and moved on to Co. Meath. By 22 August, he was at Ballydullane.[54] Before taking any further military action against Dublin, he despatched emissaries to the city once more. One of them, Dr John Travers, the dean of St Patrick's, was later deemed to have committed treason on 10 August, after joining Fitzgerald at Kilmainham.[55] In their subsequent negotiations, Fitzgerald's emissaries attempted to bring the citizens back to their former agreement, allowing the rebels free access to the city and to gain the release of John Field and his men from imprisonment. However, the citizens, emboldened by the promise of the impending arrival of a relief army from England, refused these demands and the emissaries left Dublin empty-handed, complaining of the cold hospitality they had received.[56]

Fitzgerald therefore turned up the heat. Firstly, the bark that had brought Herbert back to Ireland was destroyed, thereby hampering the city's communications with England. This vessel had been carelessly moored beside St Mary's Abbey, on the north bank of the Liffey and away from the protection of the city walls. Secondly, in order to make life more difficult for the besieged, their water supply from the surrounding countryside was cut off, which was done by

51 BL, Sloane MS 1449, fo. 295.   52 Holinshed, pp 270–2.   53 M.C. Griffith, *Calendar of Inquisitions formerly in the office of the chief remembrance of the Exchequer prepared from the MSS of the Irish Record Commission* (Dublin, 1991), pp 73–4. National Archives of Ireland, RC 10/4.   54 S.G. Elllis, 'Privy seals of the chief governors in Ireland, 1392–1560', *Bulletin of the Institute of Historical Research*, 51 (1987), 194.   55 R. Dudley Edwards, 'Venerable John Travers and the rebellion of Silken Thomas', *Studies*, 23 (1934), 693–4 n. 3. 56 Holinshed, p. 272.

breaking the 'ledys of the conductes of the water'.[57] Thirdly, Fitzgerald tried to gain entry into the castle by threatening Whyte himself. His instrument this time was John Barnewall, Lord Trimleston, who had already joined Fitzgerald with a retinue of fifty men. Barnewall appealed to Whyte to think of the city's welfare, as well as his own. He was later reported to have said:

> Sergeaunt Whitt, iff you will, you maye save this syttye; as this, to delyver the Kynges castyll to the Lorde Thomas, and you schall have lybertye to passe with bagge and baggage; and in casse you will nott, you schall dystroye this cytte, and caste away your selphe.[58]

For reasons that will become apparent later on, Whyte chose to ignore this ignominious offer, which was conveyed to him by the very man whom the king had appointed chancellor of Ireland on 16 August, although Trimleston was probably not aware of the fact at the time.[59]

Fitzgerald and Barnewall were probably encouraged to make this approach because of the familial ties of Whyte's wife to the rebels. Stanihurst tells us that in 1535, Dame Janet Eustace had been held prisoner in Dublin Castle for over a year. She died while in custody and her body was subsequently moved to Greyfriars (the Franciscan friary), where it lay unburied for five days, by command of the lord deputy, Sir William Skeffington. Lady 'Gennet' Golding, the wife of the constable, John Whyte, pleaded with the lord deputy for the body to be given a Christian burial. This was eventually granted.[60] Lady Janet's request may have been due to her compassionate nature, but it was probably driven by other concerns. Dame Janet Eustace was the wife of Sir Walter Delahyde, the steward and receiver-general of the earl of Kildare, who was imprisoned in the castle with her. She was also aunt to the earl himself.[61] Her son, James Delahyde, was said to have been Silken Thomas' principal counsellor during the rebellion, for which reason he was later attainted for treason. Another son, John Delahyde, was also attainted because of the prominent part he had played in the rebellion.[62] John was married to Elizabeth, one of the four daughters of Richard Goldyng of Piercetown Laundy in Co. Meath. On 26 November 1538, Elizabeth was granted a custodiam for three years of her husband's lands in Irishtown and Primatestown, Co. Meath, which had been escheated to the crown, for 26s. 8d. per annum, payable at the exchequer.[63] However, this custodiam seems to have been granted soon afterwards to James Barnewall of Riverston.[64] Janet Golding's parentage is not

57 Gilbert, *CARD*, i, p. 500.   58 *State papers*, ii, p. 245.   59 *Patent and close rolls*, p. 13, no. 9.   60 Holinshed, p. 282.   61 *State papers*, ii, p. 228.   62 S.G. Ellis, 'Bastard feudalism and the Kildare Rebellion, 1534–35' in W. Nolan and T. McGrath (eds), *Kildare: history and society* (Dublin, 2006), p. 223.   63 NAI 2/446/2, Ferguson MSS, vol. 4, fo. 221. Rot. mem. 30 Hen. VIII, m. 4.   64 NAI, Fergusson MSS, 'Repertory of the memoranda rolls',

known, but her request to seek Christian burial for Dame Janet Eustace's body is understandable if she was the sister of Elizabeth Goldyng and therefore sister-in-law of John Delahyde, a prominent rebel.

There is also some secondary evidence of a link between Janet Golding and the Piercetown Laundy branch of the family. One Walter Goldyng of Piercetown Laundy seems to have died shortly after he was appointed second baron to the Irish exchequer on 27 March 1535, in place of Patrick White, whom seems to have resumed his old office almost immediately and remained in it for several years afterwards.[65] Walter left a son and heir, Edmund, a minor, who had been a ward in the king's hands for at least one and a half years before Michaelmas 1537.[66] Edmund seems to have died shortly afterwards, however, for he was succeeded by his brother Walter, also a minor. At some unspecified date, probably in 1538–9 when it was enrolled in the patent rolls for that year, Francis Herbert was granted a custodiam of Walter's lands.[67] Herbert apparently had a direct interest in Walter's welfare, either before or soon afterwards, because he took one Janet Golding to be his second wife. Janet was still alive when Herbert died in 1570 and was given a life interest in some of his property. Herbert's inquisition post mortem also recites that one Walter Golding of Piercetown Laundy was one of a number of grantees named in a deed that Francis drew up in 1561. This Walter must have been Francis' former ward.[68] It is tempting to think that these two Janet Goldings are one and the same person and that she married Francis Herbert after Whyte's death. However, no evidence of this has been found to date, other than the similarity of names.

Nevertheless, there is one other possible Golding link to the rebel camp. In 1538, a correspondent from Ireland complained that one 'Golding of the Grange' had previously been 'towardes the Erll of Kildare' in his affiliations.[69] In view of the appellation, this person was probably Walter Goldyng of the Grange of Portmarnock, who only acquired this property from St Mary's Abbey, Dublin, prior to its dissolution in 1539, primarily through his connection with the then lord deputy, Lord Grey.[70] This third Walter Golding, who was occasionally described in the patent rolls as 'junior', presumably to differentiate him from his elder namesake, also followed a career in the Irish exchequer, although he occupied relatively low-ranking positions such as second engrosser, summonister and transcriptor up until the early years of Elizabeth's reign.[71] Is it possible that Whyte's wife was related to this branch of the family instead? The exact relationship between this third Walter Golding and the other two is not clear at the moment. One writer has already

Henry VII.   **65** *Patent and close rolls*, p. 15, no. 42.   **66** *Letters and papers*, xii pt 2, p. 1310 (37).   **67** *Patent and close rolls*, p. 36, no. 6.   **68** Griffith, *Inquisitions*, p. 199.   **69** *State papers*, iii, p. 13.   **70** J.T. Gilbert (ed.), *Chartularies of St Mary's Abbey, Dublin* (London, 1884), ii, p. xxviii.   **71** *Patent and close rolls*, p. 4, no. 11; p. 16, no. 46; p. 30, no. 64; p. 31, no. 70; p. 41, no. 5, p. 67, no. 16.

commented on the confused state of the genealogy of this family.[72] Until it is sorted out, the exact relationship of Whyte's wife with the Geraldines will remain unclear. It seems likely that there was such a link, however, and that this was a possible source of weakness for principals of the rebellion to exploit. The pressure on Whyte to surrender the castle must have been considerable.

SHIP STREET

Nevertheless, Whyte stood firm. After receiving his refusal, Fitzgerald launched an attack on the castle down Ship Street, on the southern side of the city. This thoroughfare would have brought his forces opposite Birmingham Tower, where the castle joined the city wall. From here, the wall led westward to the Pole Gate astride St Werburgh's Street via Stanihurst's Tower. This was a very narrow frontage on which to launch an attack, but Fitzgerald was probably using the houses on either side of the street as cover for his men, in exactly the same way that he did for his subsequent attack on the Newgate. We are not told of the method of assault, but due to his lack of heavy artillery, as well as powder and shot, he may have attempted an escalade for a quick result. However, there was no gate at this point in the castle perimeter to storm and break through. There was also a watery ditch to cross before his men could even place their ladders against the wall. The only other alternative perhaps was undermining, although this would have been very time consuming, a luxury Thomas no longer possessed, if indeed it was possible through the waterlogged soil.

We are told by our only source for this event, Stanihurst, that Fitzgerald's attack was beaten off by ordnance from the castle. However, on this occasion, we are also told that Whyte used a novel weapon called 'wildfire' to completely demoralize the attackers.[73] Apparently devised by Whyte himself, this substance was a combustible material, probably shot at the enemy by blasting it with compressed air through a hollowed trunk – a kind of primitive flame-thrower perhaps. In a set of ordnance accounts, compiled in Ireland between 1537 and 1539, six 'trompis of wyldffyer' are mentioned as having being purchased from some Bretons at 4s. 2d. Irish a piece. Some were also made locally by a turner using two quarters of ash wood purchased in Drogheda. These 'trompis' seem to have been pre-charged with the stuff, for 6s. was also paid 'for lodyng of iiij trompis of wyldffyer' at 18d. sterling each.[74] The Oxford English Dictionary describes a 'tromp' as being 'an apparatus for producing a blast, in which water falling in a pipe carries air into a receiver, where it is compressed, and then led

72 H.M. Roe, 'Cadaver effigial monuments in Ireland', *Journal of the Royal Society of Antiquaries of Ireland*, 99 (1969), 15. 73 Holinshed, p. 273. 74 B. Trainor, 'Extracts from Irish Ordnance Accounts, 1537–1539', *Irish Sword*, 1 (1949–53), 325.

to the blast-pipe; a water blowing-engine'. However, wildfire was versatile enough to be used in other ways. At the siege of Boulogne in 1544, 'sertaine balles of Wildfier', perhaps primitive hand-grenades, were used by the English to discomfit the French defenders.[75] In the following year, twenty 'tronckes' charged with 'wylde fyer', six 'morest spykes' and six 'horstakes' laden with the same, were part of the munitions carried on board the ships used to convey the Irish expeditionary force sent from Dublin to fight in Scotland.[76] Wildfire was also found on arrows stored in the Berwick and Newhaven arsenals during an inventory taken after the death of Henry VIII in 1547.

Whyte's use of this 'secret weapon' was a great success and Fitzgerald's men fled after the thatched houses in Ship Street were set alight. Three of the cottages destroyed on this occasion, together with their appurtenances, belonged to Christopher Talbot, gentleman. Eight years after the siege, he intended rebuilding them. To compensate Talbot for his financial loss, the city assembly granted Talbot remission from the chief rent for fifty-one years, saving 12*d*. Irish per annum. The city's assembly book recorded that the cottages were 'burned and destroyed at the last rebellion, trusting that the city should have been better defended'.[77]

The fighting in this area is commemorated today by the concrete façades decorating the chief state solicitor's office building in Little Ship Street. These depict various figures engaged in the attack, copied directly from those that appear in a sixteenth-century wood-print illustrating Holinshed's chronicle and which purports to represent this particular event. The great profusion of fire and smoke in the latter is noteworthy.

NEWGATE

After failing to storm the castle, Fitzgerald moved on to St Thomas' Court, on the western side of the city, and prepared to attack the Newgate instead. By now he had been joined by all his uncles and his army numbered an improbable 15,000 men.[78] Many were gentry from the Pale, together with their retainers, who had obeyed Fitzgerald's summonses to attend, but they did so reluctantly, fearful of reprisals if they did not. One unfortunate, perhaps, was James Mareward, baron of Skreen, who was killed on 14 September by one of Fitzgerald's uncles, Richard of Powerscourt, apparently at the instigation of Mareward's own wife, Maud or Matilda Darcy, who subsequently married his murderer.[79] The Mareward family had strong traditional links with the city, including holding the franchise.

75 J. Davies and M. Bryn Davies (eds), *Elis Gruffydd and the 1544 'Enterprises' of Paris and Boulogne* (Farnham, 2003), p. 65. 76 *State papers*, iii, p. 542. 77 Gilbert, *CARD*, i, pp 411–12. 78 British Library, MS Sloane 1449, fo. 295 (NLI Microfilm P2). 79 *Patent and close rolls*, p. 41, no. 49; Griffith, *Inquisitions*, pp 58–9.

New Street was burnt first of all and the partitions between the houses on
either side of St Thomas' Street were torn down to form covered ways. These
would protect Fitzgerald's men as they approached the gateway. A falcon was
also set up in the street immediately opposite the gate. However, this light
piece of artillery was just as ineffective as before, with only one shot pene-
trating the gate itself and killing an apprentice beyond as he was collecting
water from the high-pipe in the Cornmarket.[80]

There was also some sniping between the two forces, during which the
attackers seem to have come off worse. Richard Stanton, the keeper of the
city's gaol, which was located in the Newgate itself, proved to be a fine shot
with his hackbut. After shooting one of Fitzgerald's men, hitting him full in
the forehead, Stanton ventured out the wicket-gate to strip his victim bare
before endeavouring to return to the safety of the city with his clothes and
firearm. However, this impudent action seems to have infuriated Fitzgerald's
men, who took the opportunity to rush the gateway, piling up faggots against it
and setting them alight. The citizens, fearful that if the wooden gate was
consumed the city would be open to successful attack and subsequent pillage,
sallied out. However, they were also encouraged by the knowledge that many of
Fitzgerald's men had no stomach for the fight. Several had already commu-
nicated with the citizens inside by shooting arrows over the walls with
messages attached, letting them know of Fitzgerald's plans. Some of their
arrows were also without heads, rendering them ineffective. Their use may
only indicate that they had been rapidly withdrawn from store, however, where
it was not unusual to find both headed and unheaded arrows listed in the
inventories, rather than any lack of hostile intent of those using them.[81]

To heighten the effect of their impending charge and to compensate for
their smaller numbers, the citizens 'blazed abrode vppon the walles triumphante
newes, the king hys army was arriued, as it hadde bin so in dede'. Four hundred
rushed out through the burning aperture, taking Fitzgerald's men by surprise.
Disconcerted by the Dubliners' ruse, as well as by the suddenness of their
attack, the Geraldines broke and fled, with one hundred of their galloglass being
killed in the rout. Their falcon outside the gate was also taken. Fitzgerald,
separated from his men, hid overnight in the Greyfriars convent in St Francis'
Street and remained there until morning when he was able to rejoin them.[82]

Antony Mores, the prior of Kilmainham's servant, also took part in this
sortie. He was one of the first to venture out and killed a number of
Fitzgerald's best footmen with his own hand.[83] 'Dickie' Stanton was able to
regain the safety of the city, apparently unharmed after his daring and perhaps
foolish exploit. He was subsequently made one of the mayor's two serjeants at
the city assembly meeting on 2 October.[84] Francis Herbert, whose return with

80 Holinshed, p. 273. 81 Gilbert MSS, account book. 82 Holinshed, pp 273–4.
83 *Letters and papers*, viii, p. 695. 84 Gilbert, *CARD*, i, p. 398.

the king's letters had galvanized the citizens into action, also proved to be a competent shot with his gun and distinguished himself by killing twenty-four or more of Fitzgerald's men, twenty apparently in a single day, as well as one of their 'great captains'. Indeed, it was said later that Fitzgerald would rather have had Herbert delivered up to him than any amount of goods. Herbert was subsequently knighted for his efforts.[85] Christopher Plunkett, whose exact exploits during the siege are not known, was also rewarded for his good and true service to the king and city during the rebellion by being made sword-bearer for life to the mayor of Dublin from Michaelmas 1535.[86]

RELIEF

Matters were again at an impasse when news reached Fitzgerald in Maynooth Castle that a fleet had indeed arrived on 15 October, off Lambay Island, after being driven across the Irish Sea by storm.[87] In anticipation of its arrival, Fitzgerald had previously been to Drogheda to collect a 'great gun' that was lying there.[88] This was probably the 'curteill of brass beyng on the keye at Drogheda' which Kildare had in his possession on 20 October 1532.[89] This piece, a 'curtailed' (that is, a short-barrelled) cannon, was moved to Howth, probably by sea, and made ready to 'bulche' any ships that came into range.[90] Nevertheless, Fitzgerald tried one last time to negotiate a settlement with the citizens in order to obtain the munitions he desperately needed to combat the king's army in the field, once it had landed. He therefore sent further emissaries to Dublin, who were taken to William Kelly's house after being let in through the battered Newgate.[91] According to a deed drawn up on 25 March 1534 for an adjoining property, Kelly's house stood in 'Christ Church ground' to the north of St Werburgh's Street.[92] Inside, they were received by the mayor and his brethren. Fitzgerald's emissaries included Dr Travers once more, as well as William Bath of Dollardstown.[93] At his subsequent trial before Patrick Finglas, the chief justice (who had somehow managed to explain away his own defection to Fitzgerald), Bath was found guilty of treason from 24 September 1534. We are not told of the significance of that date, but it was probably when this second phase of the siege began.[94]

The mayor of Dublin was now Robert Shillyngford. If the normal traditions were observed, Shillyngford would have been elected by his fellow jureés on Holy Rood Day, 14 September, before being installed into his new office at

---

85 *State papers*, ii, pp 204–5.   86 Gilbert, *CARD*, i, pp 497–8.   87 *State papers*, ii, p. 204. 88 *Carew MSS*, i, doc. 84.   89 Ellis, 'Indenture', p. 102.   90 Holinshed, p. 276.   91 Ibid., pp 274–5.   92 H.F. Twiss, 'Some ancient deeds of the parish of St Werburgh, Dublin, 1243–1676', *Proceedings of the Royal Irish Academy*, 35C (1918–20), 292.   93 Holinshed, p. 275.   94 Griffiths, *Inquisitions*, pp 66–7.

Michaelmas, 29 September.[95] His first assembly meeting took place on 2 October.[96] By this stage, his predecessor Walter Fitzsimon had fallen out of the limelight and Shillyngford was subsequently credited with the successful defence of the city.[97] Indeed, Fitzsimon may have been ineffective as a leader for some time. The death of his kinsman at the Salcock Wood skirmish on 4 August, coupled with the fact that three of his sons were being held hostage by Fitzgerald's men, seems to have incapacitated him from playing an active role in the city's defence. He may even have been replaced in the mayoral office before his allotted time expired.[98]

In the subsequent negotiations, the Geraldines offered a truce. The terms proposed were that Fitzgerald's men captured inside the city several weeks previously should be freed; the citizens should provide Fitzgerald with one thousand pounds in ready money in a single payment, as well as five hundred pounds worth of goods. They also demanded munitions and artillery to supply his army. Finally, Fitzgerald sought a promise from the citizens that they would write to the king favourably on his behalf, seeking his royal pardon and asking that he should also be given the deputyship of Ireland in lieu of his father, who had since died in the Tower of London on 2 September.

After debating these terms, Fitzgerald's emissaries were informed by the city's recorder that the citizens agreed to the release of Field and his men in return for the sixteen or more of their sons then being held captive. These boys had been sent out into the surrounding countryside prior to the siege in order to escape the contagion then raging inside the city, but they were subsequently rounded up by Fitzgerald for use as bargaining chips. The rest of the terms put forward by the emissaries were rejected, although the citizens apparently promised to plead Fitzgerald's case for a royal pardon.[99]

Realizing that their leader's fortunes were waning fast, Fitzgerald's emissaries accepted these reduced terms. A six-week truce was also agreed, after which the city would be surrendered, if not relieved before then. The citizens also managed to gain Fitzgerald's agreement that he would not burn or destroy any part of the surrounding country for the duration of the truce. To ensure its observance, hostages were exchanged. Dr Travers remained in Dublin, together with some unnamed colleagues. They were subsequently held in the castle by Serjeant Whyte, together with other state prisoners, for which purpose he was paid £19 13s. 4d. for supplying them with food and drink.[100] For their part, the city delivered one of their jureés, Richard Talbot, as well as one Rochford and one Rery. Fitzgerald placed them into the safe keeping of David Sutton of Rathbride, but Sutton released them as soon as he considered it safe to do so.[101] The truce took effect on 17 October, but it was broken the very next day, when

95 Gilbert, *CARD*, i, p. 367. 96 Ibid., p. 398. 97 Gilbert, *CARD*, i, p. 501.
98 Holinshed, p. 272. 99 Ibid., pp 275–6. 100 *Letters and papers*, xii, pt ii, p. 1310.
101 Holinshed, p. 276.

Fitzgerald's men burned the roof of the stone-walled barn at Kilmainham that belonged to the Hospital of St John, destroying all the grain stored there.[102] This included £40 worth of Anthony Mores' corn.[103]

Rumours of the apparent surrender of Dublin quickly reached Sir William Skeffington on board the fleet. After discussing the alarming news, Skeffington was soon persuaded by his captains to send four-hundred-and-fifty white-coated soldiers immediately into the city by boat, under the command of Sir William Brereton and John Salisbury. Arriving unopposed on the evening of 18 October, they were taken to the tholsel, where Shillyngford informed them of the truce he had made with Fitzgerald. Because of the uncertain situation, Brereton immediately had the city gates secured, with some of his men posted as guards and the remainder placed inside the castle. Letters were despatched to Skeffington, pleading with him to land immediately with the rest of the army and relieve the city, rather than sail on south towards Waterford, as originally planned.[104] Skeffington subsequently landed another small force as reinforcements, but this was trounced by Fitzgerald at Clontarf, on its way to Dublin, with the loss of some twenty-five of its men.[105] Eventually, Skeffington was persuaded to land his remaining force at Skerries, because adverse winds were preventing him from sailing to Waterford in any case. He had also heard that the Butlers, the allies he was hoping to reinforce there, were now only two days away from Dublin. They had apparently responded to Shillyngford's repeated calls for help, requesting them to come to the aid of the city by attacking Fitzgerald's lands in Co. Kildare and thereby draw his forces away from Dublin.[106] Skeffington eventually arrived at Dublin by boat, landing at the slipway near the bridge on 24 October.[107] He was received with all solemnity by the mayor and aldermen, given a loyal oration by the recorder, as well as a *feu de joie* by the city's defenders.

On 17 November 1534, the king wrote to the citizens of Dublin, thanking them for their loyal and good service during the revolt, but this did not lead to an immediate, more tangible reward.[108] The mayor and citizens therefore petitioned the king in 1536, seeking either a grant of the hospital of St John in Kilmainham, or the priory of All Hallows, Dublin, in order to compensate them for the ruin and decay caused to their city by the breaking of their towers, bridges and houses and the lead water conduits during the recent siege. On the same occasion, they asked for a grant in perpetuity of a previous remission of £46, from the two hundred marks (£133 3s. 4d.) fee farm payable to the king annually. They also sought six falcons to be provided, one for each gate of the city, as well as four lasts of gunpowder to serve them.[109] The petition seems to have been carried to London, by the former mayor Robert

---

102 *State papers*, ii, pp 203–4. White, *Extents*, p. 81.   103 *Letters and papers*, viii, p. 695.
104 *State papers*, ii, p. 204.   105 Holinshed, p. 276.   106 Gilbert, *CARD*, i, p. 501.
107 *State papers*, ii, pp 204–5.   108 Gilbert, *CARD*, i, pp 496–7.   109 Gilbert, *CARD*, i,

Shillyngford, who also took with him a letter of recommendation from James Butler, dated 22 May 1536.[110] To ensure the petition's success, Thomas Stephens, Shillyngford's successor as mayor, also wrote to the duke of Norfolk (formerly the lord lieutenant of Ireland, as the earl of Surrey) on 26 May, asking him to intercede on behalf of the city for them to be compensated by the king for the great ruin, losses and decay they had suffered as a result of Fitzgerald's rebellion and siege.[111] Shillyngford's mission was not a success immediately. It was not until 4 February 1539, that the citizens were finally rewarded by the king through being granted the priory of All Hallows (which would subsequently become the site of Trinity College Dublin) in return for an annual rent of £4 4s. 0¾d., or one-twentieth of its annual value. This grant included not only the site and buildings in Dublin, but also all of the priory's extensive landholdings in the surrounding counties. The citizens also gained a £20 remission of the annual fee farm payment in perpetuity.[112] It is perhaps noteworthy that Shillyngford did not receive a personal reward for his part in the defence of the city, unlike some other participants previously named. Perhaps the truce he had made with Fitzgerald, on the eve of the city being relieved by Brereton and Salisbury, counted against him?

DISPUTED LANDS

Although Fitzgerald's rebellion had several more months to run, the siege of Dublin was effectively over. What part Serjeant Whyte had played in these final momentous days is not known. However, it is clear that his refusal to hand over the castle to Fitzgerald in the first place, coupled with his successful defence of it, probably saved Dublin from being lost to the king and his cause in Ireland perhaps being damaged irretrievably. But what prompted Whyte to remain loyal to the king, when those around him, particularly his superiors, either compounded with Fitzgerald, joined him or sought to flee from his clutches?

The answer probably lies in a letter Whyte wrote to Thomas Cromwell on 29 May 1536, requesting letters to be sent to the under-treasurer in Ireland, commanding him to allow Whyte to occupy the land the earl of Kildare had kept from him for many years and for which he had been an unsuccessful suitor.[113]

'Certain lands in Kildare, Frereton and other places' were the subject of a long legal battle between a John White, gentleman of Dublin, son of Thomas White of Haverfordwest, son of James White, and an illegitimate second cousin, James, son of Nicholas White of Kildare. This dispute came to a head

---

pp 500–1.   **110** Gilbert, *CARD*, i, pp 501–2.   **111** Gilbert, *CARD*, i, pp 497–500.
112 Gilbert, *CARD*, i, pp 33–4. *Patent and close rolls*, p. 48, no.1.   **113** *Letters and papers*, x,
p. 984. The National Archives, Kew, SP 60/3 fo. 55.

in 1521, when John brought his case before the earl of Surrey, then lord lieutenant. Surrey and his council found in favour of John and ordered that he should enjoy the lands without further impediment, under penalty of £200 payable to the king. Confirmation of this ruling was obtained three years later from the visiting king's commissioners, James Denton, Sir Ralph Egerton and Anthony Fitzherbert. However, sometime afterwards, probably between late 1532 and 1533, the earl of Kildare ordered Thomas Netterville, the chief justice of the king's bench, to re-examine the case. This was probably to the detriment of John, for Netterville was a creature of the earl's, having acted as his chief justice in the liberty of Kildare in 1518.[114] After Kildare's downfall, John sought a confirmation of the commissioners' decision, which was given on 22 November 1538. Even so, James Fitz Nicholas White was still in possession of the lands on 10 February 1540, when John obtained a final decree in his favour, establishing James' illegitimacy, and that of his father Nicholas, once more. Nevertheless, James was allowed to reap and carry away the corn he had sown come harvest time. During the third year of Edward VI (1549–50), the whole proceedings back to 1521 were copied into the Irish patent rolls, which suggests that this dispute had flared up once more.[115]

Can we be certain that the John White mentioned in this series of legal decisions is the same person who subsequently became constable of Dublin Castle? With his mention of being an unsuccessful suitor for many years (which key comments do not appear in the printed calendared version), the letter that Sir John wrote to Cromwell in 1536 seems to be conclusive proof that he was. Also, from the interpolations that John Lodge made in his own record of the entry in the patent rolls, the originals of which were still extent in his day, it is clear that this eighteenth-century antiquarian believed this to be the case too.[116]

REWARDS

In the summer of 1535, Serjeant Whyte travelled to London, for it was recommended in a letter sent from Ireland on 24 May that Cromwell should examine Whyte about the Lord Trimleston's conduct during the siege.[117] John Salisbury also wrote ten days previously, reporting the excellent service done by Whyte during the siege and that, for the encouragement of others, he

---

114 Kildare's order is not dated. Netterville had been second justice of the common bench in 1524. He was replaced in this capacity by Gerald Aylmer on 24 August 1532, but I have not found a record of Netterville's subsequent promotion to chief justice of the king's bench. See F. Elrington Ball, *The judges in Ireland, 1221–1921* (London, 1926), i, pp 159, 194, who believes that Netterville was either dead or retired in 1528.   115 *Patent and close rolls*, i, pp 194–5, no. 150.   116 National Library of Ireland, microfilm P1891 (Lodge's MSS), p. 104.   117 *State papers*, ii, p. 245. *Letters and papers*, viii, p. 755, *Carew MSS*, 52.

should be 'noticed' by the king.[118] Whyte was subsequently dubbed a knight.[119] This must have been done on or before 28 August 1535, the date on which the king's letters patent were issued, formally appointing Whyte constable of Dublin Castle for life. This is because he is described for the very first time in this document as 'Sir John'. His new salary of twenty marks (£13 6s. 8d.) per annum was to be raised from the customs and subsidy of Dublin. On the very same day, his son Owen was appointed serjeant-at-arms for life in his stead.[120] Owen seems to have died in or after 1574, when the reversion of his office of serjeant-at-arms was granted to one Richard Lawrence.[121] Another reward made for Whyte's successful defence of Dublin Castle from July until October 1534 was the payment by the under-treasurer of £81 12s. 6d.[122] Before Whyte could reap these financial rewards, however, he apparently had to borrow some money. In the very same year he was knighted by the king, Sir John was found guilty by the lord deputy and the council in Ireland of withholding the return of £18 5s., three broken crowns of gold and one gold ring to John Douse, who had decided to call in the loans he had made to Whyte and two other debtors, but which he was having problems in recovering. Whyte and the other two debtors were ordered to repay Douse the monies loaned to them, on penalty of double the amount.[123]

Whyte also seems to have used his new-found influence to build up his land holdings in and around Dublin, which he did mainly from church sources, both before and after the suppression of the Irish monasteries. On 20 September 1539, he obtained the lease for sixty-one years for forty acres of land in Donnybrook from the prior of All Hallows, in exchange for an annual rent of 40s. and a pound of pepper, payable in equal portions at Easter and Michaelmas.[124] By 31 October 1540, he was holding an *ortus* and a garden in St Andrew's parish, formally belonging to the Austin Friary of Dublin.[125] Finally, on 8 November 1540, he was also said to be holding twenty-four or twenty-eight acres of demesne lands belonging to the former nunnery of St Mary de Hogges, Dublin, for which he rendered 28s. annually. These latter lands were later known as 'Mynchons' Mantles' and encompassed the area bound today by Leinster, Nassau and Grafton Streets, and the northern side of St Stephen's Green. Further afield, Sir John also held from the priory of Christ Church, the tithe sheaf of Kilmashogue, on the marches of Dublin, payable by the priory's tenant there, although it is not known from what date.[126] Also, according to a survey made of the late earl of Kildare's lands in 1540–1, Sir John Whyte was found to be holding a messuage and certain lands in Kildare

118 *Letters and papers*, viii, p. 715.   **119** Holinshed, p. 266.   **120** *Patent and close rolls*, i, p. 25, no. 14, p. 18, no. 66; 'Fiants Henry VIII', nos 47, 48.   **121** *Patent and close rolls*, i, p. 555.   **122** *Letters and papers*, xii, pt ii, p. 1310.   **123** *Patent and close rolls*, i, p. 22.   **124** Griffith, *Inquisitions*, p. 73. NAI RC10/4, p. 72.   **125** White, *Extents*, p. 79; M.V. Ronan, 'St Stephen's hospital', *Dublin Historical Record*, 4 (1942), 146.   **126** M.J. McEnery and R. Refaussé (eds), *Christ Church deeds* (Dublin, 2001), p. 249.

from the earl, for which he rendered 4*d*. annually.[127] Whether these were the same lands he was disputing with his kinsman James White in the Irish law courts is not clear. The low value of the lands would seem to suggest otherwise.

DEMISE

Whyte's remaining life revolved around his duties in the castle, during which he was also responsible for the state prisoners incarcerated within.[128] He was occasionally involved in, or at least a witness to, their interrogation.[129] He may also have presided over their execution, for William Bath of Dollardstown and Christopher Eustace of Ballycutland, both attainted for their respective parts in Fitzgerald's revolt, met their deaths within the castle walls after due process of law.[130] Whyte was also appointed to the king's council in Ireland from 12 December 1538 at least, when he appended his name to a letter to Secretary Cromwell, together with those of his fellow councillors.[131] His last known official act was to sign the lord deputy and council's letter of 9 September 1542 to the king at Maynooth. Whyte died in the same year (or perhaps in the early months of 1543, by modern reckoning, because the year was considered by his contemporaries to start on Lady Day, 25 March) after a period of sickness. He was buried in Christ Church Cathedral, Dublin, 5*s*. being paid for his funeral and 1*s*. 6*d*. for his month's mind.[132] His office of constable of Dublin Castle was granted to John Parker of Holmpatrick, secretary to the lord deputy, Anthony St Leger, who had the reversion. Parker's fee was later increased to £20 sterling per annum, 'considering that the castle of Dublin is one of the principal fortresses that we have within that our realm'.[133]

CONCLUSION

John Whyte's family seems to have had a previous connection with Ireland, but evidence is lacking at the moment to say any more. The matter is also complicated by Whyte's common surname, which was already in widespread use throughout Ireland by the sixteenth century. Although Whyte was identified with Dublin from 1521, there seems to have been a Welsh connection here, considering that his father hailed from Haverfordwest and his own son was called Owen. The fact that the constable of Dublin Castle was expected to be

---

127 Gearóid Mac Niocaill, *Crown surveys of lands, 1540–1 with the Kildare rental begun in 1518* (Dublin, 1992), p. 151.　**128** *Letters and papers*, xii, pt 2, 1310 ii.　**129** *Letters and papers*, xiv, pt 1, 1245 ii; ibid., xvi, p. 304 iii (7).　**130** Holinshed, p. 276.　**131** *State papers*, iii, p. 111.　**132** R. Refaussé with C. Lennon (eds), *The registers of Christ Church Cathedral, Dublin* (Dublin, 1998), p. 89.　**133** *State papers*, iii, p. 486.

someone born in the realm of England also implies that Whyte was originally an outsider.

Whyte first came to notice in the early 1520s, a time that coincided with the arrival in Ireland of the earl of Surrey. In view of Whyte's later defence of Dublin Castle, he probably had some previous military experience. Whether this was in Ireland or in Henry VIII's wars in France or Scotland is not known. During the early sixteenth century, Wales was a rich recruiting ground for the Tudor armies, in the same way that Ireland and Scotland became to Great Britain in later centuries. Considering the background of his predecessors as serjeants-at-arms, it is possible that Whyte might have been a yeoman of the guard, two hundred of which accompanied Surrey to Ireland in 1520.

Whyte's appointment came at a moment of crisis, following the capture of the vice-deputy in 1528. It is possible that he may have owed his appointment to a connection with the Fitzgerald family. His duty of protecting the persons of the lord deputy and the chancellor soon included the keeping of Dublin Castle, a responsibility he never relinquished except through death.

His steadfast defence of the castle in the summer of 1534 was the high point of his career. He helped to keep alive the flames of the English cause during very bleak times indeed, until succour eventually arrived in the form of a relief army from England. During the siege, Whyte successfully used 'wildfire', a novel weapon apparently not seen in Ireland before, to beat off the most serious attack on the castle itself. He was also helped by the ineptness of the besieging forces. This was partly due to the lack of enthusiasm of many of the pressed men in Fitzgerald's ranks, but more telling was the lack of heavy artillery to batter down the city or castle walls, even though a suitable piece had been sitting on the quayside at Drogheda since 1532, although perhaps without sufficient powder and ball to serve it. Also, Fitzgerald's evident desire to get what he wanted through negotiation rather than force is an interesting facet of his rebellion, which perhaps deserves further investigation.

Whyte was strongly pressurized during the siege to give up the castle to the rebels. The principals probably relied on their previous professional relationships with him. His previous connections with the Fitzgerald family may have been counted on too. However, those of his wife, Janet Golding, with the Delahydes, were probably just as important. Nevertheless, Whyte remained loyal to the end. His defiance was probably due to a grudge that he bore against Gerald, earl of Kildare, who, for many years, had kept lands from him that had previously belonged to his grandfather, despite a string of successful legal judgments in Whyte's favour. Whyte's situation, in this regard, seems to have been the classic one of the legitimate offspring of an individual serving in Ireland failing to put down strong roots in the country, while an illegitimate line prospered in the land of their birth, hijacking the legitimate line's inheritance, thanks to obtaining good lordship from the dominant power, in this case the Geraldines. However, in view of the end result, the earl seems to have chosen the wrong man to support, with disastrous consequences for his own son, and indeed, for the whole of his house.

Whyte was well rewarded for his loyalty to the king, being granted the constableship of Dublin Castle for life, with his former office of serjeant-at-arms being given to his son. He also received a cash reward as well as a regular place on the lord deputy's council. He subsequently used his increased wealth and status to increase his landholdings in Ireland, primarily taking advantage of the impending dissolution of the monasteries to obtain leases of various lands in the vicinity of Dublin itself. When, after a period of sickness, Whyte eventually died in 1542, he was honoured by being buried in the mother church of the city, Christ Church Cathedral, where other illustrious persons connected with Dublin' history have been laid to rest, both before and since.

Christ Church Cathedral and its environs: medieval and beyond

MICHAEL O'NEILL

INTRODUCTION

Christ Church Cathedral is at the heart of medieval Dublin, whether approached from the south up Patrick Street, or obliquely from the south-east at the junction of Castle and Werburgh Streets, or from the west on High Street. Before the erection of the Civic Offices, the north flank of the cathedral and the crossing tower dominated all views looking south across the river. In terms of the cathedral's longevity, a relatively new vista is that from the east on Lord Edward Street, a thoroughfare that was opened in 1886, 'by which the steep ascent at Cork Hill and Castle Street will be avoided'.[1] The choir school at the east end of the cathedral complex was extended and embellished on the exterior by Thomas Drew in 1891–2 to take advantage of the vista provided by the new street. The new east window was inspired by that of the thirteenth-century chapter house, which had been excavated only a few years previously.[2] This was one of the last throws of the dice in the almost century-long restoration and reconfiguration of the cathedral complex employing in equal measure forensic scholarship and hardly justifiable innovations. These campaigns saw breathtaking feats of engineering, careful recording of elevations, plans and details, meticulous restoration and copying of parts and at the same time, paradoxically, a willingness to create plans and elevations based on an ideology of (creative) conformity to the building style of one period of the Middle Ages at the expense of every other.

This attitude or approach is hardly unique to Christ Church. However, what was at play in Christ Church in the second half of the nineteenth century was a coalescence of many powerful factors: the needs of a cathedral clergy and choir, a cathedral vying for metropolitan status (hence the attached synod hall), the first major restoration work of the post-Disestablishment era, a wealthy benefactor (Henry Roe) and a brilliant and busy architect, George Edmund Street. The building was well known before the restoration of 1871–8,

---

1 'Provisional order. Plan and design for New Street, from Dame Street to Christ Church Place'. Signed Parke Neville and Co. City Engineers. Approved on behalf of the dean and chapter of Christ Church Cathedral, 5 May 1882. In Christ Church Cathedral Muniments Collection.   2 Roger Stalley, 'Christ Church Cathedral' in Christine Casey, *The buildings of Ireland: Dublin* (New Haven, 2005), pp 317–37 at p. 333.

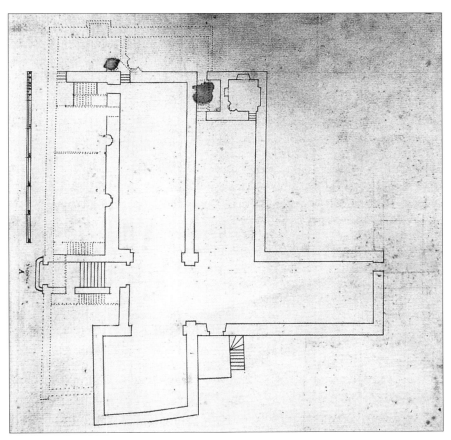

10.1 'A plan of the Four Courts' (Lady Davis-Goff Collection, photograph IAA). This is a plan of the Four Courts at ground floor level (aligned north–south). The court of chancery extends to the east (right); exchequer to the south. The courts of king's bench and common pleas are separated by a spine wall. Stairs rise up to the domed entrance lobby to the courts complex from the west, on Christ Church Lane, now St Michael's Hill (the external entrance arch is visible in fig. 10.4). In the re-entrant angle between the courts of chancery and exchequer was the baroque door case by William Robinson (visible in figs 10.4, 10.11, 10.12). The buildings to the west and north outlined by dotted lines are part of the cathedral precincts, the former west range belonging to the prior and later the dean, and to the north the vicar's room and the chapter room, built or partially rebuilt following the collapse of the north side of the nave in 1562. This implies that the north gables of the courts of king's bench and common pleas are raised on the west bays of the cathedral aisle wall. The south wall of chancery is likely to have incorporated the inner wall of the south range. Fireplaces are prominently marked on the plan, two warming the former west range and corner chimneys at the north end (the substantial stacks are visible in figs 10.3 and 10.12, those of the corner chimneys depicted as diagonal stacks by Petrie). The courts were raised over extensive cellars, and passages ran underneath the court of exchequer, under the east end of chancery, and under the north end of the other two courts (the Reading and Jebb plans, figs 10.5 and 10.7, indicate cellar or basement levels of the Four Courts and rather confusingly ground level in the cathedral).

10.2 'Inside view of the old courts of justice, Dublin' (*Gentleman's Magazine*, April 1788), as refurbished by William Robinson. The view is from the west under the domed vestibule. The court of exchequer is to the right up a flight of steps; chancery is directly ahead with the inner arch of the baroque doorway visible (see fig. 10.4). To the left are the arched entrances into king's bench and common pleas. The south wall of chancery may incorporate the inner wall of the south cloister range, the round-headed windows may therefore be medieval (for exterior views, see figs 10.4, 10.11, 10.12).

with many earlier views and descriptions. In addition, there was a full set of measured plans and elevations drawn before restoration and published by William Butler in 1874.[3] It was also the first major Irish cathedral restoration to have been fairly comprehensively photographed, interior images taken before restoration were offered for sale as souvenirs, and photography was deliberately used to record the various feats of engineering prowess employed in restoring the nave and rebuilding the north transept. Again, unusually in an Irish context, the architect produced a sumptuous volume giving an account of

3 William Butler, *Christ Church Cathedral, Dublin: measured drawings and historical sketch* (Dublin, 1874), [iv], 8p, 9pls.

10.3 View from the south-east by George Grattan, 1815–19 (courtesy of the Victoria and Albert Museum). This wonderful view is full of incident. St Michael's Church, built in 1815, is on the left, framing a view down Christ Church Lane with the whole west side of the Christ Church complex visible. It also provides a particularly good view of the crossing tower, largely rebuilt around 1600. The houses flanking the west gable of the cathedral were formerly chambers belonging to king's bench and exchequer, and court of admiralty, essentially the remodelled west range. The Four Courts had moved to Inns Quay in 1796 and the former court building complex beyond the elaborate entrance arch had become dilapidated. The entrance with blocked upper arch and four storeys over was the gateway to 'Hell' as marked on Rocque's map of 1765. A similar view by Petrie (engraved by J. Greig in 1819) shows the end bays of Skinners Row beyond this entrance. The main entrance to the former courts complex survived. The springers of the entrance doorway to the courts and the springer of the arch from the vestibule opening into king's bench is also visible, as is a window beyond, lighting common pleas. The west front of the cathedral is depicted in some detail. The four-light west window with switchline tracery is placed under a round head, indicating a later medieval date than the switchline tracery under pointed or lancet-headed windows in the south wall of the choir (figs 10.8–11). The doorway below is a post-medieval remodelling. The image captures well the near-ashlar quality of the west façade, contrasting to the dark calp limestone used on the upper nave walls and more randomly coursed crossing tower, all contrasting with the rendered inner elevations of the surviving Four Courts walls.

the restoration campaign and its achievements.[4] The necessity for Street to publish his account of the restoration and the fact that for a century following the restoration the crypt was essentially a museum for medieval cut-stone,

4 *The cathedral of the Holy Trinity commonly called Christ Church Cathedral, Dublin: an account of the restoration of the fabric, by George Edmund Street, R.A., with an historical sketch*

10.4 Edward Murphy, 'Remains of the old Four Courts', lithograph (NLI TB 532). This is a view within the court precincts. The baroque door case by William Robinson gave access to the court of chancery (see fig. 10.2). It was a virtuoso piece of architecture. Partial views of this door case can be seen in figs 10.11 and 10.12. The argument being made in the text is that this passage is through the former south range of the cloister complex and that the court of chancery incorporates the inner wall of this range; the round-headed windows may be medieval survivals. The wall to the west was the inner wall of exchequer. The arched exit below, leading west, ran under the court, one of the 'dark passages' leading into the court and cathedral complex.

serving as a sort of proof text supporting his restoration decisions, silently suggested that the restoration was not without its critics. The stone collection as presented was hardly useful or informative – cut-stone piled into heaps – and has been moved to the crypt of St Werburgh's Church, allowing the cathedral crypt to become a useful space. Some of the more interesting cut-stone pieces formerly kept in the crypt are now on display in the north transept, with accompanying interpretative panels by the present writer.

of the cathedral by Edward Seymour, MA (London, 1882). Street's text was reproduced in Roger Stalley, 'George Edmund Street's account of the architecture of Christ Church Cathedral, 1882, with commentary by Roger Stalley' in idem (ed.), *George Edmund Street and the restoration of Christ Church Cathedral, Dublin* (Dublin, 2000), pp 77–212. The quality of the reproduced images is poor.

Street's insight into the close relationship between the masonry styles of the English West Country and Irish architecture of the late twelfth and into the thirteenth century was important for the study of Irish medieval architecture.[5] The similarities in style were discussed by E.S. Prior, Arthur Champneys, Edwin C. Rae and H.G. Leask and developed comprehensively by Roger Stalley. The latter's work over several decades, particularly in the areas of the late romanesque and early Gothic cathedral, was in large part responsible for rescuing the cathedral's reputation from being considered merely a Victorian Gothic restoration.[6] There is a historiographical point to be made here. Street's insights as to the sources of Irish Gothic were scarcely developed beyond Champneys, and in the period of the Celtic Revival at the end of the century and in the university archaeology departments of the nascent Republic, the art and architecture of the pre-Anglo-Norman period received pre-eminence as subjects worthy of study. In more recent decades, and probably as likely also the influence of the glasnost following Vatican II as the work of any academic departments, the 1169 date-barrier for art and architectural studies of medieval ecclesiastical buildings has been broken. This can be seen obliquely in a related area – castle studies. In this discipline, largely the preserve of archaeologists (why?), the slim study of Irish castles first published by Leask in 1941 is nearly always the starting point and is unmercifully pilloried and criticized. By way of contrast, Leask's three volumes on ecclesiastical architecture are rarely critiqued (even though they are difficult to use), suggesting that for several decades an ideological debate (with theological levels of definitions and distinctions in relation to tower houses or small tall castles) concerning post-Anglo-Norman Irish architecture was fought in one field of medieval architecture only.

If the zeitgeist of raising awareness of medieval Dublin in the 1970s was to rightly include Christ Church Cathedral, then the arbitrary approach of Street to some of the later architecture could be swept aside or at least mitigated by the argument that the amount of architecture and architectural detail he caused to be preserved outweighed the losses.[7]

5 'I find in these buildings the most unmistakable marks of them having been erected by the same men who were engaged at the same time in England and Wales. They may be divided into two classes of the first Christ Church Cathedral in this city, and Kilkenny Cathedral may be taken as illustrations. These 2 churches possess certain features so peculiar and so exactly like what is seen in S David's, Llandaff and Wells Cathedral and Glastonbury Abbey that they must have been erected by the same group of workmen or from the designs of the same architect ... St Patrick's on the other hand, as it seems to me, to another school, and you must compare it with the early portions of Chester Cathedral if you would learn whence its builders came ...', MSS *Extracts from a Lecture delivered in 1866 in the Irish National Institution in St Stephen's Green E.* Christ Church Archives. 6 Roger Stalley, 'The medieval sculpture of Christ Church Cathedral, Dublin', *Archaeologia*, 106 (1979), 107–22; Roger Stalley, 'Three Irish buildings with West Country origins', *BAACT Conference Transactions 1978* (Leeds, 1981), 62–80. 7 Roger Stalley, 'Confronting the past: George Edmund Street at Christ Church Cathedral in Dublin' in Frank Salmon (ed.), *Gothic and the Gothic revival: papers from the 26th annual symposium of the Society of Architectural*

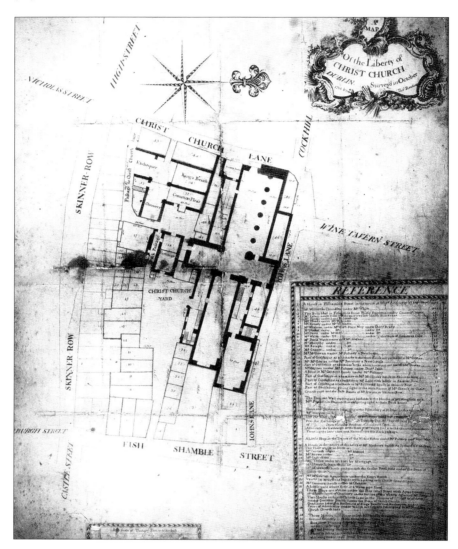

10.5 Map of the liberty of Christ Church, 1764, by Thomas Reading (Representative Church Body, Dublin), reproduced from *IHTA Dublin*. Reading's map of the whole cathedral complex gives a sense of the integrated area before the work of the Wide Street Commissioners in the nineteenth century and Dublin Corporation in the twentieth century, which has in effect turned Christ Church into an island complex surrounded by busy streets. The plan of the cathedral is at ground-floor level, but the plan of the former cloister area, the Four Courts, is at basement or cellar level; in other words, at the property level owned by the cathedral authorities. The plan of the courts is thus foreshortened, indicating, among other things, passages through the complex below court room level.

If we regretfully accept the premise that in most cases restoration of a medieval building complex of many architectural periods has generally prioritized one period, we can be on our guard that there was probably a more complex historical sequence. Following Rickman's classification of Gothic into the Early English, decorated and perpendicular styles and the contemporary biological (or teleological) notion of growth, flowering and decline or decadence, the decorated style was prioritized in English restorations, while in Ireland, post-Pugin and the Ecclesiologists, earlier rather than late Gothic forms were favoured by restorers of Irish cathedrals and churches.[8]

Having qualified and briefly contextualized Street's restoration of Christ Church, it might now be appropriate to state that his intervention was radical and more thoroughgoing than any other Irish cathedral restoration save St Finbarr's in Cork, which was a complete rebuild in French Gothic style. Such a claim for the restoration of Christ Church is dependent on an analysis of old views, maps and plans.

MEDIEVAL AND EARLY MODERN

The majority of Irish medieval cathedrals had secular chapters of one form or another; only those of Downpatrick (Benedictine monks), Newtown Trim in Meath and Christ Church Cathedral, Dublin (Augustinian canons), had monastic chapters, with evidence of monastic precincts at the latter two. The fact that Christ Church was a monastic cathedral informs not only arguments relating to the medieval building sequence, but also much of the available later visual material and map evidence. The cloister precinct at Christ Church was to the south of the cathedral, the east range of the cloister extending south from the south transept, the south range parallel to Skinners Row and the west range parallel to St Michael's Hill. The ground floor of the surviving ruined and formerly vaulted medieval chapter house is ranged beside the south transept, and the entrance doorway height is set a level above the crypt floor level and below that of the nave.

At the Dissolution of the monasteries, Christ Church Cathedral continued as the cathedral of Dublin but was reconstituted with a secular chapter headed by a dean. Properties within the cathedral precincts became part of the income

Historians of Great Britain (Manchester, 1998), pp 75–86; for an opposing view, see Sean O'Reilly, 'The arts of inference, presumption and invention: George Edmund Street rebuilds Christ Church' in ibid., 87–98. The present writer designed an exhibition of sixteen panels on display in the cathedral crypt in 2008 which celebrated the 130th anniversary of the completion of Street's restoration.   8 St Patrick's Cathedral in Dublin was also restored to its Early English form in the 1860s following Richard Cromwell Carpenter; so, too, Kildare Cathedral (also restored by Street). The earlier, 1830s, restoration of Armagh Cathedral by Cottingham favoured perpendicular Gothic as did the Pain brothers when restoring Lismore Cathedral nave.

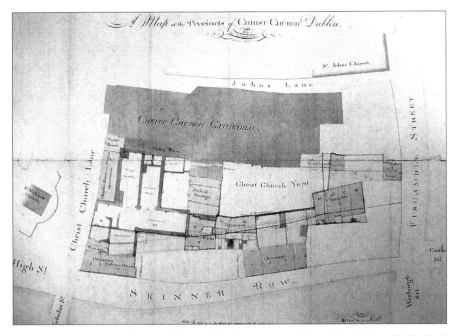

10.6 'A map of the precincts of Christ Church … survey'd by J[ohn] L[ongfield] 1817' (National Library of Ireland, map 21 F 90, no. 213). The focus of this map is on the property of the various cathedral dignities in the close, the cathedral building being only treated in outline. The former western range is here delineated as the vicar's room, the chapter room and the verger's apartments. The arched passage immediately south of the south transept is the chapter house of the cathedral. The chapter house survives unvaulted, and this map gives an indication of the ground level within the close up to the early decades of the nineteenth century. Longfield's plan of the courts is at court room level, showing the extent to which inner walls of the cloistral ranges were reused by Molyneux at the beginning of the seventeenth century. The plan also indicates the entrance to Christ Church Yard (south of the choir) through an arched passage from Fishamble Street.

and houses of the various cathedral dignitaries including the dean, chantor, chancellor, treasurer and other properties belonging to the economy of the cathedral faced onto Skinners Row and the corner with St Michael's Hill (formerly Christ Church Lane). The cathedral dignitaries built houses within the cathedral precincts, following the model of secular cathedral layouts of some three hundred years earlier. The dean, as the Augustinian priors before him, occupied the west range of the cloisters. The cellars under the dean's house are mentioned in a deed dated 1565, the chantor's house is mentioned in a deed dated 1581,[9] and that of the precentor occupied a location near the (now) main entrance gates to the cathedral.[10] While the monastic day no longer

9 M.J. McEnery and Raymond Refaussé (eds), *Christ Church deeds* (Dublin, 2001), nos 1303, 1357.   10 James Mills, 'The journal of Sir Peter Lewys, 1564–5', *Journal of the Royal Society of Antiquaries of Ireland*, 5th ser., 6 (1896), 136–41.

applied, including the focus of activity around the cloister, the vicars and choirmen lived at a common table and probably still occupied the monastic dormitories. A grant dated 1565 to Nicholas Begge, a singingman, included a chamber to sleep in the 'dorter'.[11] Other properties on Skinners Row and Winetavern Street backing onto the precincts were not owned by the cathedral.[12] The cloister garth and ranges of Christ Church would be put to a radically different use in the early seventeenth century.

FOUR COURTS

Various unsuccessful attempts were made throughout the sixteenth century to remove the Four Courts – the chancery, king's bench, common pleas and exchequer – from the king's hall of Dublin Castle to more satisfactory premises. Early in the seventeenth century, they were transferred to Carey's Hospital in College Green. A proposal to remove the Four Courts to the site of the former Dominican priory north of the river proved to be a temporary arrangement (from 1606 to 1608), as the citizens of Dublin opposed the plan of losing both the courts and potentially the parliament to locations outside the city walls. They agreed to contribute an amount towards the cost of carrying out alterations to the cloister area of Christ Church, which were considered suitable for housing the Four Courts.[13] In 1608, Samuel Molyneux, clerk of the royal works, was paid £21 10s. 4d., the final instalment of what the city of Dublin had agreed to contribute to complete these buildings, built on a cross-plan.[14] It is difficult, without any physical evidence, to determine how much of the existing cloister alley walls were incorporated in Molyneaux's design, to what extent the cloister area had been already developed by the cathedral community, and the extent to which the Four Courts were rebuilt by William Robinson in 1695. The likelihood is that Robinson built the dome over the central entrance space of the Four Courts, but it is less clear to what degree he remodelled rather than

11 McEnery and Refaussé (eds), *Christ Church deeds*, no. 1305. 12 Thomas Reading, *Map of the liberty of Christ Church*, 1764 (MSS Map, Representative Church Body Library, Dublin); John Longfield, *A map of the precincts of Christ Church ... survey'd by JL*, 1817 (National Library of Ireland, map 21 F 90, no. 213); John Jebb, 'Copy of a map of the Liberty of Christ Church Dublin surveyed in October 1764 by Thomas Reading in the possession of the dean and chapter of Christ Church' in John Jebb, 'A few observations respecting Christ Church Cathedral and its precinct', *Proceedings of the Saint Patrick's Society for the Study of Ecclesiology*, II, 1855, 18–31 (annotated version of Readings' map). 13 Colum Kenny, *King's Inns and the kingdom of Ireland* (Dublin, 1992), pp 72–3; J.T. Gilbert and Lady Gilbert (eds), *Calendar of ancient records of Dublin, in the possession of the municipal corporation*, 19 vols (Dublin, 1865–1901), ii, pp 478, 501; H.B. Clarke, *Dublin Part 1, to 1610: Irish historic town atlas no. 11* (Dublin, 2002), p. 24. 14 Rolf Loeber, *A biographical dictionary of Irish architects, 1600–1720* (London, 1981), pp 73–5. The Four Courts seems to have remained at Christ Church, Loeber op. cit., p. 75, but see Colm Lennon, *Dublin Part 2, 1610 to 1756: Irish historic town atlas no. 19* (Dublin, 2008), p. 27.

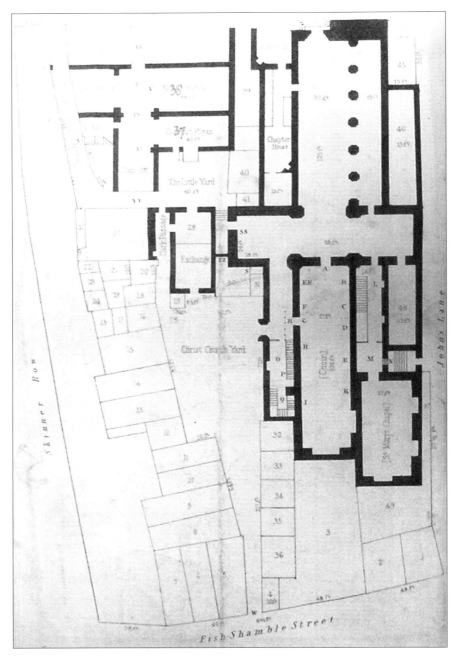

10.7 John Jebb's published version of Reading's map of the cathedral precincts. The particular value of Jebb's map is twofold: firstly, he has updated the list of tenants from Reading's list to 1855; and, secondly, he has annotated the internal layout of the choir and aspects of the topography of the cathedral close.

REFERENCES TO THE ANNEXED MAP.

[These are mere extracts from the original map, as it was not thought necessary to mention the names of all the tenants. The landlords' names are only given here, and such other notices as may illustrate the history, &c., of the church.—J. J.]

1. Captain Skeaf.
2. Mr. White.
3. *The Bull's Head*, under Counsellor Cooper.
4. House over Gateway.
5. Lord Russborough.
6, 7. Mr. Wilkinson.
8, 9, 10. Dr. Brady (Chancellor).
11. Heirs of Erasmus Cope.
12. Mr. Moland.
13, 14, 15. Ditto.
16, 18, 21. Mr. Poulteney.
20. Dr. Jebb (Treasurer).
26. Precinct Wall.
27. Prebendary of St. John's.
28. Old Exchange. Mr. Poulteney. Over the Exchange, a house fronting Christ Church yard, under heirs of Erasmus Cope. At the rear of Mr. Cope's house, the Chancery Chamber, fronting the little yard, and extending over the dark passage.

29. Mr. Poulteney & Dr. Jebb (Treasurer).
30. Prebendary of St. Michan.
31. "The place where the Stocks is."
32, 33, 34. Mr. Moland.
35, 36. Mr. Holt.
37, 43. Dean of Christ Church.
38. Apartment under King's Bench.
39. Vaults, with a passage into Christ Church Lane.
40. Mr. Fennor.
42. Shops, under Four Courts' steps and Court of Chancery.
44. Chambers belonging to King's Bench and Exchequer, and Court of Admiralty. Cellars beneath. Mr. Fleming.
45. Caleb Smalley.
46. Formerly shops. "Since taken into the church."
47. Shed, shops. — Ogle, Esq.
48. Yard.
49. Captain Skeaf, deceased.

The following references are not on the old map:—

A. Lord Lieutenant's Gallery, afterwards Organ Loft.
B. Peers' Seat, &c.
C. Duke of Leinster's Closet.
D. Lady Mayoress's Closet.
E. Peeresses' Seat, formerly Organ Loft.
EE. Seat opposite to the Peers'.
F. Archbishop of Dublin's Closet.
G. Lord Lieutenant's Closet.
H. Archbishop's Throne   No Gallery above.
I. Gallery.
K. Gallery and Staircase.
L. Staircase to A. EE. and galleries on north side.
M. Passage to St. Mary's Chapel.
N. Porch and Stairs to ditto, from St. John's Lane. Over M and N a Vestibule to the Peeresses' Seat, and a Chamber for the Sextoness.
O. In this aisle, staircases; P. to the Lord Lieutenant's Closet and the Archbishop's Closet; Q. to East Gallery.

R. Pillars, supporting Lobby to Lord Lieutenant's Closet, &c.
S. Door into Transept from Christ Church yard, now built up.
T. Over this, Dome of Four Courts, extending to Tt. The Hall extended to U. where was the screen of the Court of Chancery.
V. Curtain of the Court of King's Bench.
UU. Staircase to Courts, from the Passage to Christ Church Lane.
VV. Chief entrance to Courts, from Christ Church Lane.
W. Gateway to Christ Church yard. A House overhead.
XX. Termination of the Court of Exchequer, extending over the passage.
YY. Probable passage from Court of Chancery to Chancery Chamber, over the lane.
ZZ. Line of the Eastern Wall and Arch of the Old Exchange, before the alterations.
* Probable Southern termination of the Precinct

10.8 Watercolour view of the cathedral looking west from Christ Church Yard, dated 1824. This is one of the most intriguing and informative views depicting the state of the cathedral before the refurbishment by Matthew Price in the 1830s and the drastic remodelling by Street in the 1870s. The figures in the foreground suggest the celebration of clearance work within the precinct, perhaps in relation to the work undertaken by the Wide Street Commissioners (I owe this observation to Niall McCullough). The east gable of the cathedral is flanked by battlemented turrets, that on the south further supported by weathered clasping buttresses. The five-light east window with switchline tracery is set within a round-headed arch, presumably dating to post-1461, when a great storm blew in the east window. The switchline tracery of the south side of the choir under pointed heads is earlier. Clasping buttresses define the bays of the choir, while the hipped roof of the aisles and entrance porch into the choir suggest little integration between nave and aisles. A doorway into the transept was blocked by Jebb's time (1855) (fig. 10.7). To the south of the transept is the chapter house, the 'arched passage' of Longfield's map (fig. 10.6). Beyond are the courts of common pleas and the clerestory lighting of king's bench.

rebuilt the early seventeenth-century work. If the number of deeds relating to cellars and spaces under the various courts is anything to go by, he may have had little enough room for manoeuvre, implying that the cross-plan of the Four Courts was retained from Molyneux's design, modernized internally and brought up to date with a Wren London-church-inspired dome or copula over the entrance lobby.[15]

15 Edward McParland, *Public architecture in Ireland, 1680–1760* (New Haven, 2001), pp 116–18. Christ Church deeds mainly relating to properties around and under the Four Courts include McEnery and Refaussé (eds), *Christ Church deeds*, nos 1628 (in 1662), 1675 (1664), 1676 (1664), 1871 (1690), 1830 (1681), 1630 (1662), 1632 (1662: deanery house), 1689 (1665), 1830 (1681), 1946 (1702), 1357 (1581: chantor's house and colfabias), 1305 (1565: dortor, dormitory), 1303 (1565: dean's house).

10.9 Watercolour view of the cathedral from the south (RCB Library). This intriguing bird's-eye view into the cathedral close is possibly taken from an upstairs window at the rear of Skinners Row or some other vantage point. In the background is a highly detailed elevation of the south side of the cathedral from west to east. The stepped gable of the transept is a late medieval feature, while the clerestory windows are probably late Romanesque. The nave clerestory windows date to after the 1562 collapse of the nave. In the foreground is the naively drawn top of the baroque door case by Robinson captured in Murphy's lithograph (fig. 10.4). It suggests the artist's interests lie in Gothic rather than classical architecture. The view is looking down into the courts of king's bench, common pleas and chancery, with exchequer and the formerly domed vestibule out of the frame to the left.

A short discussion of the plan and layout of the seventeenth-century Four Courts using an early to mid-eighteenth-century plan (fig. 10.1), and an interior view published in 1788 (fig. 10.2),[16] helps clarify eighteenth- and nineteenth-century maps of the precincts and views into the cathedral complex from the south. The main entrance to the Four Courts was from the west through a cut-stone archway on St Michael's Hill and steps led up to the entrance. From within the domed entrance lobby, turning right (south) up a number of steps was the smallest room, the court of exchequer. Directly ahead (east) was the court of chancery. Immediately left (north) was the court of king's bench and parallel to that was the court of common pleas.[17] Another entrance from St Michael's Hill, further south nearer the junction with Skinners Row, gave

---

16 'A plan of the Four Courts' (Lady Davis-Goff collection, photograph IAA), reproduced in McParland, op. cit., fig. 143, p. 116. 'Inside view of the old [Four] Courts of Justice Dublin' from *The Gentleman's Magazine*, Apr. 1780. 17 Edward McParland, 'The old Four Courts, at Christ Church' in Caroline Costello (ed.), *The Four Courts: 200 years*

10.10 'Christ Church Cathedral, drawn and engraved by Kirkwood & Son, Dublin', published in Philip Dixon Hardy, *A new picture of Dublin* (Dublin, 1831). This is another intriguing view into the Cathedral Close, from street level. The houses on Skinners Row backing onto the cathedral were demolished by the Wide Street Commissioners in the 1820s. Behind the low wall there is a considerable drop to ground level inside the precinct, along the 'Passage to Christ Church Lane' identified in Reading's map. It is fairly clear that Molyneux or Robinson had never expected the south façade of the Four Courts to be visible in this way. The raised ground level in front of the south transept depicts the top of the vault of the chapter house.

access to the former cloister complex and beyond that to Christ Church Yard, an open space to the south of the choir (fig. 10.3). This entrance passage ran under the court of exchequer and immediately beyond this was a stairs leading up to a baroque doorcase (by Robinson) into the court of chancery (fig. 10.4).

The courts moved to the Gandon-designed complex on Inns Quay in 1796 and the Christ Church complex rapidly became ruinous, as is captured in various late eighteenth- and early nineteenth-century views. The extent to which Molyneaux reused or cannibalized the cloistral complex is difficult if not impossible to determine now. Any attempt to do so is reliant on Thomas Reading's 1764 survey of the cathedral precincts (fig. 10.5), the Longfield map of the precincts dated 1817 (fig. 10.6) and the version of Reading's survey redrawn by John Jebb (fig. 10.7) with valuable annotations regarding the internal arrangements in the long choir. The Reading (and Jebb) plan of the cloister area is at basement level, the plan from the Lady Goff collection is at ground floor (above cellar) level, as is the Longfield map.[18] It seems likely that Molyneaux, at the beginning of the eighteenth century, was able to incorporate the inner wall of the medieval west range as the outer wall of king's bench, with the fireplaces heating the west range clearly marked on the Four Courts plan. The north gables of king's bench and common pleas were continued up from the nave aisle wall with a passage running at cellar level from Christ Church Lane (near the cathedral west gable) through to the 'Little Yard'. The east

(Dublin, 1996), pp 23–32 and figs 1–8.   **18** See n. 10 above.

10.11 Aerial view of Athassel Augustinian priory, Co. Tipperary, begun 1200. Both Athassel and Christ Church have aisled naves, which is unusual in an Irish Augustinian context. It is argued here that the cloister complex at Athassel is close in scale to the Dublin cathedral.

gable of chancery may have incorporated the inner wall of the dormitory range, while the south wall of chancery incorporated the north wall of the medieval south range. The spine walls between the courts and other walls putatively not continuing up the medieval walls apparently rested on great baulks of oak rather than on foundations down to the boulder clay. According to Thomas Drew, who uncovered the chapter house in 1886,

> Those who built the law courts in 1610 had evidently an eye to popular feeling about the desecration of graves, for they laid a great cradle of massive oak beams on them, and built their walls on these without digging foundations. As this construction rotted, it is intelligible how these buildings fell into dilapidation, with many settlements and fissures (although solidly built) within a century after their foundation.[19]

19 Thomas Drew, 'The ancient chapter-house of the priory of the Holy Trinity, Dublin', *Journal of the Royal Society of Antiquaries of Ireland*, 5th ser., 1 (1890), 36–43 at 43.

Lighting king's bench must have been a problem with an un-fenestrated west wall, solved perhaps by clerestory lighting in the east wall, suggesting that common pleas was roofed at a lower level. Such an arrangement is suggested by the interior view of 1788, where the visible south-east window of common pleas appears to be set lower than the elaborate east window composition of chancery and the south windows of the same space.[20]

That this was the general arrangement is confirmed by later views showing the Four Courts at Christ Church in various states of ruin. West of Christ Church Yard were the lower (square-headed) windows of common pleas over-looking the 'Little Yard' with the partially buried chapter house in the middle ground. Behind common pleas were the clerestory windows of king's bench on the spine wall between the courts and behind again were visible the tall and substantial stacks of the west range (fig. 10.8). Newenham O'Callaghan shows the north-east corner of chancery in addition to the spine wall between king's bench and common pleas. Petrie, in Wright's *An historical guide to the city of Dublin*, again shows the semi-submerged chapter house and vaulted slype (the 'Dark Passage' of Reading's map), lower east wall of common pleas, and clerestory pierced spine wall between it and king's bench. The watercolour view of the south elevation of Christ Church has a quasi-bird's eye view into the ruinous Four Courts (fig. 10.9). The baroque doorcase into the courts of chancery allows an orientation of what is being depicted. The round-headed windows to the east of the doorcase are those also depicted in the Murphy lithograph. The view depicts the courts of chancery and common pleas, perhaps indicating that the joisted floor had collapsed with basement level depicted to the south and south-west in front of the cathedral nave. The George Grattan view from the south-west shows Robinson's entrance arch to the former Four Courts, the former west range to the north of this entrance. It also depicts the heavy stacks on the rear wall, in effect the spine wall between the range and king's bench, the springers for Robinson's dome over the entrance lobby and the spine wall between king's bench and common pleas are all depicted. The former west range had been remodelled, at least the facade, if not rebuilt, possibly during the late sixteenth or early seventeenth century. The ground floor had a cut-stone facade, the upper floors faced in brick with a heavy decorative cornice distinguishing the former range from both the shop-fronted houses north of John's Lane and the tall five-storey house at the corner of Michael's Hill and Skinners Row. The tall heavy stacks are another distin-guishing feature, the tall stack of the corner fireplace of the 'Vicar's Room' nearest the cathedral is a medieval or very early modern arrangement.[21]

20 In William Monck Mason's unpublished history of the cathedral, he wrote that the court rooms had been on a number of different levels, 'the courts of chancery and common pleas were on a level, there was an ascent of 10 or 12 steps or more from the chancery to the exchequer and from the exchequer there was 6 or eight steps more to the king's bench'. Quoted in McParland, 'The Old Four Courts, at Christ Church', p. 24.   21 One might

10.12 Lawrence photograph of Christ Church Cathedral and close, *c.*1900. The chapter house had been recently re-excavated by Thomas Drew. Christ Church Place is considerably wider than Skinners Row. The horse and cart in the middle ground likely mark the rear of the house plots facing onto Skinners Row (see figs 10.5–7).

The eighteenth- and nineteenth-century plans and views of the Four Courts in the former cloister area present a very different picture to the cloisters of the medieval Franciscan friaries of the West, which, in their ruined and abandoned state, are fossilized in their early modern condition (fig. 10.10). Secondly, it is very unusual for a former monastic cathedral to survive the Reformation as a cathedral church, and the use of the precincts by the secular cathedral clergy in the early modern period, as documented in the cathedral records, is a fascinating aspect of continuities and discontinuities in the use of the monastic ranges of a fair-sized cathedral complex. It has been argued that some of the courts used the inner walls of parts of the east, south and west ranges. This allows a putative plan of the extent of the cloister area to be established, including a western range, which later provided the 'passage to Christ Church Lane' as annotated on Reading's map. A comparison of the

wonder whether there was a refurbishment of the west range following the decision in 1716 to build new houses for the cathedral dignitaries. In the event, the new deanery was not built until 1733. See Edward McParland, 'Edward Lovett Pearce and the deanery of Christ Church Dublin' in Agnes Bernelle (ed.), *Decantations: a tribute in honour of Maurice Craig* (Dublin, 1992), pp 130–3. The northern part of the west range was gothicized and crennelated in the mid-nineteenth century, as can be seen in the Millard-Robinson view of the north flank of the nave.

arrangement of the Christ Church cloister to other Irish Augustinian priories points to one close similarity, that of Athassel priory in Co. Tipperary. The splendidly isolated and shattered ruins of Athassel (fig. 10.11) seem larger than the church and cloister area of urban Christ Church; nevertheless a rescaled plan of Reading's map and a scaled plan of Athassel overlaid show the closeness in overall layout and scale.[22]

The lithograph view by Kirkwood of the south elevation of Christ Church Cathedral showing the substantial walls remaining of the old Four Courts are one indication of the transformation of the precinct to its appearance today (fig. 10.12). The eastern extent of the complex is indicated by the choir school and modern chapter house complex, while the isolated pier of masonry south-east of the present choir marks the south-east corner of the later medieval long choir. It is more difficult to envisage the extent of ground lost within the close to the south of the cathedral from the transept westwards. The railings exclude at least the width of the former south range, and the canting or rounding of the south-west corner facilitates this even more. Similarly, scaled plans of the Christ Church precinct (based on Reading) and a modern plan of Athassel overlaid give a good indication of the similarities in scale if not exact detail between the medieval complexes (see note 22, below).

CATHEDRAL CHURCH

Old views of the cathedral fabric indicate that it too had a complex building history, one which old views, plans and elevations can in part recover. The fenestration, treatment of wall heads and style of the buttressing are all (surrogate) indicators of building and rebuilding dates. The discussion of the documentary and pictorial evidence has been coloured by Street's interpretation of the physical evidence available to him and his subsequent decision to drastically shorten the choir and surround it with an ambulatory and short lady chapel. That this was the original form of the choir, essentially mirroring the east end of the crypt below, does not take into account the large additional amounts of masonry introduced into the crypt at the restoration to support the canted walls of the newly built ambulatory above.[23]

Be that as it may, the surviving chevron-decorated arches of the later Romanesque choir invite the notion of a three-storey elevation to correspond with the elevation of the transepts (restored quite differently by Street). Yet it is clear that the long choir had a two-storey elevation with hipped rather than

22 Michael O'Neill, 'Christ Church Cathedral as a blueprint for other Augustinian buildings in Ireland' in John Bradley, A.J. Fletcher and Anngret Simms (eds), *Dublin in the medieval world: studies in honour of Howard B. Clarke* (Dublin, 2009), pp 168–87 at pp 168–80 and pl. 8.
23 O'Neill, 'Christ Church Cathedral as a blueprint', pp 186–7 and figs 13.13–13.16.

lean-to roofs to the aisles. Is it possible that the event of 1316 when 'a violent storm of rain and wind threw down the steeple', was indeed the crossing tower and that it substantially destroyed the cathedral choir? A 'licence to crennelate' received from Edward III, in 1329, probably indicated the intention to rebuild the tower but might equally apply to the choir. While it has been remarked that there is no evidence in the fabric for the collapse of the crossing tower, surely the most pertinent evidence of this was the resulting two-storey choir elevation with Y-tracery windows lighting the main space with separately articulated aisles. A calamitous event might better explain the radical reordering of the choir on the assumption that it originally had a three-storey elevation than whatever was accomplished in 1289 under Prior Delamore when 'the new work of the presbytery had begun'.[24] The aisleless extension of the choir eastward by Archbishop John de St Paul between 1349 and 1362 was lit by three-light windows with switchline tracery. A century later, on 19 July 1461, a great storm blew in the east window. The reference in the following year to 'the destruction of the two chief windows, commonly called Gabilles', suggests that either the north transept or the west window of the nave was also damaged. The illustrative evidence suggests that it was the west gable that had a four-light round-headed window with switchline tracery inserted. The north transept gable retained its late Romanesque appearance into the nineteenth century; the south transept gable had the east range upper storey attached. The east window was also repaired after 1462 with a five-light switchline tracery composition, again round-headed.[25] The east gable was flanked by battlemented turrets, copying a feature found in many churches in the Pale. A closer exemplar of course was the west front of the nearby and rival St Patrick's Cathedral, where the west gable was rebuilt in the late fourteenth century. In its own right, switchline tracery dating from the mid-fifteenth century might be considered retardaire, showing no evidence or knowledge of perpendicular Gothic forms. Christ Church was not completely devoid of perpendicular forms – the north choir aisle had cusped paired lights under a square head and the early sixteenth-century Kildare chantry chapel was an elaborate composition of late Gothic character. The large east and west windows might instead be regarded as evidence of the revival of round-headed forms in the late Gothic period in Ireland, particularly evident in the friaries of the west, where pointed and round-headed forms are juxtaposed in a manner which can startle the architectural historian unfamiliar with later Irish Gothic.[26] Thus, in the case of

24 In O'Neill, 'Christ Church Cathedral as a blueprint', it is suggested that the 1289 document might refer to a lady chapel, an architectural response to the recently constructed similar space at St Patrick's Cathedral.   **25** All available views clearly show the nave west window as round-headed. The *c.*1824 watercolour of the cathedral from the south-east shows the choir east window as round-headed, the more oblique view of the east façade by Petrie has the least window less emphatically round-headed.   **26** For a recent discussion of Irish friary architecture, see Michael O'Neill, 'Irish Franciscan friary architecture: late

10.13 'The north prospect of the cathedral Church of Holy Trinity in Dublin', Jonas Blaymires, 1733. Note the Romanesque doorway in the transept gable (moved to the south transept in 1833). The shoulder lady chapel is to the north-east.

Christ Church, what the pictorial evidence suggests is a relatively early revival of late Romanesque forms, which would become one of the hallmarks of late Irish Gothic.[27]

Late round-headed window forms were also found lighting the 'shoulder' lady chapel, with Y-tracery. A similarly disposed lady chapel was built at Old Leighlin cathedral in the late fifteenth or early sixteenth century. Jonas Blaymires, who illustrated Ware's *Bishops*, depicted round-headed windows with two lights and a roundel in the spandrel at Armagh, Kildare and Lismore cathedrals, the explicit depiction of Y-tracery under a round head in the lateral walls of the lady chapel at Christ Church can hardly be a misrepresentation of the roundel form (fig. 10.13). There is some evidence, however, that the lady chapel east window had the latter form, as depicted in *Monumenta Eblanae*.[28] According to an entry in the *Liber Niger*, the lady chapel at Christ Church was built after the long choir, in the late fourteenth century. The fenestration is

medieval and early modern' in Edel Bhreathnach, Joseph MacMahon and John McCafferty (eds), *The Irish Franciscans, 1534–1990* (Dublin, 2009), pp 305–27. **27** The echo between late Gothic revival forms and early thirteenth-century round-headed window forms can be seen at Kilfenora Cathedral. **28** Rolf Loeber, 'Sculptured memorials to the dead in early seventeenth-century Ireland: a survey from "Monumenta Eblanae" and other sources', *Proceedings of the Royal Irish Academy*, 81C (1981), 267–93, no. 119 at 285.

later, however, nearer the end of the fifteenth or early in the sixteenth century. Round-headed windows with paired lights and roundel appeared in the transept gables at triforium level following the 1832 restoration by Matthew Price. As he had remodelled the lady chapel to function as a cathedral school, it is possible that one of the inserted transept windows was reused from the largely demolished or heavily remodelled lady chapel. This window form had a long afterlife and was used frequently by William Robinson in the late seventeenth and turn of the eighteenth century at Lismore, Kildare and St Mary's Church in Dublin. The lady chapel of Christ Church (St Mary's Chapel) was re-roofed by Hugh Kinder, carpenter, in 1694, who was paid for 'framing and raising the roof'.[29] There is no indication that it was rebuilt or re-fenestrated at this time. Robinson may have been responsible for the lady chapel at Christ Church, but it may instead be the case that he borrowed the window motif from the Dublin cathedral for use in churches and cathedrals alike. It is intuitively more likely that Robinson would borrow the motif from a major Dublin building than from one of the more remote Franciscan friaries of the west. Rather than regarding the fourteenth- to sixteenth-century architecture of Christ Church as provincial and second-rate, it might be better to see it as being in the mainstream of later Irish architecture, particularly as an 'early adaptor' of revivalist forms. Lighting a candle, as it were, to the late Gothic elements that can be discerned from old views, is better than cursing the dark of the destructive element inherent in the nineteenth-century Gothic revival.

29 Kenneth Milne, 'Restoration and reorganisation, 1660–1830' in idem (ed.), *Christ Church Cathedral Dublin: a history* (Dublin, 2000), pp 255–97 at p. 268, quoting C6/1/7/3, 21 Apr. 1694.

Richard Stanihurst's Irish *Chronicle* and the crown censors, 1577

PATRICK JAMES HERBAGE

Holinshed's *Chronicles* were a compilation under the guidance of Raphael Holinshed, of the history of England, Ireland and Scotland. In the early 1570s, when Edmund Campion, the esteemed scholar from Oxford, was residing in the Stanihurst household in Dublin, he began to write a history of Ireland from various different sources but, due to time constraints, he could not finish it to the detail and standard it required. Therefore, it was passed to his Oxford student, the Dubliner Richard Stanihurst, who subsequently not only edited Campion's text but also made substantial additions. Stanihurst's finished work was then put forward as an invited contribution to the Holinshed *Chronicle* and was due to be published in 1577. The aim of this paper is to examine the reasons that the Elizabethan censors decided to censor Richard Stanihurst's contribution to the Holinshed *Chronicles*.

In 1559, the year after Elizabeth had been crowned queen, the acts of supremacy and uniformity had been passed, which gave the crown the right to censor any document seen to be seditious or treasonable. Members of Queen Elizabeth's privy council were delegated the task of censoring any publications in England that were deemed to be subversive of the crown's domestic and international policies. As Cyndia Clegg has pointed out, the privy council became aware in December 1577 of Richard Stanihurst's contribution to the 'history of Ireland' in the 1577 edition of the *Chronicle*, 'in which many things are falcelie recited and contrarie to the ancient records'.[1] As a consequence, Stanihurst's text was subjected to rigorous censorship by the authorities, including the excision of his introductory paragraphs.

In the first nine original paragraphs of his history of Henry VIII's reign in Ireland, Stanihurst gives an important apologia for his concept of history and the role of a historian, but it failed to appear in the text as approved by the censors. The importance of his statement of his views, complementing earlier remarks, lies in its humanistic principles in general and its revelation of his approach to contemporary Irish history in particular. As Patterson writes,

> All of the chroniclers had, as they frequently testify, good reason to
> believe that what they were doing teetered constantly on the edge of the

---

1 Cyndia Clegg, *Press censorship in Elizabethan England* (Cambridge, 1997), p. 139.

illegal – that the general constraints on public expression had particular relevance to English historiography.[2]

In what follows we will see how this applies, in the case of Stanihurst's text, to the expression of a version of Irish historiography.

This assessment of the censorship process as it was applied to Stanihurst's history entails a comparison of the text of the original version as composed by the author with that of the substituted text. The censors' intervention occurred too late to prevent some of the earlier copies of the *Chronicles* containing the uncensored text from passing into circulation, so we have the opportunity to contrast it with the changed version that the censors demanded. The bibliographer and publisher, Liam Miller, has made a study of many of the extant copies of the volume of *Chronicles* containing Stanihurst's work in Ireland, and has presented both versions in his fine edition of Holinshed's *Irish Chronicle*, as he calls Stanihurst's contribution to the great compilation.

In the first excised paragraph, Stanihurst justifies to Henry Sidney, his dedicatee and patron, his reasons for writing about near-contemporary events in Ireland, remarking that it was dangerous to give one's opinion on affairs of the state: 'How cumbersome (ryghte honourable) & daungerous a taske it is, to engrosse & divulge the doings of others, especially when the parties registred or their issue are liuing'.[3] This is especially the case when the narration of events touches the honour of living individuals and their families: 'Man by course of nature is so partially affected to himself, and his bloud, as hee will bee more agreeued with the chronicler for recording a peeuish trespasse, then hee will be offended with his friend, for committing an heinous treason'.[4] Thus, in his opening paragraph addressed to Henry Sidney, Stanihurst presciently anticipates the objections of relatives of those depicted in his history.

Stanihurst then elaborated on the perils of the contemporary historian in a characteristically anaphoric passage:

> if the historian be long, hee is accompted a trifler: if he be short, he is taken for a summister: if he commende, he is twighted for a flatterer: if he reprooue, he is holden for a carper: if he pleasant, he is noted for a iester: if hee bee graue, he is reckoned for a drouper: if he misdate, he is named a falsyfer: if he once but trippe, hee is tearmed a stumbler.[5]

In this second paragraph, Stanihurst gives expression to the difficulties in presenting an acceptable history of events. Despite his attempts to report the facts as a chronicler 'as vprightly and as conscionably as he may', he is fearful

---

2 A. Patterson, *Reading Holinshed's Chronicles* (Chicago and London, 1994), p. 7. 3 *Holinshed's Irish chronicles*, ed. Liam Miller and Eileen Power (Mountrath, 1979), appendix, p. 321. 4 Ibid. 5 Ibid.

that there will be those 'that wyll bee more prest to blabbe forth his pelfish faultes, than they will be ready to blaze out his good desertes'.[6] He was under no illusions about the possibility of harsh criticism of his work and indeed his candour did lead to his difficulties with the censors.

While Stanihurst sees it as a duty of the historian to expose wrongdoing, he is conscious of the fact that some chroniclers, wary of being accused of being too honest or else of having omitted crucial details, decide not to proceed with their chronicling. They are thus open to the charge of having altered the historical record: 'Heere, saye they, thys exployte is omitted: there that policie is not detected: here thys saying woulde haue beene enterlaced: that treacherie shoulde haue beene displayd'.[7] The issue of 'treacherie' being 'displayd' is particularly apposite in the light of Stanihurst's account of the Fitzgerald rebellion with which the censors found fault. It is thus not surprising that those whom he terms 'historiographers', 'taking the way to bee thorny, the credite slipperie, the carpers to bee many, woulde in no case bee meddlers, choosing rather to sitte by theyr owne fyre obscurely at home, than to bee bayted with enuious tongs openly abrode'.[8] By contrast,

> others on the contrary side, beeyng resolute fellowes, and trampling vnder foote these curious faultfynders, would sticke to put themselues forthe in presse, and maugre all theyr heartes, to buskle forwarde, and rushe through the pykes of theyr quipping nippes, and bityng frumps.[9]

Stanihurst's approach is to take a middle ground between the extremities. This could be misconstrued as nervousness on Stanihurst's part and he justifies himself to Sidney that he will not be extreme and neither will he sit idly by without giving his account of events. He writes that

> I, taking the meane between both these extremities, helde if for better, not to bee so feynte and peeuishe a meacocke, as to shrinke and couche myne head, for euery mizeling shoure, nor yet to beare my selfe so high in heart, as to praunce and iette lyke a proude gennet through the streete, not weighing the barking of currish bandogges.[10]

And continues

> and therefore, if I shall be founde in my hystorie sometime too tedious, sometime too spare, sometime too fawning in commendyng the lyuing, sometime to flatte in reprouing the dead: I take GOD to witness, that myne offence therein proceedeth of ignorance, and not of sette wilfulnesse.[11]

---

6 Ibid. 7 Ibid. 8 Ibid. 9 Ibid. 10 Ibid., pp 321–2. 11 Ibid., p. 322.

In these last few paragraphs, Stanihurst is tentative about his writings and the effect they will have. He takes the unusual step of defending his work in case there are any faults found. He states 'yet I must confesse, that as I was not able, vppon so little leasure, to knowe all that was said or done, so I was not willing, for sundry respects, to write euery trim tram, that I knew to be said or done'.[12] He characteristically recounts a humorous anecdote about a painter in Oxford, one Doly, who was commissioned to engrave the Ten Commandments, but omitted one. When chided by his patron about the omission, the painter declared that when his master had well observed and kept the nine commandments that were already drawn, he undertook to finish the tenth. In the last few sentences of the eighth paragraph, then, he turns his attention to the readers and pleads with them to be lenient in respect of any falsification of facts that he has recorded.

Stanihurst concludes his introduction by pleading his case to Henry Sidney, where he states

> that the worke is painefull, and I doe forecast, that the misconstruction may be perillous: the toylesomnesse of the payne, I referre to my priuate knowledge, the abandoning of the perill, I committe to your honourable patronage, not doubting thereby, to be shielded against the sinister glosing of malitious interpreters.[13]

Stanihurst then writes: 'thus betaking your lordshippe to God, I craue youre attentiueness, in perusing a cantell or parcel of the Irish historie, that here ensueth'.[14] The main text now begins for Stanihurst and this is also where the text begins in the version approved by the censors.

Many political reasons can be ascertained as to why the crown censors decided to omit Stanihurst's opening remarks on how history should be written. Firstly, the dedication to Henry Sidney who found himself embroiled in the courtly factions of Queen Elizabeth's court. In the censored text, the opening dedication to Henry Sidney is excised and the history of Henry VIII follows on from that of Henry VII without any break for dedications. Secondly, if the crown censors wanted to undermine a work they found to discredit the character of the earl of Ormond, who was the queen's relation, they may have chosen to omit the piece in which Stanihurst defends his own text and therefore allow the readers to come to their own conclusion without any influence from the writer. Thirdly, it also shows an Old English response to New English Plantation. Stanihurst as a key member of Old English society in Ireland was providing a history of Ireland to show that Ireland was conquered and did not need a new wave of settlers, as the only result would be chaos and similar events that followed the arrival of the Anglo-Normans into Ireland in 1169.

12 Ibid.   13 Ibid.   14 Ibid.

Fourthly, it shows the threat of the printed word and the length to which the authorities would go in order to keep control of the press and public opinion. Humanistic writers, like Stanihurst, tended to be more liberal in the 1570s and the crown would do everything in its power to regain authority.

Let us now turn to the actual text of Stanihurst's history of Henry VIII's reign in Ireland to examine the details of what was cut from his original text. We will see how Stanihurst's fears were realized when the privy council in London ordered that his work be censored. Among other changes, they doctored the tone of Stanihurst's personality descriptions of key characters in his narrative and made amendments relating to sensitive issues that bore upon the politics of the 1570s. There are three main elements in the section that was cut by the censors: the coverage of the career of Gerald (Gearóid Mór), the eighth earl of Kildare, that of his son Gerald (Gearóid Óg), the ninth earl, and the brief rule of Silken Thomas, Lord Offaly, before the rebellion began in June 1534. The complete removal of the introductory passage meant that the edited text flowed directly from the earlier to the later part of Gearóid Mór Fitzgerald's career, giving him the significant position of opening the narrative on Henry VIII's reign in Ireland. In the original version of Stanihurst's opening paragraph of the history of the reign of Henry VIII, there is a phrase, 'of whom mention was made in the later ende of the seconde booke',[15] referring to the eighth earl of Kildare, Gearóid Mór. This reference is rendered redundant because of the omitting of the intervening discourse of the original text that separated Book Two from a separate Book Three. Now the text runs on, without a formal division. In this opening paragraph, both the original and the censored texts give a description of Kildare and a reference to his burial place. He is recorded as being 'a mightie man of stature, full of honore and courage, who had bin deputie, and Lord Iustice of Ireland first and last, three and thirtie years, deceased at Kildare the thirde of September, and lyeth entombed in the chore of Christes Church at Dublin, in a chappell by hym founded.'[16]

The first substantial issue that Stanihurst brings to the reader's attention in this section is the intense rivalry between the earls of Ormond and Kildare. He shows how both earls became divided by the inner factionalism that was occurring over in England and the taking of sides by each between the house of Lancaster and the house of York. Stanihurst writes that 'the plot of whiche mutuall grudge was grounded vpon the factious dissention, that was raysed in England, between the houses of Yorke & Lancaster, Kildare cleauing to Yorke, and Ormond relying to Lancaster'.[17] For the censors to omit this piece from the original raises many questions concerning the motive and reasoning behind such an act. The omission of the reference to the Wars of the Roses may have been regarded as avoiding an unwelcome reminder of an era of embarrassing lawlessness.

---

15 Ibid.; this quotation followed Stanihurst's opening statement concerning 'Girald Fitzgeralde, Earle of Kildare'.   **16** Ibid., p. 322.   **17** Ibid.

Included in this long passage cut by the censors is a reference to the abiding and ongoing rivalry and hatred between the Butlers and the Fitzgeralds:

> To vpholding of whiche discord, both these noble men laboured, with tooth and nayle, to ouercome, and consequently to ouerthrow one the other: And for asmuch as they were in honour Peeres, they wrought by hooke and by crooke to be in authoritie superiours.[18]

As will be seen, there was consistently evident in the strategy employed by the censors a tendency to rectify any pro-Geraldine bias on the part of Stanihurst and a consequent protectiveness of the reputation of various members of the Ormond family, with which Queen Elizabeth was associated by blood. It may have been expedient to veil the implacable integrity of the rivalry to spare the feelings of members of the Ormond family and their connections including the queen. Moreover, reference to the virulence of the quarrel may well have enflamed inter-family passions in the present.

Stanihurst shows how

> Wherevpon, Ormonde addressed his letters to the deputie, specifying a slaunder raysed on hym and his, that hee purposed to deface his gouernemente, and to withstand his authoritie, and for the clearing of himself and of his adherentes, so it stoode with the deputie his pleasure, he woulde make his speedy repayre to Dublin, and there in open audience, woulde purge hymselfe of all suche odious crimes, of whiche he was wrongfully suspected.[19]

Stanihurst's next three paragraphs are concerned with this event of Lord Ormond marching on Dublin. For Stanihurst, this point is very important within his subtext, as it showed that Ormond was out of control and wanted to bring chaos into Ireland and challenge the power of the earl of Kildare. The city was in an uproar and it took a handshake within the confines of St Patrick's Cathedral to end the dispute between both men. Stanihurst writes that

> Kildare, pursuing Ormond to the chapiter house dore, vndertooke on hys honor, that hee should receyue no villanie. Wherevpon, the recluse crauing his lordships hand to assure hym his life, there was a clift in the chapiter house dore, pierced at a trice, to the end both the earles should haue shaken hands, and bee reconciled.[20]

This paragraph not only shows that peace has broken out between both noblemen, but also that, for Stanihurst, Kildare has been the appeaser in this

18 Ibid.   19 Ibid., p. 323.   20 Ibid.

situation and Lord Ormond the aggressor. From the point of view of the censors, the omission of this piece of Stanihurst's text shows that they were uncertain about how this rivalry would impact on contemporary events in Ireland. This episode of factionalism reflected credit on neither side, harking back to the baronial conflicts of the pre-Tudor era, and thus may have been regarded by the censors as of less than pressing interest for Elizabethans.

In his portraits of the eighth earl of Kildare and James, Lord Ormond, Stanihurst obviously favoured the former, humorously depicting his larger-than-life personality and mercurial temper. He describes an occasion where Kildare was professing to use violence when Boyce (one of his gentlemen) approached the earl and said

> So it is, and if it like youre good lordshippe, one of youre horsemen promised mee a choice horse, if I snippe one heare from your berde. Well quoth the earle, I agree thereto, but if thou plucke anye more than one, I promise thee to bring my fyst from thine eare.[21]

Stanihurst then balances this story with the earl showing signs of good nature against one of his servants when he uses the wrong sauce on a partridge but when he enters the kitchen to berate the cook he changes his mind and instead he commends the building of such a room.[22] He writes that the

> olde earle beeyng, as is aforesayde, soone hote and soone colde, was of the Englische well beloued, a good iusticier, a suppressor of the rebels, a warrioure incomparable, towards the nobles that he fanysed not, some-what headlong and vnruly.[23]

After the censors' work, that passage reads

> Kildare was open and playne, not able to rule himself when hee was moued, desperate in hys moody displeasure both of word and deede, of the English welbeloued, a good iusticier, a warrioure incomparable, towards the nobles that he fancied not, somewhat headlong and unruly.[24]

Perhaps the involvement of the family in rebellion in 1534–5 rendered it less deserving of the accolade of being a suppressor of rebels.

We find that, just as they excised the narrative of the battle between Butler and Geraldine partisans in the streets of Dublin, the censors cut Stanihurst's

---

21 Ibid., p. 324.   22 'who being in a chafe, for the wrong saucing of a Partridge, rose suddenly from the table, meaning to haue reasoned the matter with hys cooke: hauyng entred into the Kitchen, drowning in obliuion hys chalenge, hee began to commende the buyldyng of the roome, wherein hee was at no tyme before, and so leauyng the Cooke vuncontrold, he returned to his guests merly': ibid., p. 324.   23 Ibid., p. 324.   24 Ibid., p. 253.

account of Kildare's freewheeling campaigns against the Gaelic clans: 'In hys warres hee vsed, for policie, a retchlesse kynde of diligence, or a headye care-lesnesse, to the ende hys souldyers shoulde not faynte in theyr attempts were the enimie neuer of so great power.'[25] These vestiges of bastard feudalism and coign and livery were out of fashion in the 1570s. The tribute paid to Gearóid Mór is perfunctory, the award of the knighthood of the garter being mentioned, but the following passage was cut:

> hauing triumphantly vanquished the Irishe in that conflict, hee was shortly after, as well as for that, as other his valiant exploytes made knight of the garter, and in the fifth yeare of Henry the eyght in that renowne and honoure hee dyed, wherein for the space of manye years hee lyued.[26]

For Stanihurst, this point is crucial to his subtext because he wants to show that the crown did recognize the earl of Kildare as a defender of the king's lands in Ireland against the Irish native. For the censors, however, any piece describing the political turmoil in Ireland would be a deterrent for the new settlers travelling to Ireland in the 1570s. Ormond is again in the next paragraph shown in a bad light by Stanihurst when he describes how Ormond accused the citizens of Dublin of being treacherous and looked to the court of Rome for help. As Stanihurst writes,

> the heathenish riot of the citizens of Dublin in rushing into the churche armed, polluting with slaughter the consecrated place, defacing the images, prostrating the reliques, racing downe aultars, with barbarous outcries, more like miscreant Sarazans then Christian Catholiques.[27]

From the above passage, the censors had reason to omit some lines from Stanihurst's text as Ormond was an ancestor of the queen. For Stanihurst, however, it showed Ormond looking for outside help in dealing with major events, while Kildare would have dealt with the situation himself.

The career of Gerald (Gearóid Óg), the ninth earl of Kildare, is censored less dramatically, but nonetheless the authorities took the opportunity to make some significant changes. An ominous addition to the character description of Gerald as being 'a gentleman valiant and well spoken' occurs in the statement: 'yet in his latter time overtaken with vehement suspition of sundry treasons'.[28] Stanihurst certainly had not written that in his original account. Some less than flattering references to Lady Margaret, Gerald's sister, and her husband, Piers Roe Butler, are cut, perhaps out of deference to their grandson, Earl Thomas of Ormond, to whom Elizabeth was close, as cousin and patron. In the succeeding passage, the censors again censored a piece that contained recordings

25 Ibid., p. 325.   26 Ibid.   27 Ibid.   28 Ibid., p. 253.

of events that show Ireland in turmoil. Stanihurst writes that 'While the lord lieutenante sate at dynner in the castle of Dublin, hee hearde news that the Moores with a mayne army were euen at the entrie of the bordures, readye to inuade the English Pale'.[29]

The substance of the account of the confrontation between Gearóid Óg and Cardinal Wolsey in London is left unchanged in the amended version of the *Chronicles*. That the exchanges reflected poorly on the cardinal would not have been contentious in the 1570s. But the involvement of the duke of Norfolk may have been considered more politically fraught, and perhaps this is why the following passage of Stanihurst's original is excised:

> The duke of Norffolke who was late lieutenant in Ireland, perceyuing the cardinal to be sore bent against the noble man, rather for the deadly hatred hee bare his house, than for anye great matter he had wherewith to charge his person, stept to the king, & craued Kildare to be his prisoner, offring to be bound for his forth comming, ouer and aboue all his lands, bodie for bodie. Wherevpon to the cardinall his greate grief, the prisoner was bayled, and honourably by the duke enterteyned.[30]

The importance of this quotation from Stanihurst can be seen in the following point where he suggests that when the earl of Ossory is made lord deputy, in place of Kildare, then the Irish rise in open rebellion. Stanihurst records that 'During his abode in the duke his house, Oneyle and Oconor and all their friends and alyes, watching their time to annoy the Pale, made open insur- rection against the earle of Ossorie then lord deputie of Irelande'.[31] Stanihurst continues by 'purporting that all these hurly burlies were of purpose raysed by the meanes of Kyldare, to the blemishing and steyning of his brother Ossorie his gouernment'.[32] Even with this quotation, Stanihurst is showing that Kildare has complete rule in Ireland whether he is lord deputy or not.

A mandatum was then conjured by the cardinal to bring about the execution of the earl, but an interception by the king himself gains a reprieve for the earl of Kildare. The following year, Wolsey was out of favour and the earl of Kildare looked forward to a triumphant return to Ireland. As Stanihurst writes, 'thus broke vp the storme for that time, and the next yeare Woolsey was cast out of favour, and within few years, sir William Skeffington was sent ouer l.deputie and brought with him the erle pardoned and ryd from all his troubles'.[33] This sentence is also contained in the censored text, but another sentence is added to the point of Kildare returning to Ireland. The censored version goes: 'Who would not thinke but these lessons should haue schooled so wise a man, and warned him rather by experience of aduersities past to cure olde sores, than for ioy of this presente fortune to minde seditious driftes to come'.[34] Again, this

---

29 Ibid., p. 327.   **30** Ibid., p. 332.   **31** Ibid.   **32** Ibid.   **33** Ibid.   **34** Ibid.

portentous note reflects more the views of the authorities who censored the text rather than those of Stanihurst himself who was consistently supportive of the ninth earl of Kildare.

Stanihurst's account of the speech made before the municipal community of Dublin by William Skeffington in praise of the earl of Kildare when they arrived back in Ireland was cut in the altered version, perhaps because it was too flattering of the Kildares:

> Master maior, and maister recorder, you haue at length this noble man here present, for whom you sore longed, whylest he was absent. And after many stormes by him susteyned, hee hath nowe to the comforte of his friends, to the confusion of his foes, subdued violence with pacience, iniuries with sufferance, and malice with obedience: and such butchers as of hatred thirsted after his bloud, are nowe taken for outcaste mastiues, littred in currish bloud.[35]

From Stanihurst's point of view, this quotation is highly significant to his subtext, as it shows the king's representative in Ireland in complete support of the earl of Kildare. Also taken out is a narrative of some of the events of Skeffington's tenure as lord deputy, including an account of a riot in Dublin caused by a conflict between Skeffington's soldiers and some city apprentices. It may not have been appropriate to depict the haplessness of an English governor who was suffering by comparison with the native candidate, the earl of Kildare.

The final section of Stanihurst's text that came under scrutiny by the queen's censors was that concerning the causality of the rebellion of Thomas, Lord Offaly. Stanihurst's text described how both the earl of Kildare and Skeffington, who becomes jealous of Kildare, now find themselves on opposite sides:

> Skeffington, supposing that he was put beside the quishion by the secrete canuassing of Kildare his friends, conceyued thereof a great iealousie, being therein the deeper drenched, bycause that Kildare hauing receyued the meane priuate person, to dance attendance among other suiters in his house at Dublyn, named the Carbry.[36]

This rivalry gives a context to the letter-writing campaign of rumour and innuendo that later prompted Thomas Fitzgerald into revolt, but this essential background is missing from the sanitized version, rendering the reasons for the breaking out into rebellion less acute.

Kildare is again called to London to answer treasonable charges against the crown. In Stanihurst's text, he writes: 'Wherevpon Kildare was commanded by

---

35 Ibid.   36 Ibid., p. 334.

sharpe letters to repayre into Englande, leauing such a person for the furniture of that realm, and the gouernance of the lande in his absence, for whose doings he would answere'.[37] The censored text changed Stanihurst's quotation by continuing 'Wherevpon he was agayne commanded by sharp letters, to repayre into England'.[38] Stanihurst continues by recording in full the speech made by the earl of Kildare to his heir and son, Thomas. Anything, however, that elicited sympathy for the Fitzgerald family in these circumstances is removed. Thus, Gearóid Óg's lengthy and moving farewell to his son, Thomas, is completely excised. Stanihurst may have wished to separate the earl of Kildare from any responsibility for Lord Thomas' actions in the mid-1530s, with the speech containing a warning to the young man against any rash or ill-considered actions. Stanihurst, writing in the 1570s, was trying to downplay the role of the house of Kildare in the rebellion: 'my will is that you behaue your selfe so wisely in these greene yeares, as that to the comfort of your friendes, you may enjoy the pleasure of summer, gleane and reape the fruite of your haruest'.[39] The censorship of this piece indicates unwillingness on the part of the authorities to countenance any exculpation.

The original version of the History contained a highly unflattering description of four 'belwethers and caterpillars'[40] of Thomas' overethrow. Firstly, he describes John Alen, archbishop of Dublin, whose 'firste grudge towards the Giraldines, proceeded from the great affection he bare his lorde and maister the cardinall'.[41] The second enemy was 'Sir Iohn Alen, knight, first secretarie to this archbishop, after became mayster of the rolles, lastly lorde chancellor',[42] 'reputed by such as did stomacke his proceedings as little more than a villaine'. The gratuitous information is added that Archbishop Alen had a long-running affair with Sir John Alen's wife, being the father of some children by her. Thomas Canon, secretary to William Skeffington, was the third agent of Thomas' downfall, 'who thinking to be reuenged on Kildare for puttyng his Lord and maister beside the cushen, as hee surmised, was very willyng to haue an oare in that boate'.[43] Fourthly, Stanihurst describes Robert Cowly, 'first baylife in Dublin, after seraunt to the Ladie Margaret Fitz Giralde countesse of Ormond and Ossorie, lastly maister of the rolles in Ireland',[44] as 'a sower of discord'. As Stanihurst records, 'These foure as byrdes of one feather, were supposed to bee open enimies to the house of Kyldare, bearing that sway in the common wealth, as they were not occasioned, as they thought, eyther to craue the friendshippe of the Giraldines, or greatly to feare theyr hatred and enmitie'.[45]

As a result, Kildare's enemies began conspiring in Dublin and London and, according to Stanihurst,

---

37 Ibid., p. 335. **38** Ibid., p. 261. **39** Ibid., p. 335. **40** Ibid. **41** Ibid., p. 336. **42** Ibid.
43 Ibid., p. 337. **44** Ibid. **45** Ibid.

> The enimies therefore hauing well nighe knedded the dough that should
> haue beene baked for the Giraldines bane, deuised that secrete rumors
> should sprinkle to and fro, that the earle of Kildare his execution was
> intended in Englande and that vpon his death the Lorde Thomas and all
> his bloud should haue bene apprehended in Irelande.[46]

None of this conspiracy involving leading officials in the Irish administration
is retained in the final version, apart from the story of the fateful letter from an
anonymous source among Skeffington's entourage. This paves the way for the
actions of 'the Lorde Thomas who, being youthfull, rash and headlong, and
assuring himself, that the knot of all the force of Ireland was twisted vnder his
gyrdle'[47] rushed into rebellion.

As far as is known, the rest of Richard Stanihurst's text of the history of
Henry VIII's reign is uncensored and he continues detailing the events of the
Kildare rebellion. The events of 1534 and 1535 seem, within this new framework,
to have been caused by irrational fear and misinformation, and are not now
ascribed to conscious plotting by high-placed members of the regime, whose
reputations are therefore intact. The Kildare dynasty could be seen to have
brought its ignominy upon itself. This could be contextualized in the later
1570s by reference to the restiveness of the restored eleventh earl. The history
of the events of the 1530s as doctored in 1577 might serve as a warning to him
or any other recalcitrant lord as to the consequences of disobedience. To those
such as Stanihurst who hankered after the restoration of native governance, the
message was that the days of autonomous lordship of the earlier Tudor period
were over. The thrust of this apologia in the excised version of the aims and
methods of contemporary history was borne out: 'how cumbersome and
daungerous a taske it is, to engross and divulge the doings of thers, especially
when the parties registered or their issue are liuing'.[48]

46 Ibid., p. 338.   47 Ibid.   48 Ibid.

Printing in Dublin: the first sixty years

DERMOT McGUINNE

Anyone conducting research into early printing in Dublin must, in fairness, pay tribute to Earnest McClintock Dix for his authoritative work on this topic conducted one hundred years ago. So thorough were his efforts that followers are often left having to satisfy themselves with identifying some oversight or minor error on his part. In this regard, I wish to acknowledge my own indebtedness to him.

Printing came relatively late to Dublin, with Humphrey Powell setting up his press in 1550, roughly seventy-five years after a similar development in England and one hundred years following the invention of printing in this manner by Gutenberg in Mainz. The acts of the privy council of England, in an entry dated 18 July 1550, inform us that 'A warrant to deliver xxli [£20] unto Powell the printer given him by the king's majestie towards his setting up in Irelande'. Prior to this date, he seems to have carried on his business at Holborn in London.

The patent of king's printer entitled the holder to certain privileges of publishing and printing such works as bibles, prayer books and other works like official orders and proclamations approved by the privy council. It provided a certain status that improved business potential. In Ireland, this position initially had a greater significance for, in addition to establishing exclusive rights to printing

> Books, statutes, grammars, almanacks, acts of parliament, proclamations, injunctions, bibles and books of the New Testament and all other books whatsoever as well in the English tongue as the Irish,

it also allowed the holder to confiscate such works that may have been printed by others or imported from abroad without permission.[1] The power of print technology was greatly feared by some in those early days, leading one nervous cleric to declare that 'we must root out printing or printing will root us out'.[2]

The fact that Powell's name was not entered on the patent rolls has led to some suggestions that he did not officially hold the position of king's printer in Ireland, but the fact that he received royal sponsorship from the court of

---

1 Proclamation by the lord deputy and council dated 15 July 1620. See E.R. McClintock Dix, 'The law as to printing in Ireland before the Act of Union', *Irish Book Lover* (Sept.–Oct. 1934), 111. 2 The vicar of Croydon from the pulpit of St Paul's Cross, quoted in 'The king's printer in Ireland, 1551–1919' by J.W. Hammond, *Dublin Historical Record*, 11 (1949), 29.

fol. Cxl.

☞ Certaine notes for the moze plaine explication and decent ministracion of thynges, conteyned in this booke.

 N the saiyng oz syngyng of Mattens and Euensong, Baptizyng and Buriyng, the minister, in parishe Churches and Chapels annexed to the same, shall vse a Surplesse. And in all Cathedzall churches and Colledges, the archedeacons, Deanes, Pzouostes maisters, Pzebendaries and felowes, beyng Graduates, maie vse in the quier beside theyz Surplesses, suche hoodes as perteineth to their seuerall degrees, which thei haue taken in any vniuersitie within this realme. But in all other places, euery minister shall be at libertie to vse any Surplesse oz no. It is also seemely that Graduates, when thei doe pzeache, should vse suche hoodes as perteineth to theyz seuerall degrees.

And whensoeuer the Byshop shall celebzate the holy Communion in the Churche, oz execute any other publike ministracion: he shall haue vpon hym, besyde his Rochette, a Surplesse oz Aulbe, and a Cope oz Uestment, and also his Pastozall staffe in his hand, ozels bozne oz holden by his Chapelepne.

As touchyng kneelyng, crossyng, holdyng vp of handes, knockyng vpon the bzeast, and other gestures: they maie be vsed oz left, as euery mans deuocion serueth, without blame.

Also vpon Chzistmasdaie, Easter day, the Ascension day, Whitsondaie, and the feast of the Trinitie, maie be vsed any part of holy scripture hereafter to be certainely limitted and appointed, in the steade of the Lateny.

If there be a sermon, oz foz other great cause, the Curate by his discrecion, maie leaue out the Latenie, Glozia in excelsis, the Crede, the Homely and the exhoztacion to the Communion.

FINIS.

Impzinted by Humfrey Powell, Pzinter to the Kynges Maiestie, in his hyghnesse realme of Ireland, dwellyng in the citee of Dublin in the great toure by the Crane.

Cvm priuilegio ad imprimendum solum.

ANNO DOMINI.

M. D. Li.

12.1 Colophon of *The Book of Common Prayer*, the first book printed in Ireland, 1551.

Edward VI would suggest that he was sent to Ireland as the approved state printer. Indeed, he claimed this privilege himself – for example, the imprint to his first important work, *The Bok of Common Prayer*, states

> Imprinted by Humfrey Powell, printer to the kyngs maiestie, in his hyghnesse realm of Ireland, dwelling in the citee of Dublin in the great toure by the crane.

Dix suggests that this location 'may have been in the vicinity where Crane Lane is today'[3] – but Crane Lane led down to the location of a later crane. The tower in question was that which became known as Prickett's Tower alongside an earlier crane at the bottom of present-day Winetavern Street, roughly at the point of the Liffey entrance to the Civic Offices. Complaints regarding the commercial presence along the wall and towers led to concerns that the military defence role of the wall was being diluted. Efforts were made to restore it to its intended purpose, resulting in the eviction of many traders. We can only speculate that this resulted in Powell's removal, but, whatever the circumstances, the next known book printed by him was in 1566, at which time he was operating from his address in St Nicholas Street.

Following the English Act of Uniformity in January 1549, the use of the Edwardian *Book of Common Prayer* was imposed. To begin with, it is most likely that copies were imported from England to meet the requirement here until such time as copies could be made available by Powell. He completed this in 1551 and, by any standard, it was a most sophisticated production (fig. 12.1). It demonstrated that Powell was a highly accomplished printer not inclined to take the easy solution. In fact, some features of his typography would present a challenge to present-day typographers sitting at their computer keyboards. His type repertoire consisted primarily of black letter later often referred to as old english style. He used three sizes in the setting of the *Book of Common Prayer* together with italic for margin notes and on the title page together with roman and a display roman main title.

Dix states that 'the most interesting discovery I ever made in Irish bibliography was the finding of so many sheets of a copy of the *Book of Common Prayer* ... in the Royal Irish Academy'.[4] Just two complete copies of this book remain – one in Trinity College, Dublin, and the other in Emanuel College, Cambridge. The partial copy, discovered by Dix in the Royal Irish Academy, contains just thirty-four pages out of 140.

His next piece of work was the Proclamation against Shane O'Neill. The imprint states that it was 'Imprinted in Dublyn, by Humfrey Powell'. No date

3 E.R. McClintock Dix, 'Humfrey Powell, the first Dublin printer', *Proceedings of the Royal Irish Academy*, 27C (1908), 215.   4 E.R. McClintock Dix, *Printing in Dublin prior to 1601* (2nd ed., Dublin, 1932), p. xxiii.

is given, but evidence is provided in the state papers establishing 1561 as the date of printing.[5] Powell uses his black letter with a display roman for the heading and a decorative initial capital letter similar to those used in the *Book of Common Prayer*. There followed another notice, a Proclamation against the O'Connors 'Imprynted at Dublyn by Humfrey Powell, the 16, of August, 1564'. This followed the same general design layout. The fourth and final work extant printed by Powell was an eight-page booklet titled *A brefe declaration of certain principal articles of religion* also in black letter: 'Imprynted at Dublyn in Saint Nicholas Street, by Humfrey Powell, prynter appointed for the realme of Irelande'. Undoubtedly he printed other works that have not survived.

We are informed of a number of financial considerations from the Fitzwilliam papers at Milton and enrolled accounts, where it is recorded that Powell was lent £40 in 1556 'to furnish himself with print and letters for the imprinting of the acts of parliament of this realm and other necessary books'. It adds that by October two years later he had repaid just £10. In May 1564 he was lent a further £13 6s. 8d. which, together with the earlier balance, does not seem to have been repaid. Sometime between May 1560 and June 1567 he is recorded as being in receipt of a government pension.[6]

What precisely happened to Powell is unknown, for his name does not appear in any official context in Ireland following this date. One thing I feel certain of is that, had he the means of continuing his business and printing in the Irish language, we would have heard of him, for it was about this time that efforts focused sharply on producing reformed religious texts directed at Irish speakers.

At the time, Irish was the principal language spoken throughout the country. Even within the Pale it was widely used among the native classes – a fact that did not go unnoticed by Queen Elizabeth and the administrators of the reformed church. At a personal level, it is said of Elizabeth that she had a particular interest in languages and enjoyed being able to converse with visitors to her court. To facilitate her, Baron Delvin (Christopher Nugent) prepared a manuscript at her request, an 'Irish–Latten–Englishe primer', which set down the Irish alphabet, together with some words and phrases in Irish with Latin and English translations. Nugent pays tribute to Elizabeth for her interest in the language:

> Among the manifold actions … that beare testymonie to the worlde of your maiestyes great affection, tending to the reformation of Ireland, there is noe one (in my opinion) that more euydent showithe the same,

5 The year of printing is suggested as 1561, since this is the date established by a contemporaneous letter confirming the sending of the Proclamation to England: see *Calendar of state papers, Ireland*, 1561.   6 Historical Manuscripts Commission, *De l'Isle and Dudley*, 1, p. 397, quoted in 'Information about Dublin Printers, 1556–1573, in English

then the desyer your highnes hath to understand the language of your
people there.

It is recorded in the Fitzwilliam abstract of accounts from 1559–69 that a
payment was made for the making of irish type. It involved the provision of
£66 13s. 4d. 'for the making of carecter to print the New Testament in Irish'.
There followed a repayment demand in the absence of the promised work.[7]
Three years later, however, with the help of John O'Kearney and Nicholas
Walsh, later treasurer and chancellor of St Patrick's Cathedral in Dublin
respectively, who were studying at the time at Cambridge, an irish font type-
face was produced at about one-third the cost of the earlier consideration.
Elizabeth, in this way, initiated the preparation of the first irish character
printing type, thus setting in train a process that in typographic terms at least
contributed to the isolation of the language and fated its expression through
print to a continuous fiscal struggle.

Produced sometime shortly prior to 1571, it used a combination of Irish
letters and the roman type of Pierre Hautin together with an italic capital and
lower-case a. It was used for the first time to print a broadsheet poem *Tuar
ferge foighide Dhé*. The only known remaining copy was left by Archbishop
Matthew Parker to Corpus Christi College, Cambridge, with the inscription
written across the top 'This Irishe balade printed in Irelande who belike use
the olde Saxon carecte'. The link between Parker and the printer type-founder
John Day, whom he sponsored, together with the archbishop's interest in the
Irish language and the resemblance of some of the irish letters to those of
Day's anglo-saxon type has led some bibliographical historians to argue that
the irish were taken directly from the anglo-saxon. Dix contributed to this
theory, stating: 'I venture to submit that this type was simply anglo-saxon type
cast by John Day in 1567 for Archbishop Parker, and used as if irish type'.[8]

A comparison of the two faces clearly establishes the inaccuracy of this
opinion (see fig. 12.2). While both combine traditional script-like forms with
existing roman letters, the roman and the newly cut special characters differ in
the irish from the anglo-saxon font significantly. While it may seem surprising
that no effort was made to use the anglo-saxon font, the fact remains that the
irish characters were cut independently and consequently it is unlikely that
Day played any role in this operation. Furthermore, the font contained an
extensive range of ligatures found in Irish manuscripts and quite foreign to the
anglo-saxon font.

Financial Records' by D.B. Quinn, *Irish Book Lover* (May 1942), 113.   **7** *Calendar of state
papers, Ireland, 1509–73* (London, 1860), p. 356.   8 E.R. McClintock Dix, 'William Kearney,
the second earliest known printer in Dublin', *Proceedings of the Royal Irish Academy*, 28C
(1910), 157.

A B C D E F G Ꟈ I L ꟼ N O P R S T V

a b c ꝺ e ꝼ ʒ h i l m n o p ꞃ ꞅ ꞇ u

a b c ꝺ e ꝼ ʒ h ɟ l m n o p r s ꞇ u

a b c ꝺ e ꝼ ʒ h ɟ l m n o p ꞃ ꞅ ꞇ u

12.2 John Day's anglo-saxon type (above) and the Queen Elizabeth irish type (below), enlarged to facilitate comparison.

It was also used to print the catechism *Aibidil Gaoidheilge & Caiticiosma*. In the preface, the author Seán Ó Cearnaigh (John O'Kearney) paid tribute to Elizabeth for providing the type:

> Here you have, O reader, the first fruits and progeny of that good and very laborious work which I have been producing and devising for you for a long time, that is, the true and perfect type of the Irish language which will open to you that road which leads you to knowledge and which, nevertheless, has been closed to you formerly ... I have undertaken (as I saw no one else who would do so) the labour and toil of bringing this type to the form in which it is now seen, at the cost of the high, pious, great and mighty prince Elizabeth.

The title page indicates that it was translated into Irish by O'Kearney and printed in irish type in Dublin at the expense of Alderman John Usher (at his house) at the head of the bridge on 20 June 1571 (fig. 12.3). The date is significant, for forty years later, to the day, the Irish Franciscans printed their counter version of the catechism in Antwerp on 20 June 1611.

Perhaps immediately prior to the catechism, the abovementioned broadsheet poem was printed also using this irish type. The poem gives an account of God's anger on the day of the Last Judgment by Pilib Bocht Ó hUiginn, a fifteenth-century Franciscan friar. The only remaining copy is in Corpus Christi College, Cambridge. It is a single sheet measuring 39 by 28cm, printed one side with an under inked same impression on the reverse, leading many commentators to conclude that the poem was simply a sample test piece printed in preparation for the catechism. In addition to the text type, both works incorporate the decorative capital letters that had earlier been used so

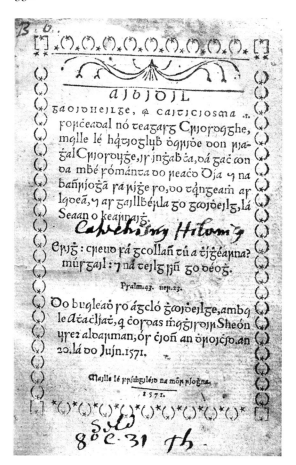

12.3 Title page of *Aibidil Gaoidheilge agus caiticiosma* (*Irish alphabet and catechism*), the first book to use the Queen Elizabeth irish type, 1571.

effectively by Powell, suggesting that at least that part of Powell's type supply had been moved to Usher's premises.

No printer is named on either the broadsheet or the catechism. This has led to much deliberation regarding the identity of those involved. With their academic and administrative backgrounds, neither O'Kearney nor Walsh, nor indeed Usher himself, would likely have been directly involved in the printing. There is no evidence of any other printer working in Dublin at this precise time. One likely candidate, however, William Kearney, a nephew of John (Seán), did emerge later, but 1571 is a little early for him to have been practising as a printer in Dublin.

William is first mentioned as a printer in the acts of the privy council of England in 1587, in which he is recommended as printer of the long-awaited New Testament in Irish. The record describes how his training as a printer and his knowledge of irish type had developed over the previous fourteen years.[9] Calculating back fourteen years takes us to 1573, just two years short of the year in which the catechism was printed. A warrant dated October 1591 records permission for William's passage to Ireland and exhorts all to facilitate him in the printing of Irish bibles. An undated letter from the Irish privy council intended for the attention of all bishops, adds further testimony to William's familiarity with irish type. It confirms William as a suitable printer who had trained over the previous twenty years.[10]

Remarkably, despite such strong recommendation and a career full of trouble and controversy here, the only extant piece of printing that carries his imprint is the Proclamation against Hugh O'Neill, the earl of Tyrone: 'Imprinted in the cathedral church of the blessed Trinitie by William Kearney printer to the queenes most excellent maiestie. 1595'. It is printed in black letter save for the heading, the introductory text and imprint which are in roman type. His black letter font is different from that used by Powell, as is the initial decorative capital letter. It is recorded that an Irish version was also printed, but in one account it is noted that the Irish copy had not been received.[11] Dix comments: 'there is a statement written, I believe, in pencil upon the original proclamation in the Public Records Office in London that there was an Irish edition of this proclamation. No doubt William Kearney was competent to execute such printing'. Indeed, my own examination of the original did reveal written in pencil in a modern hand on the reverse the statement that 'There was an Irish one sent' dated curiously 12 January 1895, just five years or so prior to Dix's comment. The word *sent* rather than *printed* is of interest in that the original reference to the Irish version in a letter from Sir Geff Fenton to William Burghley in 1595 mentions that he had 'sent your lordship one proclamation in English and another in Irish'. The pencilled inscription, therefore, in my opinion, does not suggest that the Irish version had been seen by the author of the pencilled note. Nor indeed is it recorded as having been seen by anyone at any time.

Kearney worked as a printer at the newly established Trinity College after 1593. During this time, it seems, he encountered certain problems. It would appear that he had a falling out with his employers, for, after setting up his press there, he left shortly afterwards, taking with him his press, type and also certain furniture that belonged to the college, as well as the printed sheets that he had promised to deliver to them.

While there, Kearney must have been engaged in preparation work for printing the Irish Testament. The state papers for 1595 indicate that the New

---

9 J.R. Dassent (ed.), '20–21 August 1587: letter from the council to the lord deputy and council of Ireland', *Acts of the privy council of England*, new ser., 15 (London, 1897), p. 201.
10 Letter undated [1592–3], TCD, MS.MUN/P/1.14. See E.R. McClintock Dix, *The earliest Dublin printing* (Dublin, 1901), p. 26.

12.4 Title page of *Leabhar na nUrnaightheadh gComhchoidchiond* (*The Book of Common Prayer*), 1608.

Testament was then being set up and printed in Irish. A proposed set of terms for Kearney's re-employment at the college, issued in 1596, lists a number of conditions.[12] They provided for his professional and personal accommodation in the college. Item 3 provides: 'The allowinge you a boy his lodginge and his diet among the loer scholars you paying for it when you are able'. They continue by requiring him to pursue his craft to the best of his ability during his lifetime and to train an apprentice to continue after him. It is interesting to speculate as to the identity of the trainee, for the next name that appears as printer in Dublin was that of a John Francton. It is possible that he accompanied Kearney to Dublin about 1592, and after serving his time, succeeded him as the official printer here.

The proclamation against Hugh O'Neill was the first work to carry Francton's imprint 'Printed in Dublin at the Bridgefoote, by John Francke, 1600'. It made use of roman and italic type and a hitherto unseen initial capital letter used in the familiar layout style.

In the introduction to the New Testament, William O'Donnell (Daniel), then archbishop of Tuam, indicates that he together with Maoilín Óg MacBhruáideadha, who was fluent in Irish, shared in the translation of the Gospels working in the new college, and that the Gospels of Matthew, Mark and part of Luke were printed there. The printing was most likely done by Kearney. Following this, there was a delay of five years. During this time, Daniel, with the help of a Domhnall Óg Ó hUiginn, translated the remainder of Luke and the Gospel of John. The printing was completed by John Francton in William Usher's house – the site where the catechism was printed in 1571 with the assistance of William's father John. It carries the imprint 'printed in Dublin in the house of Master William Usher beside the bridge, by John Francke, 1603'. Does this mean that a printing press remained at Usher's house over the thirty years? Unlikely!

I began this paper with an account of Powell's *Book of Common Prayer*, so perhaps it is appropriate that I should conclude with the Irish language edition of the same book translated into Irish by William Ó Domhnaill, which bears the imprint 'Printed in Dublin, at the house of John Francke *alias* Francton king's printer in Ireland 1608' (fig. 12.4). While the dedication is to the lord deputy, Sir Arthur Chichester, who had commissioned the translation in 1605, it is dated 20 October 1609. It is stated there regarding the translation:

> it pleased your lordship to impose upon myselfe, the burden of trans-
> lating the Booke of Common Prayer … into the mother tongue … And
> having translated the booke, I followed it to the presse with jelousy, and

---

11 Letter from Sir Geff Fenton to Burghley, 24 June 1595: *Calendar of state papers, Ireland: Elizabeth, 1592–1596*, p. 332.   12 Proposed terms between Trinity College, Dublin and William Kearney, 18 Mar. 1596, TCD, MS MUN/P/1.25.

daily attendance, to see it perfected, payned as a woman in travell desirous to be delivered.

An entry under William Daniel in the *Dictionary of National Biography* refers to Francton in this manner: 'In 1608 he [Daniel] put it [*The Book of Common Prayer*] to the press, employing the same printer as before, who now had an establishment of his own, and called himself John Francke, *alias* Francton, printer to the king of Ireland'. It used the same irish type and incorporated a particularly lavish title page. Francton, who was never a member of the Company of Stationers of London, was specially appointed for life in 1604 as king's printer in Ireland. He was paid £40 'for his enabling to buy paper and other necessaries for printing the Book of Common Prayer in the Irish tongue'.[13]

The New Testament and *Book of Common Prayer* are the only known works printed by Francton which use the irish font; however, not unlike many current printers in Dublin, he either by necessity or otherwise engaged in pursuing other sources of income – there is a record of the Dublin Common Council having purchased one dozen fire buckets from him in 1610.[14] He continued as a printer until 1617, at which time it would appear that he was in poor health and, to use a term all too familiar nowadays, was considered unfit for purpose. His death is recorded in the funeral entry of the office of arms in Dublin Castle: 'John Francke or Francton, printer and sometime shrife of Dublin, deceased about the 7 or 8 of October 1620'.

13 *Calendar of state papers, Ireland, 1608–1610*, p. 75.   14 *Calendar of ancient records of Dublin*, ed. J.T. Gilbert and Lady Gilbert, 19 vols (Dublin, 1889–1944), ii, pp 468, 534, quoted in T. Percy C. Kirkpatrick, *Notes on the printers in Dublin* (Dublin, 1929), p. 5.